UNIVERSITY OF
WOLVERHAMPTON

WITHDR

D0806887

WP 2099923 2

SUTTON STUDIES IN MODERN BRITISH HISTORY

WORKHOUSE
CHILDREN

SUTTON STUDIES IN MODERN BRITISH HISTORY

General Editor: *Keith Laybourn,*
Professor of History, University of Huddersfield

1. The Rise of Socialism in Britain, *c.* 1881–1951
Keith Laybourn

2. Workhouse Children: Infant and Child Paupers under the Worcestershire Poor Law, 1780–1871
Frank Crompton

3. Social Conditions, Status and Community, *c.* 1860–1920
edited by *Keith Laybourn*

Forthcoming Titles

The National Union of Mineworkers and British Politics, 1944–1995
Andrew J. Taylor

The Age of Unease: Government and Reform in Britain, 1782–1832
Michael Turner

SUTTON STUDIES IN MODERN BRITISH HISTORY

WORKHOUSE CHILDREN

FRANK CROMPTON

UNIVERSITY OF WOLVERHAMPTON
LIBRARY

Acc No. 2099923

CLASS
362.
732
0942

CONTROL
0750912812

DATE
28 FEB 1997

SITE
DY 44

CRO

ae 362.5094244

SUTTON PUBLISHING

First published in 1997 by
Sutton Publishing Limited · Phoenix Mill
Thrupp · Stroud · Gloucestershire · GL5 2BU

Copyright © Frank Crompton, 1997

All rights reserved. No part of this publication may be reproduced, stored in a retrieval system, or transmitted, in any form, or by any means, electronic, mechanical, photocopying, recording or otherwise, without the prior permission of the publisher and copyright holder.

The author has asserted the moral right to be identified as the author of this work.

British Library Cataloguing in Publication Data
A catalogue record for this book is available from the British Library

ISBN 0 7509-1281-2 (hardback)
ISBN 0-7509-1429-7 (paperback)

Cover illustration: feeding the poor at the Conder Street Mission Hall, Limehouse (Mansell Collection)

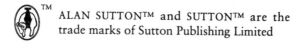
ALAN SUTTON™ and SUTTON™ are the
trade marks of Sutton Publishing Limited

Typeset in 11/14pt Sabon.
Typesetting and origination by
Sutton Publishing Limited.
Printed in Great Britain by
Hartnolls, Bodmin, Cornwall.

CONTENTS

LIST OF PLATES

PREFACE

Writing 'history from below' might be seen as a reaction to what has been called 'Great Person History', the dominant style of historical writing before Marx and Engels changed the whole nature of this discipline. *The Condition of the Working-Class in England in 1844*, published in 1845, in which Friedrich Engels explored the condition and nature of Manchester's working-class population, was not, however, unique in its subject-matter, because many people in the first half of the nineteenth century had already written about the poor, the problems they posed and possible solutions to the implied threat. What was unique about Engels' work was its polemical nature and the perspective from which it was written. Perhaps for the first time, the notion of a conflict between two apparently irreconcilable parts of society was offered as an explanation for the parlous state of the working class. The result of this analysis, based on the philosophical stance of Karl Marx, Friedrich Engels' mentor, was that an attempt was made to empathise with the plight of the poor working class. It was for this reason that Engels' work appeared to be the first social commentary truly written from the perspective of the poor.

Writing this particular kind of history is not an easy task, not only because before the era of extensive elementary education the working classes were often illiterate, but also because their writing was not valued and was usually lost. This means that sources for such history in mid-nineteenth century Britain are scarce. For this reason 'history from below' uses oblique approaches to develop an understanding of working-class people in this period. Typically such history is written from a mass of disparate sources, using a process of aggregation to develop an understanding of the lives of such people.

The workhouses created after 1834 by the New Poor Law were

institutions imposed on the destitute poor by the ruling élite of society and a great deal is known about the way the system was administered. Nevertheless, we know little of what these institutions were like for the destitute individuals incarcerated there. This book is an attempt to write a 'history from below' of these institutions from the perspective of child inmates, taking an approach through the huge mass of detailed evidence from locally available sources for the thirteen Poor Law unions of Worcestershire, between 1834 and 1871. The early chapters of the book identify how destitute children were dealt with under the Old Poor Law, between 1780 and 1834. The result is a more detailed description than is usually presented by an historian of the Poor Law and describes the way that the workhouse treated and educated child paupers. The author hopes that the result of this approach allows some appreciation of the plight of such children, who in some cases spent the whole of their childhood in the general workhouse, a total institution designed to deter adults – not children – from lifelong pauperism.

Frank Crompton
Worcester
May 1996

ACKNOWLEDGEMENTS

Grateful acknowledgement is given to Dr John Hurt, Professor Roy Lowe and the late Dr Richard Szreter for their help and advice during the research phase of this book; Worcester College of Higher Education for its support in both its research and preparation; my colleagues in the History Department at Worcester College for their continued support; the staff of Worcester, Hereford and Dudley Record Offices, and the Birmingham Central Library Archives Department for their help in locating and interpreting the sources that play such an important part in this publication, and the staff of the Public Record Office at Kew for their help and advice.

I would also like to thank Mr Tony Wherry, Chief Archivist of Worcester County Record Office for his help and advice, and for permission to reproduce material from the sources held by that Office; Mr David Hickman, Principal Librarian of Stourbridge Library for permission to reproduce the photograph of Stourbridge workhouse; Mr Robert Ryland, of the Local Studies and History Department of Birmingham Central Library for permission to reproduce a lithograph of the Birmingham Asylum for Destitute Children and the photograph of King's Norton workhouse; Berrow's Newspapers, Worcester, for their permission to reproduce photographs of Worcester workhouse and the Group Librarian of *Building*, the successor journal to *The Builder*, for permission to reproduce the lithographs of Birmingham workhouse.

Mr William Meadows also kindly gave his permission to reproduce the photograph of Martley workhouse, as did Mr L.E. Hartman for the reproduction of the photograph of Tenbury Wells workhouse; Mary Furlong, of the Media Services Department of Worcester College of Higher Education, also gave her expertise in producing some of the photographic material in this book. Last but not least, my grateful thanks go to my wife for her forbearance while this book was being researched and written.

INTRODUCTION

Several generations of the English working class grew up in the shadow of the workhouse, with those individuals who were in insecure employment, were lowly paid, or unfortunate enough to be widowed, orphaned or deserted, fearing incarceration there and thus being tainted by the epithet 'pauper'. For ninety-five years, from 1834, the poorest members of the working classes – or the 'dangerous poor' as they were known – feared the workhouse, whereas their middle and upper-class contemporaries apparently believed that there was also danger if destitute poor people readily accepted the illusory advantages that workhouse life offered. However, this indicated the supreme ignorance of the motivations and aspirations of the lower orders that their social superiors had. Even after the abolition of the Local Government Board in 1929, in the eighteen years before the National Health Service was created in 1947, the working classes still feared the taint of the workhouse.

Regarding the overall basis of the workhouse, the Poor Law Report of 1834 stated that: 'The first and most essential of all conditions, a principle which we find universally admitted, even by those whose practice is at variance with it, is that his [the pauper's] situation on the whole shall not be made really or apparently so eligible as the situation of the independent labourer of the lowest class.'[1] The pauper's situation referred to was known as Less Eligibility, which formed a major tenet of New Poor Law administration, which the Report referred to again. It stated:

Uniformity in the administration of relief we deem essential as a means, first, of reducing the perpetual shifting from parish to parish, and fraudulent removals to parishes where profuse management prevails from parishes where the management is less profuse; secondly, of preventing the discontents which arise among the paupers maintained under the less profuse management of adjacent districts; and, thirdly, of bringing the management, which consists in detail, more closely within the public control.[2]

This Principle of National Uniformity was the other major tenet of Poor Law administration, so that although between 1780 and 1834 child paupers were treated differently, dependent on where they lived and what was available under the Old Poor Law, after 1834, all paupers, no matter what their parish of origin, were to be treated uniformly, in a fashion that would not make their condition desirable to other individuals in a similar situation. One significant result of this was that rural mendicants were to receive the same treatment in the workhouse as their more threatening urban contemporaries, although the circumstances of such rural places differed considerably from urban ones. This system soon proved impractical, with the treatment, administered fairly quickly, being adapted to local conditions, which effectively demonstrated that the administration set up under the New Poor Law was an essentially reactive system.

This book investigates the treatment of children in the workhouses of the thirteen Worcestershire Poor Law unions, in the period 1834 to 1871, although it also refers to their situation between 1780 and 1834. It seeks to examine the ways in which children were treated, educated and trained, by whom they were cared for, and the outcome of their treatment. It also examines whether the management of such children was indeed uniform and less eligible, which necessitates an understanding of Worcestershire between 1780 to 1871 and of the considerably revised attitude to poverty and its changed definition that developed in this period. It also demonstrates that the workhouse, as a total institution, had a profound and continuing influence on child inmates and that this influence continued into adulthood.

Under the Old Poor Law, Worcestershire had been administered as separate parishes, for the purpose of relieving the indigent poor, although there were exceptions to this at Kidderminster, Upton upon Severn and Worcester, where, most unusually, a union of parishes had been formed under Gilbert's Act of 1782.[3] In a few other cases, Worcestershire parishes were enclaves within adjacent counties, but for the purpose of Poor Law administration these places were regarded as parts of Worcestershire. This was because, when Poor Law unions were created in 1834, county boundaries were ignored and some unions contained parishes from more than one county. For example, Martley union contained parishes from Herefordshire, Dudley union parishes from Staffordshire, and Shipston on Stour union parishes from both Gloucestershire and Warwickshire. The thirteen Poor Law unions chosen for investigation in this book were those named after places in the county of Worcestershire. Worcestershire was a predominantly rural county in the early nineteenth century. It was divided from north-east to south-west by the River Severn and from north-west to south-east by the Rivers Avon and Teme, with high ground to the north and west of the county, and undulating countryside elsewhere. The river valleys were extremely fertile and were used for market gardening, with good arable and grazing land for cattle on the lower slopes in south and east Worcestershire and good sheep-pastures on high land in the north and west. Enclosures in lowland Worcestershire were carried out early – by 1790 over half of the county's farmland was enclosed – so the county became rich agriculturally, with the products of the farms used to support various industries. Worsted and woollen cloth was made from the abundant supply of wool and at Kidderminster this fibre allowed the development of carpet making during the mid-eighteenth century. Carpets were also made at Worcester and at Bewdley, but the industry eventually became established in factories and centralised in and around Kidderminster after 1820. Leather was tanned in all parts of the county, although Bewdley became the centre for this trade, but Worcester used fine soft leathers to make gloves, a craft that had existed in the city since the fourteenth century and which by the late eighteenth century was said to employ over 4,000 citizens. The county was not a rich source of minerals, although salt – particularly brine – was extracted at Droitwich from Roman times onwards. In the early nineteenth century this town was developed as a spa, when the medicinal properties of its saline springs were discovered. Elsewhere, at Stourbridge – another source of salt – good sand deposits led to the founding of the glass industry there, which from about 1750 onwards made specialist glasses and by 1800 had developed techniques to toughen glass by an annealing process. Plate-glass, flint-glass and crown-glass, all made by adding various mineral salts to the glass, were also produced and worked in that area. Later still, the addition of lead oxide to the glass-melt created crystal-glass and the trade of glass cutting, to produce decorative objects, was introduced in the first quarter of the nineteenth century. The coal necessary for glass production, and as a source of power generally, was available to the north of Stourbridge, but prior to 1800 it had also been mined to the south and east of the town, although these areas became exhausted by the end of the eighteenth century. However, at Dudley, coal seams coincided with the discovery of iron-ore deposits and iron-smelting became a staple trade in that area during the eighteenth century. Iron was wrought, moulded and cast into tools or made into nails and chains. Nails were also made in Bromsgrove, while needles were made at Redditch, although these trades remained as cottage industries and were never fully mechanised and centralised into factories.

The canalisation of the rivers Severn and Avon in the mid-eighteenth century and the building of additional canals, between 1760 and 1830, improved the transport of both raw materials and finished products within Worcestershire. Of all the county's trades, fine-china production was the one with no logical basis, as the raw materials for this were not found in the area and neither was there a trained and skilled workforce available. In spite of this, the Royal Worcester Porcelain Company was founded by Dr John Wall in 1750, in a successful effort to revitalise Worcester's economy. China clay was now brought to the city from Cornwall by barge and local labour was trained as skilled china-moulders and painters, so that new techniques of china decoration were introduced and the trade flourished. Clearly, Worcestershire's industrial base was not substantial, although the county did have major industries at Kidderminster, Stourbridge and Dudley. This caused labour to migrate towards these urban places in the second half of the eighteenth century and the movement continued after 1800. Birmingham, outside the county, but contiguous with it in the north-east, also began to develop as an industrial centre. It eventually acted as a magnet for migratory labour from agricultural areas in Worcestershire. Only places near to manufacturing centres became urban, with the majority of the county remaining rural; some of it very rural. For these reasons, Worcestershire was a very suitable place to investigate the administration of the New Poor Law, as both rural and urban areas existed within the county and could be compared. This analysis appeared very worthwhile, as many generalisations about the New Poor Law have been based on the evidence of urban Poor Law unions, with the rural Poor Law often ignored.

Nineteenth-century demographic statistics and population

distribution patterns were useful in demonstrating the contrasting nature of various areas of the county. While the population of Worcestershire as a whole grew by over 130 per cent between 1801 and 1871, from 146,441 to 338,837, certain places grew very rapidly. For instance, in this period, the population of Dudley increased by 330 per cent, from 10,107 to 43,791 and that of King's Norton, contiguous with Birmingham, by over 670 per cent, from 2,807 to 21,845.

In contrast to this, rural places, particularly some parishes in the west of the county, grew only slightly. For instance, the population of Martley grew by only sixty-six people, from 1,192 to 1,258, between 1801 and 1871. Even more rural places on the uplands in the west of the county lost members of their population, as at Cotheridge, Hanley Childe and Kyre Magna. In many parts of England and Wales in the 1780s the distress of the poor, particularly in urban areas, led to civil disturbances which were sometimes said to press the need for a reform of the Poor Law system. Within Worcestershire there were small-scale disturbances, for instance at Stourbridge and Redditch in the early nineteenth century, but local newspaper reports indicated no organised or substantial demand for Poor Law reform here. Indeed there appeared to be no such pressure even after 1834, when the passing of the Poor Law Amendment Act caused agitation and the creation of a national Anti-Poor Law pressure group. In spite of these docile responses by the population of the county, local Poor Law unions approached the task of Poor Law administration with varying degrees of enthusiasm. The highly urban Dudley union was noticeably the least enthusiastic out of all county Poor Law unions in adopting the New Poor Law. However this was likely to be the case, because the methods, approaches and ideologies of the Overseers of the Poor under the old legislation were continued under the New Poor Law after 1834. Changes in attitude to the New Poor Law did occur, but only very slowly and for this reason it appeared imperative that this book investigate the Old Poor Law, to show the developments in the treatment of children under the New Poor Law.

Nineteenth-century statistics, which were notoriously inaccurate and difficult to interpret, did give some impression of the condition and situation of child inmates in workhouses. Such figures suggested that throughout the period from 1834 to 1871, over one-third of workhouse inmates were under sixteen years of age. Initially, during this period, workhouses were administered by the Poor Law Commission, which existed until 1847, and then by the Poor Law

Board which was abolished in 1871. Inmates under sixteen years old were classified as children from the outset in the workhouses of most Poor Law Unions and they soon formed a large and recognisable group. Such inmates were likely to be incarcerated in the workhouse for up to sixteen years, because, while adults were voluntarily in the workhouse, children had no choice about being there. If they were dependent on their parents, they entered and left the workhouse with them, but if their parents were dead or they had been deserted, such children became the responsibility of the Board of Guardians. These permanent inmates were most likely to be profoundly, and probably permanently, altered by their institutional experience.

As many as 20 per cent of workhouse inmates, or about 60 per cent of inmate children, were in the category of being orphaned and deserted and Guardians were most assiduous in their care of these groups, as they were immediately responsible for children born in the workhouse or those who were foundlings soon after birth. This was particularly important as these individuals might thus spend their whole upbringing in the workhouse, until they became members of the class of adult pauper. However, most Boards of Guardians wanted to avoid this eventuality at all costs and for this reason most parentless children were found employment as apprentices as soon as possible. This was because Guardians were at worst motivated by a desire to rid Poor Rate payers of the burden of unwanted dependent children – for whom they would have had responsibility until the child was sixteen years old – and at best by the desire to avoid the lifelong pauperism of such individuals. Such children were apprenticed when they were as young as seven years old, although most usually they were between nine and twelve years of age. In spite of this, some children spent over ten years continuously in the workhouses in Worcestershire and this must have left an indelible mark on them.

Many historians have studied the New Poor Law in individual English counties, while others have investigated specific aspects of the Poor Law system, such as the workhouses or the officers who dealt with paupers, but a large scale study of inmate pauper children in a county has not been attempted. An extensive study, produced by Alec Ross in the 1950s,[4] was related to the administration of Poor Law children from a national standpoint and this was partly replicated and extended in the early 1980s by S.P. Oberman.[5] However, these were administrative histories, concentrating on the central management, which only used Metropolitan examples when referring to the local authorities. One important conclusion emerged from this. It appears that the nature of the sources used will make a fundamental difference to the findings of any study. While national Poor Law papers allowed the nature of the developing official Poor Law policy to be illustrated, which could then be exemplified from selected Poor Law Guardians' Minute Books, what was produced from these studies was a somewhat clinical examination of the New Poor Law, from an administrator's viewpoint. A contrary approach, used in this book, uses Boards of Guardians' Minute Books as its major source. These were elucidated from national Poor Law papers. While Guardians' Minute Books are a biased source, because they were written from a particular point of view, this was seen as a virtue in the case of this book, because what emerged was an account of how individual pauper children were treated in Worcestershire workhouses between 1834 and 1871. This was arguably a description that was closer to the reality of life for these children than the somewhat clinical official accounts provided elsewhere. This also means that the descriptions in this book are in greater detail than is perhaps usual. However, this is intended to be a social history which gives a flavour of workhouse life in the mid-nineteenth century, rather than an administrative history that concentrates on the administrator's point of view. It also seeks to alleviate the south-eastwards official bias of previous work and provides a useful comparison with Anne Digby's work on Norfolk.[6] It also draws on the ideas posited by Gertrude Himmelfarb in her book, *The Idea of Poverty*,[7] and those of Erving Goffman in his classic sociological study *Asylums*.[8] Both of these works are used to provide an analytical framework for this book.

CHAPTER

1

CHILDREN UNDER THE OLD POOR LAW, 1780–1834

Under the New Poor Law, the system of administration set up after the Poor Law Amendment Act of 1834, there was a residuum of Old Poor Law thought still present. The New Poor Law was informed by Benthamite utilitarianism and had a central authority, the Poor Law Commission, led by its first permanent secretary, Edwin Chadwick, who was strongly associated with Jeremy Bentham, having been his personal private secretary. Accordingly, this Commission could be assumed to be orthodox in its adherence to the new utilitarian principles for treating the poor, as were the men initially appointed to the department. The same was not true of local administrators and locally elected Poor Law Guardians, who were often recruited from among existing Overseers of the Poor. They often continued to use their previous practices for treating the indigent poor. Many of these men also remained unconvinced of the need for a new Poor Law, particularly in a rural area such as Worcestershire, as the new legislation was intended to solve problems caused by urbanisation. However, with the possible exception of Dudley, the county had no urban places to generate such problems and disaffection with the new law was almost inevitable.

In these circumstances, it was interesting that Dudley Guardians were the most intransigent group in the county in their dealings with the central Poor Law administration, throughout the period to 1871. They effectively prevented proper implementation of the New Poor Law in their urbanised union, which was a common occurrence in the north of England, but was unusual in the Midlands. Elsewhere in the county,

Guardians apparently considered the New Poor Law a costly irrelevance, but one that they implemented. However, they continued to hold attitudes implicit in the Old Poor Law, an accretion of legislation developed over 450 years and this much influenced their interpretation of the New Poor Law. Understandably, where a poorhouse pre-existed the 1834 Poor Law Amendment Act, officers whom had proven ability in coping with Poor Law institutions were appointed to the new workhouses. This effectively ensured the continuing influence of the Old Poor Law, a tendency further accentuated by the local financing of these facilities from the Poor Rates, the expenditure of which was overseen by locally elected Boards of Guardians. These bodies had great influence over the implementation of the new rules and regulations. This new code of practice continued to be interpreted from previous experience, so that entrenched local attitudes towards the poor endured. For these reasons, this book, which is mainly about inmate children in the English county of Worcestershire between 1780 and 1871, begins with a description of the evolution of the Old Poor Law.

Children were implicated, but not mentioned, in the Statute of Labourers,[1] the first Poor Law legislation passed in England in 1350. In this legislation, children were assumed to be the responsibility of their parents, which was an emphasis that continued into the era of the New Poor Law after 1834. From their inception in the fourteenth century, Poor Law measures were definitely intended as social control to moderate the behaviour and movements of labouring men, who were to be restrained in turn by their social superiors. However, this probably ensured what M. MacKissack called a 'united . . . hostility to the government'[2] by working men and proved a cohesive influence among this section of society. The need for social control continued to influence governments. They sought to regulate the geographical distribution of an increasingly unified class of labouring men until the sixteenth century, when industrialisation, particularly of the metal industries, changed matters. New stresses were now created in society by industrialisation and its concomitant urbanisation, which led to the passing of the Statute of Artificers in 1563.[3] This legislation attempted to control the wages and behaviour of craftsmen, but it also inadvertently controlled the lives of their young offspring. The living conditions for these children were adversely affected, because the standard of the living conditions for the whole family was reduced. This statute also unsuccessfully sought to control apprenticing, but because a source for the financing of this system was unclear, another Act of Parliament was necessary.[4] This was passed in 1572 and attempted to make the local community corporately responsible for the financing of apprenticeships and other Poor Law facilities in their area, although a flaw was that no individual was made directly responsible for organising almsgiving locally. This problem was solved in 1597, when an Act of Parliament[5] required that Overseers of the Poor be elected, who were to be responsible for poor relief in a particular locality. They also administered the system for the apprenticing of orphaned and destitute children in the area and were the antecedents of the Boards of Guardians under the New Poor Law after 1834.

By 1600, the existing Poor Laws were inappropriate to the needs of a rapidly changing society and an Act of Parliament passed in 1601[6] attempted to tidy up existing legislation. However, drastic social changes continued and by 1662 another Act[7] was necessary to cope with urban destitution, which was an increasing problem. The principle that destitute individuals were the responsibility of their parish of birth was reconfirmed. Therefore such individuals were removed to their parish of origin if they became dependent on poor relief, taking with them any dependent children they might have, who also became a burden on that parish. Such children were often strangers in their parent's birthplace, which was even more likely with abandoned and orphaned children removed to the parish of settlement of their actual, or supposed, parent after that parent had died or disappeared. Thus, these children often had no apparent connection with the parish to which they had been removed and this caused great resentment. These destitute children were now liable to be apprenticed at their host parish's expense, an arrangement that was quite popular, even though it cost the ratepayers money. This was because the settlement of the apprentice was automatically transferred to the parish where craftsman training was to be undertaken, so that the newly qualified craftsman became a parishioner of their new abode and never returned to the parish paying the pauper apprenticeship fee. This arrangement was re-emphasised in an Act of Parliament of 1698,[8] although it was now assumed that a workhouse for the destitute would be provided and that the problem of orphaned and deserted children would be reduced.

This optimism was misplaced and yet another Act of Parliament, passed in 1722,[9] attempted to encourage the development of workhouses. Only four out of over 300 Worcestershire parishes were encouraged to provide these, all in places where poorhouses already existed. Inevitably, by the beginning of the nineteenth century, these workhouses or shelters for destitutes, where they existed, were in the least appropriate places; in rural parishes, like Ombersley and Chaddesley Corbett, and not in the burgeoning industrialised urban parishes of the Black Country, or near to the growing industrial town of Birmingham. This was because these places had created workhouses to accommodate destitute people in a very different context from that pertaining in the early nineteenth century. It was in these newly urbanised places where the industrial revolutions of the eighteenth and nineteenth centuries caused most stress and where workhouses were most needed. This need was also emphasised because existing social structures, such as the traditional relationship between master and servant, were dramatically altered by industrial change. It was in such areas that a 'new middle class',[10] a management class, was created. Social relationships were also altered by new ways of financing businesses, which made masters more remote from their employees and made workers more free to migrate elsewhere. Thus, the restraints provided by the Law of Settlement were now ignored, so the increasing numbers of workers, demanded in industrial towns and urban places, were able to migrate to them, causing a redistribution of the population.

The censuses, from 1801 onwards, revealed that urban places were growing, while the proportion of people dwelling in rural areas was a lot smaller. It also revealed that migration occurred in a 'stepwise' fashion,[11] so that villages surrounding towns grew in size, while small hamlets in outlying rural areas became depopulated.[12] This was a tendency repeated nationally, so that virtually no area of England remained unaffected. The result of all this was that new pressures were placed on the already inadequate Poor Law system. Essentially, workhouses, where these existed, became even less appropriately located and in the circumstances it was no surprise that traditional child-rearing practices, involving 'extended families', were forced to change. Inevitably, extended families disintegrated,[13] which caused even more problems, although there was some evidence that these social organisations may have reformed within two generations in the new urban areas. Urban child neglect and abandonment now became a common and pressing problem, with destitute children often found in urban workhouses, which were ill-equipped to cope with them. Hanway's Act of 1762,[14] was a response to this problem in London, where 'a number of boarding establishments [were created] in the suburbs to which they relegated the younger children whom they were not legally permitted to keep in the workhouse'.[15] Such children from the Metropolis, when moved to suburban boarding houses, needed a task to keep them occupied, so a system of education was introduced. This was the origins of workhouse education, which was facilitated by an Act of Parliament in 1767,[16] that made it possible for schools to be established in children's departments. These were to be available to all pauper children within a fifteen-mile radius of such a school, but these schemes were inappropriate in non-Metropolitan areas, such as Worcestershire. Here destitute children were left in the workhouses or cared for in some other way.

This unsatisfactory state of affairs continued and caused great concern, which certainly exercised the mind of Jonas Hanway, the philanthropist and promoter of the Metropolitan Poor Act, who was contemporaneously considered to be a great expert on the poor. He wrote in 1766: 'Many of the children instead of being nourished with care, by the fostering hand or breast of a wholesome country nurse, are thrust into the impure air of the workhouse, into the hands of some careless worthless young female, or decrepit old woman.'[17] Although this comment related to a Metropolitan workhouse, Hanway's writings certainly made it clear that his concern was not just for urban areas. He emphasised the problem of destitute children throughout England, by using infant mortality statistics, showing that infant death rates were higher in workhouses than elsewhere. He was then able to assert that mortality in children aged under two years in the workhouses of the Metropolis, between 1756–8, was 46.9 per cent, which meant that out of 43,101 infants in the workhouse, 20,232 would die before they were two years old. These sorts of statistics made the people employed in parish poor relief defensive, so much so that the workhouse master of a large suburban parish had to defend his apparent inhumanity, when he was challenged for forcing a child from the breast of the mother and sending it to a foundling hospital. He stated, 'we send all our children to the foundling hospital, we have not saved one alive for the last fourteen years – We have no fit place to preserve them in; the air is too confined.'[18] He went on: 'Of the same nature was another parish, some years before the foundling hospital opened, where it appeared, that of 54 children born in or taken into their workhouse, not one outlived the year in which it was born or taken in.'[19] It was this sort of evidence that caused the dislike of workhouses to persist and led to the continuance of Hanway's propaganda. For these reasons, he also successfully promoted the Poor Law Acts of 1762[20] and 1767,[21] both of which attempted to remove destitute infants from apparently lethal conditions. By the 1780s the insatiable demand for labour created by industrial change was reduced in some places, so that some of the problems associated with the Poor Laws were altered. Now, adult unemployment led large numbers of able-bodied individuals to apply for poor relief, so that the Act of 1723[22] proved totally inappropriate and indeed it may have made matters worse, because it banned Outdoor Poor Relief completely and assumed, unrealistically, that workhouse accommodation was adequate. Palpably, the workhouse accommodation available was wholly inadequate, with the few workhouses that existed almost always inappropriately located. This was certainly true in Worcestershire, where the accommodation available, although appropriate for Tudor times, was now wrongly placed for the distribution of population prevailing in the later eighteenth century. Another Act of Parliament of 1782,[23] usually known as Gilbert's Act, was intended to alleviate this situation, as it was intended to encourage the building of new workhouses and to ensure that they were used. This legislation stated that, if paupers refused to work, the justices 'on conviction shall punish such offenders by committing . . . [them] . . . to the house of correction for refusing to work', where they were sentenced to 'hard labour'[24] for between one and three months. However, in spite of this intention, such regulations could only apply where workhouses were available, which was certainly not the case in most places in Worcestershire. Even where such institutions did exist they were in need of an overhaul and sufficient staff to ensure that inmates would be compelled to work. Overseers of the Poor, in the eighteenth century, also quite frequently misapplied money raised for poor relief, whereas if this money had been correctly used it might have built, purchased or rented sufficient workhouses. This would have almost certainly been the case in Worcestershire, although even when a new workhouse was built and a Board of Guardians appointed, there were still problems. Indeed, the hope of the sponsors of the 1782 Act – that poor relief would be applied uniformly – proved a vain one, because this legislation was only permissive. It presumed a demand from a locality to build workhouses in response to the needs of the poor that was usually absent. Indeed, of the county's towns, only Worcester city provided a new workhouse, financed by the creation of a union of parishes. Admissions to and discharges from this workhouse were carefully registered, with the aim of regulating the pauper problem locally. It attempted to ensure that: 'no person shall be sent to such poor house or houses, except such as become indigent by age, sickness, or infirmities, and are unable to obtain maintenance by their labours;

and except such orphan children . . . [and] . . . such children as shall necessarily go there with their mother thither their sustenance'.[25]

A strict régime was now to be enforced in the workhouse, which was to be enhanced by the depersonalising effect of registration; intended to further emphasise institutionalisation. In spite of the scarcity of workhouses, even in the later eighteenth century, they were now considered inappropriate accommodation for unaccompanied children. This was hinted at by the 1782 Act, when it stated 'infant children of tender age . . . may either be sent to such poorhouse . . . or placed by the Guardians of the Poor . . . with some reputable persons in or near the parish . . . until such child . . . be of sufficient age to be put out to service, or bound apprentice'.[26] Thus, it was clearly hoped that the influence of the child's natural parents, who by their destitution had proved themselves unsuitable to care for their own offspring, would be ameliorated. This belief led to the fostering of children in some areas, but not in Worcestershire. The respectable poor, who fell on hard times, were to be cared for and it was stated that 'any person able and willing to work, but who cannot get employment . . . [was] . . . to be properly maintained, lodged and provided for until such employment shall be provided',[27] which also gave the union responsibility for providing work. However, where tasks were provided in the workhouse, children also had to be taken into the care of the Guardians, which was sometimes seen as to the child's advantage.[28] It was only at Worcester that a new workhouse was provided, and elsewhere, at Kidderminster, Pershore and Upton upon Severn existing institutions were remodelled to replace poorhouses set up in Elizabethan I's reign. In most other places in the county, no new or remodelled workhouses were provided. Here, there was continued reliance on outdoor relief, which continued to be thought of as the only possible solution to the pauper problem in a rural area. For this reason, while some county parishes had great problems with indigence, few had the will to finance institutions to alleviate the situation and they certainly did not appoint local Guardians to replace Overseers of the Poor. However, this may not have been the situation nationally, because at about this time Sir George Nicholls, one of the Poor Law Commissioners after 1834 and a zealous proponent of reform, referred to: 'New returns of parochial expenditure, which revealed the widening range of Poor Law administrators, with the increase in population, and with the steady growth of the burden.'[29] Metropolitan and larger urban areas appeared to be very different, because here pauperism was an increasing problem, in spite of the provisions of Gilbert's Act[30] and a further attempt to provide a stimulus for the financing of workhouses made in 1783.[31] This also failed, which led William Pitt's administration to legislate again. In 1786,[32] they attempted to re-legalise outdoor relief, because urban workhouses, where these existed, were so overcrowded. However, if local Guardians placed those seeking relief in the workhouse, local justices could overrule them, although this seldom happened. Such attitudes were indicative of the dominant philosophy of the upper middle and upper classes towards the poor, which was well illustrated by the Reverend Joseph Townsend, who somewhat complacently wrote in 1785: 'The wisest legislator will never be able to devise a more equitable, or in any respect a more suitable punishment, than hunger is for a disobedient servant. Hunger will tame the fiercest animals, it will teach decency and courtesy, obedience and subjection to the most brutish the most obstinate the most perverse.'[33] Such views were informed by the economics of Adam Smith, in *The Wealth of Nations* (1776) and by the philosophy of Jeremy Bentham, usually called 'Utilitarianism', in his book on the management of the indigent poor, *Pauper Management Improved* (1785). In this work, Jeremy Bentham suggested abolishing the existing Poor Laws and replacing them with a profit-making company, which would provide accommodation for paupers and others deemed to be menaces to society, who had not broken the law, but whose labour was seen to be of value. They would be made to work and do more than earn their keep, as it was envisaged that the institution would make a profit. Thomas Malthus' ideas about population were also invoked in support of these principles; it was believed that no matter how much money was given to the poor, if there was no increase in the quantity of meat available, the price of meat would rise, causing an increase in population to accentuate these problems. In real terms, therefore, the poor would be no better off, although it was also suggested that: 'An increase of population without a proportional increase of food will evidently have the same effect in lowering the value of each man's patent. The food must necessarily be distributed in smaller quantities, and consequently a day's labour will purchase a smaller quantity of provisions.'[34] For this reason, Thomas Malthus thought that the Poor Laws increased population unnecessarily, by giving security to paupers, but without increasing the food supply available. Yet, what was more important was that he regarded 'the quantity of food consumed in the workhouse upon that part of society that cannot be considered the most valuable part, diminished the share that would otherwise belong to the most industrious, and more worthy members'.[35] The result was that the poor were feared and resented by the middle and upper classes even more than previously and any alteration in the system to deal with mendicancy became even more contentious. This tendency was enhanced still further when it was suggested that previous Poor Law legislation had 'alleviated little of the intensity of individual misfortune'.[36] Instead it had 'spread the general evil over a much greater surface'[37] and for such reasons it was logical that a prime aim of the Poor Law reforms of 1834 was to provide a deterrent, in which the workhouse was to be made as unpleasant as possible. Inevitably this intention caused opponents of these social, economic and philosophical stances, which have already been discussed, to create an 'Anti-Poor Law Movement'.[38]

In the later eighteenth century, country parishes were much concerned about their former inhabitants who applied for parish relief anywhere in England or Wales, because now they were automatically removed to their parish of origin. This proved particularly problematical where young and active individuals had migrated from these parishes, leaving an ageing poor population there, on whom they became dependent several years later, but even worse was that some young paupers were removed to the birthplace of a parent and were thus unknown in the parish to which they were sent. For this reason, there were tremendous pressures placed on local rural economies, with individuals removed there placing an unreasonable burden on that parish, a tendency enhanced by Boards of Guardians in industrial towns eager to remove individuals to their parish of origin as soon as possible after they became destitute. This reduced the burden on their own Poor Rates. This problem was greatest if a woman was pregnant, a likely eventuality, as young women migrating from rural places were often at the beginning of the fecund period of their lives. Even more complications occurred if the woman was also unmarried or was in dispute about the paternity of her unborn child. Such women were commonly removed to their parish of origin, where they were to be cared for by their families, who it was presumed still lived there. However, many such women had no family remaining where they had been born and thus the commonly held belief that they would be shamed by their return, particularly if they were unmarried, was ill founded. Such destitutes and their children only compounded the pauper problem in rural places, so another Act of Parliament of 1795[39] attempted to alleviate this. It delayed removal until the pauper was chargeable, that was until actually in receipt of poor relief, but this solution also failed, as urban parishes wished to rid themselves of potential paupers as soon as possible.

Other attempts at reform of the Old Poor Law followed. For instance, an Act of Parliament of 1809[40] made it illegal to remove individuals to their parish of origin if they were sick, so that seriously ill people were prevented from being transported around the country, thus avoiding the well-publicised deaths that had occurred in such circumstances. Compassion meant that this regulation was acceptable, whereas under another Act, passed in 1810,[41] mothers of illegitimate children were to be sent to the house of correction, with the offspring left to be cared for in the workhouse. However, this was usually impossible as such corrective institutions were rare outside Metropolitan areas and unknown in Worcestershire. Where such treatment was possible, the havoc created by unattended pauper babies left alone in the workhouse can only be imagined. In spite of these efforts at legislation, the pauper problem increased and Sturges Bourne's Act, of 1818,[42] can be seen as a radical reaction to this. It amended the Law of Settlement,[43] to make outdoor relief available in the parish of residence, as opposed to the pauper's parish of origin, so that in 'sudden and urgent necessity . . . adequate relief'[44] was to be given. This met the immediate needs of the individual, a change in emphasis for the Poor Laws and arguably a movement away from Benthamite utilitarianism. This change was taken further by another Act, passed in 1819,[45] that specifically aimed to rescue the poor from pauperism rather than to deter them from it. Under this legislation, the cost of poor relief was to be reclaimed from the individual's wages, when they found employment, but this proved almost impossible to administer and a return to deterrence as a major aim of the Poor Laws appeared inevitable. In 1820, another Act[46] attempted to ensure that residence for one year became a prerequisite before relief could be claimed, which led the poet George Crabbe to acerbically comment, about an overseer's perplexity:[47]

> There is a doubtful pauper and we think,
> 'Tis not with us to give him meat and drink;
> A child is born and 'tis not mighty clear,
> Whether the mother lived with us a year.

These were difficult problems for the Poor Laws, which were compounded by a transient workforce of men 'on the tramp', who simply slept rough, or took to, what the Webbs referred to in their retrospective text, published in the early twentieth century, as 'social parasitism'.[48] These men simply used workhouses as convenient lodging houses and added to the size of the pauper population by doing so. To combat this supposed problem, another Act of Parliament, passed in 1824, attempted to make workhouse conditions most unpleasant of all for transient inmates. Indeed, it was this Vagrancy Act,[49] that was incongruously invoked by the Thatcher Government in the late 1980s in an attempt to control late twentieth-century homeless people. It failed in the early nineteenth century, as it did in the 1980s, because the whole problem of homelessness of all types increased, outstripping the amount of institutional accommodation available. However, overcrowding was not just confined to adult pauper inmates. In the 1820s there were more young workhouse inmates than ever before and this created huge problems, as indicated by one Overseer of the Poor, who wrote in 1800: 'I was at our workhouse near the whole of yesterday. The number of the paupers in the house was four hundred and twelve. It be considerably more than full. We were obliged to put them three in a bed, and in some cases four to a bed.'[50] In spite of such cases, overcrowded workhouses were not found everywhere in England, but even where they did exist the idea of getting rid of destitute children as early as possible was an attractive one.

In Tudor times the poorhouses had been emptied of destitute children by apprenticing them, sometimes when they were as young as seven years old, and this practice became even more common as society industrialised. However, the market for apprentices fluctuated and sometimes appropriate placements for such children were difficult to find. In there circumstances, apprenticing away from the home parish developed, so that some pauper children from London were apprenticed in places as far away as Lancashire, in the cotton mills there. In spite of this practice, the newly industrialised town of Birmingham, which had dramatically increased its size in the later eighteenth century, did not follow suit, although it did begin to apprentice pauper children to the merchant marine, which apparently constantly demanded young apprentices. In spite of such developments in urban areas, the rural parishes of Worcestershire had no comparable large source of apprentices and therefore they had no need for such schemes. The parishes invariably continued to apprentice small numbers of pauper children locally. However, nationally, it was large scale apprenticeship schemes that were most problematical. Thus, the 1802

Act,[51] began by attempting to regulate the treatment of pauper apprentices sent in batches to employers, particularly to the cotton industry in Lancashire. The 1802 legislation suggested that 'it hath of late become the practice in cotton and wool mills, and . . . factories to employ a great number of male and female apprentices . . . [and that] . . . certain regulations are becoming necessary to preserve the health and morals of such apprentices and other persons'.[52] Thus, in the cotton and wool industries – where iniquities were at their greatest – regulations about hours of work, living conditions, the clothing supplied to apprentices and the nature of their education were specified. However, such rules were never implemented uniformly, particularly because there was no factory inspectorate to enforce these regulations. Thus, for instance, the education clauses of the Act, which specified 'half-time education' and 'instruction in the usual hours of work in reading, writing and arithmetic', for 'at least one hour every Sunday in the principles of the Christian Religion'[53] were implemented in only a few places. Consequently, in spite of high hopes for the 1802 legislation, it proved wholly ineffective and those few employers interested in improving the lot of their pauper apprentices had to tackle such problems piecemeal.

Clearly, all was not well with parish apprenticeships, as John Moss, master of the Preston workhouse, revealed in his evidence to the 'Select Committee on the State of Children Employed in Manufactories' in 1816.[54] Moss had previously been employed as master of the apprentices' house at Backbarrow Mill, Cartmel, Lancashire, where apprentices mainly from London, and particularly from Whitechapel, St James's and St Clement's parishes, were employed, together with a few apprentices from Liverpool. He stated that children from London 'were from seven to eleven, and those from Liverpool were eight or ten to fifteen'[55] when apprenticed. Theoretically, therefore, the 1802 Act[56] meant that parish officers should visit these apprentices to ensure that they were properly treated. However, Moss claimed to be completely unaware of this legislation and furthermore he asserted that the apprentices from London were certainly never visited, while those from Liverpool received 'some visits'. He went on to demonstrate that such visits were important, for example when complaints were made by Liverpool officials, particularly about the dirty condition of the apprentices' bedding, there was some immediate improvement in conditions. However, what he thought even more important was the annual fee, paid by the children's home parish, which could be withheld if the conditions under which they were kept proved unsatisfactory. The fees for these apprentices were eventually not paid and 'the children were [now] turned out on the high road to beg their way to their former parishes . . . [so] . . . they were taken from the mill in a cart and then turned adrift near the sands on the Lancaster Road'.[57] This led to some of these apprentices being taken in by another factory, while others found their way to the workhouse at Lancaster, where the Guardians demanded the boys be taken back to Backbarrow. When returned there, they were forced to accept an additional six-week term of apprenticeship, 'on account of running away', which was a complete fabrication of the situation under which they left the mill.

Elsewhere, parish apprentices out of their period of indenture, were sometimes considered unfit for future employment and were dismissed, which probably indicated their lack of skills and it appeared likely that many gained nothing from their craft training. Indeed, such training often appeared to be a subterfuge for cheap, or nearly free, labour which must have been the attraction to some apprentice masters. In spite of the inadequacies of parish apprenticeship from the recipient's point of view, it remained an attractive proposition to the parish burdened with pauper children, because an individual's settlement moved to the parish where they had attained craftsman status at the end of their apprenticeship, which was seen as a wholly desirable outcome that rid the Poor Rates of an unwanted burden. The aftercare of pauper apprentices under the Old Poor Law was a perpetual problem, with abuses common. This situation worsened as positions with local apprentice masters became more difficult to obtain, so that now apprentices were sent much further afield; this increased supervision problems and compounded abuses. Legislation passed in 1802[58] was intended to curb such problems, but it was ineffective and did nothing to regulate conditions in textile manufacturing, including the wool and silk industries. A further Act passed in 1819[59] attempted to resolve the problem of very young pauper apprentices being accepted in the textile trades. It confirmed that 'no child shall be employed in any description of work . . . until he or she shall have attained the full age of nine years',[60] which was important because children as young as seven years old had been apprenticed previously. However, this Act also attempted to regulate hours of work for apprentices in all textile industries, although perhaps inevitably these measures proved ineffective, as there was no enforcement agency to ensure proper implementation. Indeed, until there was an inspectorate to ensure compliance with apprenticeship regulations, there would be no development of effective control. The cotton industry remained the largest employer of pauper apprentices in the country, so another attempt was made to regulate this industry in 1820,[61] when legislation specifically attempted to regulate apprenticings in the Lancashire cotton trade. This was also in vain as this law was largely ignored. It appeared that if the cotton industry could not be regulated, the problems in other industries – where apprentices were more widely dispersed and fewer in number – were insuperable, so that that no real attempt was made to legislate for other industries.

By 1831 the control of apprenticeship was thought to need complete revision and a Factory Act was prepared to do this.[62] It was to repeal previous Acts and stated that 'certain regulations have become necessary to preserve the health and morals of such people',[63] referring particularly to young persons of both sexes employed in the cotton mills. Night work, considered morally damaging, was outlawed for those under twenty-one years of age, while a twelve-hour day was made the maximum for all those under eighteen years old. The minimum age for apprenticeship was also reaffirmed at nine years, with factory owners now made responsible for ensuring that no one under that age was employed, although they could claim in their defence that parents had certified the child old enough. This temptation, for parents eager to obtain work for their child, was great and such false certification went unchecked again because of a lack of inspection.

Another Factory Act was necessary in 1833;[64] this act appointed the first two full-time paid factory inspectors to visit industrial premises 'to examine therein the children and any other persons employed therein, and make enquiries respecting the condition of employment and education'. However, these men were also 'authorised and required to enforce attendance at school and factory'.[65] At last legislation materially affected the condition of pauper apprentices, ensuring that conditions 'be regulated . . . [with] due regard being had to their health and education',[66] but improvement remained slow until more Factory Inspectors were appointed. The 1833 Factory Act also specifically excluded children employed in certain processes, such as 'fulling, roughing and boiling',[67] which were continuous processes and from night work, but another clause of the Act meant that children under nine years old could still be employed in silk manufacture, because their nimble fingers were considered essential for that work. There was one other novel innovation in the 1833 Act, which had an immediate effect. This was the requirement for a certificate 'that such child . . . be of ordinary strength and appearance at the age of nine years . . . the child to personally appear before some surgeon or physician . . . and shall submit itself to his examination'[68] before being employed. According to extant parish apprenticeship indentures for Worcestershire, this regulation was applied immediately.

The New Poor Law, after 1834, was intended to be a new beginning. It represented a thoroughly modern approach, initially influenced by Edwin Chadwick, first secretary to the Poor Law Commission, who oversaw the new system and ensured the influence of utilitarianism and the orthodoxy of the early servants of the central administration. Nevertheless, this orthodoxy was not all pervasive, because the Old Poor Law still had influence in the post-1834 Poor Law system. Old workhouse premises, now overseen by Boards of Guardians, successors to the Overseers of the Poor, were in many cases in the same premises and overseen by the same officers, who had proven ability to cope with the considerable problems of the day-to-day care of pauper inmates. The new rules for running a Poor Law union and a workhouse, after 1834, may have been developed in the totally orthodox atmosphere of Somerset House, the offices of the Poor Law Commission in London, but they were interpreted locally by Guardians and officials steeped in the traditions of the Old Poor Law. Thus, when added to the inappropriateness of the New Poor Law to rural places, such as those in Worcestershire, and to the realisation that the Poor Law was financed and controlled locally, the influence of the Old Poor Law was inevitably to continue, although this influence gradually diminished as older Guardians disappeared and union officials were replaced, retired, or died. Of the methods available for dealing with children under the Old Poor Law, apprenticeship was most important. It was suspended for a time, after 1834, but was reinstated by the Poor Law Amendment Act of 1844,[69] which meant that the type of child who was a pauper apprentice under the Old Poor Law, between 1780 and 1834, was liable to be a workhouse inmate after 1834. It is these children who are the subject of the remainder of this book.

CHAPTER

2

APPRENTICESHIP UNDER THE OLD POOR LAW, 1780–1834

Of the methods available for dealing with pauper children under the Old Poor Law, only the parish apprenticeship system was useful in resolving the problems of rural areas such as Worcestershire. Workhouses were rare in the county prior to 1834, although even if they had existed they were considered inappropriate places for children, as was the child's home with its pauper parents, on outdoor relief. However, the Poor Law Commission's preferred solution to the problem, the children's establishment, which had been adopted in the Metropolis, was impossible in a rural area, because of the low density of population. This meant there were insufficient children to sustain such an institution, so that parish apprenticeship remained the only viable solution to the problem.

Parish apprenticeship has received relatively scant detailed treatment in historical work on the Old Poor Law, apparently because the evidence available is disparate, difficult to analyse and generally confusing. In spite of this, some historians of the Old Poor Law have indicated[1] that it was impossible to assess the intentions of Overseers in apprenticing pauper children anyway. However, it appeared that quantitative methods, which have been little used in this context before, might provide information about some aspects of pauper apprenticeship.

It was certainly the case that the sort of child found in workhouses after the 1834 Poor Law Amendment Act would have previously been apprenticed at parish expense and therefore a detailed quantitative analysis of the sources available on parish apprenticeship in Worcestershire appeared worthwhile. It was hoped that this analysis would provide information about the potential clientele of the workhouses of the New Poor Law. This chapter investigates pauper apprentices, in Worcestershire between 1780 and 1834, to provide a comparison with the treatment of destitute children after the reform of the Poor Law system. However, the treatment of destitute children who were not apprenticed prior to this reform was not documented and therefore details of this procedure remain a matter of conjecture.

The pauper child was a cause for concern in Worcestershire, as elsewhere, prior to 1834, but because there was no central administration for the Old Poor Law there could be no unified action on the problem. The destitute were the responsibility of the Home Department, who apparently never communicated with parish authorities about measures to alleviate the situation of pauper children. However, an Act of Parliament,[2] intended to alleviate the problems of destitution, had been passed in 1782. This allowed unions of parishes to be formed to finance the building of workhouses, but few parishes availed themselves of this opportunity, which meant that in most places only poor-houses established under the Elizabethan Poor Law were in use. Where these existed, children accompanied their parents into them, thus joining deserted or orphan children who were already accommodated there. By the last quarter of the eighteenth century there was a growing belief in the endemic and contagious nature of mendicancy, a belief that made the workhouse even less acceptable as a means of dealing with pauper children. It was now thought that if young individuals had contact with afflicted adults, it would cause them great harm. It was this belief that also led to the questioning of the practice that allowed the offspring of afflicted families to remain in their homes, as the nature and condition of parents who accepted outdoor relief, made them unsuitable people to care for their own children. For this reason removal from their home was even more desirable.

In spite of this, as has already been suggested, the children's establishment – the accepted best solution to the pauper child problem – remained impractical. Hanway's Act of 1767[3] had encouraged the building of these establishments in Metropolitan areas, so that by the early nineteenth century most parts of London had separate children's establishments, but such schemes proved impossible in rural areas. Elsewhere in non-Metropolitan England, the cost of paying for the upkeep of pauper children placed a great strain on local Poor Rates and this pressure increased as the belief that workhouses created pauperism found favour.

The attractions of pauper apprenticeships were now even more obvious, so much so that the Parish Apprentices Act of 1698[4] was increasingly invoked as a means of ridding parishes of the burden of unwanted pauper children. Under this Act, children could be apprenticed at seven years of age, while younger individuals were left with their parents. By 1780 there had evolved three distinct types of parish apprenticeship. These were:

1. The binding of individual children to a master in consideration of a fee, so that a premium was paid by the Overseers of the Poor to the parish of origin for the child.
2. The allotment of pauper children to the ratepayers of the parish, selected in rotation, who were compelled to take such children, with failure to accept them leading to a fine.
3. The binding of batches of children to manufacturers to work in their factories.

In relation to this latter type of apprenticing – batch apprenticing – Sidney and Beatrice Webb, writing in the early twentieth century, asserted that in 1833: 'Changes in the distribution of the textile manufactories, and in the character of the machinery, together with increasing legal restrictions, had practically killed out (except in a few districts such as Worcestershire and Staffordshire) the device of wholesale apprenticing of pauper children to capitalist manufacturers.'[5] They based this opinion about batch apprenticing, on the evidence of Charles Pelham Villiers, who referred to the West Midlands counties, but not just to Worcestershire and Staffordshire, in his statements to the Poor Law Inquiry Commission of 1833.[6] In spite of this, nowhere could Sidney and Beatrice Webb have found proof of this assertion. It appeared that they thought that because Kidderminster had a thriving carpet industry, Stoke-on-Trent a pottery industry and the Black Country a multitude of different industries, there was a large market for child labour and that batch apprenticing must have been possible. A search of extant material on apprenticeships in Worcestershire and of carpet industry records, revealed no evidence of batch apprenticing in the county, including Kidderminster, or in the Severn Valley to the north of that town.[7] The area of Worcestershire from Kidderminster up the Severn Valley as far as Bridgnorth in Shropshire, had cottage-based handlooms for the weaving of carpets and carpet weavers from here certainly took apprentices, probably including some parish apprentices, but the numbers involved hardly warranted the description 'mass apprenticing'. Traditionally, the products of these cottage manufactories in the Severn Valley around Kidderminster were marketed through carpet proprietors, such as Henry Brinton, who operated from Kidderminster and established the first carpet mill in the town in 1821. After this date the industry became more centralised, although this reorganisation of carpet manufacture into factories, with the enlargement of scale that inevitably occurred, did not mean adopting the wholesale employment of parish apprentices. The Black Country, often considered the part of England where the Industrial Revolution began, was partly in Worcestershire, as Dudley was a detached enclave of the county within Staffordshire. This area was renowned for its small workshops making metal goods, but these industries were essentially small scale and while pauper apprentices were certainly bound to Black Country manufacturers by county parishes, the numbers involved were again always small and insufficient to be termed wholesale apprenticing. Worcestershire thus had no industry using large-scale modes of production that took batches of parish apprentices and in any case there were insufficient numbers of destitute children in the area to sustain such a system.

Sidney and Beatrice Webb understandably cited C.P. Villiers' evidence again, this time with reference to Kidderminster, where he had suggested that: 'One fifth of the inhabitants, were said, during my visit, to be non-parishioners, but who would soon acquire settlement.'[8] This apparently substantiated statement was used by the Webbs, together with evidence from an unnamed bookseller in Tewkesbury, who referred to the 'frameknitting trade' at some unidentified date in the past, to suggest vast apprenticing of pauper children in the carpet industry in Kidderminster. However, Villiers did not state what he meant by 'non-parishioners' and it remains uncertain whether he meant a person born outside the parish or one who had not obtained settlement there. A person born in a parish had an automatic right of settlement there, while outsiders could only alter their settlement if they bought property within their new parish or completed an apprenticeship there. However, even this did not prevent attempts – some of them successful – to remove individuals applying for poor relief to their parish of origin, or sometimes to the parish of origin of their parent. Therefore it was worthwhile to examine the evidence about the population of Kidderminster, contained in the 1851 census, the first to specify place of birth accurately. A sample of 10 per cent of the entries on the 1851 census was taken, which revealed that 58.1 per cent of the sample had been born outside Kidderminster, which had itself grown dramatically between 1801 and 1831, during which time its population doubled in size. Between 1831 and 1841 the population of the town fell slightly, but there was another increase between 1841 and 1851.[9] Clearly, a natural increase in population could not have sustained this high level of growth and there must have been substantial immigration into the town, but this migration could not be identified from the census, which did not indicate settlement, it only indicated place of birth.

Information about a sample of individuals born after 1834 was used to investigate natives and non-natives of the town and this cast doubt on Villiers' estimate of 20 per cent non-parishioners, which appeared a gross under-estimate. The percentage of persons born outside Kidderminster, was 58.5 per cent from this survey, which accorded well with the estimate taken from the sample of the whole population of the town in 1851. A survey of carpet workers, who were above twenty-five years old at the time of the 1851 census – who would thus have been over seven years of age in 1834, and would have been liable to be apprenticed under the Old Poor Law – gave some equally revealing results. Of the 1,834 natives of Kidderminster in this category, two-thirds were employed in the carpet industry, in stark contrast to non-natives of the town. Of these 2,586 individuals only 19.7 per cent were employed in the carpet industry. Also, out of the 508 individuals born outside Kidderminster who were employed in the carpet industry, over 100 were born in Wilton, Wiltshire, where carpet mills had been established in the 1780s: noticeably the youngest of these individuals were in their late forties at the time of the 1851 census, which suggested that they were imported as ready-trained technicians when Kidderminster established its carpet mills in the 1820s. Of the other 400 carpet industry employees from outside Kidderminster, there was no apparent pattern in their places of birth. If, as the Webbs had suggested, batches of apprentices had been sent to Kidderminster from the Gloucester area it would have been expected, less than twenty years later, that a group of Kidderminster inhabitants would have had places of birth in Gloucester; but this was not the case. Alternatively, there might have been two types of apprentice; craft apprentices, who received training that enabled them to become the next generation of carpet craftsmen, but who were not locally recruited and parish apprentices, who did not receive such training and thus did not become journeyman carpet weavers. The few parish apprentices engaged in the carpet industry were employed as drawers, setting up the frames on which carpets were woven, which was a relatively unskilled occupation for girls and young boys with nimble fingers. However, such children were certainly not classed as carpet weavers and they were apparently dismissed when their fingers became too plump to continue the work. Thus, while some of these individuals, possibly born in the Gloucester area, probably found alternative employment in the Kidderminster area, this was undetectable from their census entries; others probably left Kidderminster altogether. Craft apprentices were recruited in the Kidderminster area, where there grew up a tradition that one generation arranged employment for the next, a suggestion supported by an employee of Brinton's Carpets since 1926,[10] who was the third generation of his family employed in the carpet industry. His grandfather had first been employed in Brinton's carpet mill in the 1860s, where a system of internal recruitment had certainly operated for several generations. The term parish apprenticeship was somewhat of a misnomer, as destitute children appeared simply to be a source of cheap unskilled labour, which had advantages for the child's home parish. It rid them of a potential long-term burden, at the cost of a premium, usually of no more than £5, which meant that the apprentice's settlement was transferred away from their parish of birth, to the parish where they attained quasi-craftsman status. The community accepting the parish apprentice was now responsible for individuals pauperised in later life. This apparently caused severe problems for urban parishes, with industries that attracted so-called parish apprentices who apparently had a greater propensity to later become pauperised than did normal citizens.

The only exception to the internal recruitment of Kidderminster natives to the carpet industry was from parishes contiguous with the town, for instance Wribbenhall, the Mittons, Bewdley and places to the north and west of the town, extending into Shropshire. These were parishes that had traditionally been associated with cottage industry carpet weaving, where the pre-existence of skills made such people obvious recruits to centralised carpet manufactories in the Kidderminster area. Of carpet industry employees in 1851, around 70 per cent were born in Kidderminster, another 5 per cent at Wilton in Wiltshire, and the other 25 per cent outside Kidderminster, mainly from parishes near to the town. In other occupations the situation was virtually reversed, with only 23 per cent of people employed in other trades born in Kidderminster and 77 per cent born outside the town. Thus the carpet industry, the prime industry of Kidderminster, usually recruited from known individuals who were also normally related to existing employees in the industry. Other historians have found a similar tendency in other industries. For instance, among printers' apprentices in the eighteenth century, craftsmen also caused 'the exclusion of foreigners from the trade'.[11] It was thus the 'artisan élite' of the Kidderminster area who were recruited from within the town, or from parishes close by. For this reason, parish apprentices were never given access to these coveted occupations and thus the Webbs' suggestion of batch apprenticeship in the carpet industry in Kidderminster was totally unfounded, unless such apprentices habitually left the vicinity on completion of their training, which was a very doubtful proposition.

There was another example of suspect evidence about Kidderminster given to the Poor Law Inquiry Commission in 1833, when J. Gough Jnr, High Bailiff of the town, asserted that girls were never apprenticed in the carpet industry, a statement that was not substantiated by extant parish apprenticeship indentures. These showed two girls apprenticed to carpet weavers, which was a significant inaccuracy in evidence given to the Commission, demonstrating again that circumspection was needed when examining evidence from this Commission and any comments based on it. For this reason the work of Sidney and Beatrice Webb also needs careful reinterpretation.

Having discovered trends towards internal recruitment in the carpet trade it appeared worthwhile to conduct a comparative study of another prime trade in another area of the county. Glovemaking, in the city of Worcester, appeared to provide a suitable comparison. This trade had been conducted as a cottage industry from Tudor times and eventually it became the prime industry of Worcester, although glovemaking factories were not established before the 1880s. The trade employed men who cut the leather for gloves and women who sewed them. An analysis of those employed in the trade revealed a situation not unlike that of the carpet trade in Kidderminster. The same type of internal recruitment was seen to operate, with around three quarters of those employed in 1851, coming from Worcester parishes. Among Worcester men, glovemaking was a minority occupation, as the majority of skilled gloving labour was employed in the women's work of sewing gloves. For women such gloving work provided almost a quarter of all occupations within Worcester city at the time of the 1851 census. Among the whole population of the city, 63 per cent of males and 60 per cent of females were not born there, whereas approximately three-quarters of both sexes employed in glovemaking were Worcester born. Thus, as with carpet weaving there was no suspicion of batch apprenticing, even though glovemaking was a large scale employer, which meant that both towns had prime industries that recruited new labour predominantly from the families of workers already employed in the trade by a system of internal recruitment.

For the fifty or so years from 1781, there are still about 900 extant parish apprenticeship indentures, from 27 of the 302 county parishes. However, while it was difficult to justify the belief that these surviving documents are in any sense representative, none the less an analysis appeared worthwhile. Parish apprenticeship indentures changed design and wording several times between 1780 and 1834, but they were always recognisable from private apprenticeship indentures, which tended to be smaller and very differently worded. In some cases, parish apprenticeship indentures had remained attached to a bond of agreement between the master and the apprentice, which provided additional information. Realistically, however, an individual apprenticeship for a pauper child was analogous to the arrangement made by independent parents for their own offspring. Thus, when an individual pauper child was apprenticed to a master to learn a trade, a fee was often payable, the amount of which was recorded on the indenture. Such fees apparently made apprenticeships outside the parish of birth possible. While a parish apprenticing a pauper child gained the advantage of altering the apprentice's parish of settlement, this usually had to be paid for, so that the accepting parish gained revenue in aid of its Poor Rates. In spite of this, apprenticeships continued to be arranged without a fee, even outside the child's parish of origin, with no incentives offered apart from obtaining cheap labour. Sometimes clothing had been given with apprentices, for instance in Devon in the seventeenth century,[12] but there was no indication that this was done in Worcestershire before the 1840s. Usually, what the apprentice gained from its training was impossible to ascertain. In other cases, apprenticings were irregular and there was no suspicion of such an illegal system of apprenticing as that described to the Select Committee in 1818,[13] where apprentices were sent without indentures. Ironically, this would probably have made them a very attractive proposition as they would certainly have never been inspected.

Only 162 extant indentures were endorsed with a fee, a much lower proportion than expected, as a fee would normally be necessary to attract suitable masters. Nevertheless, of apprenticeships where an apprenticeship fee was paid, 75 were for places in the child's parish of origin, although 43 of these were in the parish of Hallow, where a fee of £1 10s 0d was habitually paid. None the less, it appeared likely that where an apprenticeship fee was paid, an employer felt more obliged to teach the apprentice certain skills, although there was no evidence to substantiate

23

this view. Husbandry was the most common occupation apprenticing pauper boys, while housewifery was most common for girls. In 19 out of 891 cases, the only occupation recorded was 'useful' and in a further 44 cases the occupational description was left blank, which probably meant that some apprentices described in this way were taught no trade at all.

The allotment of apprentices to ratepayers in rotation, a system made possible by an Act of Parliament of 1696,[14] which was eventually made completely illegal after 1834 because it was believed to be a source of 'much abuse', was certainly in use in Worcestershire between 1781 and 1834. This was a kind of enforced boarding out or fostering which resembled true apprenticeships only in that an indenture was used, on which the apprentice's trade appeared to be a description of the ratepayer's occupation, rather than of the training to be given to that pauper child. It was Charles Pelham Villiers who suggested to the Poor Law Inquiry Commission in 1833, that this form of apprenticeship was wholly unsatisfactory and that: 'The system compelling the ratepayers to receive apprentices according to the amount of their assessment has generally been discontinued, owing to the opportunity which manufacturers offer in the county for early employment, and the dislike of the ratepayers themselves of the practice.'[15] However, apprentices were still allotted in a few parishes in Worcestershire in the early nineteenth century, although this arrangement appeared to be unsatisfactory, as the individual apparently learned no skills and ratepayers only gained an additional burden.

Powick parish was late in adopting parish apprenticeship as a solution to child destitution. In fact, 89 per cent of its apprenticings were in the period 1817 to 1820, at a time when there was no economic crisis in the area and when 'real wages' were more or less static. Thus, it was difficult to understand why this parish suddenly apprenticed over fifty pauper children and particularly why it chose allotment apprenticing, a system that had already proved so unpopular elsewhere. Within Powick this dislike was apparent in 1818, when three ratepayers refused to accept such apprentices. In two cases the intended masters were 'Fined £10 for not taking an apprentice', while another man was 'Fined £10 for returning a (husbandry) apprentice'. Thus, some Poor Rate payers clearly deemed it better to pay a £10 fine, a considerable sum of money at that time, than take an unwanted apprentice for at least seven years. The system was shown to have little use to the master in another way, because no master demanded more than one apprentice. Surely, had they benefited from this arrangement they would have asked for more apprentices.

Parishes apprenticing pauper children varied considerably in size and character, from the extremely small parish of Besford, with a population of 102 at the 1801 census, to the thirteen parishes of Worcester city, with a combined population of 14,036. There was no indication however that a *pro rata* 'apprenticeship rate', analogous to 'marriage rate', could be computed. However, this was to be expected, as local conditions determined the need for pauper apprenticeships and these conditions varied considerably from place to place and from time to time. The parish of Alvechurch, with a population of 1,288 in 1801, apprenticed the most pauper children, 208, between 1780 and 1834, while several small parishes apprenticed very few children indeed. For instance, Warndon, close to Worcester, with a population of 126 in 1801, apprenticed only three children and Huddington, with a population of 108, apprenticed only one child, although the much larger parish of Evesham All Saints, with a population of 1,197, apprenticed only two children. Yet, it would have been expected that such a large and relatively urban parish would have apprenticed more youngsters. Clearly, the matter of pauper apprenticeships was more complicated than it at first appeared. In all parishes apprenticing over 100 pauper children, between 1780 and 1834, males outnumbered females. Assuming that there was a 50:50 proportion of males to females in the population, this was unexpected and there must have been a reason for this disparity. Such inequalities varied between parishes, so that in the city of Worcester there was an 87:13 proportion of males to females, with the proportion only approaching 50:50 at Hallow, which, as has already been discussed had a peculiar apprenticing policy. In most county parishes there was a smaller number of girls requiring apprenticeship, which was probably due to the relative ease with which they obtained domestic employment. For instance, Worcester city had a great demand for such domestics and in this circumstance it might have been expected that the contiguous parish of Hallow would have been similar. However, as 87 per cent of apprentices recorded in Hallow, including girls, received a fee, this probably disturbed this trend.

The nature of a parish was clearly important in determining how often parish apprenticeships were used as a solution to the problem of destitute children. Certainly, places in Worcestershire varied considerably in terms of size and remoteness. The county was most developed down the valleys of the Rivers Severn and Avon, which had market gardens along them and in the urban and industrial areas bordering the Black Country and

Birmingham. It was in these areas that population densities were greatest and increasing. They acted as magnets for country people in search of work, which caused 'stepwise migration'[16] and some pauper apprentices were among these migrants. Meanwhile, the area of upland in the extreme west of the county, around the Clee Hills, depopulated, so there was no need for pauper apprenticeship there. However, perhaps rather surprisingly, it was not the highly urban and industrial Poor Law unions that accepted most pauper children as apprentices, presumably because there was a plentiful alternative supply of cheap labour there. Rather, it was intermediate places that found the acceptance of parish apprentices most attractive. Over half (56.8 per cent) of male parish apprentices went to farming or husbandry, while two-thirds (66.7 per cent) of females went into housewifery, particularly in rural parishes. When the relationship between rurality and the numbers of parish apprenticeships in husbandry and housewifery was computed, by means of a correlation coefficient, a strong relationship was established between the proportion of boys apprenticed to husbandry and girls to housewifery and the population size in 1801. This was presumably because apprenticeships in these occupations were easiest to find in rural areas, where a solution of the child destitution problem was most pressing. Nevertheless, the problem was less pressing for girls, even in rural areas, because domestic occupations were easily available without the need for apprenticeships. Thus, both husbandry and housewifery apprenticeships were very different from craft apprenticeships and indeed they probably hardly warranted the epithet apprenticeship at all, because the skills taught were easily available elsewhere.

Glovemaking, shoemaking and weaving, which were crafts well represented in the county, provided genuine craft apprenticeships. Glovemaking, the prime industry of Worcester, was unusual because girls employed in the women's work of sewing gloves outnumbered boys as apprentices, whereas other trades connected with leather, such as leather grounding, loathing and tannery work employed only men and thus these trades apprenticed only boys. Around half of all cordwainer's or shoemaker's apprentices were in the city of Worcester, although shoemakers were present in most communities, but some of these apprentices were employed in shoe repair as opposed to shoemaking. Elsewhere, weaver was an occupational title used to include individuals employed in textile industries including carpet making, although five of the thirty-eight individuals described as weaver's apprentices were certainly employed in making cloth. The other thirty-three were carpet weavers and bombazine weavers, who respectively made pile carpets and closely woven carpets with uncut piles of superior quality. Bombazine weavers appeared to have greater status in the carpet trade than did ordinary carpet weavers, partly because of the greater measure of skill required, but also because these carpets were more expensive to buy.

The need to apprentice pauper children also varied according to the economic climate prevailing in an area. For this reason apprenticeship numbers fluctuated wildly, apparently as the cost of living increased, pressure was exerted on personal economic circumstances, which was felt by the poor most keenly. Individuals on the margins of pauperism were now in most danger from destitution and thus any increase in the cost of living caused the number of individuals applying for parish relief to rise. This in turn made their children liable to be apprenticed at parish expense and for this reason parish apprenticeships were often clustered around times of economic crisis.

The *Worcester Herald* gave cereal prices in local markets that were very similar to those found nationally. These prices were critical to the poor as bread remained a staple in their diet, and therefore, not surprisingly, cereal prices were related very closely to the cost of bread, the cost of living and to real wages. National real wage levels[17] were used to compute cost of living and real wage indices, which were then employed to investigate the relationship between the state of the local economy, the level of destitution and the rate at which pauper children were apprenticed at parish expense. There proved to be a strong relationship between the cost of living and the tendency for parishes to apprentice destitute children: this was also true for any substantial sub-group of the main sample, such as the numbers of male or female apprentices, the numbers of apprentices in urban as opposed to rural areas and the numbers of apprentices to husbandry or housewifery. Pauper apprenticing increased when the cost of living increased and the mechanism initially postulated, where a rising cost of living plunged more families into accepting poor relief, thus exposing their children to the possibility of becoming a parish apprentice, appeared most reasonable. By correlating male apprentice numbers against those for females in particular quarters of years, a very strong relationship between apprenticing patterns for both sexes of apprentice was revealed in spite of the large numbers of pauper girls finding employment in domestic work other than by apprenticeship. However, this tendency was to be expected, as local circumstances, and particularly local economic conditions, were common to all children no matter what their gender.

Given these findings, it was not unexpected that the age distribution of apprentices also altered as economic circumstances varied, so that younger children were apprenticed in times of financial hardship. The minimum age for apprenticing had been set at seven years by an Act of Parliament in 1698,[18] but usually children were not apprenticed this young. However, the number of seven and eight year olds apprenticed, when related to real wages, indicated that the apprenticing of younger children coincided with a worsening local economic climate. Thus, as real wages fell, individuals became financially distressed and younger children were offered for apprenticing. Most parishes waited until a child was at least eight years old before apprenticing them, but some places waited even longer, with the age range for apprenticing usually being between eight and twelve years old. The lowest mean age for apprenticing, of under nine years old, was at Leigh, a rural community, while the highest mean age, of around twelve years old, was at Kidderminster St Mary's, one of the most urban parishes in the county. None the less these discrepancies also related to the availability of husbandry and housewifery apprenticeships in a parish, as very young children could cope with some of the menial tasks involved in these occupations. The average age for the commencement of apprenticeship in such places was depressed by the preponderance of younger children apprenticed to these trades.

A minimum duration of seven years for an apprenticeship was laid down under the Elizabethan Statute of 1563,[19] but by the late eighteenth century male apprenticeship indentures showed twenty-four years as the age for apprenticeships to end, whereas females were apprenticed until they were twenty-one years old or until they married. Whilst these age limits were usually applied in Worcestershire, one parish, Welland, was an exception. This very rural parish, in the south-east of the county, turned to apprenticeship as a means of dealing with pauper children only after 1820; in the seventy years beforehand there had been no apprenticing, and unusually they chose allotment apprenticing as their favoured approach, a system which had caused great resentment when it was tried in other places. However, they also chose a completion age of sixteen years of age for both male and female apprentices, which was clearly encouraging, because fourteen apprenticeships were arranged almost immediately. Of these cases, twelve were to unspecified trades, with the occupational description left blank. In the other two cases, one as a butcher's apprentice, the other as a tailor's apprentice, the completion age was specified as twenty-one years old. Why Welland should use sixteen years old as the age to end most apprenticeships remained a mystery, although this conscious decision would have alleviated the anxiety of parishioners allotted apprentices and it was equally unclear why other parishes, using similar apprenticeship schemes, did not adopt the same expedient of a shorter period of apprenticeship to quell the anxieties of their Poor Rate payers.

The age of commencement for apprenticeships in various occupations also varied, with the mean age of commencement clearly indicating the nature of the age-distribution of apprenticing in that trade. A low mean age of commencement indicated a tendency to apprentice younger pauper children and a higher mean age, older individuals. Husbandry and housewifery apprenticeships, which taught some skills that could be managed by younger children, on average apprenticed children one year younger than did other trades, a pattern that was most apparent when rural and urban housewifery apprentices were separated. Here, it was found that the average age of commencement for housewifery apprentices in towns was 10.7 years, compared with 9.9 years in country areas, which supported well the earlier contention that housewifery was a suitable occupation for young girls in rural areas. Glovemaking, nailmaking, tailoring and carpet weaving were all trades with a higher element of skill, for which very young children were considered unsuitable, so that the mean age of commencement for apprenticeship in these trades was about eleven years old.

When the date at which various trades ceased to recruit pauper apprentices was investigated it was found that while most of the occupations surveyed began apprenticings well before 1780, there was no commonality about when recruitment ceased. Thus, some trades stopped recruiting apprentices much earlier than did others, possibly because these trades became mechanised. Service[20] and housewifery were trades that were never automated, so that the demand for girl apprentices in these occupations continued unabated throughout the period to 1834. On the other hand, occupations for boys in agriculture became much less common after 1800, as an agrarian revolution took place. Carpet weaving, which became centralised in factories from the 1820s onwards, having previously been a cottage trade, was forced to alter its mode of apprenticing in about 1820, after which cottage industry tradesmen, who had previously employed their own apprentices – sometimes parish apprentices – ceased to be regarded as suitable masters by parish authorities. Former masters were now employed by carpet manufacturers, such as Henry Brinton, which meant that pauper apprentices were no longer employed, even as drawers, in setting up the carpet looms.

The dates at which parishes began apprenticing pauper children also proved revealing; some parishes, particularly Hallow, Powick and Welland did not use parish apprenticeships to solve the problem of destitution among children before 1800, although there was no evidence available to suggest a reason for this. Most rural county parishes stopped apprenticing children much earlier than this, long before their urban counterparts did so, possibly because the need for such apprenticeship disappeared in rural places. This was particularly a problem where children and fecund women, likely to bear offspring, migrated from these areas in the second half of the eighteenth century, which left an ageing population with no children to be apprenticed. However, in towns, the need for parish apprenticeship continued.

The geographical placement of apprentices also differed, with rural places tending to apprentice inside the home parish whereas urban places often sent destitute children some distance away. Hallow was an exception to this, as only 26 per cent of its parish apprentices were sent to masters inside the parish, an aberration probably explained by the fee that was habitually paid there. It may also have been that its parish apprentices were relatively more attractive to employers than pauper children from other places, although the nearness of Worcester, a city with a demand for parish apprentices, may have disturbed the expected pattern of apprenticing. Perhaps significantly, around two-thirds of the total pauper apprentices from Hallow were arranged after 1808, the date when the parish authorities began habitually to pay an apprenticing fee, which probably attracted hesitant apprentice masters.

The dates at which various parishes were willing to accept apprentices were also revealing. Birmingham, Wolverhampton and other places in Staffordshire and Warwickshire, outside the county, took pauper apprentices from Worcestershire parishes and some parish authorities appeared to favour apprenticing pauper children to places over twenty miles from the their home. This was probably because the Law required that such children be reported on by the host parish, whose responsibility these apprentices now became, which was administratively ensured by having duplicate copies of the apprenticeship indentures, one for the apprenticing parish, the other for the parish accepting the child. This system apparently worked, as there was no indication that such children returned to their parish of birth once they had been sent away as parish apprentices.

Apprenticeship fees were sometimes paid by parish authorities to employers to take pauper apprentices, but these varied considerably in amount, although as might be expected, in nineteenth-century England, these also differed for male and female apprentices. Where apprenticeship fees were paid, the mean fee paid for boy apprentices was £4 4s 6d, compared with an average £2 18s 10d for girls. However, if the fees for Hallow parish, where fees were habitually paid, were ignored, the average fee paid was £5 0s 3d for boys and £4 8s 10d for girls. When a rank order of mean fees paid in various trades was compiled, it was unexpectedly found that the average fee for husbandry apprentices was £5 4s 7d, which was above the average fee paid for pauper children bound to carpet weavers, glovemakers and shoemakers, which were all trades with a higher skill content. While this was difficult to explain, it was perhaps the case that a higher fee was necessary to gain such employment with a large-scale farmer, who could provide better employment opportunities. Certainly, genuine craft apprenticeships usually attracted a high average fee, so that tailors were, on average, paid £7 5s 6d, shoemakers £4 12s 4d, glovers £4 6s 8d and carpet weavers £4 5s 9d to take pauper apprentices. These were fees that apparently indicated the prestige of the craft involved, while the status of the individual to whom the apprentice was to be bound was also probably important. Such fees ensured that access to artisan élite trades was tightly regulated for all apprentices, paupers or not. This was the most likely reason for the largest fee paid with pauper apprentices, fifteen guineas, paid when two fourteen-year-old boys, both from Claines, were apprenticed in the city of Worcester, one to a cordwainer, the other to a breeches maker. These fees were certainly sufficient to make these apprenticeships approximate to those arranged privately by a parent for their own offspring. However, it may also have been that a larger fee was necessary to get an older child apprenticed, as both of these boys were fourteen years old when bound apprentice, which was towards the top end of the age range for parish apprentices.

Another aspect investigated was the distances that pauper children travelled from their home parish to be apprenticed. Only one child from the county travelled over fifty miles, when a ten-year-old boy from Droitwich, was sent to a glass-cutter in Rotherham, Yorkshire, although why he went so far afield to be bound apprentice remained unclear. In most cases, apprenticeships were within Worcestershire, with 80 per cent within the parish of the child's birth, although some places in Herefordshire, Gloucestershire, Shropshire, Staffordshire and Warwickshire accepted apprentices from Worcestershire parishes.

Birmingham, Kidderminster and King's Norton provided many housewifery apprenticeships, which was to be expected, as these places were growing urban centres and attracted labour like a magnet, but also because they were places where even the upper working classes could afford cheap servants, many of them former child inmates from workhouses. Of pauper children sent to Worcester city to be apprenticed, about 82 per cent came from the contiguous parish of Claines. However, the mean distance migrated by male apprentices in the county, as a whole, was 4.5 miles, while girls migrated an average 3.5 miles. This discrepancy was expected, because, as was suggested, it was easier for girls to obtain employment. In spite of this, in broad terms, the patterns of migration revealed were similar for both boy and girl apprentices.

In Worcestershire, before 1834, as in many other rural counties, workhouses were relatively uncommon and outdoor relief was used as the main means of dealing with large numbers of paupers. Children, who were dependants of these paupers, were also given outdoor relief, but where institutions existed dependent children were inmates along with their parents. However, orphans and deserted children were automatically placed in the workhouse, if one existed, or they were given outdoor relief and placed with foster parents, if there was no suitable institution available. Nevertheless, both of these methods of dealing with destitute children were considered unsatisfactory and countenanced only as long as pauperism was regarded as an unfortunate chance happening. When a theory developed that pauperism was disease-like, endemic and contagious, a means of sanitising society was sought and nowhere was the need for this more urgent than in the treatment of pauper children, who continued to be seen as blameless for their plight.

This chapter has investigated pauper apprenticeship as an aspect of the treatment of destitute children, in the fifty years before the Poor Law Amendment Act of 1834,[21] which abolished parish apprenticeships altogether for more than a decade. What it has also done is to identify the type of child dealt with by parish apprenticeship under the Old Poor Law, who after 1834 was to be maintained and treated in the workhouses of the New Poor Law. These are the children who are described in the remainder of this book.

CHAPTER 3

THE TREATMENT OF CHILDREN

As has been suggested, under the Old Poor Law children were given outdoor relief and were liable to be apprenticed as parish poor children, but, after 1834, under the New Poor Law such children were liable to be found in workhouses, although they were still regarded as their parents' responsibility, including when they were admitted to the workhouse. Here treatment was determined by the rules and regulations of the Poor Law Commission, between 1834 and 1847, and by the Poor Law Board, between 1847 and 1871, with local interpretation of policy varying considerably. By using sources relating to the Poor Law locally, an image develops of the relationship between the bureaucracy and its clientele, including the children, and while we cannot reconstruct what life was like for an individual child in a particular workhouse on a specific day, what we can gain is an enduring impression of the conditions and treatment obtained.

The 1834 Poor Law Amendment Act[1] made the Poor Law Commission, described by Elie Halevy as the 'Somerset House dictators',[2] responsible for administering the Poor Law in 396 unions.[3] Originally the Commission's regulations had been inflexible, but correspondence between local and national administrators was still full of reinterpretations of policy, constantly altering the situation and accentuating local differences, in spite of the intention that this should not happen. Eventually, this led the Commission to become unequal to its task, not in the sense of inadequacy, but in the sense that its bureaucracy had outgrown its administration. The Commission was replaced, in 1847, by the Poor Law Board and Norman Gash has commented that the central authority, at this time, was 'primarily concerned with the administrative structure rather than the policy it was to administer',[4] a comment that was very appropriate, so that replacement appeared inevitable.

The New Poor Law was based on two guiding principles; National Uniformity and Less Eligibility, on which all of its practices, including the treatment of children, were based. The Principle of National Uniformity, in which all paupers, in all unions, were to be treated equally, was introduced in 1834, but by 1847 the ideological context had altered and the treatment of children and aged paupers, was radically different from that originally envisaged. The reason for this was that the definition of pauperism, particularly in the case of these two groups, had significantly changed, so that Gertrude Himmelfarb's notion of the nature of poverty altering,[5] because of its revised definition, was demonstrated.

In the north of England there was a resistance to the New Poor Law, so that in some places it remained unimplemented, but the Worcestershire unions – like most of southern England and Wales – complied with the new Law, although unions like Dudley applied a version of the Law acceptable to the local Guardians. Almost immediately, it became obvious that some of the basic principles of the new Law were unworkable, particularly in dealing with children, a situation that resulted in a constant flow of orders and regulations to remedy impracticalities. In spite of this, the administrators at Somerset House, the headquarters of the Poor Law Commission, were reticent to sanction any formal change of the rules and regulations by which the New Poor Law was administered, although it was clear from the outset that flexibility was necessary to cope with the very different needs of unions in their many different local contexts. National Uniformity hampered this and inevitably the principle was speedily abandoned, for all but able-bodied male paupers, although even in their treatment some discretion was allowed. By the 1850s, in the majority of unions, outdoor relief for able-bodied paupers had been abolished,[6] apart from in the most exceptional of circumstances, for instance, during periods of severe frost in parishes bordering the River Severn, where watermen were laid off for considerable periods. Here, outdoor relief continued to be allowed, which was a sensible decision in the circumstances, because otherwise the workhouses would have become overcrowded and their systems unworkable, although it appeared to be practicality rather than compassion that led to such unofficial decisions.

The Poor Law Report of 1834 largely ignored children and the comment by Sidney and Beatrice Webb, writing in the early twentieth century, that 'apart from apprenticeship the report deals only incidentally with children . . . It assumes throughout that the children go with their parents'[7] appeared an appropriate summary. Some adults entering the workhouse brought their children with them, but from the outset there were roughly twice as many children on outdoor relief as in the workhouses, in spite of an attempt to outlaw all outdoor relief. The condition of such children was to remain largely undocumented, except in the special case of medical relief, which will be dealt with in the next chapter.

Despite the general unpreparedness of the Poor Law Central Authority for many situations common after 1834, large numbers of dependent children in the workhouse were expected, and to some extent, planned for. This was particularly so in Metropolitan and densely populated urban areas, where such children were to be placed in separate institutions and to be given special treatment including education '. . . by a person properly qualified to act as a schoolmaster'.[8] However, even in 1834, it was apparently considered unsatisfactory that children should be exposed to the atmosphere of the general workhouse, although the only viable alternative, in most places, including the whole of Worcestershire, was that the various classes of pauper be strictly segregated. Again this decision was apparently based on morality rather than on practicality. In the large general workhouses created in Worcestershire and elsewhere, which were to be administered by one set of officers, with a workhouse master in charge and responsible for all inmates, complete segregation proved impossible to enforce. It was the workhouse master who determined the behaviour of his subordinate officers, including the schoolmaster and schoolmistress, which invariably meant that the special needs of child inmates were effectively ignored. Understandably, chief officers became preoccupied with the needs of able-bodied adult paupers, who were seen as more threatening and whose needs were thus perceived as being paramount in general workhouses.

The initial intention, regarding the administration of paupers in workhouses, had been that: 'Each class might . . . receive an appropriate treatment; the old may enjoy their indulgences without torment from the boisterous; the children to be educated, the able-bodied to be subjected to such course of labour and discipline as will repel the indolent and the vicious',[9] but in most cases in county workhouses the complete separation deemed necessary to accomplish this was impossible. The cause of this was not the quality of the workhouse officers, or their fulfilment of their duties, but rather it was the design and the state of the old workhouses, which still housed paupers under the New Poor Law. These buildings were seen as totally inappropriate to the needs of the system developed after 1834. The exception to this was Dudley union,[10] which provided separate departmental workhouses, fortuitously adapted from the four old workhouses available in the union. Sedgley workhouse became the children's department, after 1834, so that child inmates in Dudley union were only tolerated in the general workhouse for three or four weeks, before being transferred to Sedgley. This was a system that endured until 1858, when ironically, a new workhouse was built and the union ceased to have a separate children's department. Thus, the treatment of children in most of the county's workhouses remained inappropriate throughout the period to 1871.

In 1834 the intention had been to maintain the twin principles of the New Poor Law, National Uniformity and Less Eligibility, at all costs and for all classes of pauper. This it was hoped would secure the purpose stated in the Report; that 'his [the pauper's] situation on the whole shall not be made really or apparently so eligible as the situation of the independent labourer of the lowest class',[11] thus maintaining the deterrent effect of the workhouse. This rationale was further buttressed by the belief that 'as the condition of any pauper class is elevated above the condition of the independent labourers, the condition of the independent class is depressed; their industry impaired, their employment becomes unsteady, and its remuneration in wages diminished'. Thus, potential paupers were 'under the strongest inducement to quit the less eligible class of labourers and enter the more eligible class of paupers'. The reverse proposition was also thought to be true, because: 'Every penny bestowed that renders the condition of the pauper more eligible than that of the independent labourer, is a bounty on indolence and vice.'[12] These aspects of the new Poor Law administration, after 1834, had Jeremy Bentham's utilitarian philosophy as their progenitor, so that Gertrude Himmelfarb's thesis[13] that it was morality that initially lay at the base of all such policy, also appeared reasonable.

Thus, the workhouse, with its provision for less eligible treatment, was seen as a disincentive to pauperism and by 1847, when the Poor Law Commission was replaced by the Poor Law Board, the principle had come to be achieved by a régime of confinement in such institutions. Life was monotonous and inmates, including children, were given menial and degrading tasks to perform, thus impressing on them their lowly condition. Such treatment probably hastened the pauper child's institutionalisation, particularly as some children lived in such a restricted environment for up to sixteen years, which much concerned both supporters and opponents of the Poor Law from among the middle and upper classes. For this reason, it was stated in the House of Commons, in 1848 that: 'Too many of those brought up in the workhouse were marked by a tendency to regard the workhouse as their natural home. They had been accustomed to the workhouse from early infancy . . . and when they were adults there was nothing to deter them from entering it',[14] a tendency that inevitably caused consternation, as hereditary pauperism, which was considered endemic in the workhouses, was increasingly feared. Because of this further action about the incarceration of children in the workhouse was demanded.

Probably inevitably, support for Less Eligibility was initially strongest among Poor Rate payers, so that Poor Law Commission orders, regulations and circulars coming soon after 1834, were supportive of this principle. However, this phase came to an end with the removal of the first secretary Edwin Chadwick, to the Poor Law Commission, after 1841. This was referred to by S.E. Finer, Chadwick's biographer, as 'dropping the pilot',[15] in a significant use of Tenniel's phrase,[16] with regard to the first secretary's influence on the Poor Law Commission. At this point Edwin Chadwick was said to have lost his 'personal battle' with George Cornewall-Lewis, one of three Poor Law Commissioners, so that 'utilitarianism',[17] most associated with rigid adherence to Less Eligibility, lost favour and, according to Finer, Chadwick now 'withdrew from Poor Law affairs completely',[18] until the Andover workhouse scandal of 1845. After this case, in which paupers were definitely treated less eligibly, public opinion altered and Chadwick's influence was temporarily reinstated, which might have led to the decline of Cornewall-Lewis's power, but nepotism saved him. Chadwick, the so called 'victor'[19] of this competition for influence again lost importance, which caused the emphasis on Less Eligibility in the treatment of paupers, including children, to be reduced; this time for good. The Poor Law Board Act of 1847[20] was to confirm the reduction of the importance of this principle, but some county Guardians continued to insist that all inmates be treated less eligibly. Thus, for instance, the Guardians at Martley[21] continued to insist on no erosion of the principle and they ostentatiously refused to implement orders and regulations that they considered ignored Less Eligibility. Elsewhere in the county, other Guardians adhered to what Sidney and Beatrice Webb were to refer to, at the beginning of the twentieth century, as 'supplying whatever was necessary',[22] sometimes in direct contravention of Poor Law Board orders. However, after 1848, there was certainly no demand for the continuance of the Principle of Less Eligibility in relation to children, but in some cases it was still applied to able-bodied adults.

In undifferentiated general workhouses, according to G.D.H. Cole and Raymond Postgate, children were exposed to the same régime as adult paupers, to dissuade them from a life of indolence and mendicancy and being kept in what has been described as 'sluggish sensual indolence'.[23] Segregation in workhouses, including those in the county, was maintained to prevent contamination of the young by adults, who were presumed to be tainted by mendicancy. To ensure this, after 1836, children were classified on the basis of:

1. Boys between 7 and 13 years.
2. Girls between 7 and 16 years.
3. Children under 7 years old.[24]

This system of classification was logical and legitimated the existing situation in Worcestershire workhouses, where the classification ages of boys and girls had always varied, probably because girls obtained employment more easily than boys. However, the presence of unchaste women, such as known prostitutes, in the workhouse, would also have meant that girls of thirteen years old, or less, in general wards, would be liable to contamination by these undesirables. Clearly keeping pubescent girls apart from such women was thought essential, whereas the situation where boys of a similar age resided in adult male wards posed no comparable danger. Segregation in workhouses was obviously not always as complete as the separate treatment of youngsters – recommended by the Poor Law central authority – demanded, but such officially approved practices were not always to the liking of local Boards of Guardians. Those at Droitwich showed this when they stated: 'This Board does not think it right either to compel the separation of children from their mothers before the age of seven years, or to offer the workhouse to mothers, themselves not being paupers – while on the other hand the Board consider it highly inexpedient to accord to all such children on application for relief, an indiscriminate payment of eighteen pence.'[25]

However, the 1836 national classification system was clearly not regarded as satisfactory by the Central Poor Law Authority, because it was revised in 1838 to:

changed

1. Boys between 7 and 15 years.
2. Girls between 7 and 15 years.
3. Children under 7 years old.[26]

However, this new system was not seen as necessary, or desirable, by some county Guardians, because these changes were not immediately adopted everywhere. For instance, Worcester union did not use it until 1840,[27] ostensibly because good employment prospects in the area made it unnecessary and perhaps significantly the Poor Law Commission did not question this decision, although had these central administrators been totally convinced of the need to change workhouse classification, they would surely have been more assiduous in applying the revised classification nationally. Now, the treatment of children continued to depend on their age, but also on their health, so that sickly children were treated differently from the rest from the outset.

Initially, the workhouse system was strict, rigid and unchanging, with segregation between pauper classes to be as complete as possible, but this aspect of the workhouse régime was imperfect from the start. This was well illustrated at Pershore, in 1837,[28] where communication over the walls of the yard occurred, which resulted in a costly alteration to the workhouse, which raised the height of the walls by two feet; an unsuccessful attempt to prevent such events happening. Elsewhere, the Kidderminster Visiting Committee, in 1846, made substantial alterations to their workhouse. Here it was recorded that 'in consequence of the entrance to the vagrants' ward' opening into the boys' yard and thus affording a means of communication between the vagrants and the boys, they recommended that the doors and windows should be removed to the opposite side, opening into the garden, and also that the privy be divided and the door put on the garden side.[29] In spite of such extensive alterations, imperfect segregation in the county's workhouses continued throughout the period from 1834 to 1871. Whilst many piecemeal attempts were made to improve matters, problems continued.

Kidderminster, like several other unions, had an old workhouse which progressively became over-used as the New Poor Law was implemented. The major problem here, as elsewhere, was the general layout of the workhouse, which was based on outdated ideas, not surprising as the ideology of 'pauper management' had been drastically altered by the philosophical stance of Jeremy Bentham and the other utilitarians. Thus, after 1834, in hard winters when men were thrown out of work, the Poor Law institutions filled and the only solution available to Guardians was to resort to outdoor relief which thus prevented overcrowding. This measure was used regularly at Worcester, where the annual report of the Poor Law Commission, in 1847,[30] recorded that the workhouse was full during the winter months, with outdoor relief adopted to alleviate the problem. Whilst the central authority could not have approved of this, because it ran contrary to official thinking, they were forced to accept the solution. However, in 1842, they did act and made an uncharacteristically pragmatic decision,[31] allowing unions to classify children over ten years of age in any way they chose, so that classes of inmates could be mixed together, which was completely contrary to the Commission's previously professed beliefs. Not surprisingly, therefore, this decision was reversed in 1847,[32] although the problem of overcrowding persisted. However, in some unions, other solutions were tried. For instance, at Bromsgrove workhouse, where seasonal overcrowding was common, it was found worthwhile to open a temporary workhouse whenever this was necessary.

In spite of such attempts to solve these administrative problems, workhouses continued to be, 'as disagreeable as was consistent with health',[33] according to Sir George Nicholls, one of the Poor Law Commissioners, but it was obvious that this statement referred to the treatment of able-bodied adult paupers, because children continued to be strictly segregated by gender. Under the regulation of 1848, children were to be kept where 'separation must be entire and absolute between the sexes, who are to live, sleep and take their meals in totally separate parts of the building, with an enclosed yard for each'[34] and where a specially designed régime of treatment, different from that for adult paupers, could be applied. Infants were also to be treated as a separate class, but for practical reasons, relating to the problems of having unattended infants in the workhouse, it was decided they 'are to be kept by their mothers until they are of an age to receive instruction . . . [after which] . . . they are to be sent to school' and to 'live in the children's wards'.[35]

In 1851, after the recasting of the Poor Law Commission as the Poor Law Board, Lord George Cornewall-Lewis asserted to another Poor Law Commissioner, Sir Edmund Head, that the Board had become 'purely administrative, and had no character or policy of its own',[36] which ironically was redolent of the criticisms levelled at its predecessor, the Poor Law Commission. These criticisms had led to its replacement only four years earlier. Such problems were probably inevitable and arose because decisions about administration and policy were now determined outside the Poor Law Board, by politicians accountable to Parliament. The effect of this was that the central administration turned in on itself and became preoccupied with the minutiae of workhouse administration, although concentration on the matter of the segregation of the classes of paupers continued. Now, because of changes in opinion about mendicancy, children were regarded as blameless for their predicament and were deliberately treated differently from adult paupers. Thus, the few new workhouses designed at this time attempted to make communication between classes absolutely impossible, so that children would be treated differently in isolation from the rest of the workhouse. However, of the county unions, only Dudley built new premises, which were opened in 1858.[37] Thus, in spite of the diligent application of separation rules by efficient workhouse officers, communication between children and adult paupers continued to happen, but because of staff diligence there was a slow continuous improvement in this aspect of workhouse administration.

This approach to segregation was clearly a success because, by 1871, when the Poor Law Board was replaced by the Local Government Board, such problems had disappeared, so that local Guardians were told to concentrate on minute details, such as the composition of the asphalt used to surface yards or the height of outside walls, to ensure that workhouses were 'slightly less prison like'.[38] Noticeably, however, inmates continuously remained protected from outside influences, an emphasis that may have been explained by an alteration in the prevailing attitude toward pauperism or more likely by the belief that segregation was now as complete as was practicable. Patently the workhouses were still closed institutions, but the conditions for individual inmate paupers incarcerated in them had been much improved. Children now had extra facilities for play and recreation, and additional industrial training was now also available.

The creation of the Poor Law Board, in 1847, caused little change in

41

the mode of administration for indoor paupers and classification remained unaltered. Paupers under the age of sixteen years continued to be classified as children, which was in stark contrast to the situation outside workhouses. There, at sixteen years of age, such an individual could have been employed for over five years. Inside workhouses, the need for the separation of children was re-emphasised by the final consolidated order of the Poor Law Commission in 1847,[39] in the continuing belief that even the sight of an adult pauper was detrimental to the child. While ideally the Central Poor Law Authority would have liked separate children's establishments, in a rural county like Worcestershire they had to be content with general workhouses, because separate children's institutions were impossible.

Assistant Poor Law Commissioners continually drew the Guardians' attention to the inadequacies of separation, as at Droitwich in 1848, when J.T. Graves[40] indicated the possibility of the girls seeing into the female vagrants' ward. To solve this, the windows were equipped with shades, but three months later[41] Jellinger C. Symons, the inspector of workhouse schools, re-emphasised the need for complete separation in a marginal comment on the Poor Law Board's copy of the minutes.[42] Thus, one national official reinforced the opinion of another and within a week Assistant Commissioner Graves returned and again found the workhouse filled with paupers. He clearly regarded the workhouse as inadequate, but his visit was in the autumn, when inclement weather often caused the institution to be full. To cope with this, the boys had been placed with the able-bodied men, which Graves regarded as 'detrimental to the morals of the children so placed'.[43] The visiting committee, a group of Guardians responsible for day-to-day decisions about the workhouse, was immediately asked to investigate the situation. They reported that there was indeed a problem and to solve this the 'present store room [was] to be thrown into the boys' sleeping room, which will give an increase of five beds . . . [and that] . . . The one half of the men's infirm ward be converted into a store room.'[44] Significantly, this proposal was adopted immediately, in spite of the fact that it involved a cost to the Poor Rates, which Guardians were usually reluctant to countenance.

The situation at Worcester union in 1855, was similar. Here, HMI Jellinger C. Symons again drew Assistant Commissioner J.T. Graves's attention to 'certain irregularities', because: 'The rules affecting the classification of girls . . . proved very imperfect for their separation from depraved adults of their own sex.'[45] The Worcester Guardians responded, by stating that they always attempted to improve classification 'knowing how essential it was to keep the necessary discipline of the workhouse',[46] but they attempted to turn these official criticisms in their own favour, by suggesting that the existing workhouse was inadequate and should be sold to the War Department as a barracks, so that a new workhouse could be built. However, this idea was not new, because the War Office had previously refused such an offer, but the Guardians still attempted to use this old proposal as a convenient prevarication. Elsewhere, at Shipston on Stour in 1862, there were also some problems relating to communication between children and adult paupers[47] and it was decided that the solution was to alter the workhouse,[48] which undoubtedly enhanced its effectiveness as a total institution. This in turn further enhanced the institutionalisation of long-stay inmates there. This continued to be seen as desirable, but elsewhere problems regarding separation of the pauper classes continued, so that there was a complaint about segregation, as late as in 1869, at Worcester.[49]

Immoral females were considered to be a very dangerous influence on girl paupers, with unchaste women thought most dangerous of all. Immorality was believed to be proven in any woman who mothered a bastard, although interestingly the bastard itself, in the isolation of the workhouse children's ward, was not discriminated against. This probably demonstrated that it was contact with immorality, not heredity, that was thought to be the danger. In other cases, the influence of unchaste women was more direct, as in the case of a girl called Isabella Robinson, who, in 1847 at the age of fourteen years had been 'induced to leave the workhouse on Holy Thursday Fair Day last, with a girl named Braggington, by whom she was taken to a house of ill fame, kept by a person called Taylor in Blackwell Street', in Kidderminster. Whilst there, she 'had connexion with twenty different men, and had contracted venereal disease',[50] after which the proceeds of her prostitution were taken from her, by Braggington and Taylor, the person who kept the house. This was regarded as exploitation of the child, as well as destruction of her morals, so that Braggington and the keeper of the brothel were successfully prosecuted.

In other county unions, workhouses sometimes dealt with girls corrupted before they became inmates. For instance at Martley, in 1865, a girl called Emma Hinton, described as 'very forward in disposition, and likely, if left without proper restraint, to turn out badly',[51] was recommended, by the Guardians, to be sent to a special institution.[52] However, the Poor Law Board refused to allow this, because the chosen institution was not 'certified' by them.[53] In spite of this the Guardians persisted, as they regarded Hinton's case to be 'a peculiar one'[54] but still the central authority refused to pay the fees. There was a similar case at Upton upon Severn, in 1861,[55] where again the Poor Law Board's rules were invoked. In this case, this may have been functional, as it protected the child from being sent to an unsuitable place. Arguably, however, such decisions were better explained by the Poor Law Board's desire to save money, a notion well supported by a case at Shipston on Stour in 1859,[56] where no objections were raised when a local benefactress paid the fees for a mother, who left her child in the workhouse, to enter a reformatory for 'Unfortunate Women' in London, which was not registered by the Poor Law Board.[57] Thus, it appeared that such treatment was acceptable if paid for by someone else, but not if financed from the Poor Rates.

The number of immoral inmate girls was always small, but the scale of the problem was undoubtedly over-emphasised, because of a common preoccupation among the Victorian upper and middle classes with overt morality. Thus, while there were very few cases of venereal disease among adolescent inmate girls, or among similar children entering county workhouses, such cases were well publicised and an impression was clearly given in contemporary literature that overstated the case. Apart from the case of Isabella Robinson,[58] there was only one other case of a girl child inmate suffering from venereal disease, at Kidderminster in 1857.[59] Here, significantly, an unnamed girl was sent to the infectious diseases ward immediately on entry to the workhouse, so that she did not infect other inmate girls with the disease, but probably what was even more important was that she did not infect them morally. This emphasis was enhanced by people such as 'The Rt Hon Mrs Emmeline Way',[60] who might have been appropriately described as a 'middle-class do-gooder', who expressed the view, at Martley workhouse in 1853, that girls must be kept 'away from women of bad character'.[61] She repeated this view in her statement to the Select Committee on Poor Relief in 1861,[62] where she was invited to give evidence. She had been a founder member of the Workhouse Visiting Society, a branch of the National Association for the Promotion of Social Science and a workhouse visitor for over thirteen years, so that she was considered to be an expert on such institutions. The Workhouse Visiting Society had played a major part in encouraging the middle and upper classes to visit workhouses, where it was believed their mere presence would have a miraculous curative effect. The work of this group supposedly encouraged an objective approach to the workhouse and to its pauper inmates, but they produced material that was far from objective. Its *Journal* articles[63] related not so much to the treatment of paupers, but to middle- and upper- class attitudes towards that treatment, particularly with regard to children, who were often regarded in a very paternalistic and patronising way. For instance, an article entitled 'Christmas Day in the Workhouse', published in 1859; M.J. Roberts's article 'A Plea for Workhouse Children', of 1861, and 'A Railway Trip for Workhouse Children', written anonymously, in 1863,[64] were all particularly paternalistic.

The interest of individuals of high social status was usually regarded as beneficial to the Poor Law system and to pauper inmates of workhouses in general, but at Bromsgrove, in 1858,[65] this influence was clearly deemed in need of control. Here, the chaplain recruited 'respectable ladies' to visit the workhouse, but he also created regulations to ensure that all visits were sanctioned by him, on behalf of the Guardians. Such a lady visitor was initially only allowed 'to read and converse with any of the inmates in the hospital, or those not at work, to interest herself in the school and if she got an opportunity, to seek situations for the inmates of the house, particularly the children, when they were old enough'. She was also told 'not to listen to, or mention complaints from any of the inmates, or to interfere in any manner with the management and discipline of the house'.[66] Thus, while middle-class interest was welcome, interference was not to be tolerated. However, within three years, these rules were not regarded as sufficient, so that in 1861 they were made stricter. Now a lady visitor was not to converse with adult inmates at all, merely to confine 'her attention to the school and to do what she may for its benefit'.[67] The visitors, at Bromsgrove, were apparently not members of the Workhouse Visiting Society, founded by Mrs Way and others, and although the Guardian's attention was drawn to this society's annual conference in 1846, no one attended it. Workhouse visiting by ladies at Bromsgrove continued until after 1871. The importance of the influence of a person of high social status on pauper inmates was emphasised even more clearly in October 1865, when Bromsgrove workhouse was honoured by a visit from Baroness Windsor,[68] who was definitely an upper-class personage. Her visit was seen as 'enormously beneficial', according to the Guardians, although precisely why remained unclear.

Soon after the passing of the Poor Law Amendment Act, in 1834, there were so many children in the workhouses of England and Wales that a special report was commissioned to review the working of the legislation.[69] Thus, as part of this inquiry in 1836, a census of inmate children was conducted, which revealed that there were over 42,000 children, under sixteen years old, in the nation's workhouses, or 43.9 per cent of the workhouse population. This statistic was surprising and it led to continued monitoring of numbers. Another similar census in 1840 revealed that there was then over 68,000 inmate children, of whom 88 per cent were above the infant class. Thus many of the nation's workhouses, including some of those in Worcestershire, were thronged with children, but not every workhouse was overcrowded. For instance, the workhouse at Tenbury Wells in 1844, had so few children that the Guardians ordered the clerk to 'communicate with the Poor Law Commissioners as to the propriety of removing the schoolmistress from the workhouse, it being the opinion of this Board that it is not necessary she should continue in her situation owing to the small number of children now, and likely to be in the future, in the workhouse of sufficient age to receive instruction'.[70] From such disparate evidence, it was clear the workhouse child population was unevenly distributed across the country, and that major problems of overcrowding were mainly confined to urban areas, the very area on which previous studies of the New Poor Law have concentrated.

In the most overcrowded and urban parts of Worcestershire large numbers of children in workhouses led to discussions of separate children's departments and district schools, so that when a survey of orphan paupers in the three counties of Worcestershire, Herefordshire and Gloucestershire was conducted in 1841,[71] it revealed 377 boys and 338 girls in workhouses, with a further 73 boys and 12 girls in prisons, such provision appeared appropriate. However, overcrowding of workhouses was seasonal, with most inmates there in the autumn and winter, whereas, in the spring and summer the workhouses could cope with their youthful clientele and a district school appeared unnecessary for that half of the year. This was in spite of evidence that Stourbridge workhouse had received 2,057 children in 1842,[72] or that on 26 September 1842[73] Worcester workhouse contained 64 boys and 66 girls, or 39.5 per cent of its inmates, together with 16 infants. Such contrary evidence illustrated the huge seasonal fluctuation in child pauper numbers, which made separate institutions for children inexpedient and it was thought that to spend a large sum of money to cope with a problem that only existed for half of the year was inappropriate. Other evidence, collected later, revealed that there were only 45 child inmates in Worcester workhouse in June 1845,[74] compared with 133 young individuals there in March 1847,[75] so that the decision not to provide a children's department or district school in the county was again vindicated. For this reason, the majority of pauper children had to remain in county workhouses, in spite of the opinion held by central administrators and Guardians alike, that such institutions were injurious to them.

In spite of recriminations against unchaste women, including at one stage their wearing a distinctive garb,[76] pregnant women, including unmarried ones, found the workhouse the most acceptable of the alternatives available for their confinements at childbirth. Certainly, the option of having a baby outside the workhouse, without medical aid, was most hazardous of all and was to be avoided at any price, including the cost of being humiliated as an inmate of the workhouse. The children of these women, who were born in the workhouse, accentuated the already acute problem of the large numbers of young infants already there. While the 1834 Act had made no provision for this, the Poor Law Commission quickly made an obvious decision; that mothers with children at their breast were to be allowed regular and constant contact with their offspring. This decision was very significant as it gave, for the first time, discretion to Boards of Guardians over an aspect of workhouse management. There were very few other such decisions during the whole term of office of the Poor Law Commission, between 1834 and 1847. Thus, in most cases, by 1836, mothers were allowed access to their infants 'at all reasonable times',[77] which was a logical arrangement, reaffirmed in 1842[78] and again in 1847.[79] In 1842,[80] a further order allowed a mother and her child not yet weaned to occupy the same bed and later the rule that there should be no contact between mothers and their children over two years old, was also relaxed, so that the severe problems of bringing very young children under the rigid control of the workhouse disciplinary codes, without the constant supervision of an adult, disappeared. Although such issues as these became apparent very quickly after 1834, it took over two years for children up to the age of seven years to be allowed in able-bodied women's wards, a strict breach of the segregation[81] that came to be ignored.

Orphaned and deserted children sometimes remained in the workhouse until they were sixteen years old, or until they were apprenticed, sent to service, or adopted, while a few other children were sent to orphanages, a few more lodged with relatives, while others absconded. The most common procedure was for such children to remain in the workhouse until they were bound apprentice, unless some relative was induced to look after them.[82] If relatives did this they were paid outdoor relief, which usually happened when older siblings accepted this responsibility. However, grandparents, and even aunts and uncles, sometimes took children, although if a more distant relative asked for such orphans from the workhouse, this was treated with suspicion, lest their relative's intention was to exploit the child. Generally Guardians did not allow such arrangements, again demonstrating their care for inmate children. The relieving officer normally investigated the circumstances of applicants for such children, so that at Shipston on Stour in 1850,[83] when a woman domestic servant, living some fifteen miles from the union, asked for the custody of her niece, she was investigated. This adoption was only allowed when her employer vouched for her maid and offered to supply the child with clothes, so that outdoor relief was allowed, although this probably did not cover the cost of keeping the child adequately. What was most significant about this case was that it was the intervention of a middle-class employer that assured the Guardians of the suitability of this relatively poor applicant to look after her niece. Without such middle-class surety Guardians were reluctant to allow children to go to more distant relatives. This sort of care for the welfare of pauper children by Guardians was shown again at Worcester in 1852,[84] when a man applied for his two nephews, but in this case the uncle was regarded as 'a bad example' and the Guardians were told that they could refuse permission for the boys to go if they wished, which they did. Shipston on Stour Guardians were equally careful, in 1863,[85] they ordered the return of a seven year old from her cousin's home in London, because she was too far away to be regularly inspected by the relieving officer, while a relative taking an orphan at Kidderminster in 1864, had to 'maintain and educate the child',[86] apparently without outdoor relief being paid. Here, as in other cases, this child's condition was regularly monitored by the relieving officer.

In spite of the onerous burden of looking after such children, sometimes without financial support, this was not a total disincentive to relatives accepting more than one orphan or deserted child. At Pershore in 1860,[87] a man accepted three of his brother's orphaned children, apparently caring for them without any payment being made from public funds. Clearly, arrangements like these saved Poor Rate payers' money and were to be encouraged, but only small numbers of children were ever involved. The reason why Guardians were most ready to send children under nine years old to relatives was because the Central Poor Law Authority usually would not agree to older children being sent, particularly when outdoor relief was to be paid. There was an example of this, at Pershore in 1860,[88] when the Poor Law Board objected to the Guardians there paying 2s 6d per week outdoor relief, to allow a ten year old girl to go to her aunt. They suggested that the girl was employable and should be found work, but they eventually relented after eight months and agreed to her going. Similar cases of adoption by relatives, however, were rare in the county between 1834 and 1871. There was a peculiar decision at Kidderminster in 1857,[89] that might cause assertions made earlier about the Guardians' level of care of inmate children to be questioned. Here, a girl was sent to school in Ireland, where she would never be inspected by the union relieving officer, but significantly this was at her sister's expense, which probably absolved the Guardians of any responsibility.

Very occasionally non-relatives asked for children out of the workhouse and such requests were treated analogously with apprenticeships, particularly after 1844.[90] Now the social status of the applicant for a pauper child appeared imperative. Such children were asked for by name and not selected by the Guardians, but most children in the workhouse were, by definition, at or near the destitution level, as were acquaintances liable to ask for them from the workhouse. For this reason, such applicants were inevitably regarded as unsuitable, which severely limited the number of applications of this type. However, workhouse officers who knew the pauper children in their care, were regarded as suitable custodians and they sometimes asked to take children as servants when they left their workhouse employment. There were such cases at Kidderminster in 1865,[91] and at Pershore in 1868,[92] where on both occasions a schoolteacher applied for a child as a servant. Both requests were quickly granted, which indicated the raised prestige of the workhouse teacher, who by the 1860s was regarded as a respectable working-class individual and a very suitable master for a workhouse child. Workhouse servants were only regarded as suitable applicants if they intended to move relatively short distances from the home union, so that when Droitwich Guardians were asked by a retiring workhouse officer in 1871,[93] if he could take a child as a servant to Yorkshire this was refused. Here, once again, the Guardians demonstrated a good level of care for their young pauper charges. In a few other cases, children who left the workhouse with former workhouse officers were legally adopted, which was an arrangement strongly approved of by Guardians, because this meant that they ceased to have any legal responsibility for the child. Thus, when the master of King's Norton workhouse asked to adopt an inmate girl when he retired in 1867,[94] the arrangement was quickly agreed and the child was even supplied with a suit of clothes as an incentive to this sort of adoption.

It had been the practice in some Gilbert's Act workhouses before 1834[95] to educate pauper children, particularly in urban areas. After the Poor Law Amendment Act, such schemes continued, with academic education used as a means of occupying pauper children's time. Inevitably this created problems, because the children were usually not placed in the charge of specially appointed school staff, but instead such education was left to ordinary workhouse officers, many of whom were completely unsuitable for the task, because often they were themselves illiterate. These same officers also supervised the children when they were set to work, an action taken because labour was seen as having a reforming influence, as well as being a deterrent. Such a custodial role was not specific to children, as the same task officers also oversaw the work of adult paupers. For this reason, when the Poor Law Commission enquired in 1835, 'are the youths, and the boys and girls, properly set to work; and is care taken to fit them to become useful members of the community?[96] the response was usually an affirmative one, but the precise interpretation of what this statement meant remained a problem. However, after 1834, workhouse tasks were much altered. Kidderminster Guardians in 1837,[97] were able to use pauper labour to drive machinery by hand crank and treadmill, a scheme of which the Poor Law Commission apparently approved, but while the Guardians at first suggested that children might be employed in this labour, such youthful labour was apparently never used. At King's Norton in 1844, a flour mill was indeed installed, which was worked by boys[98] and it was stated, '1.5 bushels of flour per period, delimited by meal times' was to be ground by each child. This mill proved inefficient, with the set targets impossible to reach, so that the whole project of grinding corn by this means was abandoned. Elsewhere, at Droitwich, also in 1844,[99] another mill was provided, but this equipment also remained untried, because there were too few paupers to work the system and here flour had to be bought from a local miller.

The Poor Law Commission required that older boys be employed at some labour within the workhouse, so that at King's Norton in 1838,[100] the Guardians there resolved 'that boys above 14 years of age are to work with the men', which was technically an infringement of segregation. In spite of this, marginal comments on the Poor Law Commission's copy of the minutes made it obvious that this decision was noted and indeed approved of, which provided a good early example of the pragmatic relaxation of central authority rules. Here task work outside the workhouse, including stonebreaking and roadbuilding to maintain the local roads, was used. Indeed, such tasks were apparently more interesting to paupers than the more usual workhouse occupations, which were all deliberately monotonous. For example, this was undoubtedly the case, when half a ton of coconut fibres for mat making was purchased by King's Norton Guardians in 1839.[101] Elsewhere, at about this time Kidderminster union introduced oakum picking[102] that involved paupers, including children, tearing apart the fibres of old ropes with their fingers, which often caused abrasions and bleeding. Indeed, this task became so popular with Guardians in other unions that the supply of old ropes sometimes was exhausted and this workhouse occupation had to be abandoned, which was the case at Bromsgrove workhouse in 1841.[103] While these were popular tasks with Guardians, because they were hard, tedious work and demeaning to paupers, they were intensely disliked by inmates. When at a loss as to how to occupy pauper inmates in workhouses, Guardians sometimes turned to peculiar occupations. Thus, at Droitwich in 1845,[104] when the price of potatoes was very high, rotten ones were procured and grated to obtain farina[105] or potato starch, which was then made into a sort of soup and fed to the inmates. This was a very attractive idea to the cost-conscious Guardians, who were initially congratulated for their resource by the Poor Law Commission, but within five weeks they were told by the union medical officer that 'grating potatoes was injurious to health',[106] a view probably not based on objective evidence, but because of the infamous Andover bone grinding scandal, which occurred at about this time. In this *cause célèbre*, bones had been pounded by paupers, which adversely affected their health, so that when the medical officer's opinion that grating potatoes bore some similarity to bone grinding reached the Poor Law Commission they wrote immediately, stating that farina extraction could be abandoned if the Guardians wished and the practice ceased.

From 1834 onwards, the child inmates of county workhouses were taught a trade and the schoolmistress or schoolmaster was usually made responsible for this duty, although sometimes these officers were incapable of giving such instruction. Thus, occupational instructors came to be appointed, so that a tailor or shoemaker was sometimes employed as a porter, who could then instruct boy inmates in his trade. This was first done at Bromsgrove in 1839.[107] The training of girls was less problematic, because older girls could simply be employed in domestic tasks which were automatically considered female vocational training. Such domestic work was menial, but it did arguably give relevant training to workhouse girls and it was assumed that schoolmistresses were capable of teaching this. It was mentioned for the first time in the Poor Law Commission regulations of 1836,[108] when it was emphasised that such work was to be strictly controlled by the mistress of the house and this was reaffirmed in 1842,[109] when the new regulations attempted to ensure that complete segregation was maintained, so that no girl pauper was allowed to undertake domestic tasks in the male wards. Girls from workhouses were cheap to employ as domestic servants outside the workhouse, in fact so cheap that even working-class people could afford them and they were especially attractive in this role, as they were partly trained and very subservient. Indeed, if they were not subservient enough they would be returned to the workhouse, so that at Droitwich in 1840,[110] a girl, who had been sent as a servant, was returned to the workhouse to be punished for an undisclosed misdemeanour. The Guardians here were now unsure of what to do, so they asked the Poor Law Commission its opinion.[111] However, when the central authority suggested that the girl 'should be placed with the adult women, rather than with girls of her own age', which was clearly against strict classification, the Guardians were outraged and refused to follow the official suggestion. This demonstrated well that the Poor Law central authority's thinking was sometimes at variance with that of local Guardians. Other workhouse children were very transitory and giving satisfactory education and training to these youngsters was difficult, if not impossible. There was insufficient time to accomplish effective training, even if these children had been receptive to such instruction, which they were usually not. Thus, at Droitwich in 1847, it was stated that 'an attempt was made some time ago to teach shoemaking, but it had been discontinued in consequence of the smallness of the numbers and the frequent change among the boys'.[112]

Orphaned and deserted children were generally the most permanent workhouse inmates, possibly being institutionalised for up to sixteen years, and it should therefore have been possible to provide successful training for them, but this proved more difficult than expected, because of the disturbing presence of 'ins and outs', as transitory child inmates were known. For this reason it became quite popular for orphaned children to be sent to orphanages. The one most often used by county unions was at Ashey Down, Bristol. Here, Guardians made an initial *per capita* payment to the orphanage, after which the child was kept there free of charge, although the Guardians did sign a declaration, that they would re-admit the orphan to the workhouse if they were dismissed from the orphanage for any reason. However, this never happened. In spite of the success of such arrangements, the Central Poor Law Authority still questioned the legality of payments to orphanages, but Evesham Guardians successfully contested this interpretation of the Law in 1869.[113] Elsewhere, at Stourbridge in 1870,[114] a more unusual approach to ridding the union of unwanted children was used. Here, the Guardians paid £12 per head to send orphan children to Canada with a Miss Ryle, a scheme devised under the Pauper Emigration Act of 1849,[115] but the scheme was rarely used by county unions.

Deserted children, who were also in the workhouse for prolonged periods of time, were little different from the orphans incarcerated there. They were of two types: the foundlings deserted when they were a few days old, and older children, deserted by parents in situations of distress. It was King's Norton union that had the greatest number of foundlings, probably because the union was contiguous with the growing industrial town of Birmingham. Illegitimate babies were often abandoned just over the town boundary, where the Birmingham town police force would not investigate. In such circumstances, the King's Norton Guardians usually offered a £10 reward to apprehend the deserting mother, but in the period 1834 to 1871, none were ever found. This same approach was used at Droitwich[116] and at Kidderminster,[117] both in 1868, but there was no success here either. In other cases the effects of desertion sometimes went further than mere incarceration in the workhouse and indeed so traumatic was the experience of one young child, found wandering at Droitwich in 1848,[118] that he had lost his memory. The Guardians were so concerned about this boy's condition and the crime committed against him that they unsuccessfully advertised for information. This boy remained in the workhouse for the next six years, before he was apprenticed.

Other children, usually known as 'ins and outs', were often in the workhouse with their destitute parents for only a single night, a short period, or very occasionally for a more prolonged stay. In a few cases, just one child from a family was taken into the workhouse as a form of relief to the whole family, an action which was officially illegal but had been practised in the county under the Old Poor Law. In spite of its known illegality, the Guardians at Pershore in 1852[119] demonstrated their independence by taking several children from the same family into the workhouse, to enable a woman, whose husband had been transported for a felony, to obtain employment. In a similar case, at Upton upon Severn in 1862,[120] a man, whose wife suddenly became an imbecile and was unable to cope with his family, had his children taken into the workhouse, until he could care for them again. Elsewhere, at Shipston on Stour in 1856,[121] similar problems of coping with a family in circumstances of distress, led a woman, who was confined for the birth of her ninth child, to bring her eight other children into the workhouse with her. In another case, which was unique in the county, the Guardians at Stourbridge in 1855,[122] admitted a boy to the workhouse without his parents. He had been so badly treated that he was placed in the workhouse in 'a diseased and dangerous state' to keep him safe. Meanwhile, the Guardians sought to prosecute his parents for ill-treating him. Thus, the workhouse was utilised by the working classes to cope in otherwise impossible circumstances and the utility of the institution to these individuals was clearly demonstrated. Whilst there were disadvantages to the pauper inmate, including the affixing of pauper status to these individuals, sometimes such illegal actions by Guardians proved worthwhile.

Inadequate workhouse accommodation for children sometimes proved a problem in some county unions, but ironically it was only at Dudley union, which had the county's only children's department until 1858, where overcrowding of pauper children was really critical. Whilst urban unions sometimes had more problems than did rural unions, this was not always the case. Thus, Stourbridge union, the second most populous Poor Law division in the county, had an adequate workhouse, which never had an overcrowding problem, whereas Martley workhouse, in a rural union with an inadequate workhouse, had continual overcrowding and administrative problems. It therefore appeared that it was the design and level of usage in the workhouse, rather than the urban or rural nature of the union, that caused the differential treatment of pauper children in the various union workhouses of the county. This was in clear contravention of the Principle of National Uniformity, which theoretically applied in all unions. Thus, such an analysis would suggest that if a union had an adequate workhouse – a judgement based on a number of architectural and design factors and on the staff and facilities available – then administrative and overcrowding problems were reduced, whereas unions with inadequate workhouses, judged by the same criteria as above, continued to have problems. For these reasons, Dudley, the most populous county union, with its four old workhouses, inevitably had problems with many aspects of pauper administration, but these difficulties were not only attributable to the urban nature of the union, but rather to the overuse of its inappropriate and inadequate old union workhouses. This illustrated well the efficacy of this analysis, a judgement further supported by the fact that after a new, adequate, workhouse was built at Dudley in 1858, problems relating to pauper administration disappeared.

Dudley union had been created under Gilbert's Act in 1782,[123] by amalgamating four parishes, each urban and highly industrialised and each with its own workhouse. Whilst the accommodation then available had been suitable for the pauperised poor population of the town in the eighteenth century, by the 1840s the population had tripled and the arrangements there were totally inadequate, so much so that the working class demanded a public meeting to discuss the matter,[124] but the Guardians refused this. However, by 1853[125] the Poor Law Board inspector was also publicly critical of the workhouse accommodation provided, so that a special committee of the Guardians was set up to enquire into the need for a new workhouse.[126] This committee concluded that a new workhouse was indeed necessary, but the Board of Guardians, as a whole, ignored this advice and refused to sanction one. The Poor Law Board's response to this was swift and effective. They threatened unique action, by saying that they would hive off the parish of Sedgley from Dudley union and amalgamate it with Wolverhampton union, if the Guardians refused to cooperate, which would certainly have solved the problem of overcrowding, but it would also have drastically reduced the Poor Rate revenue of Dudley union, an eventuality that the Guardians clearly wanted to avoid. This threat brought them quickly to heel. Thus, in 1854, they found it 'desirable to agree to the erection of a new workhouse',[127] which after considerable discussion, and one false start – due to the incompetence of a local builder in wrongly costing a grandiose 'Italianate design' by a London architect – was built. It opened in May 1858,[128] which ironically caused the closure of the only children's establishment in the county, but solved the problem of workhouse overcrowding in this populous union.

The design of the floor plan of a workhouse and the disposition of its rooms was imperative in deciding whether a building provided adequate accommodation for paupers. However, the method of assessing the adequacy of workhouse accommodation used by the Poor Law Commission after 1834, was by the volume of the building. For this reason, the size of bedrooms in the workhouse at Martley in 1859,[129] were deemed inadequate, which indeed they probably were, but it was because of an inappropriate design rather than the volume of the rooms that this judgement should have been made. Under Poor Law Commission's regulations, each child was allowed 300 cubic feet of volume, so that it was calculated that there was bedroom accommodation for twenty-six boys and eighteen girls, but there were usually more inmate children than this in the workhouse.[130] For this reason the Guardians agreed to alter the accommodation, so that three bedrooms replaced four,[131] which allowed between 295 and 315 cubic feet per child respectively. However, there was to be no increase in the volume of the building and therefore any alteration within the Board's regulations was futile and these changes caused a drastic reduction of bedroom accommodation, to fourteen places for each sex, which demonstrated the absurd nature of the rules operating at this time. In spite of this, the Poor Law Board expressed themselves satisfied, thus clearly illustrating that following central authority rules and regulations was more important than satisfying the needs of the most vulnerable class of paupers – the children. It was these same regulations that were applied at Upton upon Severn in 1868,[132] where there were sleeping places available for fifteen boys and twelve girls, which caused perpetual overcrowding. It was resolved to increase accommodation to twenty places for boys and nineteen for girls,[133] but again the alterations implemented deteriorated the conditions for pauper children. They created only ten beds for each sex, so that bed sharing continued, in spite of the fact that the Poor Law Board and the Lunacy Commission had opposed this practice ten years previously.[134] In a slightly more optimistic context, King's Norton Guardians planned a new workhouse in 1868,[135] on a site at Selly Oak, which was not completed before the replacement of the Poor Law Board by the Local Government Board in 1871.[136] However, this new building, to accommodate 150 men, 150 women and 150 children, was planned on the same basis and conformed to the same building regulations used by the Poor Law Commissioners in planning workhouses between 1834 and

1840. Thus, seemingly, Poor Law administrators had learned nothing in the intervening period.

The state of the workhouse was normally the responsibility of the visiting committee, an elected group of Guardians, who dealt with the mundane matters of everyday institutional life, as well as with some major issues. For instance they were consulted about the relatively trivial matter of alleviating the offensive state of the children's privies, at Bromsgrove in 1855[137] and at Pershore in 1856.[138] In both cases the solution was to move the privies a greater distance from the workhouse rather than to make them more hygienic. Objectively, however, these committees usually attempted to ensure continual improvement to workhouse premises. Thus, gas lighting was fitted at Kidderminster workhouse in 1856[139] and in other county workhouses at about the same time, an innovation that certainly provided more adequate lighting and must therefore have improved living conditions for inmates, including children, but which almost certainly infringed the Principle of Less Eligibility, as few independent labourers would have afforded such lighting. In spite of such improvements, it has still been suggested, by George Kitson-Clark, that 'even a well-administered late nineteenth-century workhouse could be a very dreary and degraded place'.[140]

The visiting committee's responsibilities were varied, so that at King's Norton workhouse in 1851,[141] the committee were consulted about a faulty chimney, which caused smoke to come into the schoolroom, creating a great nuisance. This resulted in an inquiry, at which the builder of the schoolroom blamed its architect, who in turn blamed the builder, an impasse that was eventually resolved by the visiting committee. They fitted 'Dr Arnott's patent ventilating apparatus', which they later recommended to Droitwich union, describing it as 'an excellent sanitary instrument and very cheap'.[142]

Amongst their other duties, visiting committees carefully monitored the conditions under which workhouse children lived, which included ensuring that the school staff and the individual's mother kept inmate children clean, which was not always successful. For instance, at Pershore in 1853,[143] a woman was called before the visiting committee and admonished for failing to keep her child clean. Yet another aspect of the visiting committee's responsibilities was to ensure that children were adequately clothed, usually in a garb of the cheapest quality, bought from specialist wholesale clothiers. However, the Guardians, who were very cost conscious, inevitably wanted value for money, which was also expected by Poor Rate payers, who had elected them for this very purpose. For this reason, at Bromsgrove in 1861, the visiting committee returned some fustian jackets, which were 'not up to standard',[144] saying that they could acquire better quality jackets at the same price from another source. This event contrasted with the practice at Birmingham workhouse, where costs were minimised by employing pauper labour to make workhouse clothing, under the management of a tailor employed to oversee this activity. This was considered ideal, but in spite of this, Worcestershire Guardians maintained that they could not afford such an extravagance and only repair tailoring was taught in county workhouses. In another decision relating to workhouse clothing, most Worcestershire visiting committees adopted the expedient of having clothing for children over ten years of age 'conspicuously marked with the union name' to prevent absconding, whereas the clothes of inmates under ten years old was left unmarked, because such youngsters were regarded as not responsible for their own destitution. This was certainly done at Bromsgrove in 1863.[145]

Initially, after 1834, inmate children were definitely treated according to the Principle of National Uniformity, to provide and maintain a common disciplinary code in all workhouses. Thus, hours of work were theoretically uniform, so that children over seven years old were to work for precisely the same hours as adults, a totally impractical decision, as young children were incapable of working for the same length of time as adults. However, these regulations were soon changed, so that the workhouse times were now prescribed by the master of the workhouse. In this circumstance the workhouse hours now inevitably varied, which ran contrary to the Principle of National Uniformity. In turn this led to renewed pressure for prescribed hours for all workhouses. These were reapplied in 1836,[146] when the Poor Law Commission issued an order setting out new uniform workhouse hours. Paupers were to rise at 5.00 a.m. in summer and 6.00 a.m. in winter and to work for ten hours per day in summer, and nine hours in winter, with meals to be consumed in silence and simultaneously by all paupers, a demand that created huge catering and control problems. At the end of the day, all paupers, no matter what their age, or workhouse classification, were to be in bed by 8.00 p.m. In spite of these rules, there developed a flexibility in application, so that from the outset, workhouse masters continued to determine precise details of times, which was certainly a logical decision. It was thus no surprise that these formal regulations were abandoned after two years as impossible to enforce.

At about this time, children were also expected to attend school for three hours per day and to work for all but one hour of what time remained, an arrangement that was intended to enhance institutionalisation, but which also must have been very fatiguing for young children. Even then, their one hour of free time was restricted to certain leisure activities, that could only be pursued in an exercise yard intended for child paupers, so as to ensure that segregation was easily maintained. In spite of intended uniformity, some unions made their own arrangements, so that the master at Droitwich workhouse in 1839, determined that 'the hours during which the male children in the house shall daily be engaged in employment . . . shall be until the end of the quarter; viz, from 8 till half past ten O'clock and in school from half past ten till twelve O'clock noon, in work under the instruction of the porter and schoolmaster respectively, and from 2 until five O'clock p.m. – also in work under instruction'.[147] This was changed in 1840, when the Worcester Guardians[148] belatedly agreed the 'National Hours of Work'. Elsewhere, at Bromsgrove, the Guardians were even later than Droitwich in accepting the national workhouse hours and indeed it was not until 1842 that they came into line with national policy.[149] In the same year the Poor Law Commission amended the hour of rising to 5.45 a.m. in summer and 6.45 a.m. in winter.[150] Whilst in modern terms these work hours appeared to be excessive for children, they did compare very favourably with the hours worked by youngsters outside the workhouse and for this reason, workhouse children were thought not to have been treated less eligibly compared with their non-pauper contemporaries. Thus, in 1840, Worcester Guardians reported: 'One evil is apparent from the circumstances (these times) that when the Board puts out girls and boys to service, they have invariably to work three hours longer each day than in the workhouse, the consequence is, that the greater part so put out come back to the workhouse because they have more hours work than they have had before',[151] although there was little evidence to suggest that children were returned to the workhouse for this reason, and it appeared likely that such opinions were based on little more than prejudice.

In spite of the belief made explicit in the 1834 Poor Law Amendment Act,[152] that paupers should not be allowed out of the workhouse, the question of inmates leaving workhouse premises was discussed by the Poor Law Commission in 1837, when Boards of Guardians were asked 'to what extent, and under what regulations, and subject to what control, may permission be safely and advantageously be given to aged persons and children, occasionally to go beyond the limits of the workhouse, and what are the existing practices in this respect?'[153] However, it took until 1842 for regulations to be officially relaxed,[154] so that now, children under fifteen years old, were sometimes allowed out of the workhouse for exercise, under the charge of the schoolmistress, schoolmaster or another officer. Kidderminster Guardians were the first to adopt this practice, apparently for health reasons. They noted: 'It is the opinion of this Board that the children of the workhouse should go out in fine weather once or twice a week under the care of the governess, if the medical officer agrees.'[155] This was in line with the Commission's decision of 1842,[156] but in spite of such relaxations of workhouse rules, rigid discipline remained, which created and maintained a tightly ordered and controlled 'total institution'[157] in which compliance was assured.

Another matter of constant concern to Guardians was the sanctions imposed to punish inmate paupers in workhouses. Such punishments were supposedly uniform, but, in spite of this, there were inevitable variations, even within the same workhouse. In the early years of the New Poor Law, diet was commonly reduced as a punishment for children, which was an issue that the Poor Law Commission debated in 1837. At this time they decided on 'the expediency of adopting a regulation for preventing children in the workhouse from being punished by reduction of diet',[158] because they recognised the potential dangers of this form of punishment. This matter remained unresolved and no new regulations were issued, although the central authority's concerns were clearly known to local Guardians. Indeed, at King's Norton in 1838, it was suggested that 'when the governor punishes any inmate, such be inflicted by giving him/her food of less palatable or coarser description, not by depriving them of food, in addition to other punishments that are inflicted'.[159] In spite of such caution, events at Fareham workhouse in Hampshire in 1839, where reductions of diet had been so severe that near-starvation had resulted, the problems of this form of punishment were brought to public attention. This was an eventuality that caused the Poor Law Commission to re-emphasise its policy on this matter, which caused all Guardians to think again about the use of a reduced diet to punish paupers.

Lack of uniformity regarding discipline, was partly the result of the idiosyncrasies of individual workhouse masters in determining sanctions and partly because of the freedom of Boards of Guardians to act independently. To monitor differences in punishment, the Poor Law

Commission sent Guardians a circular in 1841, asking for
'punishments administered to children'.[160] This survey l[
order[161] theoretically making sanctions across the whole P[
system uniform, but cases of cruelty and over-reaction w[
inevitable. Usually sanctions on children were within the central
authority rules, although over-punishment remained a problem,
particularly as such cases almost always went unrecorded. However, a
case at Droitwich in 1838,[162] was the subject of an official complaint,
when the nurse complained about the severe punishment of a girl by
the schoolmistress. When this was investigated by the visiting
committee, it proved to be exaggerated, although the schoolmistress
was still told to cease using corporal punishment on girls, which was
an affirmation of the national rules. These stated that while boys,
between seven and fourteen years old, could be beaten, no girl could be
similarly chastised. False alarms about maltreatment were quite
common, but complaints were always investigated, which again
demonstrated care on the part of local Guardians and Poor Law
officers. However, punishments, some of them extreme, will inevitably
have gone unrecorded. A case of gross maltreatment, at Kidderminster
in 1840, probably only came to light because of gossip. The Clerk to
the Guardians later reported that 'in consequence of the porter John
Stokes putting a boy named —— Perks aged 6 years in a sack, tying
him up, and hanging him up in one of the rooms of the workhouse for
nearly an hour, he (the clerk) had taken out a summons against Stokes,
who had been fined by the magistrates for assault'.[163] This
maltreatment led to the porter's immediate dismissal, which clearly
demonstrated that any such inhuman treatment towards a pauper,
particularly a child, would not be countenanced.

In other places, the Central Poor Law Authority's attention was
drawn to children confined for long periods in darkened rooms, a
sanction often used when a child soiled its bedlinen, in spite of new
regulations in 1841[164] that outlawed such punishment. Essentially, the
Poor Law Commission sought to normalise the punishment of child
inmates, although they inevitably remained powerless to prevent
unauthorised maltreatments. The workhouse master was the local Poor
Law officer nominally responsible for punishing pauper children,
although he often delegated this power to school staff, who were in
constant contact with the children. This was in spite of the particular
problems of disciplining these children and the likelihood of over-
reaction by the teacher. This delegation of authority caused the Poor

Punishment

Law Commission to tighten its regulations regarding punishment still further. The punishment regulation of 1841 resulted. This stated that no corporal punishment 'shall be inflicted on any boy except by the schoolmaster or master of the workhouse', and it was 'to be inflicted [with] a rod or other instrument such as shall be approved by the Board of Guardians or visiting committee'.[165] There was also to be an element of premeditation in inflicting corporal punishment, which was not to be administered within six hours of the offence, presumably in the hope that this delay would remove any malice from the situation. These rules also required that the workhouse master be present when punishment was inflicted and that every such sanction was recorded in a punishment register, which was inspected regularly to ensure accuracy and accountability. The instructional letter that accompanied the 1841 punishment regulations made some very revealing statements about the Poor Law Commission's expectations. They stated, in terms well ahead of their time and in comparison with other contemporary thinking that: 'The Commissioners are satisfied that good temper joined to firmness and self command will enable the skilful teacher to manage children with little or no corporal punishment. The frequent use of corporal punishment is the common resource of the teacher who from idleness or other defects is incompetent to acquire a command over children by knowledge of their character, and gentle means.'[166] However, in spite of this officially expressed belief, the punishment rules caused problems in practice, as all teachers were not competent and many found huge difficulties in disciplining workhouse children. For instance, the schoolmistress at Kidderminster in 1842, attended a Guardians' Meeting at her own request to convey her inability to preserve order and obedience in the school 'without resorting to corporal punishment on the girls'.[167] The Guardians sympathised and expressed 'their opinion' to the Commissioners, that corporal punishment was essential for proper management and discipline. They even went as far as asking 'if correcting with a rod on the hand would be deemed corporal punishment'. The Commission inevitably replied that this would be an infringement of the rules.

In the context of punishing boy miscreants, King's Norton Guardians suggested in 1850 that the governor 'procure one dozen birch rods for the purpose of inflicting chastisement on boys of the workhouse who may deserve chastisement'.[168] This also contravened the punishment regulations of 1841,[169] that specifically forbade the master from laying hands on male paupers, although the porter or another subordinate officer was empowered to apply violent punishment to such individuals, if this was necessary. However, the schoolmaster or schoolmistress remained responsible for restraining child miscreants, with those who damaged workhouse property or who were violent towards a fellow inmate treated most severely. Such miscreants could be brought before the magistrates for such offences. In the period from 1834 to 1871 this happened on only three occasions. The sanction used for lesser offences was an appearance before the Guardians, which was an equally rare event. From this summary of serious discipline problems in Worcestershire Poor Law institutions, between 1834 and 1871, it is apparent that misdemeanours were fewer in number than might have been expected, as were recorded punishments, which undoubtedly bore testimony to the effective social control imposed by the county's workhouses. In spite of this, workhouse children still had the ability to misbehave and to be mischievous, but unlike the punishments given to children of the independent poor, punishments in workhouses were circumscribed by tight regulations, which were eventually formalised in the consolidated order of 1847.[170] Nevertheless, there were undoubtedly unofficial punishments used in workhouses, which because they went unrecorded were impossible to quantify in terms of amount, type or severity. It was only when these punishments were gross, where injury was inflicted, or where the matter was reported to a senior officer, that such punishments were noticed, although there were fewer complaints about such illegal treatment between 1847 and 1871 than there had been between 1834 and 1847. This probably indicated the increased effectiveness of workhouse officers, or of the Poor Law bureaucracy in controlling individual officers as time passed, although an improved ability to cover up offences may also have explained this change.

The removal of privileges was often used as a punishment for child, as well as for adult, paupers, and some miscreants lost their free time – with hard labour added – for between seven to fourteen days. This punishment was also often associated with locking up the offender and for this reason Worcester Guardians applied to build a 'lock-up' in the boys' yard in 1853, with the purpose of 'confining such of the boys there as may be liable . . . instead of using the lock-up in the able-bodied men's yard'.[171] This arrangement had infringed segregation and allowed communication between boys and men to continue, which inevitably led the Poor Law Board to agree to the immediate building of the boys' 'lock-up'. Plans were submitted by the Board of Guardians to the central authority, but a letter in July 1853[172] announced that the intended structure was too small. It stated that the lock-up must be at least 4 feet 9 inches square.

Within the Poor Law System punishment was expected to fit the crime, so that the nature of an offence determined the punishment given, although the age, sex and physical condition of the offender were also important, as was the child's previous disciplinary record. At Bromsgrove in 1847, two girls were given the same punishment, 'fourteen days hard labour',[173] for persistent misbehaviour, whereas at Droitwich, nine years later,[174] two girls found to be disobedient, were differentially punished. One girl, aged thirteen years, was confined to the refractory ward for twenty-four hours with a changed diet, but with permission that she be released after twelve hours if she apologised, whereas her colleague, who was fifteen years old, was sent back to the normal children's ward, provided she apologised to the master for her disobedience. This decision was clearly tempered with discretion as the older girl, who probably had no previous record, was apparently treated much more leniently than her younger partner in disobedience. There was only one special refractory ward in a county workhouse, at Droitwich, where it was used in 1861[175] to accommodate a boy, aged fourteen years, for using bad language and assaulting his younger brother, but his punishment appeared ineffective, because within fourteen days the offence was repeated.[176] The boy was this time placed in the able-bodied men's ward, but he was clearly a recidivist, because in 1863 he was again confined in the refractory ward for a similar offence.[177] This type of punishment could only be given at this one workhouse, where a special ward was provided, so that any notion of equal treatment between unions, to maintain National Uniformity, was questionable. However, beatings were a quite widely-used punishment, apparently reserved for minor damage to workhouse property. This was certainly the punishment inflicted at Droitwich in 1849, where a boy, aged thirteen years old, who 'burned and otherwise injured the stockings given him to wear'. He was ordered to 'be well flogged', a punishment to 'be inflicted with a birch rod'.[178] Elsewhere, three boys who 'damaged the playroom floor' at Bromsgrove,[179] were beaten, whereas during the same week that this offence occurred three other boys, who seriously assaulted another youth, were not beaten. This revealed an interesting paradox, as damage to property was apparently considered more grievous than damage to persons. Where property was seriously damaged, or there was a threat to life, offenders were taken before the magistrates, so that at Pershore in 1853, three boys who were 'detected by the master's son making a fire on the privy seat in the boys yard, that could have set the workhouse on fire',[180] were dealt with by the local magistrates, found guilty of arson and sent to prison.

Absconding from workhouses by children was not common in Worcestershire between 1834 and 1871, but where it did happen it was usually treated very seriously. Indeed, whereas adults who absconded were always taken before the magistrates, children were sometimes treated with discretion, so they were often simply returned to the workhouse for punishment. Only a few children, all boys, absconded from five county workhouses, at Bromsgrove, Droitwich, Kidderminster, King's Norton and Shipston on Stour, with the main incidence being at Droitwich, where twenty of the twenty-nine cases took place. This was probably related to the design of the workhouse there, because it had been found necessary to raise the height of the walls of this institution to prevent absconding. This was done in 1856,[181] but the solution was unsuccessful and it became apparent that without building a replacement workhouse this problem was insoluble, although this was not the case elsewhere; in other workhouses fairly minor redesign helped prevent absconding. For instance, at Bromsgrove in 1853,[182] the windows of the boys' bedroom were barred on the outside and latticed on the inside to prevent escape, a solution that immediately reduced incidents of absconding at this union. Of the twenty cases of absconding from Droitwich workhouse, six were second attempts, while a boy called Samuel Rogers tried to abscond on three occasions. He was eleven years old at his first attempt in 1861;[183] he made another attempt in the same year,[184] and a year later he got as far as Sculcoates in Leicestershire, before he was caught.[185] On each occasion the police searched for him, as they did when two boys absconded from King's Norton workhouse in 1850. This pair were caught very quickly and one of them, Michael Golding, insisted that he had escaped because he had been ill-treated in the workhouse, by being unnecessarily and severely beaten. This claim was investigated, when it was revealed that he had been beaten for scaling the workhouse wall and stealing onions from the gardens, an offence for which the Guardians believed his chastisement to be 'perfectly satisfactory'.[186] Golding and his fellow escapee, George Benyon, were eventually dealt with by the magistrates.

The magistrates were also used at Shipston on Stour in 1858,[187] with expenses allowed from public funds, to prosecute four boys for absconding, but elsewhere boys who absconded were simply returned to the workhouse and punished there. Indeed, there was sometimes unequal punishment within the same union, apparent at Droitwich in 1861,[188] where three boys, who absconded, were treated differently on their return to the workhouse. However, this was explicable because John Smith, aged fourteen years, who had been punished previously for swearing and hitting his brother, assaulting a girl inmate, and rudeness to the master, was punished by being 'dieted' for forty-eight hours. Another boy, aged thirteen, just had his diet reduced for twenty-four hours and a third boy, Samuel Rogers, was severely reprimanded.[189] When another four boys absconded from the same workhouse in 1862, they were caught at Fearnall Heath,[190] after four hours of freedom and their leader, the eldest, was beaten and kept in solitary confinement for twelve hours, with his fellow escapees merely reprimanded. Corporal punishment was also used at Bromsgrove in 1864,[191] to punish a boy who absconded and individual punishments were given again at Droitwich in 1868,[192] when four boys absconded from there. When he was returned to the workhouse, Frank Newman, who was the oldest boy, was substantially punished by being placed in the able-bodied mens' ward, but his compatriots were merely reprimanded. However, these punishments may have been unjust, because these two younger boys absconded again in 1870[193] and this time one of them was never caught, whereas the other, who was brought back to the institution by his uncle, was flogged. It was certainly the case that escapes by boys from workhouses were rarer than might have been expected and that individuals who did get away were usually apprehended and returned. Only Michael Golding never came back to the institution.[194] Of the three other cases of absconding from Droitwich workhouse, one was in 1856,[195] the other two in 1863.[196]

The design of most county workhouses was clearly usually satisfactory in preventing the escape of child inmates, but absconding while out of the workhouse was obviously much easier. After 1848, when children were allowed out more often – to take walks, to attend lectures, to go to church and to visit fairs and art exhibitions – they were always accompanied by an officer, but this did not prevent escapes. Thus, two boys from Kidderminster escaped while visiting Habberley Valley with the porter. These children, said to be 'out for recreation . . . rambled about', although they were clearly not under the control of the porter, who later sent two other children after them,[197] but the searchers returned later saying that they could not find the absconders. At a subsequent Guardians' inquiry, held when the boys were not found, the porter was dismissed for his negligence.

Another very important aspect of the treatment of pauper children was how and what they were fed, so that an examination of the normal workhouse dietary appeared essential for the purposes of this book. Most worryingly, manipulation of the pauper's diet was used as punishment, usually for gross infringements of workhouse discipline, which was extremely effective: any reduction of diet, from an already minimal standard, led even the most intransigent inmate to observe the workhouse rules. Such institutionalised starving was certainly used for child miscreants, in the county and elsewhere, early in the Poor Law Commission's era. However, the normal diet of child paupers was already inadequate, with even seasoning removed, so that M.A. Crowther has suggested: 'The workhouse diet was stripped of everything that made similar food acceptable to the poor; sometimes even salt was not offered at the table.'[198] Under the 1834 Act, the nature of the workhouse diet had initially been left to the Guardians discretion and they relied on their experience under the Old Poor Law to determine what was fed to the inmates of their workhouse. National Uniformity eventually demanded more control over diet than this, so that in 1853, county Boards of Guardians received six national dietaries,[199] from which they had to choose one. A modern computerised dietary analysis[200] revealed a 29 per cent deficiency in energy content for the most satisfactory diet offered, whereas the diet chosen by all county unions, probably because it was the cheapest, revealed[201] a 56 per cent shortfall in energy, a 50 per cent deficiency in vitamin C, an almost total lack of vitamin D and a serious deficiency in calcium. This almost certainly meant that pauper children in Worcestershire's workhouses suffered from malnutrition and had a reduced resistance to diseases. With hindsight, and by chance, the County Guardians made a poor choice of diet for their pauper child charges, but how this diet compared with that of the children of independent labourers, and whether the workhouse child was Less Eligible in these terms, was impossible to assess. Evidence from an Assistant Poor Law Commissioner in 1835, cited by R.G. Hodgkinson, might have thrown light on this. He suggested that, 'the average quantity of food consumed by an agricultural labourer did not exceed 20 oz per day or 15 oz of nutritive substance . . . It was stated that 18–24 oz or 16 oz of nutritive food per day was requisite to support life in a sound and healthy state, and 24–30 oz for those doing hard labour.'[202] Whilst this sort of evidence was probably uppermost in the

Guardians' minds when choosing a dietary plan, its simplistic reliance on weights of various foods did not make it an adequate benchmark for making comparisons between diets.

It appears probable that the independent labourer was usually in poor physical condition, because his normal diet was inadequate, but the Guardians at Dudley in 1838, demurred from this view with regard to the working class population of that town. They stated:

> From his very boyhood the labour of the working man from this part of the country (and that holds good for females too) is of a much harder description and his strength cannot be kept without generous diet: this naturally includes the continuance of a similar diet to support him in his declining years. This support is a state of freedom, if not driven by the hand of God from his own purpose within the poor house, he for the main part continues to enjoy, but if his future be to become a parish pauper, the staff of life be taken from under him; he sinks with accelerated pace into the chambers of the grave.[203]

Hence, these comments provide an alternative view of the workhouse dietary in the most urban of all Worcestershire unions, although this opinion was probably not representative of other county unions. There was continual tinkering with workhouse diets during the period from 1834 to 1871 and details of only some of these changes were conveyed to the Poor Law Central Authority. Thus, some workhouse masters altered the paupers' diet without informing anyone, because they regarded such changes as minor culinary adjustments, but on other occasions drastic alterations were made. For instance, at Bromsgrove in 1840,[204] the Guardians reduced the weight of the supper from five ounces to four ounces and in 1843[205] these same Guardians chose to replace twenty ounces of bacon and potatoes with eight ounces of bread and cheese, and fourteen ounces of boiled rice and treacle was replaced by a similar weight of bread and cheese for the evening meal. This meant that the energy content of the diet, which was already inadequate, was further reduced, although throughout such changes one matter remained constant, the woman's diet continued to be used for children between seven and sixteen years of age, while children below seven years of age were dieted 'at discretion', with the precise meaning of this phrase a matter of conjecture. Sometimes, dietary changes were made on medical advice, as at Droitwich in 1846, where it was 'resolved that the children of the workhouse have treacle and dripping cake instead of cheese for supper, which was recommended by the visiting committee and the medical officer',[206] because cheese was regarded as injurious to the young, especially if eaten in the evening.

Other changes of diet were forced by external circumstances. For instance, when the potato crop failed in the autumn and winter of 1845 and 1846, expensive potatoes were replaced with rice, which made the diet marginally more satisfactory nutritionally.[207] However, as suggested earlier, Droitwich union kept potatoes in the diet at this time, which was a unique action, when farina, extracted from rotten potatoes, was fed as soup to the workhouse inmates.[208] This practice was stopped however, not because of the unwholesome quality of the soup but because of the supposed injurious nature of the grating process. Elsewhere, official comments about diet – at both local and national levels – were reasonably common, but unofficial comments went largely undocumented and thus the events, at King's Norton union, starting in 1839, were of interest because they may have given some slight indication of pauper opinion about institutional food. When, in 1839,[209] a complaint about the thinness of the porridge came before the Guardians, it was dismissed, but some two years later in 1841,[210] the soup served in the same workhouse was the subject of complaint, with the inmates refusing to eat it and throwing it around the room – such was their disgust. In spite of this serious infraction of workhouse rules, the Guardians, present at a meeting in the workhouse at the time, examined the soup, and determined that it was 'of excellent quality',[211] but significantly, and uniquely in such a serious case of indiscipline, they did not even admonish the paupers concerned, which may have indicated that they agreed with the inmates about the poor quality of the food provided. In spite of M.A. Crowther's suggestion that 'although the poor were inadequately fed, their preferences differed strongly from the institutional diet, which therefore seemed harsh and punitive',[212] the inmates probably regarded the workhouse diet as preferable to starvation, the likely plight of some of those seeking relief. However, the few children who were infirm in body or mind and who may have spent their entire childhood in the workhouse, had no alternative to the workhouse diet, as part of a régime described by Kellow Chesney as 'a harsh measure, designed to inspire fear'[213] and these individuals were probably malnourished, but probably so too were their non-inmate contemporaries.

Religion was another very important consideration in workhouses, probably because God-fearing paupers were considered less threatening than Godless ones. Thus, the Poor Law Commission included religious education in their armoury to be used against paupers from 1834, which was not surprising in a predominantly Christian culture. The Poor Law Amendment Act had been drafted to protect adult paupers from proselytism, so that no pressure was to be applied on them to attend church. However, the dangers of proselytism were apparently ignored when a circular, issued by the Poor Law Commission in 1835, laid down that a chaplain could be appointed 'to examine and catechise the children at least once every month; and after every examination to record the names and general progress, and the state of the children, and the moral and religious state of the inmates'.[214] The Commission's intention was plain. In spite of this, when a Nonconformist Guardian suggested that no replacement be appointed when the chaplain left, at Pershore union in 1837,[215] this idea gained quite substantial minority support. A replacement was soon appointed, although this incident probably indicated a common tension between Anglicans and other churches regarding the religious training offered in workhouses.

In spite of the freedom of adult paupers not to attend church, it was made compulsory for child inmates to attend. From 1836,[216] dependent children had to go to church on Sundays, to a service of the denomination determined by the creed their parent was declared on entry to the workhouse. This caused immediate problems because although Anglican chaplains were appointed to workhouses, pauper parents could declare themselves, and their dependants, to be of any other denomination they liked. For this reason, an order, published later in 1836,[217] inevitably attempted to simplify this situation by allowing Nonconformist ministers to visit workhouses to provide religious instruction and spiritual guidance to dissenters, a principle that was reaffirmed in 1838.[218] However, Worcester union had allowed paupers to attend Nonconformist churches outside the workhouse from 1837,[219] and initially this even included able-bodied inmates. These paupers attended Pump Street Chapel, in St Helen's parish, but the Poor Law Commission soon objected to this and able-bodied attendances ceased within a month. Aged and child paupers continued to attend, in line with the 1838 regulation, which stated that church attendance outside the workhouse was officially intended only for aged and child paupers, who had to be accompanied by an officer. Yet, this system also caused problems, because workhouse officers were invariably Anglican,[220] the religious affiliation most favoured by Guardians, so these Poor Law Commission servants, who were protected by a conscience clause in their contracts, could not be compelled to attend Nonconformist churches either. In spite of this, even where the arrangement was workable, it was clear that aged paupers and not children were troublesome. The Poor Law Commission confirmed this in a letter, sent to Kidderminster Guardians in March 1838.[221] It stated that 'the children would be more easily conducted to and from church and would be less likely to abuse the privilege than certain aged paupers'. An alternative experiment was now tried. The minister of the church attended by the pauper now certified the unsupervised pauper's attendance, but inevitably some paupers absconded and the only possible alternative was to invite Nonconformist ministers back into workhouses, so that inevitably the old resentments reasserted themselves.

Adult paupers, on entering the workhouse, were asked their creed, which was entered into a creed register and was immutable on subsequent admissions to any workhouse. Thus, the head of the family determined the creed for the whole group and once professed this religious denomination was difficult to change, particularly for children. Ministers of religion now became possessive about 'their flock', whom they guarded zealously. Thus, disputes inevitably arose and interdenominational competition developed, with pastors now ensuring that paupers attended only the services of their professed creed. Nevertheless, in 1842,[222] apparently in a gesture of uncharacteristic ecumenicalism, adult inmates were allowed to contact ministers of other faiths and more proselytism inevitably occurred. In all of this, the implications for orphaned and deserted child inmates went unnoticed and they invariably continued to attend Anglican services. As suggested earlier, the initial intention was that a chaplain be responsible for the religious instruction offered in the workhouse, including that given by the schoolmaster and schoolmistress. However, he was initially to be appointed only 'if the Guardians think fit', a freedom re-emphasised by a consolidated order in 1836[223] and reaffirmed in 1838.[224] On this occasion the Solicitor General reminded the Poor Law Commission of their responsibility to ensure religious freedom, apparently for officers and paupers alike. Thus, from the outset, it was an official intention to create ordered Christian communities in workhouses, which would give them an atmosphere considered most likely to fulfil the expectations of the New Poor Law. Indeed, except for the sick and dying, the chaplain was not to administer the Sacrament in the workhouse, although the Bishop of the diocese in which the workhouse stood could give permission for the Sacrament to be administered in special circumstances, under a regulation of 1842.[225] While it was also inevitable that Sunday should be strictly observed as the Lord's Day by inmates, with all labour – apart from household duties and cooking – not allowed, ironically this had one useful, but unintentional effect, when it gave hardworking paupers some respite from the monotonous toil of workhouse life.

During the period from 1834 to 1871, the treatment of child paupers in Worcestershire workhouses altered in nature, a change arguably caused by an altered definition of poverty, in line with Gertrude Himmelfarb's ideas, expressed in *The Idea of Poverty* (1984).[226] Thus, the middle and upper classes locally – via their elected representatives, the Board of Guardians – still imposed a morality on these poorest members of the working classes. However, while there was a clear difference in the treatment of children from union to union, an urban versus rural division in treatment was not apparent. More likely, differences in treatment in various Poor Law institutions were due to the relative level of usage of the workhouses and their design. Such an institution in an urban context was therefore invariably under stress, particularly because of seasonal destitution, which led many inappropriately designed workhouses to be overcrowded. In such circumstances they could not cope and the Poor Law Central Authority's rules and regulations proved inflexible and unworkable in such a context, so that differential treatment appeared inevitable. Such differentiation was also accentuated by unofficial and illegal treatment, sometimes bordering on the criminal, which further eroded the Principle of National Uniformity, but inevitably most illicit maltreatment went unrecorded. In spite of this, the uniform treatment of children in workhouses was attempted, where external factors allowed this to be done. Whilst an institutionalised ill-treatment of children, by feeding them an inadequate diet, continued at the fiat of the Central Poor Law Authority, inmate children were probably treated more fairly, humanely and hence more eligibly than their contemporaries outside the institution. Inmate children were deliberately institutionalised in a total environment designed to make their behaviour acceptable to their social superiors, which was an effect aided by the adoption of Anglicanism as the preferred creed in the workhouse. Thus, any analysis of relative eligibility is impossible, because meaningful comparison of their freedom involved determining the value of liberty to an individual, but in most cases such freedoms related to 'negative liberties'.[227]

THE MEDICAL TREATMENT OF CHILDREN

The availability of independent medical treatment for the poor in the nineteenth century was rare and unless Poor Law medical relief was accepted, the poor remained untreated. However, to receive such medical charity was seen as a sure sign of poverty and was therefore stigmatised. Indeed it came to provide one facet of a definition of destitution, or even pauperisation, and was regarded as the first step towards a loss of independence, so the acceptance of medical relief was resisted except in dire emergency. For this reason, it appeared essential that this form of Poor Law aid be considered in any investigation of the treatment of pauper children, because health was clearly important in determining the inmate child's quality of life. This material also partly filled a gap in the coverage of this book, as the documentary evidence about Poor Law medical relief gave some insight into the treatment of outdoor pauper children. Here, uniquely, there was plentiful evidence about this group, whose treatment otherwise went undocumented.

Whilst the general treatment of pauper children influenced their physical condition, so too did the medical treatment they received. Rudimentary medical care for all paupers was largely paid for by the middle and upper classes, via the Poor Rates and this greatly influenced how medical care was provided and regarded. Self-interest was undoubtedly one reason for the willingness of the ruling élite to pay for such treatment, but they also expected public health legislation to be passed to protect them against those diseases that attacked the rich as well as the poor. They also expected that there would be effective treatment for these afflictions, as this was clearly necessary to complete their own personal protection. However, the treatment of diseases that attacked the poor, which were associated with inadequate diet and poor living conditions and posed no threat to the ruling élite, remained relatively neglected. Conversely, contagious diseases which were a threat to all, had to be dealt with and for this reason the medical treatment of these afflictions was relatively better developed. Thus, this analysis suggests that the speed of medical treatment development, and the order in which the alleviation of diseases and afflictions were tackled, depended on the perceived threat to the ruling élite, who, in nineteenth-century English society, directly or indirectly, paid for these scientific developments.

Medical assistance was always unequally available in nineteenth-century England. The upper classes used fashionable doctors, while other medical gentlemen treated the middle classes, sometimes including the 'artisan élite',[1] with the working classes often not catered for at all. It was the population size of the place where an individual resided which determined the social mix of a medical practitioner's patients and the likelihood of working-class people gaining treatment. In urban areas there were often sufficient middle-class patients for a doctor to specialise in treating them, but in the countryside there were too few middle-class individuals to make this possible. Here, doctors' lists may have included artisans and even some of the more wealthy skilled working classes. Effectively, this meant that medical treatment was only available to the poorer working classes if they could afford it, which some managed by belonging to sick clubs. Elsewhere special dispensaries and infirmaries were available, but these were almost exclusively established in densely populated urban areas. For the majority of the working classes, unable to afford such facilities, and for most of the rural poor, living in areas where sick clubs did not exist, this affordable medical treatment was not possible. For such people, Poor Law medical relief was the only alternative available, but this was often unacceptable, because it was stigmatised as charity. For this reason, many very poor individuals relied on self-medication, quack doctors and folk remedies, so that serious maladies afflicting the poor often went untreated. Apparently, outdoor medical relief was only sought by the poor when the patient was beyond treatment, so most people were already very seriously ill before they were seen by a doctor. Thus, R.G. Hodgkinson's suggestion that: 'The most noxious result of pauperisation through medical assistance was that the sick poor, unwilling to suffer from the stigma, tried to do without adequate attention'[2] was reasonable. In contrast to this, pauper inmates of workhouses had their health monitored by trained staff, who ensured that any health threats were promptly minimised. They had no choice about accepting medical treatment, it was provided for them and they were forced to accept it, which conferred improved health, but also clearly indicated their personal loss of liberty. In spite of this, the medical treatment provided to the poor was not of the same quality as that provided to their richer contemporaries. Thus, George Cornewall-Lewis, appointed as a Poor Law Commissioner in 1834, expressed a view pertinent to this in 1844, when he suggested that he did 'not see how it is possible for the State to supply medical relief to the poor of as good a quality and to as great an extent as the richer classes enjoy'.[3] Whilst he clearly believed that it was impossible to provide adequate medical treatment for the poor, this was ironical, because it was those least able to pay – the poorest members of society – who needed the most expert and expensive treatment, although they seldom obtained it outside the workhouse.

In contrast, the medical treatment of sick inmates in workhouses became a major facet in the management of paupers, including children, between 1834 and 1871. Thus, the poorest members of society, who demonstrated their parlous state by entering the workhouse, were offered medical treatment and health care. Edwin Chadwick, initially the custodian of the utilitarian basis of the New Poor Law, intended that medical relief should be available only in workhouses, so that to gain such relief would automatically entail entering the workhouse and becoming a pauper, therefore maintaining the so-called workhouse test. For this reason, there had been no mention of outdoor medical relief in plans for the Poor Law Amendment Act of 1834,[4] although Earl Grey's cabinet, elected in November 1830, saw this as electorally inexpedient. This opinion was accentuated when Grey resigned in July 1834. He was replaced by Viscount Melbourne, who Sir L. Woodward has described as 'contemptuous of Benthamism'.[5] Melbourne's attitude probably determined the Government's antipathy to the utilitarian Poor Law policy envisaged by Chadwick, which led to a relaxation of medical relief provisions in the new legislation. Lord Melbourne's cabinet clearly believed that the Poor Law would become an issue in the next General Election, which was probably a realistic fear, because the 'Anti-Poor Law Movement' was becoming vociferous at this time. In these circumstances Chadwick's proposals were not completely adopted, but medical relief was still to conform to the major tenets of Poor Law administration, with the problems of applying these principles apparently ignored. Thus, outdoor medical relief was still only used in cases of absolute destitution, because acceptance of such aid meant that the individual and their family submitted to the indignities involved. The result of their unwillingness was that the poor often went untreated until they were critically ill, so that it could be argued that the Poor Law remained a deterrent. When the very poor had no other choice but the acceptance of Poor Law medical relief they gained the epithet 'pauper', which between 1834 and 1885 meant losing one's right to vote. Paupers were then disenfranchised for life,[6] which was seen by the ruling élite as an important symbol of lost liberty and as a potent deterrent to mendicancy. However, this loss probably had little impact on poor individuals, who had no vote anyway.

Orphaned and destitute children, often alone outside the workhouse, were sometimes apprehended and admitted there, while others applied to enter the workhouse of their own free will. It was these children, together with aged persons unfit for work, who were found in workhouses in large numbers. These groups also had the greatest propensity for illness, a situation that the 1834 Poor Law Amendment Act chose to ignore. However, to do this proved impossible, as inmates already in the workhouses were sometimes taken ill and they had to be treated. This was regarded as an acceptable situation by orthodox utilitarians, because these sick inmates had succumbed to the workhouse test before becoming ill. The decision demanding that poor, sick individuals enter the workhouse to gain medical relief, taken in 1834,[7] was made at a time when there was little alternative to the workhouse for poor sick individuals: for this reason there were very large numbers of individuals needing urgent treatment resident in the workhouse, because it had become a refuge for the chronically sick poor and a lying-in hospital for poor women during their confinements at childbirth. These new functions of the workhouse were recognised contemporaneously, but a leading article in *Lancet*, in 1842, raised another issue, when it referred to the Poor Law medical system as 'a vast machine' that had 'no throbbing heart, no voice of tenderness, no human soul'.[8] In short, it had become a bureaucracy soon after its inception, although this organisational development did not prevent the workhouse having great utility to its poor clientele.

In spite of the apparent administrative success of the Poor Law Commission, which according to R.G. Hodgkinson[9] promoted improvements in medical treatment soon after 1834, it was replaced by the Poor Law Board in 1847. This was partly because of the non-accountability of the Commission to Parliament and partly because of its administrative inefficiency. However, its replacement either caused a basic shift in the ideology of Poor Law administration, or this development occurred at the same time as such a change; coincidental with the demise of Edwin Chadwick's utilitarianism as an organising principle for the new Law. In spite of such changes to the central administration, local pauper management had been successful from the outset and in as early as 1836, the Chairman of the Board of Guardians at Pershore, described encouraging developments. He referred to 'improvements that the new medical system had brought about',[10] in a very positive comment about the working of the new Law. The increasing bureaucracy of the Poor Law system, after 1847, had a beneficial effect: it created a stratified administrative structure, which led to increased professionalism among administrators, including medical men, at both national and local levels. Centrally written medical regulations were now reinterpreted and implemented by a medical profession more aware of its status. This was demonstrated by the creation of the Provincial Medical Association, founded in Worcester in 1832, which became the British Medical Association in 1856. Further improvement was encouraged in 1859, with the founding of the General Medical Council, which was set up to oversee and maintain professional standards among doctors. This meant that pragmatic, but professional, decisions about medical treatment were now made and these were responsive to local circumstances, although they sometimes ignored the original tenets of the New Poor Law. Guardians now controlled such decisions locally, but their influence was not constant, which caused National Uniformity to be difficult to sustain and the deterrent effect of the workhouse – for recipients of medical relief – varied. In spite of this, Poor Law medical relief remained a last resort for most poor people.

Medical relief was not mentioned in official papers before a Poor Law Commission's order of 1842,[11] which laid down practices for the future and it is usually assumed that such relief did not exist before this date, although there was little doubt that medical aid was available for the poor in Worcestershire workhouses from 1834 onwards. It was regularly referred to in Guardians' Minutes and was apparently provided both inside and outside the workhouse. In urban areas this need for medical treatment for the poor led to the development of sick wards, although there were few of these in Worcestershire before 1850. However, by 1852, Martley workhouse had a sick ward for adults, but the Guardians there determined that a separate sick ward for children was not necessary,[12] which possibly meant that sick children shared this facility with adult paupers.

Within ten years of the introduction of the New Poor Law in 1834, the costs of medical relief nationally had risen dramatically, which in turn drew attention to the need for financial restraint. This led Guardians to attempt to cut the salary they paid medical officers. The Poor Law Commissioners apparently disapproved of this, because in 1840, according to Ruth Hodgkinson, they suggested 'that Guardians neglected the qualifications of candidates and appointed incompetent practitioners on the grounds of the lowness of their tender',[13] thus minimising costs. Soon after this, Edward Baines, President of the Poor Law Board spoke for the central administration when he stated that it was the quality of the treatment provided that was more important than its cost. He insisted that the 'qualifications of Poor Law medical officers ought to be such as to ensure for the poor a degree of skill . . . equal to that which can be commanded by the more fortunate classes'.[14] In spite of such assertions, the Webbs later described workhouse infirmaries in the early 1840s, as 'few and far between',[15] so that medical treatment was clearly still being given in the general wards of workhouses, where there were no special facilities.

The quality of the treatment received by pauper patients was clearly directly related to the efficiency and professionalism of their doctor, but it was also determined by the sort of medicines and equipment used. Thus, an order in 1865 which made 'quinine, cod-liver oil and other expensive medicines'[16] available to pauper patients, replacing the cheap and ineffective union medicines, which had been traditionally supplied by union druggists, who catered for the special needs of Poor Law unions, was important. This was particularly so, because medicines were paid for by the medical officer, who then charged his pauper patients for the medicines used, a system hardly designed to make more sophisticated remedies common in the treatment of the ailments of the poor. Indeed, this tendency to use cheap and ineffective medicines continued for at least thirty years after 1834, particularly in rural and semi-rural areas. However, by 1867, the Metropolitan Poor Act[17] had allowed dispensaries to be set up in London, which replaced the system of doctors dispensing for their own patients. This practice was now also common in some large towns, but not within Worcestershire, where the old inadequate system of doctors dispensing their own medicines for pauper patients persisted.

Medical officers were recruited from among the doctors in a medical district, who applied for posts advertised in local newspapers. An election was then held by the Board of Guardians if there was more than one applicant, although in Worcestershire this was often not necessary, as only one doctor applied. Indeed, occasionally there were no applicants, in which case a doctor from an adjacent union could be appointed, but this invariably meant that medical relief for a seriously ill poor person was delayed. Doctors were apparently also reluctant to become Poor Law medical officers because they feared the taint of the poor, which they believed would make them less acceptable to their more respectable patients, who would then refuse to be treated by them. However, the low salary offered was undoubtedly another consideration in making these posts unattractive, which was indeed an important factor that led to adverse comments about the unattractive nature of Poor Law medical posts being published in the correspondence columns of *Lancet*.[18]

Once appointed, a medical officer held his post 'until he resigned, or died, or until he became legally disqualified to hold such office, or was removed by the Guardians',[19] with the Poor Law Central Authority regarding the potential to remove an unsatisfactory medical officer from his post as such a threat that it would ensure his compliance. Thus, he would take care not to displease the Board of Guardians, men who were sometimes, but not always, his social superiors. In 1834, the salaries of Worcestershire's Poor Law medical officers varied between £30 and £60 per annum, which was contrary to a suggestion, made by R.G. Hodgkinson,[20] that salaries in most county parishes were only between £15 to £20. However, these lower average salaries were probably computed by dividing the total medical relief expenditure for the county by the number of medical officers employed, while the first assessment quoted was based on the range of actual salaries received, with the implication that small Poor Law unions, such as Tenbury Wells, paid only small salaries to their medical officers. A national average salary of £65 was cited in 1837,[21] but this figure was probably inflated by the inclusion of large city and Metropolitan salaries in the sums, so that the average for non-Metropolitan England and Wales would have been less. Higher medical fees than this were certainly paid in some county parishes before 1834, with fees as much as £300 per year sometimes quoted.[22] The reason for obvious discrepancies in quoted salaries after 1834[23] was probably that medical officers' pay was limited on the direct orders of the Secretary of the Poor Law Commission, Edwin Chadwick. Indeed, the central authority was said to have envisaged[24] that the salaries offered to medical officers should not exceed those paid before 1834, which they certainly did not. Indeed, Edwin Chadwick's directive also probably lay behind an attempt by Robert Weale, the local Assistant Poor Law Commissioner, to reduce expenditure on doctors' salaries. In 1836, he tried to set the salary of medical officers in Worcestershire at 3*d* per patient, with an addition of 10*s* for maternity cases,[25] in a covert attempt to reduce average salaries. Medical officers' salaries increased, but not by as much as they might have done had Robert Weale not intervened. By 1850 they were said to average only £50.[26]

Edwin Chadwick had always insisted that medical officers were servants of the Board of Guardians and were to maintain a correct relationship with other officers and with the Guardians themselves. This proved unacceptable to some medical men, who regarded themselves as having higher social status than this implied, which was an opinion that was quite commonly held in society at large. For this reason it was inevitable that *Lancet*, the journal that represented medical opinion most closely, should suggest in 1835[27] that it was the efforts of Poor Law medical officers that were bringing relief to the poor. However, *Lancet* suggested, in carrying out this duty, doctors were being exploited, which was a deplorable action simply intended to save Poor Rate payers' money by cutting expenditure on medical relief; also at the expense of pauper patients.

Initially Poor Law unions were divided into as many medical districts as the Guardians saw fit, which invariably meant that these areas were not uniform. This was because Poor Law unions differed in terms of population density, major industry and physical size. Such anomalies led to an investigation into the feasibility of uniform medical districts in 1847,[28] when it was concluded that uniformity of medical districts was desirable, but difficult to attain. It took until the late 1850s before any attempt at reform was made. The sort of problem encountered in attempted reforms of medical districts was well illustrated by the comparison of Dudley union, a compact and densely populated urban union having only one medical district, with Martley union, a very sparsely populated rural union, covering a massive area, that also had only one medical district. Clearly, attaining genuine uniformity in these circumstances would be impossible.

The medical treatment of workhouse inmates, as opposed to the poor population of a Poor Law union, was dealt with by a workhouse medical officer, often the same doctor responsible for the treatment of the sick poor in the medical district surrounding the institution. After 1844,[29] such an officer was given a salary for undertaking his institutional duties, although extra duties were added later in the same year.[30] These extra duties included examining children to be apprenticed, who were now to be certified medically fit, which was a regulation that remained in force until after 1871. The duties of the district medical officer, as opposed to the workhouse medical officer, were not stated before 1849,[31] which was the first occasion on which the existence of such an officer was admitted, even though Boards of Guardians' minutes had regularly referred to outdoor medical treatment, by such officers, since 1834.

The workhouse medical officer examined individuals entering the workhouse and recorded medical information in a register. At Dudley these admissions and discharge registers, in which the condition on entry of the paupers was entered, are extant.[32] Entries in the admissions register there stated either 'clean', 'dirty' or 'very dirty', which probably referred to the condition of the pauper's head and body. However, in Dudley, the most densely populated of all county unions, which was associated with metal and mining industries, it was possible that those coming to the workhouse were untypical of the rest of the county, most of which was rural, agricultural and sparsely populated. Fortunately workhouse admissions and discharge registers for Bromyard[33] in Herefordshire, close to the Worcestershire border, are also extant. Whilst not in the county, this very rural area was contiguous with the western border of Worcestershire and it provided an effective comparison with urban Dudley. At Bromyard, the condition of paupers entering the workhouse was little different from those in urban Dudley, although infant mortality rates were higher in Dudley union than in Bromyard union, possibly because of the incidence there of contagious disease and malnutrition among neonates. The overall death rate in Dudley was also much higher, probably because it was a more dangerous place to live and particularly to work. Accidents were more common and indeed accident victims were sometimes found in Dudley Workhouse. The net result of these mortalities was that the average age of death in Dudley, in the 1840s, was only around seventeen years of age, compared with more than forty years of age in Bromyard. In spite of such differences, both unions applied the same Poor Law regulations, including medical regulations, as the rest of the country, but the interpretation of these rules and regulations undoubtedly differed, which was probably related to the level of usage of the workhouse.

As about 30 per cent of the sick in the workhouse were children, who were usually kept in the ordinary children's wards, the supervision of sick youngsters was a major part of the workhouse medical officer's work. Indeed it was only at Dudley and Kidderminster that separate sick wards for children were provided, but occasionally even here sick children were found in the same wards as sick adults. Elsewhere, ill girls were occasionally in the same wards as unchaste women, although these wards did not usually contain diagnosed venereal disease sufferers; these individuals were always carefully segregated, regarded as most dangerous to young girls. However, it appeared to be moral infection, rather than the spreading of venereal disease, that explained the reluctance to mix these classes of pauper. In spite of such care, some women afflicted with these sexually transmitted diseases must have gone undiagnosed. Indeed they probably did their best to hide their symptoms, to avoid the stigma of having the disease, so that they were placed in the able-bodied women's ward of the workhouse, where they might contact impressionable younger inmates.

Sometimes epidemic diseases caused vagrant wards to be emptied for use as isolation wards and sick children were removed to these wards, together with adult paupers. This was seen to be a necessary evil, although the dangers of this practice eventually led unions to establish special isolation hospitals, some built in the grounds of the workhouses, but more usually at a distance from the institution. Thus, in times of epidemic these isolation hospitals came to be used for non-pauper patients, as well as for paupers, which indicated the seriousness with which such diseases were regarded. In such cases, the threat of the contagious diseases was seen as a greater threat than that of pauperism and social pressures forced even non-pauper sufferers to enter these Poor Law hospitals.

Insanity was defined, in the nineteenth century, as a disordered functioning of the mind that could happen at any stage in life. Whilst insane adult paupers were sometimes kept in the general wards of workhouses, pauper children did not encounter them, as segregation ensured that this could not happen. However, insane, idiot and imbecile children were kept in the normal children's wards, being tolerated if they were not dangerous or disruptive. Idiocy and imbecility were usually afflictions from birth; idiocy implying a failure to develop intelligence, while imbecility was a weakness of mind, intelligence being displayed in some aspects of behaviour but not in others. Imbeciles, in particular, were apparently regarded as very cunning. The workhouse medical officer sometimes attempted to treat mentally infirm children, as at Kidderminster in 1840, when a boy called Henry Webb, an 'idiot . . . from birth', who was not disruptive was treated.[34] The Guardians had considered sending this boy to the lunatic asylum but this would have been costly, so when he was successfully treated for inflammation of the brain – the diagnosed cause of his idiocy – by 'bleeding', placing him on a 'low diet' and keeping him quiet by undisclosed means, they were happy for him to remain in the workhouse, where he improved.[35] Paupers in Webb's position were not specially inspected before 1845 and the treatment they were given may sometimes have been inappropriate. However, there was an attempt to solve this in 1844, when the Poor Law Commission's Annual Report stated: 'Paupers of unsound mind should, where there is a chance of cure, be sent to an asylum as soon as possible after the commencement of the malady.'[36] The Lunacy Commission created in 1845, following the Lunatic Asylums' Act[37] and the Lunatics' Act,[38] made such treatment more likely. These pieces of legislation were intended to alter the way in which lunatics were treated. Six Lunacy Commissioners were appointed initially, each with experience of treating the mentally ill. They were to inspect the lunatic asylums. A few pauper lunatic asylums pre-dated the 1845 Acts, which encouraged the building of about fifty more institutions in the next eight years. Worcester City and County Pauper Lunatic Asylum at Powick, was one of these. It opened in 1852 and immediately took mentally infirm inmates from the county's workhouses and from a private madhouse at Droitwich, which had apparently been used by some Poor Law unions to cope with their more severe cases of pauper insanity. The appointment of the Lunacy Commissioners was in stark contrast to the appointment of Her Majesty's Inspectors of Elementary Education and of Assistant Poor Law Commissioners, who had little experience of what they were inspecting and who like most civil servants were appointed by patronage. The Lunacy Commissioners were given a salary of £1,500, plus travelling expenses, a financial arrangement thought likely to attract well-qualified and knowledgeable applicants, with experience of caring for lunatics.[39] These Commissioners applied the provisions of the 1845 Lunatics' Act,[40] which required that only two lunatics were to be kept in a house (including a workhouse) which was not an asylum. However, Guardians often ignored this regulation, because of the cost of implementing it and indeed it has been suggested by D.J. Mellett that this was because the Poor Law Commissioners regarded 'pauper lunatics . . . [as] . . . first and foremost paupers'.[41] Pauper child lunatics continued to be kept in workhouses, unless they were considered dangerous, which was the case for only a few of them. This was the situation that prevailed until the inspection of workhouses by Lunacy Commissioners became more widespread.

Before 1857 only workhouses close to pauper lunatic asylums were inspected by the Lunacy Commissioners. Droitwich and Worcester workhouses, close to the private madhouse on the Worcester edge of that town, may have been inspected between 1845 and 1852, and only Worcester and Martley workhouses, close to Powick, were inspected between 1852 and 1857. However, after 1857, new regulations ensured that all workhouses were regularly scrutinised, so that theoretically, at least, all lunatics in workhouses were now removed to the lunatic asylums created under the 1845 Lunatic Asylums' Act. In spite of this, not all lunatics in workhouses were sent to asylums and indeed after 1860, it has been estimated by R.G. Hodgkinson,[42] that 4 per cent of paupers were lunatics, but only a minority of these were in lunatic asylums. The Lunatics' Amendment Act of 1862[43] again attempted reform, this time making the relieving officer of the Poor Law union responsible for bringing each case of pauper lunacy before the magistrates, who were expected to commit lunatics to the asylum. However, few were committed there and it has been suggested by D.J. Mellett that 'the vast proportion of lunatic paupers were [still] detained in workhouses'.[44] Even as late as 1871, while there were probably child pauper lunatics in all county unions, there were very few pauper children in the county lunatic asylum.

Responsibility for lunatic returns made to the Poor Law Commission was transferred in 1847 to the Lunacy Commission, but somewhat surprisingly there was initially no increase in the numbers of lunatics reported. Thus, it appeared likely that the only accurate returns made to the Lunacy Commission continued to be from inspected workhouses. The first returns for Worcester workhouse were made in 1847, when a boy called William Noinent, aged thirteen years,[45] was the only child reported to the Lunacy Commissioners. He was said to be not dangerous and not dirty, but he was described as an idiot. However, the fact that he posed no threat meant that the Guardians were willing to maintain him in the workhouse. Thus, it was a temptation for Guardians to record lunatics as not dangerous and avoid the cost of commitment to a lunatic asylum, a situation that was tacitly accepted by the Lunacy Commissioners. When they visited Worcester workhouse they were aware of Noinent, but did not insist that he was removed to an asylum. Many Poor Law unions made no returns on lunatic children in their workhouses, although they must have existed in these institutions and therefore there must be some question about the accuracy of lunacy statistics. In fact, D.J. Mellett's study[46] cited statistics that demonstrated that these official figures were underestimates. Thus, when lunatic children were recorded as present in a workhouse they were regarded as containable within the institution, avoiding pressure to remove them to an asylum. In this way the Poor Rate payers incurred no additional expense and money was saved, although there were cases where Poor Rates were spent on treatment in a lunatic asylum for pauper children. This occurred at Martley in 1851,[47] when a boy was committed to the asylum at Fairford in Gloucestershire,[48] at a cost of 2s 2d per week. This was a peculiar case, as the cost of maintaining the same boy at Worcestershire asylum, Powick, would have been 12s per week. Clearly, the Guardians, who wished to save money, used Fairford asylum because it was cheaper, although why the charge for these two institutions was so discrepant was difficult to know. Another case, at about the same time, was even more bemusing; when Leah Timms, a thirteen-year-old girl from Shipston on Stour union,[49] then part of Worcestershire, was sent to Fairford asylum the charge for her was 8s 6d per week. It thus appeared likely that it was the nature of the insanity of the inmate that determined the cost of care at Fairford asylum.

Quite often, child lunatics were kept by parents or relatives, who were paid outdoor relief to maintain them, and were thus hidden from the Lunacy Commissioners, so that the Guardians evaded the expense of maintaining such children in lunatic asylums. However, when such children were in workhouses, the Lunacy Commissions inspected them there and sometimes improved the conditions under which they were kept. For instance, the Lunacy Commissioner objected to the way in which two idiot boys shared a bed at Upton upon Severn workhouse in 1858,[50] and it was eventually recommended that bed sharing there be banned. The Guardians acted swiftly to ban this practice and to improve other aspects of the treatment of these boys, definitely making them more eligible. Such cases led Sidney and Beatrice Webb to comment, some fifty years later, that the Lunacy Commission was not as conscious of Less Eligibility as was the Poor Law Board, who regarded many suggestions made by the Lunacy Commission as 'preposterously extravagant',[51] so the Guardians actions at Upton upon Severn on this occasion may not have been welcomed by the Central Poor Law Authority.

Bed sharing by idiot boys was considered normal by the Poor Law Board and by most Guardians, but in this case it was quickly abandoned following the Lunacy Commissioner's comments[52] and when next visited the boys were cared for by an aged pauper, so that the Guardians were complimented on the level of care now provided.[53] Whilst comparison with idiot children outside the workhouse was impossible, because sources to make this feasible were not extant, it appeared likely that the lowest level of independent labourer would have found it impossible to provide an individual bed, permanent attendance and additional food for his idiot children. Thus, inmate idiot children appeared more eligible than their non-pauper contemporaries.

County Pauper Lunatic Asylums, described in various historical studies,[54] generally did not differentiate between lunatics of various social classes, so that lower middle-class and working-class patients were often committed to the same licensed asylums and regarded as paupers. Thus, when the medical officer of Shipston on Stour union was diagnosed insane in 1863,[55] he was committed to Powick asylum, along with his own pauper patients. However, some non-pauper poor families will have kept insane relatives at home for as long as possible, only committing them to an asylum when they became troublesome. They were thus similar to the pauperised poor, except that destitute individuals may have received outdoor relief to look after their relatives and this may have induced some poor individuals to become paupers, wholly for the purpose of receiving outdoor relief to support their insane relative. Indeed this was a chance worth taking, because insane inmates were unwelcome in workhouses and therefore the individual was unlikely to be forced to become a workhouse inmate to gain such relief for their relative. While, in most places, National Uniformity was ignored for mentally ill paupers because the utilitarian principles on which the Poor Law was based proved impractical when applied to lunatics, idiots and imbeciles, some fundamentalist Guardians insisted on a rigid application of the rules. In many cases a sort of administrative sleight of hand meant that by the 1860s mentally ill and defective children had virtually disappeared from the county's workhouses. They were probably now at home with their parents or relatives, out of sight of the Lunacy Commissioners.

As well as his responsibility for the general health of workhouse inmates, the workhouse medical officer was responsible for their diet, classification and treatment. He was able to supplement the ill child's diet[56] to treat a range of medical conditions, because an altered diet was often thought to prevent illnesses in general. For instance, at King's Norton in 1853,[57] the medical officer removed cheese from the children's diet because it was thought to be injurious to their health. Initially medical officers advised workhouse masters about the diet of sick inmates, but in 1860 they were made solely responsible for the diet of the sick.[58] However, there was no consensus about the matter of diet, even among medical experts, and inevitably this led to disputes about dietary changes. Thus, when Dr E. Smith conducted a national survey of workhouse diets in 1871, there were disagreements among so-called experts about his findings. For instance, when Dr Smith suggested that bacon be removed from the workhouse child's diet because it was injurious to their health, a correspondent to *Lancet* disagreed. He stated: 'when there are so many evils to redress in the workhouse it seems perfectly monstrous that inspectors should be employed at large salaries to cut down the meat supply to growing children'.[59] In spite of such differences of opinion, diets were usually altered for a specific purpose. For instance, measles was often treated by a general addition to the diet, which while it did not aid the cure of the disease in specific terms, it will hardly have hindered the patient's recovery.

Whilst special diets appeared to benefit the sick inmate child, even these diets remained inadequate. This was graphically illustrated at Bromsgrove in 1859, when a sick boy, named James Clarke, ate 'some flesh and marrow of the leg of a horse'.[60] Although it was apparently not normal to eat horsemeat, one major cause of anguish was that the horsemeat was raw. Significantly, the medical officer ascribed the boy's action to hunger, which was surely a cause for concern. But in spite of this the Guardians ignored the incident, as did the Poor Law Board. Whilst the sick pauper child's diet was still inadequate it was probably more adequate than the diet of the independent labourer's sick child. In this respect inmate children were still more eligible than their independent contemporaries. However, some Guardians, such as those at Martley, still assiduously maintained Less Eligibility, but even they did not challenge the medical officer's decisions about alterations to the diet of ill children in spite of this infringment of this otherwise inviolable principle. The medical profession developed in competence between 1834 and 1871, and in doing so they gained credibility and acceptance, although the methods they used sometimes remained idiosyncratic, so that any notion of uniformity of treatment was also impossible to sustain.

Another responsibility the medical officer gained in the first few years after the passing of the Poor Law Amendment Act was the presentation of a written Annual Report, which in populous towns became lengthy, particularly after the Commission on the Health of Towns in 1842.[61] Only the most populous towns were compulsorily reported on, so that within Worcestershire only the medical officers of Dudley, Kidderminster, Stourbridge and Worcester unions had to produce reports. Although there was no requirement for rural unions to produce such reports, some were written and some of these are still extant. Medical officers' reports commented on the health of workhouse inmates and on such health factors as the purity of drinking water in workhouses, which was usually obtained from a well, although where this supply failed surface water, invariably contaminated with sewage, was used. In spite of this, it was only at Bromsgrove workhouse in 1861,[62] that a serious health threat was caused by contaminated drinking water, although it appeared likely that there was a background level of sewage contamination in drinking water in all workhouses. However, as the lower-working-class areas of towns, from which most workhouse inmates came, had a water supply often taken from surface water or from contaminated wells, the inhabitants of these areas already had some resistance to some of the bacteria they consumed in workhouses. Such inmates were probably relatively unaffected by the slight contamination of the drinking water in the workhouse.

The workhouse medical officer was initially ill-equipped to deal with the public health aspects of his duties, but as these increased in importance between 1834 and 1871, his expertise developed, so that now the visiting committees accepted the efficacy of the medical officer's solutions to health problems without question. Now, workhouse drains were relaid, fever wards constructed and the general sanitary conditions in the workhouses improved, all at considerable cost to the Poor Rate payers, on the sole recommendation of the medical officer. Clearly the Poor Rate payers were willing to countenance such expenditure because their self-interest demanded a healthier environment.

Epidemic diseases were most severe in the poorest areas of densely populated towns and cities, but Worcestershire had few of these, mainly because most of its population lived in the countryside or in small towns and villages. Only the Black Country fringe of the county was densely populated, in towns like Dudley, Kidderminster and Stourbridge.

Although cholera and typhoid fever caused panic in these towns and among all sections of the community, these diseases were never a problem. Whilst the working classes were fatalistic about such epidemic diseases, the middle and upper classes were afraid of them and wanted the threat combated. Thus, it was self-interest, rather than the altruism of the middle and upper classes, that led to various public health measures and to legislation. However, it was the working classes who remained most vulnerable to these contagious diseases and it was the young who were most vulnerable of all. Indeed, F.B. Smith has stated that: 'From the 1840s onwards . . . about one quarter of all deaths recorded in England and Wales were of infants under one year'[63] and it was considered, contemporaneously, by Henry Butler, that the illegitimate child, the 'offspring of degraded parents' was most exposed to 'constitutional weakness . . . violence, and the diseases that ensued from neglect'.[64] The workhouses contained many such children who were thus considered most in danger from epidemic diseases. When these occurred in Worcestershire, they were invariably blamed on vagrants, who were said to bring diseases to the area in the summer months, when casual agricultural work was available. This was certainly thought to be the case at Kidderminster in 1848.[65] Thus, when vagrants applied for casual indoor relief, this was thought to cause a health hazard for non-vagrant inmates, so that itinerant paupers were now placed in special wards, where separation was vigorously applied. In this way ordinary inmates, including children, were thought to be protected even from the sight of such dangerous individuals.

Of all the epidemic diseases, cholera was the most feared, although there were relatively few cases of the disease in the county between 1834 and 1871 and fewer cases still in the workhouses. There was an outbreak of the disease at Kidderminster in 1848,[66] when the medical officers prescribed brandy to treat the disease and advised that sanitary precautions be taken in the workhouse, so that bedpans were introduced to prevent the soiling of bedclothes. In other cases, the mere suggestion of a potential outbreak of cholera produced immediate action; this happened in Pershore in 1854,[67] at about the same time as 'the last outbreak of cholera in Britain . . . when the disease was still feared'.[68] The Guardians here had the workhouse water supply analysed, but no pathogenic organisms were found on this occasion. At this time other Poor Law unions demanded vigilance[69] and special committees of Guardians were set up to monitor the progress of the disease.[70]

Victims of epidemic disease at Droitwich were usually given an improved diet and were often isolated in special wards kept fumigated, ventilated and whitewashed.[71] Typhus, which was initially indistinguishable from the far more serious typhoid fever – both diseases initially caused diarrhoea and vomiting – was the most common epidemic disease. The Poor Law Board suggested in 1848,[72] that the victims of such epidemic diseases be lodged away from the workhouse, which in some cases meant that outdoor relief was paid to relatives to look after victims in their homes. However, this was not done in Worcestershire, where epidemic disease sufferers were still admitted to workhouses. Vagrants were blamed for introducing typhus to the Worcester area in 1847,[73] while some children contracted this disease at Bromsgrove in 1862,[74] where one boy died and several other children were ill.[75] On this occasion, the medical officer prescribed milk pudding instead of cheese in the children's supper diet to combat the disease, which was obviously thought of as a preventive measure, as well as a treatment, because non-sufferers were also given this diet. The wards, where the children suffering from the disease were kept, were later fumigated with chloride of lime to ensure that a further outbreak of the disease was prevented.

Measles, which is today regarded as a normal childhood ailment, was, according to F.B. Smith, a disease of the poor in the nineteenth century.[76] However, surprisingly, there were only two cases recorded in a county workhouse between 1834 and 1871, at Droitwich on both occasions.[77] In spite of its apparent rarity in Worcestershire Poor Law institutions, measles was the childhood disease that killed more children than any other in nineteenth-century society in general. Diphtheria, also regarded as a serious childhood disease, was apparently brought to England from Europe in 1855. In 1859, Stourbridge Guardians recorded the disease as 'common in the union'.[78] This was only two weeks after they had responded to a Poor Law Board circular, stating that there were no cases locally.[79] Whilst this disease could also afflict adults, it was children who were its main victims, which was the case in the county's most serious outbreak of diphtheria at Bromsgrove in 1866.[80] Outside workhouses, croup and whooping cough were common childhood ailments, afflicting those under two years old. Croup was a debilitating inflammation of the respiratory system, which was treated by inhalation of steam,[81] although some doctors recommended using opium as a treatment.[82] Whooping cough was a serious bacterial infection of the lungs, that killed between 8,099 and 13,612 children annually, between 1841 and 1910.[83] However, in spite of being a widespread fatal disease among children generally, it was only a problem at Droitwich workhouse in 1868,[84] where there were twelve cases, none fatal. Scarlet fever was also rare in county workhouses, with the only reported outbreak being at Kidderminster workhouse in 1865,[85] where no one died. However, this disease was considered such a threat to Worcestershire's society generally that at Bromsgrove in 1870,[86] a special fever ward was opened to victims of the disease from outside the workhouse.

Children permanently in the workhouse, such as orphans, deserted children and long-term child inmates, were thus more eligible than their non-pauper contemporaries, because they were constantly scrutinised for signs of diseases and immediately treated if any were found. Also, because they lived in complete isolation, this conferred the advantage of isolation from infection, which was further ensured by suspending visits from non-inmates when epidemic diseases were present in an area. Workhouse children were thus kept in isolated, relatively hygienic conditions, which reduced the liability of catching diseases, so that children in Worcestershire's workhouses probably caught diseases less often than did their contemporaries outside the workhouse. However, inmate children were considered weak and they were said to be suffering from 'dibility',[87] possibly because of undiagnosed tuberculosis, which was ever present among the poor. There were two types of tuberculosis; phthisis (or consumption) which affected the lungs and scrofula that affected the bones, muscle and skin. In the case of phthisis, tubercles caused swelling of the tissues, irritation in the lungs, coughing and irreparable damage to lung tissue. In scrofula, tubercles in the skin and muscles caused swellings, which restricted blood supply, so that sometimes limbs had to be amputated.[88] Usually the only treatment given for either form of tuberculosis was an improved diet, as a cure was seldom possible. While this appeared minimal treatment, at least the pauper child with tuberculosis gained an improved diet. Their non-pauper contemporaries, who were the offspring of independent labourers on the margins of destitution, did not even obtain this minimal treatment and the Principle of Less Eligibility was again violated in this context.

In spite of the relative advantages afforded by incarceration in the workhouse, there were some diseases accentuated by institutional living, such as the skin disease known as itch which was most difficult to cure, a situation worsened by the ambivalence of medical men about the cause of the complaint. An article in *Lancet* in 1834 asserted: 'The manner of contagion . . . is not well known, and physiologists have not yet decided whether a peculiar animal exists in the morbid secretions and reproduces the disease.'[89] However, a year later, another doctor was certain that the scabies mite was the cause of the disease and he recommended sulphuretted hydrogen as a possible cure,[90] but there was no consensus about treatment either. By 1871,[91] medical opinion held that itch was scabies and because of this children's diets were sometimes altered to treat the complaint.[92] Thus, tea, sugar and butter were sometimes added to the diet of children with itch, although at other times one food was substituted for another.[93] Cheese was often seen as responsible for the continuance of the disease, a belief that an outside expert,[94] brought in to investigate an outbreak of the disease in a county workhouse, agreed with. He suggested that children became susceptible to itch when enfeebled by lack of nourishment, so an improved diet was indeed the key to treatment. Descriptions of itch appeared to suggest that it was several different skin infections. It was described as 'a lichenous rash, which created ulcers and scabs on the limbs, between the fingers, on the buttocks, and sometimes the face'.[95] Papules full of pus formed which infected and reinfected the children. While vitamin deficiency probably aided infection by itch, lack of cleanliness appeared to be the most important factor causing the continuance of the complaint. This would explain why the disease was so contagious in the institutional setting of the workhouse, so much so that the medical officer at Kidderminster in 1856,[96] believed that mere physical contact with visitors to the institution was sufficient to spread the disease. Bed sharing was thought to be another cause of the spread of the disease, which it almost certainly was, and so this practice was banned where itch was a problem. While medical officers commonly disagreed about the treatment of many diseases, locally there was a consensus about the treatment of itch, so that children with the disease were often isolated and only allowed back into the children's ward when completely recovered. While itch must have been a constant infection among the poor outside the workhouse, it was probably regarded as inevitable, so there was no apparent attempt to alleviate the complaint in the community at large. For this reason, the transient child inmate was liable to be infected with itch and would introduce the disease to the workhouse every time they were admitted there. Thus, new entrants to the institution were closely scrutinised for signs of infection and isolated within the workhouse for treatment if symptoms of the disease were found, although hygiene was also improved to eradicate itch, a remedy recommended by the Poor Law

Commission in 1847.[97] After this date, clean bedding was given regularly, but because bed sharing continued, there must have been cross infection from this source. The attraction of sharing beds was obvious: children could be packed into inadequate sized wards, as at Martley in 1858,[98] where three children shared a bed in the workhouse there. This meant that itch continued to be considered 'inevitable'[99] in this problematical union, where workhouse facilities for children were known to be inadequate.

Lice were also considered 'inevitable', which was worrying as both typhus and typhoid fevers were thought to be spread by bacteria in lice faeces. Bedlinen, at Droitwich in 1839,[100] had been washed weekly to reduce infection from these parasites, but at Bromsgrove in 1842,[101] another approach was used. Here, the bedlinen was dipped in chloride of lime and then into mercuric chloride to kill lice,[102] which undoubtedly worked, although it ruined the sheets, made them uncomfortable to use and almost certainly poisonous. In spite of such drastic measures, lice and vermin in bedclothes were considered 'an abominable nuisance' at Kidderminster in as late as 1862,[103] where the bedlinen was also treated with mercuric chloride, a chemical recommended by *Lancet* in 1836 to be applied to the skin as a treatment for itch.[104] As we have seen, isolation was more usually used in an attempted treatment for this skin complaint, so that fever hospitals were sometimes opened to receive sufferers, as at Droitwich in 1857.[105] However, only children were ever treated for itch, with adults apparently left untreated, possibly because the disease required long-term treatment, so that it was only children, permanently in the workhouse, who remained long enough to be cured. Ironically, it was the 'ins and outs', children who were transitory visitors, who were undoubtedly the source of reinfection by the disease. The most serious outbreak of itch was at Kidderminster in 1861, where it was described as 'obstinate and taking time'.[106] Here, sixty-five children were afflicted with the complaint. Other unions treated this skin infection by taking afflicted children to rented accommodation at 'a healthy spot', so that King's Norton union used a house on the Lickey Hills in 1862,[107] where they employed a nurse to care for the children, with the schoolmaster or schoolmistress continuing to be responsible for educating them there. Elsewhere, at Droitwich in 1868,[108] children suffering from itch were isolated in an old barn, where the medical officer provided old clothes, which were worn and then burned to prevent cross-infection. This scheme caused the disease to slowly succumb to treatment, but the Guardians were impatient. They asked for an outside expert's advice and were told that this treatment was satisfactory.[109] In spite of this, they proceeded with a case of negligence against the medical officer.[110] He was found guilty at the Guardians' inquiry, but refused to resign, although a similar charge brought against the same medical man in 1871[111] led to his resignation.

The most drastic treatment of itch was at Bromsgrove in 1842,[112] where a boy, named Henry Cartwright, was 'immersed in a solution of sulphuret of potash', a treatment often used to kill the smell of paupers, but on this occasion the child died, possibly from drowning. The medical officer who ordered the treatment, but who was not present when the matron administered it, was found guilty of neglect. However, at a subsequent enquiry conducted by the Assistant Poor Law Commissioner, the Guardians did not demand the doctor's resignation, because of 'his previous zeal in performing his duties', but the matron, who was simply following the medical officer's orders, was found guilty of neglect and was dismissed. A similar treatment of itch was used at Kidderminster in 1863,[113] and at Droitwich in 1868.[114] Cures for itch were generally unsuccessful and the disease persisted in most unions, although its virulence fluctuated, probably due to changing climatic conditions. The disease was usually common in the summer months, but was almost absent in the winter. Other treatments used included outdoor exercise and preventing sunlight entering children's rooms, although all such remedies proved unsuccessful. Eventually it was only improved diet and better hygiene in the workhouse that was successful in containing and treating itch. It was these measures that eventually eradicated this institutional disease from workhouses.

Ringworm or scaldhead was similar to itch, and it appeared likely that the two complaints were sometimes confused, although ringworm was definitely caused by a fungoid infection. Kidderminster workhouse had the highest incidence of both diseases, as indicated by extant medical records and an altered diet, as suggested as a treatment in a letter to *Lancet* in 1835,[115] was adopted there in 1841.[116] However, while this treatment certainly improved the general health of inmate children it probably did little to cure ringworm. Elsewhere, sufferers from this fungoid infection were often segregated, although the Guardians at King's Norton in 1840, refused to accept the medical officer's advice to do this.[117] Other unions attempted isolation in the workhouse, a treatment that also generally proved ineffective as the disease recurred, although the problems of ensuring that a small group of children were truly isolated in a large workhouse must have been huge. From all this it must be concluded that, as with itch, chance alteration of climate reduced the virulence of ringworm, although doctors continued to use a variety of treatments for the complaint. These included sulphuret of potash baths, as recommended in *Lancet* in 1835,[118] the treatment of itch that killed the boy at Bromsgrove;[119] tincture of opium,[120] sulphuric acid washes[121] and lemon juice,[122] all of which were suggested in *Lancet* in 1835 and all of which apparently assumed that ringworm was allied to scurvy. However, in as late as 1861 at Kidderminster,[123] fresh-air walks were the only treatment prescribed by the medical officer for ringworm. Isolation, improved diet and particularly improved hygiene was the most successful measure in curing and preventing both ringworm and itch among workhouse children.

Ophthalmia, an infection of the conjunctiva of the eye, was interestingly not reported in any workhouse in Worcestershire before 1847, although the complaint must have existed. It was first reported at Martley workhouse in 1847,[124] after which it became a problem in most Poor Law unions in the county. A very large body of medical literature soon developed on the complaint. Blood letting was recommended as a treatment in *Lancet* in 1835,[125] for a disease, which by this time was causing huge concern, not because of its distressing physical effects, but according to S. Liveing, in the same year, because it recurred 'again and again . . . [so that] . . . the eyesight was permanently damaged; and the child who might otherwise have been lifted out of pauperism, would be dependent on state relief throughout life'.[126] The severest outbreak of this extremely contagious disease was at King's Norton in 1855,[127] although it was most persistent at Martley, starting there in 1857.[128] Here, it was said to have been caused by 'the unhealthy position of the workhouse', so that the inmate children were temporarily removed to other premises in the hope of effecting a cure. Here, as elsewhere, it was only children who were treated. Adults, who must also have been afflicted, were never treated, possibly because their short stay in the workhouse made effective cure impossible. When J.T. Graves, the Assistant Poor Law Commissioner for the area, visited and inspected the Martley workhouse in March 1857, he concluded that the disease was caused by ammonia generated from 'urine left overnight in the sleeping rooms', which were unventilated. When Graves returned to Martley again, to inspect the children's education there, he found that the children were understandably learning nothing, because their eyesight was so impaired. This situation led him to suspend the schoolteacher's certificate, which unjustly threw her out of work for the duration of the ophthalmia outbreak.[129] Two months later Graves was very self-satisfied about the way that the situation had improved and he clearly believed that his suggestion that urine no longer be left in the bedrooms in uncovered dishes was the cause of the improvement. He now reinstated the schoolmistress, which demonstrated the insecurity of tenure of employment of workhouse school staff. At the whim of an Assistant Poor Law Commissioner this schoolmistress was put out of work for perhaps ten weeks, because of a chance happening, over which she had no control.

Whilst ophthalmia did recur in Martley union, it was never a severe problem there again, although Graves's complacent belief that he knew the cause of the disease there was doubtful, as it appeared most likely that it was climatic changes that led to the eradication of the infection at Martley rather than the removal of urine from the wards. Ophthalmia afflicted children at Kidderminster, almost continuously, between 1863 and 1865,[130] and in December 1864 it was so severe that the schoolmaster there was also dismissed: 'Because the boys were incapable of doing school work.' This time the affliction was treated with cod-liver oil and an altered diet,[131] but later in the same year, sunlight in the children's rooms was blamed by the same medical officer for another outbreak of the disease,[132] so the ward windows were whitewashed to prevent sunlight entering the room and, fortuitously, the disease abated. However, ironically, the apparent effectiveness of this cure led to the medical officer being called upon to explain his 'extravagant treatment' of his previous patients, apparently because he had used expensive cod-liver oil in their treatment. His response was to insist that it was 'to the economy of the ratepayers in general' to have the disease cured by whatever means, which was a response that clearly satisfied the Guardians as they took no further action on this matter. This disease did not recur at Kidderminster, possibly because the medical officer there heeded an article in *Lancet* in 1851, that had pointed to 'wretched hygiene conditions' as the root cause of ophthalmia and suggesting that improved hygiene measures would 'arrest the problem'.[133] With hindsight, this treatment would have eradicated the disease, but with the exception of Kidderminster workhouse it was not adopted elsewhere in the county before 1871. However, elsewhere in the country, workhouse towels became the pauper's personal property and were marked with the pauper's workhouse number. Now paupers always used the same towel, which reduced cross infection with ophthalmia, itch and ringworm, diseases that were all accentuated by communal living.

There was a great disparity in the treatment given by workhouse doctors for the same diseases and this was further complicated by disagreements about diagnosis. This situation was highlighted in a circular from the Poor Law Commission in 1844, which asked for 'apparent cause of death' for all deaths within the institution.[134] According to R.G. Hodgkinson there was no consensus about diagnosis before 1847, when an order stated that the standard statistical nosology used by the Registrar General to record deaths[135] should also be used by workhouse medical officers, which clarified matters considerably. There are extant mortality records of pauper children for four of the thirteen county unions, for 1841, with no distinction made in these records between pauper deaths that occurred inside the workhouse and those happening outside it.[136] From the evidence that these records provide, tuberculosis, which was thought to be highly contagious, was surprisingly rare among pauper children in the county's workhouses, but the disease may have been considered inevitable and may have been left untreated and possibly unrecorded. All fatal cases of respiratory tuberculosis, usually known as consumption, were recorded in Stourbridge union, where environmental factors may have accentuated the disease. Wasting diseases, such as marasmus, were only common in Worcester union; here it was the major cause of death among infants, whose condition was possibly worsened by the inadequacy of the diet of the mothers, who were probably ineffective in suckling their offspring.

In spite of relatively high infant and child mortality rates in the county, workhouses were physically relatively safe places, with only one inmate child killed in the thirty-seven years surveyed. This was when a boy was burned to death at Stourbridge workhouse in 1841.[137] Death rates were, generally, greatest of all among infants and diminished as children approached adulthood. This was well illustrated in statistical trends after 1836,[138] which showed Worcestershire slightly above the national average for death rates of infants under five years old; 22.9 per cent of males and 20.2 per cent of females dying before they were five years old. These figures compare with an average for England and Wales of 22.5 per cent and 19.9 per cent respectively. Further, it has been suggested by F.B. Smith, regarding mortality in society as a whole, that: 'The incidence of infant deaths was highest among the poor and lowest among the comfortable',[139] with the highest death rate of all among illegitimate children. This has been well demonstrated by Michael Armstrong for York between 1841 and 1851[140] where illegitimate children died in the largest numbers, although there was no attempt made here to distinguish pauper deaths, but it might reasonably be presumed that a similar pattern applied here too. The poorest working-class individuals, on the margins of pauperism, undoubtedly had the highest mortality rates and this pattern was replicated among infants and children, some of whom were undoubtedly saved from death by being inmates of workhouses. However, infant mortality in workhouses was inevitably inflated because adult women's wards were used as a lying-in hospital for the confinement of poor women at childbirth, which were said to produce sickly and vulnerable children. Significantly, according to F.B. Smith, such women accepted a pauper status to obtain the right to enter the workhouse to give birth there, which demonstrated well the threat posed by the alternatives available to such women.[141] This practice clouded the issue of neonate and infant deaths in workhouses; where a child was stillborn or died soon after birth, this was recorded as a pauper death, but because such deaths were regarded as inevitable, and the infants were most vulnerable, having a low expectation of life anyway, no cause of death was ever recorded in these cases.

With regard to Poor Law medicine in general, not just that provided for workhouse inmates, George Cornewall-Lewis, one of the Poor Law Commissioners, suggested in 1844 that: 'From so large a number of attendances, 717,200 . . . it was only reasonable to expect some instances of neglect should occur.'[142] This was a likelihood that was accentuated by the large size of medical districts. Thus, some medical officers in Worcestershire undoubtedly neglected their child pauper patients, sometimes grievously so, with the only protection for the patient being the suspension, by the Guardians, of neglectful and negligent doctors, although clearly this could only happen after the event.

There was a whole catalogue of neglect cases in the county after outdoor medical relief became common in the 1840s, although prior to this such cases must have existed, but were never mentioned in Guardians' Minute Books. In 1846, at Martley,[143] a doctor was found guilty of 'shameful neglect', when two boys, aged three and five years old, died of scarlet fever after he refused to visit them. This doctor resigned when a charge of negligence against him was substantiated,[144] although this was unusual, because most medical officers charged with neglect neither resigned nor were dismissed. Thus, when the medical officer at Pershore in 1851,[145] simply sent medicines, but did not bother to attend a five-year-old girl pauper patient, who later died, he was charged with neglect, but the Guardians simply recorded their 'disapprobation' and the doctor continued in office. In another case, at Shipston on Stour in 1851,[146] the medical officer there who refused to attend a child with severe burns, who later died, was censured by the Coroner for neglect, but no action was taken about this matter by the Guardians, and he continued in office. He refused to attend another child in 1856[147] and when he was called again the next day by the parents, he did attempt to visit the child. However, as he reported to a subsequent Guardians' inquiry, he 'immediately attended with leeches and c', but the child died half an hour before he arrived. On this occasion the doctor's actions were regretted, but again no blame was found. In another case of inaction by a medical officer, at Droitwich in 1857, another child died, but here too the medical officer was 'found guilty of practical, but not intentional neglect'.[148] Perhaps the most blatant case of neglect by a medical officer was at Hindlip, in 1870,[149] where a girl was neglected for ten days. The doctor here sent medicines only on the eleventh day, but when the girl died there was no action taken against him, even though the Guardians had noted the case and the Poor Law Board had received their minutes. From this evidence, it appeared impossible for medical officers to be dismissed for neglect, no matter how culpable they were. Thus pauper child patients were clearly less eligible in this case, compared with even poor private child patients, as non-paupers were always treated ahead of paupers, with the seriousness of the illness concerned appearing immaterial.

The onerous system of medical tickets was probably also to blame for the inefficiencies of medical officers, although it was surely not the Poor Law Central Authority's intention that pauper patients should be neglected in this way. However, it was the manner in which the system operated that was not intended by the authority. Medical tickets were supplied to paupers by the relieving officer, theoretically on demand, and were then taken to the medical officer, who gave treatment in return for the ticket. In spite of being logical, this system apparently seldom worked smoothly. Indeed, the medical ticket system was particularly at fault at Worcester, in as late as 1871,[150] in a case reported in *Lancet*, where the relieving officer left an aged pauper to give out medical tickets. This man misused his delegated authority, so that some individuals not entitled to treatment received it, although the doctor was unaware of this situation. In spite of this, it was the doctor, rather than the relieving officer, who was charged with neglect. *Lancet* publicised the case and claimed that the medical officer had no charge to answer, an opinion with which the Guardians agreed and the doctor was acquitted.[151] This case, this late in the era of the Poor Law Board, probably indicated that the system of medical tickets was at fault throughout the period from 1847 to 1871.

By the late 1840s, there were clear tensions in the Poor Law medical system which caused problems in recruiting suitable doctors as Poor Law medical officers and it was at this time that unqualified assistants were employed – the eventual cause of the whole medical system becoming discredited. The sparsity of Poor Law medical provision was a problem from its inception so that in 1846,[152] the Poor Law Board accepted these unqualified assistants as a cheaper alternative to raising medical officer's salaries to attract more applicants. One doctor writing retrospectively about this situation in 1887, long after this strategy had been adopted, recognised the inadequacy of the system. He commented that: 'were it not for this system . . . the poor would not be placed in the hands of incompetents, and the Board of Guardians would not be enabled to obtain Officers at the prices that are but too often merely nominal',[153] which were views that were certainly reflected in contemporary editions of both *Lancet* and *The British Medical Journal*. In the 1840s and 50s, medical officers apparently willingly accepted the help of such unqualified medical assistants, although perhaps understandably when problems arose, these doctors refused to accept responsibility for the neglect or incorrect treatment of patients by these assistants.

There was a serious case of neglect at Stourbridge in 1855, where a medical assistant gave inadequate treatment to a seriously ill infant who died. A subsequent inquiry found the assistant to be responsible, but stated that the doctor, who had 'over many years performed his duties in an exemplary manner',[154] was blameless. However, there were no proceedings against the assistant either, because he had left the union, presumably fearful of the consequences of his actions. In another case at Kidderminster in 1858, another medical assistant was found 'guilty of grievous neglect',[155] but again because he had left the employ of the doctor, a disciplinary case was not proceeded with. In such circumstances, it was no surprise that there were belated attempts to control the use of such unqualified medical assistants. This was done by a Poor Law Board circular in 1868,[156] but it continued to prove virtually impossible to attach blame to either a doctor or his assistant when a patient died due to negligence or malpractice. In spite of all this it was probably true that poor non-pauper patients were just as neglected as pauper ones, because the same doctors and assistants treated these individuals. Nevertheless, local newspapers apparently only took up and publicised pauper cases[157] where public funds were involved, so that ironically, paupers were probably more protected than their independent contemporaries against such malpractices. In spite of this, according to R.G. Hodgkinson, late in the Poor Law Board era medical officers continued to go unpunished even in clear cases of neglect and it was the contemporary opinion that: 'Nearly all cases of complaint against doctors were centred on neglect rather than malpractice.'[158] In spite of this assertion, neglect killed just as surely as did maltreatment although in the case of pauper patients the Central Poor Law Authority did at least monitor medical treatment, while non-paupers could be neglected and maltreated to death, apparently without any redress.

Medical science had developed sporadically in the period from 1834 to 1871, with both anaesthetics and antiseptic surgery evolving in this time, but the medical profession was reluctant to use these new techniques, preferring to rely on previous tested methods. This meant that union medical officers, who treated the whole range of diseases and medical conditions afflicting pauper patients, were reluctant to use surgical techniques, probably because even with anaesthetics and antiseptic surgery, these procedures were regarded as too hazardous. Thus only in dire emergency was surgery used, with an additional fee sometimes paid in such cases, presumably for the extra skill required and for the medication used. At Droitwich in 1853, when the additional fingers and toes of a ten-week-old child were removed in an emergency operation, probably given urgency because this medical condition was regarded as 'the work of the devil',[159] a fee was paid. However, in an apparently analogous case at Kidderminster in 1854,[160] when a boy's finger was amputated after an accident, no fee was paid. Another fee was paid at Pershore in 1854 to 'repair a [boy's] hernia . . . [unusually] . . . under chloroform',[161] although in the same union eleven years later[162] no anaesthetic was used to remove a bladder stone from another child. However the technique used on this occasion may have involved no surgical incision, as a technique to crush such *caniculi* using an instrument introduced via a catheter was available from about this time.

Unusually between 1865 and 1870 at Droitwich,[163] all cases treated by the medical officer were recorded and these records show that a fractured leg was treated here using surgery, as was a case of peritonitis. These records also demonstrate that prolonged illnesses were rare among pauper children, although there were some children suffering from life-long ailments, as in one case of hydrocephalus and one of a serious heart complaint, both of which were treated in the workhouse. Thus there appeared to be little difference between pauper and non-pauper poor children regarding the alleviation of serious medical conditions caused by disease and physical abnormalities, but it did appear that because accidents were much more common outside the workhouse than inside it, the institution was a much safer place to live in.

Parsimony was probably the major consideration in all Poor Law medicine, with decisions about treatment often made on the basis of saving money, but in spite of this some Guardians decided to subscribe to hospitals, presumably because they believed it would save them money in the long term. Dudley union subscribed two guineas to Birmingham Eye Infirmary and £21 0s 0d to Birmingham General Hospital in 1846,[164] although this latter sum was a very large fee, paid again in subsequent years, which was inexplicable, because the facilities available at the General Hospital were apparently never used by indoor paupers. The hospital was possibly used by paupers in receipt of outdoor relief, with this usage undocumented. More normally, hospital subscriptions were between £2 0s 0d and £5 0s 0d. Thus King's Norton union subscribed £2 0s 0d to the Birmingham Children's Hospital, in 1869,[165] for the use of the facilities there. Specialist institutions, some distance from the county, were sometimes used to treat children with special problems and individual fees were paid in such cases. Thus in 1868, Upton upon Severn Guardians paid for a six-year-old boy with a burned throat to be equipped with a special instrument to aid his breathing at a hospital in the north of England[166] and elsewhere children were sent for sea-bathing treatment, used to alleviate many medical conditions. Thus in 1868,[167] a boy from Kidderminster who was suffering from a strumous wrist was sent to Scarborough to a sea-bathing establishment, partly at the expense of the chairman of the Board of Guardians, Mr Brinton the carpet manufacturer. Kidderminster union paid the boy's railway fare and the remaining four shillings per week to support him while he was treated was paid by Mr Brinton. However, such treatment was clearly an erosion of Less Eligibility, because few poor children outside the workhouse would have been sent away for treatment, unless a benefactor paid, as their parents would have been unable to afford it. Thus acceptance of poor relief was the only way in which such treatment could have been obtained.

In the early years of the New Poor Law workhouses were sometimes used as convalescent homes for poor private patients; this happened at Kidderminster in 1839,[168] when a boy had a leg amputated there. He was placed in the workhouse to recover, while his parents were charged three shillings per week for this service. Soon after this in the same union, a boy's arm was amputated and he too was placed in the workhouse at his parents' expense, which the Guardians again allowed[169] in spite of this being against the Poor Law Commission's regulations. A Minute recording this case was sent to the Poor Law Commission who made no adverse comment about this irregular arrangement, although after about 1840 the practice of parents paying for such care ceased. Only at Droitwich in 1868[170] was another child convalesced in the workhouse, when a boy's hand was amputated, although no payment was made for this service and he eventually became destitute and a permanent inmate in the workhouse.

Public indifference to the medical treatment of paupers early in the New Poor Law era was altered in 1865 by what Sidney and Beatrice Webb have called an 'outburst of public indignation'[171] at workhouse scandals. At this time, Dr Edward Smith, a leading dietician, was sent with H.B. Farnall, a workhouse inspector, to inspect all workhouse infirmaries. Their findings were included in the Annual Report of 1866–7 and suggested that: 'The sick wards of the workhouses were originally provided for cases of the paupers of the workhouse who might be attacked by illness; and not as a State Hospital into which the sick poor of the country would be received for medical care.'[172] This inevitably meant that the deterrent effect of the workhouse was being eroded, but indications from Worcestershire unions were that this was an overstatement of the situation, as there was little evidence from the county that workhouse infirmaries, where they existed, were being used in this way. In Parliament, in 1867, it was stated that: 'the evils complained of have mainly arisen from workhouse management, which must to a great extent be of a deterrent character, having been applied to the sick, who are not proper objects for such a system'.[173] Critics were clearly concerned that the workhouse medical system should not create 'State Hospitals', but this was not apparent in Worcestershire, where the system was not changed to accommodate such people, at least not before the abolition of the Poor Law Board in 1871.[174]

In Worcestershire the major tenets of the New Poor Law, the twin Principles of National Uniformity and Less Eligibility, had been initially adhered to, but almost immediately there was a realisation among local

Poor Law officials that uniformity was impossible to attain. This was particularly the case for medical relief as each medical case was different and each doctor probably differed in his treatment of the same ailment. Yet in spite of this, the central Poor Law administration still desired uniformity, but when this proved impossible to attain, the Principle of National Uniformity was quietly dropped with regard to medical relief. Initially communications with the Poor Law Commission mentioned the principle, but eventually even here, Assistant Commissioners became less aware of the need for uniformity, only requiring of medical officers that they stay within their budgets for union drugs.

There were few sick wards in county workhouses during the period 1834 to 1871, with ill children usually remaining in their normal wards, but treatment in these was not uniform either. Medical officers now prescribed 'whatever was necessary' to treat ill pauper children, a decision that was never questioned by the Poor Law Central Authority. From this standpoint and from many others, the inmate child was more eligible than their non-pauper contemporaries. They had better treatment with more medicines, rudimentary nursing, clean bedlinen, regular attendance by the medical officer and an improved diet. These were conditions that were certainly not available to the poor outside the workhouse because of the costs involved. The workhouse itself also conferred advantage on all ill and infirm pauper inmates, but particularly on children, with the diseases that killed youngsters, such as measles and scarlet fever, rare inside the workhouse. Thus these institutions acted as isolating agencies, with most Guardians swift to close their workhouse to further admissions if epidemic disease was present in the union. Thus, workhouses were generally much safer places for children to live in, as they had an independent water supply that was clean and monitored by rudimentary biological tests, thus protecting the inmates from water-borne diseases.

In spite of such protection, there was one class of diseases that may have afflicted pauper children more than their non-pauper contemporaries. These were institutional diseases, such as the skin complaints itch, ringworm or scaldhead and scabies, as well as the troublesome eye infection ophthalmia. These complaints were almost constant nuisances in many county workhouses and in a few cases they were so serious that they caused the removal of children from the institution. However, while itch was an irritant, ophthalmia was regarded most seriously because, at its worst, it caused temporary blindness and sometimes impaired vision which could cause permanent pauperisation.

Successful treatments for these institutional diseases were eventually found, largely by trial and error. Yet it was eventually discovered that these ailments succumbed best to strict hygiene measures and when these practices became normal in workhouses these diseases disappeared.

Thus excepting for institutional diseases, early in the New Poor Law era, ill inmate children were again more eligible than their non-pauper contemporaries, although this was not because of conscious decisions, it was merely fortuitous. Insane and mentally defective children were also clearly at a great advantage over similar poor children outside workhouses, and these advantages increased as the treatment of mental infirmities, other than incurable conditions like idiocy and imbecility, became more effective. Now lunatic asylums ceased to be 'mere pens for the insane' and after 1845 workhouses were inspected by the Lunacy Commission, which improved the conditions for mentally infirm children who, all too often outside the workhouses, were merely kept in a squalid untreated state. This, theoretically, also ensured that curable mentally disturbed inmates were removed to the pauper lunatic asylum, although this often did not happen.

From the evidence available, it was difficult to discern differences in medical treatment in rural as opposed to urban workhouses in Worcestershire, with all medical officers, no matter what the nature of the union, varying in the way they treated inmate patients. No pattern could thus be perceived based on a rural to urban dichotomy, but as with other aspects of pauper treatment, the longer ill pauper children stayed in the workhouse, the greater the advantage they gained. This was accentuated when medical relief for inmate children was freed from the strictures of the two basic tenets of Poor Law administration, which altered the definition of the ill pauper child's plight and allowed medical treatment to alter. This development conformed exactly to Gertrude Himmelfarb's suggestion about a changed definition of poverty[175] causing changed treatment. However, ill child inmates were still in total institutions, of the sort analysed in Erving Goffman's classic sociological study *Asylums*.[176] This causes huge problems in equating the gains in health and protection from disease afforded by incarceration in the workhouse with improved medical treatment, to the loss of liberty endured by children accepting relief in the workhouse.

5

THE WORKHOUSE STAFF

Education was considered fundamental to the treatment of hereditary pauperism and was otherwise linked, according to Richard Johnson, to the suppression of 'crime, public order and economic and social discipline in general'.[1] This was because, again according to Johnson: 'These were all issues which orthodox opinion designated moral and with which, therefore, education could deal.' Such ideas relate well to notions expressed by Gertrude Himmelfarb in her book *The Idea of Poverty*,[2] about a morality being imposed on the working classes by the middle classes under the New Poor Law, which she has also referred to as 'social control'. Certainly, as David Roberts has suggested, Poor Law activists in the nineteenth century thought 'instinctively of controlling the lives of those underneath them'[3] in a truly paternalistic way, which resulted in what Brian Simon has called 'the prostration of the masses to those classes above them'.[4] This situation was also encouraged by workhouse staff, who were one facet of what Johnson has called the 'Social Police'[5] and had a vested interest in the maintenance of order in Poor Law institutions. For this reason the control function remained a major focus in the treatment of pauperism arguably until 1929, when the workhouses were closed. The concept of conditioning was thus most relevant of all to children who were seen as being in most danger from contagious disease-like pauperism. This affliction was to be treated with education, religious instruction and later by industrial training, which were palliatives recommended by the Poor Law Inquiry Commission in 1834, who assumed that such education was essential to 'healing the wounds' inflicted by the Old Poor Law. This was because the lack of such training was seen as one explanation of the pauper's parlous state. Thus workhouse education was regarded as remedial action included in the workhouse régime, which had been intended by Jeremy Bentham, whose utilitarian principles lay at the base of the New Poor Law, to create a controlled atmosphere in the closed 'total institution'[6] that was the workhouse. A 'total institution' was later defined by Erving Goffman in his classic sociological study *Asylums*, as 'a place of residence and work where a large number of like situated individuals, cut off from the wider society for an appreciable period of time, together lead an enclosed, formally administered round of life'.[7] This modern definition exactly described English and Welsh workhouses between 1834 and 1871.

In this circumstance, workhouse schoolteachers were of great importance to the process of educating, or conditioning, pauper children, but opinions expressed about them in the 1830s were not generally complimentary. They were seen as ignorant and lazy and not worthy of the important task they were set, but similar comments were also made about other elementary schoolteachers in general at this date. Those best equipped to be potential teachers did not find elementary schoolteaching an attractive career but, in spite of this, the Poor Law authorities would still not pay higher salaries to attract the few qualified and trained teachers available. The workhouses thus coped with inadequate teachers who needed very close supervision by the chaplain, although according to M.A. Crowther this plan was seen by Sir Francis Head, one of the Poor Law Commissioners, as giving 'dignity to the whole arrangement'.[8] In spite of this, Crowther has suggested that the chaplain 'unlike the medical officer, was a professional man of standing',[9] although the epithet 'Sunday gaoler'[10] was applied to this officer in the nineteenth century, presumably because this was seen as an appropriate description of his duties in a workhouse. Initially, after the Poor Law Amendment Act, Assistant Commissioners were responsible for workhouse schools and their staff, along with other aspects of the workhouse, but in 1837 an Inspector of Workhouse Schools was appointed. He was now made responsible for inspecting the workhouse school annually, to determine the level of certificate available to the teacher and hence the level of government grant payable to the school. In the first nine years of his appointment, this inspector reported only to the Central Poor Law Authority, but after 1846 a copy of his report was also sent to the Privy Council Committee on Education, which was the beginning of an attempt to relate education inside the workhouse to that going on outside it. This was arguably the single most important influence of all in improving workhouse teaching.

In most Worcestershire unions, from the outset of the New Poor Law in 1834, the chaplain was responsible for ensuring that the workhouse school was regularly attended by the schoolmaster and schoolmistress, so that the 'youths and girls [were] properly instructed and set to work . . . [so that] . . . care [was] taken to fit them to be useful members of the community'. However, education was not given such priority everywhere, so that a Poor Law Commission order had to be issued in 1835[11] to enforce the workhouse education that was offered. It restated that the 'Duties of the schoolmaster and schoolmistress . . . [were] . . . to instruct the boys and girls of the house . . . and assist the master and mistress of the House in the performance of their several duties, and in the maintenance of order and due subordination in the house.' This order also suggested that school instruction was to be given 'for three working hours every day',[12] with teachers ensuring that 'they [the children] were instructed in reading, writing and the principles of the Christian Religion'. However, this appeared already to be the norm in most Worcestershire Poor Law unions.

Clearly the intention was that the chaplain should be responsible for the day-to-day administration of the workhouse school, which was thought desirable because he would then be able to comment on religious aspects of the school curriculum, although his ability to do even this was sometimes in doubt. His competence to comment on other aspects of the school was even less certain. However when the Poor Law Commission made rules about workhouse schools, which they regarded as inviolable, it was the chaplain who was responsible for interpreting them. In spite of this, such rules and regulations were often regarded locally merely as guidelines and thus open to interpretation, so in many cases the chaplain was simply carrying out the Guardians' wishes and not those of the Poor Law Central Authority, although on other occasions he was undoubtedly incapable of making the complex judgements necessary because he did not have the basic knowledge of Poor Law administration required. An order produced in 1844 stated that the teachers' duties were to 'instruct the boys and girls according to the instructions expressed . . . [and to] . . . regulate the discipline and organisation of the school and industrial and moral training of the children, subject to the instructions of the Guardians',[13] who were apparently now controlling workhouse education, although in Worcestershire it was the workhouse chaplain who usually retained this responsibility. However, he was still admonished by the Assistant Poor Law Commissioner if he wrongly interpreted central authority guidance, which he regularly did. This situation persisted until after the Royal Commission on the Poor Laws of 1909.

In spite of central authority guidance about the duties of workhouse schoolteachers, Boards of Guardians made unacceptable demands on some teachers. For instance, the schoolmaster's duties at Kidderminster in 1848[14] were simply to teach the inmate children, whereas the schoolmistress there was also to undertake duties outside those laid down by the Poor Law Board.[15] Indeed this iniquity was so great that the HMI for workhouse schools stated in his annual report on the school, that this schoolmistress 'performed duties incompatible with her situation',[16] which prevented her from being an efficient teacher. He sought to rectify this situation by suggesting that the schoolmistress's duties outside the schoolroom were to deal only with female children, to supply 'such attendance [to these children] as is necessary to their bodily comfort', which was a restatement of central authority policy. This sort of misuse of teachers, particularly of schoolmistresses, was clearly not unique, so the Poor Law Board was eventually to insist in 1849[17] that school staff of both sexes were 'regularly to reside in the workhouse and to devote the whole of their time to the duties of the office', duties that were now very carefully and specifically defined. A system of double insurance was now used to ensure that the Poor Law Board's orders and regulations were adhered to. However, some Guardians, such as those at Dudley, incessantly questioned orders and regulations, so that the Central Poor Law Authority now sent one copy of an order directly to Boards of Guardians and another to workhouse officers. This second copy was in a strengthened form, so the officers, as employees of the central authority who were only paid salaries supplied centrally, were placed in an invidious position. By doing this it was hoped to exert pressure on Guardians to comply with rules and regulations, although the chaplain, the only officer to attend board meetings, was deemed most important in this respect – he was the only workhouse officer able to express an opinion about such Poor Law Board policy. For this reason the chaplain was the most influential workhouse officer, but his power was further emphasised by his social status, his influence and his position as a spiritual pastor. Whilst in hierarchical terms he was subordinate to the master of the workhouse, in all other ways he was superior to him and he regularly demonstrated this by organising Guardians, workhouse officers and inmates alike. In spite of his power, initially a chaplain was not considered important. Indeed in 1836 it had been suggested that a chaplain needed to be appointed 'only if the Guardians think fit',[18] although most Worcestershire Poor Law unions appointed one from the outset. The duties of the chaplain, envisaged at that time, were apparently minimal. They were to catechise the children and to 'state the general progress and state of the children'.[19] The right not to appoint a chaplain was removed by the late 1830s probably because, according to Anne Digby, by this time the chaplain's usefulness had been recognised by the Poor Law Commission and his duties were increased.[20] This action coincided with the introduction of school inspection which was no accident as the chaplain now became the local official responsible for the workhouse school and effectively the eyes and ears of the central authority locally. He now assessed and reported on the abilities and efficiency of the school staff, a task for which he was still often ill-equipped, as he seldom had much knowledge of elementary education, although his understanding improved with experience. Such problems were even greater where a new chaplain was appointed. He was usually the curate of the parish in which the workhouse stood and was thus young and inexperienced, with little knowledge of elementary schools. Even where the chaplain became efficient in overseeing the workhouse school, his advice and judgements were still overlain by moral and religious considerations that were typically Anglican, which made him far from objective.

Clearly this development of the chaplain's role was intentional because, according to Digby, James P. Kay (later Kay-Shuttleworth) suggested in as early as 1839 that the Poor Law Commission deliberately 'developed the function of the chaplain in the workhouse rules . . . into a more active supervisory and advisory role'.[21] Kay was appointed first permanent secretary at the Education Department in 1839, having been an Assistant Poor Law Commissioner in East Anglia where he had introduced the idea of pupil-teachers recruited from the most academically able workhouse schoolchildren. He thus had insights into Poor Law education that were invaluable in making judgements about education generally. Kay also emphasised social control as a purpose of workhouse education and was undoubtedly aware that by appointing a Church of England clergyman as chaplain, the continuance of an Anglican dominance over Poor Law educational administration was ensured. School inspection, instituted in 1837,[22] began the process of enhancing the power of the chaplain who had an important local inspection role, as he reported his opinions directly to

HMI. Indeed by the early 1840s he could be said to have had almost complete control over the workhouse school and its curriculum. For instance he chose reading material for the workhouse school which invariably reflected his personal ideology, being religious in character and particularly emphasising the Anglican point of view; he also controlled other aspects of education in the workhouse. The chaplain's influence was most apparent at Kidderminster in 1839, when he chose the 'elementary books for the instruction of the children'[23] that were to be purchased. Similarly at Worcester a year later,[24] the chaplain there was said to be responsible for all books allowed in the workhouse. This level of control by an individual chaplain was usual in the county workhouses, with the only exception being at Tenbury Wells, the smallest county union,[25] which eventually had no workhouse school because there were insufficient numbers of pauper children to make one worthwhile. These other local clergymen were consulted by the workhouse chaplain about instructing the inmate children in religious matters, although this arrangement was hardly calculated to reduce the Anglican Church's influence over the education offered in this workhouse. Therefore, realistically in the 1840s, chaplains took autocratic decisions about the education offered in individual workhouses which Guardians found impossible to overturn and even HMI found difficult to circumvent. Thus an entrenched cleric, determined to maintain his influence over what he regarded as his school, was impossible to shift from his very secure position. He, unlike the school staff, was not open to inspection, so no county workhouse chaplain was removed from office between 1834 and 1871.

While early school inspections, soon after their inception in 1837, revealed workhouse schools in a poor state, it was thought by the Poor Law central authority that an assiduous chaplain could be relied upon to ensure a minimum standard of education. This judgement was based on his supposed reliability and the belief that he was controllable, so he was more likely to follow orders and regulations exactly. For this reason the chaplain became a key member of the bureaucracy controlling the workhouse school, with the hierarchy among workhouse officers most apparent in this context. He inspected subordinate officers including the school staff and had the power to order their dismissal, which enhanced his status considerably. This was an arrangement deliberately created by the Poor Law Central Authority to gain control over workhouse officers in a manner far more effective than by an annual inspection, because the chaplain was a daily visitor to the workhouse, whereas workhouse inspectors probably visited only once a year. The chaplain could thus ensure that central authority's regulations were adopted and adhered to, but inevitably his judgement was coloured by his ideology, so religious matters regarding workhouse inmates, particularly children, were given the greatest priority of all. This influence was exerted early in the pauper's workhouse career as on admission their religious denomination was entered in a creed register and it was this entry that determined all aspects of that inmate's subsequent religious experience in the workhouse. Thus the inmate was theoretically protected against proselytism, because once professed the inmate's creed could not be changed, although the system appeared to favour the Anglican Church. This was because the creed register was sometimes treated in rather a cavalier fashion, with new entrants not professing any faith recorded as Anglican. This worried non-Anglican churchmen, because this process was difficult to change once it had been completed and only fervent Nonconformists and Roman Catholics escaped being classified as Anglican and ministered to by the Anglican chaplain. As an indication of the Anglican influence over a workhouse, the chaplain at Kidderminster in 1838[26] determined that *Cotterill's Book of Prayers*, an Anglican publication, be used in daily prayers for all inmates, except those who had proved that they were not Anglican. In these ways a chaplain continually determined that his will be done regarding religious matters, but worryingly they exhibited a certain amount of social class control. Chaplains were mainly recruited from the middle and upper classes and thus had hegemonic power over the workhouse community, which was made up almost exclusively of working-class individuals. Thus these minor clerics who were paid a salary of £60 to £80, a similar sum to that paid to the workhouse master and about three times the salary of the schoolmistress, for comparatively light duties, had an inordinate amount of power over the Poor Law institution to which they were appointed.

In some unions the chaplain was so powerful that he overruled the judgement of the Assistant Poor Law Commissioner. He did this by influencing the attitudes of the Board of Guardians, the group that controlled the Poor Law locally and in a case such as this, the Poor Law inspector could only invoke a complex procedure to get a decision changed. Whilst this sometimes led to the Poor Law Central Administration ordering the local Guardians to comply with orders and regulations, this procedure was very protracted and was only

1. Birmingham asylum for destitute children.

2. Worcester House of Industry.

3. Article of Agreement to set up Evesham Poor Law Union in 1834.

4. Kidderminster union workhouse.

5. King's Norton union workhouse.

6. Bromsgrove union workhouse.

7. Shipston on Stour union workhouse.

8. Advertisement for a workhouse chaplain at Bromsgrove.

9. Kidderminster union: schoolmistress'
   certificate.

BROMSGROVE UNION.

APPOINTMENT OF SCHOOLMISTRESS.

THE BOARD of GUARDIANS of this UNION, at their Meeting on TUESDAY, the 9th day of May next, intend to elect a SCHOOLMISTRESS for the WORKHOUSE. The person appointed will be required to instruct both boys and girls, and to perform such duties as are set forth in the General Consolidated Orders of the Poor Law Board. The salary will be £2, per annum, subject to such increase as may be awarded by the Committee of Council on Education, with Rations, Lodging, and Washing in the Workhouse.

Applications in the handwriting of the candidates, with testimonials as to character and ability, to be sent to me on or before Monday, the 8th of May next, and the applicants will be expected to attend at the Board Room on the following day (Tuesday), at Eleven o'clock in the Forenoon. No travelling expenses will be allowed.

By order of the Board,

THOMAS DAY, Clerk.

Board Room, Bromsgrove, 25th April, 1865.

10. Advertisement for a workhouse schoolmistress at Bromsgrove union.

11. A general view of Worcester union workhouse.

12. Stourbridge union workhouse.

13. Martley union workhouse.

14. Tenbury Wells union workhouse.

15. An individual ward at Worcester union workhouse.

16. Birmingham union workhouse; an ideal for Worcestershire unions.

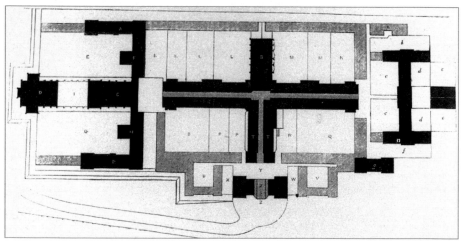

17. A plan of Birmingham union workhouse.

invoked in cases of serious disagreement. Thus in most cases the Guardian's decisions, often much influenced by the opinion of the chaplain, were not questioned by the inspector. This was well illustrated in the case of workhouse schoolteachers appointed on one month's trial, who were assessed by the chaplain and often recommended to the visiting committee to be permanently appointed. Such decisions officially had to be ratified by the Assistant Poor Law Commissioner who sometimes disagreed with the chaplain, although this seldom led to a changed decision about the appointment of a schoolteacher.

In spite of such support, schoolteachers were still vulnerable, particularly when a chaplain changed his opinion about them. This happened at Kidderminster in 1844,[27] where the chaplain found fault with the schoolmistress several months after he had recommended that she be appointed because he thought 'it would be as well for them [the children] to continue school till half past four for this month instead of ... shoe leather and making a great ... agreed with the cleric's opinion, so ... work the new hours, even though ... Poor Law Commission regulations. ... nor HMI objected to the new ... workhouse chaplain was also ... teacher more favourably than did ... employed by the Poor Law Central ... in elementary education. This ... a schoolmistress was considered ... n, but was only given a lowly ... of £8 by HMI, which indicated his ... ever, the Guardians accepted the ... nce she [the schoolmistress] has ... ced the children both in religious ... casion the chaplain's opinion may ... ernment grant was subsequently ... workhouse chaplain to overturn ... ectors with supposed expertise who ... w central administration. There was a ... nis at Bromsgrove in 1852,[31] where the ... schoolteacher criticised by HMI, who on this occasion had withheld her certificate. This would have invariably led to her dismissal, but in this case the chaplain supported the schoolmistress because he regarded the inspector's report as 'unfair'. He demanded a second inspection to confirm HMI's opinion, although he initially received the response that while the inspector was eager to do justice to the school, 'if the evidence of defective teaching remains as at his last visit he should regret his inability to alter his present judgement'.[32] No improvement was found and no government grant was paid for that year,[33] although the schoolmistress was not dismissed and was paid by the Guardians, solely out of union funds. In this case the chaplain's influence undoubtedly prevented this teacher's dismissal and a year later[34] HMI reported a great improvement, so a grant was paid.[35] However, when the same situation was repeated five years later, HMI again threatened to refuse a grant[36] and the chaplain again defended the schoolmistress, on this occasion because 'she was under the disadvantage of the frequent comings and goings of the workhouse children who were generally of a very tender age'. The union visiting committee, a subcommittee of the Board of Guardians, supported this view, but on this occasion HMI changed his opinion, apparently without reference to the Poor Law Board. This particular schoolmistress continued in office until 1859.[37]

Such situations of disagreement between the chaplain and various workhouse inspectors were not unique. There were many such cases nationally and some other local ones. For instance, the schoolmistress at Droitwich in 1862 was refused a certificate 'on account of the very unsatisfactory state of her school',[38] but the chaplain persuaded the Guardians that this criticism was unfair. They found the schoolmistress 'very satisfactory',[39] but still HMI withheld the government grant and she too was paid out of union funds for that year. Again the chaplain's judgement appeared reasonable, because on his next visit in 1863 HMI stated, 'the children appear to me to have improved and made progress since my last visit, several can read and write fairly, and were correct in their sums'.[40] He now issued a certificate and a grant was paid. On such occasions, the chaplain's opinion undoubtedly saved the workhouse schoolteacher's job and he could be regarded as a guardian of fairness, but while his view of this woman's abilities as a teacher was vindicated, she resigned within a year[41] because of improper behaviour with the porter.

Such cases as these were only a minority, because usually there was a concurrence between the chaplain and inspector about the schoolteacher's performance and other matters of workhouse administration, which ensured that the central authority's policy was applied. This, it was assumed, would lead to an improvement in the standard of teaching in workhouse schools. Logically, however, what was reported in Guardians' minutes was an accommodation between the HMI's and the chaplain's opinions and what appeared to happen was that the officer and the inspector would agree on a report for the teacher in a particular workhouse school, although there was sometimes no consensus regarding the conditions found in a particular school. For instance, at Bromsgrove in 1852,[42] HMI regarded the overcrowding of the schoolrooms there as 'intolerable' and he suggested mixing boys and girls together in the school, a solution considered absolutely inexpedient by the chaplain, an opinion also inevitably accepted by the Guardians. Clearly this cleric felt very strongly about this matter, because he persuaded the Guardians to commit themselves to spending £1,500 on a new school to alleviate the situation of overcrowding. Such a commitment may have been regarded as extremely rash by the local Poor Rate payers, particularly as the Poor Law Board would not have objected to HMI's suggestion. Kidderminster union mixed boys and girls within their school in 1869,[43] when the schoolmaster there resigned because of illness and there were too few boys to justify a separate school. On this occasion the Poor Law Board welcomed this solution to what was a temporary problem. Mixed workhouse schools had been commonplace in small Poor Law unions from 1834 onwards and the reticence of the chaplain at Bromsgrove to allow the mixing of boy and girl paupers in the workhouse school there in an emergency was unusual.

Conflicts sometimes made the relationship between Central Poor Law Authority officials and workhouse chaplains fraught, as for example at Droitwich in 1851,[44] where the chaplain reported HMI for not inspecting the workhouse school. This charge was denied, with no further action taken, but it appeared somewhat peculiar as Assistant Poor Law Commissioners quite often relied on chaplains' reports in the absence of a recent visit from HMI. Thus the Assistant Poor Law Commissioner at Stourbridge in 1860 stated: 'I have no other means of offering an opinion . . . [other than] . . . the entries in the chaplain's book, which are favourable to both schools.'[45] However, in a few cases there was severe distrust between the local union authorities and the inspector, so that at Dudley in 1857[46] the situation was such that the chaplain was ordered, by the Board of Guardians, to accompany HMI in inspecting the workhouse school. In a few other cases the chaplain performed other functions to those described. For instance he sometimes represented the schoolteacher's interests with the Guardians, so that at Pershore in 1851[47] when the schoolmistress there expressed doubts about the sufficiency of time allowed for schooling, she was invited to discuss the matter at the next Guardians' meeting. This she attended with the chaplain[48] who gave her moral support. Therefore in most cases chaplains had wide duties and responsibilities, which made them powerful members of the local Poor Law administration. Indeed within the county, only at Stourbridge were the chaplain's powers eroded. Here a school committee was set up in 1848[49] that operated until 1871, to oversee the running of the school in co-operation with the chaplain, who maintained an oversight of its day-to-day operation.

Clearly, one major facet of the work of the chaplain was to oversee the work of the workhouse schoolteachers, the linchpins of the Poor Law education system, but according to the Central Poor Law Authority regulations these men and women were also given an annual school inspection by HMI. On the basis of this inspection they were awarded certificates at one of three levels in four categories: 'efficiency', 'competency', 'probation' and 'permission', but usually the chaplain had little to do with this process. Nationally, 'competency' was said to be the median standard of certificate for schoolmasters, with schoolmistresses, on average, attaining a marginally lower level of certificate than this. Fewer men than women were also refused certificates or given the least prestigious award – 'permission'. However, such statistics may have been misleading, because according to some authorities women teachers were of better quality than their male contemporaries. These reports suggested that only 26 per cent of schoolmasters attained above the median level of certificate, compared with 44 per cent of schoolmistresses. This disparity of views was only explicable if poor quality female entrants to workhouse schoolteaching, rejected after a month's trial, were included in the collation of statistics. Workhouse schoolteachers' certificates assessed intellectual competency, which was defined by the Privy Council Committee on Education in 1849 as the ability 'to read fluently, write from dictation and from memory, [and] work sums in the first four simple and compound rules of arithmetic'.[50] Noticeably, there was no attempt to estimate teaching ability and this may well have explained the discrepancy in the assessment of teachers by HMI and chaplains. As suggested earlier, school inspection by HMI has conventionally been presumed to have raised the standard of workhouse education and this certainly appeared to be shown in Worcestershire when HMI reports, first included in Poor Law union records after 1850, were compared with the lowly standards reported in the 1830s and 1840s. However, a close scrutiny of HMI's reports after 1850 showed no clear pattern in the levels of certificates awarded, but there was some variation between unions. Noticeably rural unions with fewer children attracted teachers who obtained marginally higher levels of certificate, but lower salaries, than those in urban unions.

Workhouse schoolmistresses often stayed in office for only a very short time and it was difficult to identify the effect of inspection on these teachers, indeed if they were influenced at all. However, after 1850 the standard of teaching by schoolmistresses who taught for more than a few weeks was maintained at its previous moderate level and arguably this was because of the influence of HMI's inspection. In the country it was more difficult to evaluate the teaching performance of workhouse schoolmasters, as only the two largest Poor Law unions, which were both very urban, had sufficient children to warrant such an appointment. For this reason a comparison between rural and urban unions regarding schoolmasters' teaching performance proved impossible. In general terms, schoolmasters were given certificates of 'efficiency' or 'competency', but as with schoolmistresses there was no demonstrable pattern of improvement in the level of certificate awarded. Here again, the influence of HMI's inspection appeared to be beneficial, in as much that it maintained workhouse teaching at its moderate level standard.

The national salary scales of workhouse schoolteachers in 1849[51] showed a minimum of £5 and a maximum of £50 for male teachers, rising to £15 and £60 respectively by 1856, with women teachers receiving 80 per cent of these sums at both dates. All workhouse teachers' salaries, paid once their trial period was over, were related directly to the level of certificate awarded by HMI. It was, however, deliberate that male teachers were paid an additional 20 per cent compared with their female contemporaries, in spite of the fact that female workhouse teachers gained a higher level of certificate, on average, than did male teachers – a situation that continued until after 1871. Potentially, the biggest change in the way salaries were paid to workhouse teachers was the capitation system for government grants introduced in 1856. This paid a flat rate salary, which was then augmented by an amount for each child in attendance at inspected workhouse schools. This same system was adopted in non-pauper schools after the 'Revised Code' of 1862, which was given a trial in the

Poor Law system, before it was adopted in elementary education. This innovation appeared to have had little impact on the pattern of wages paid to workhouse teachers between 1850 and 1871, although there was an overall rise in wage rates during this period, but the disparity between male and female teachers' wages and between the salaries offered in different unions continued, as it did outside the Poor Law system. Comparing an individual workhouse schoolteacher's remuneration across time proved very difficult because of the thirteen levels of certificate awarded, a teacher could be paid on a different salary scale from one year to the next. However, the overall rise in average salary rates of workhouse schoolteachers demonstrated that they continued to be considered very important in the prevention of the spread of mendicancy to the young. While the need for careful selection was obvious, recruitment problems were compounded by the relatively low salary offered, which usually attracted unsuitable applicants for workhouse teaching posts.

Of the workhouse schoolmasters appointed in Worcestershire between 1834 and 1871, only two, at Worcester union[52] and Stourbridge union[53] in 1843, had previous teaching experience. Most other applicants had worked in artisan occupations but as M.A. Crowther suggested, official sources stated that the average salary paid to workhouse schoolmasters was only £26 in 1849,[54] and it was thus understandable why qualified and experienced applicants did not apply. In spite of this, it had been contemporaneously suggested that talk of 'low salaries' paid in workhouse schools was misleading, because amounts paid varied so much. For instance according to Anne Digby, salaries for well-qualified staff in East Anglian workhouses in the 1840s,[55] where James P. Kay had been an Assistant Poor Law Commissioner prior to his appointment to the Privy Council Committee on Education, were as much as £35 per annum. This was in contrast to those in the south-western division of England, including counties not unlike Worcestershire, where the average salary for male workhouse teachers in 1847 was, according to S.P. Oberman, £25 15s 0d.[56] Whilst 17 per cent of workhouse schoolteaching incumbents earned more than this amount, a further 11 per cent earned less than £15 per annum. In spite of this, HMI Thomas B. Browne believed that the improvement in workhouse teachers between 1847 and 1861 was attributable to salaries being increased. He stated, 'you cannot get a good man in this country to work for a low salary',[57] but still only £10 was paid to the schoolmaster appointed at Evesham in 1847, although it was raised to £16 within two months[58] after it had been described by the Assistant Poor Law Commissioner as 'too low'. However, this salary was exceptionally low, as usually schoolmasters were paid at least £20 per annum.

According to M.A. Crowther, the national average salary for workhouse schoolmistresses in 1839[59] was £16 per annum, although according to S.P. Oberman, by 1847, one woman teacher was earning more than £35.[60] However, 10 per cent of her contemporaries earned £10 or less, with the average salary paid being only £15 per annum. This undoubtedly went some way to explaining the poor quality of the applicants for workhouse teaching posts, but in spite of this, HMI Jellinger C. Symons justified low salaries for workhouse teachers as 'preferable to fluctuating ones',[61] a distinction probably not understood by workhouse teachers who had to live on such wages. The arrangement for appointing workhouse staff in most unions was for the master and matron of the workhouse to be appointed, who were usually a man and wife. The rest of the staff were then appointed as subordinates. Nevertheless at Pershore in 1838, there was a peculiar arrangement made. Here, the workhouse master's daughters helped their mother, the unpaid matron, run the workhouse school, while their father, the master, arranged for all of the other officers' posts to be fulfilled, either by himself acting as porter and chaplain or by using members of his family, all of whom were unpaid.[62]

The effectiveness of workhouse schools must have varied considerably and the preface to the 1851 *Educational Census*[63] made this obvious by suggesting that the efficiency of workhouse schools depended most on the teacher, 'much more than on any other circumstance'. Where the workhouse teacher could not cope, the workhouse school was said to be hopelessly ineffective. HMI Thomas B. Browne agreed that there were good teachers available, when he suggested that 'there are persons who can teach admirably, and exercise an extraordinary influence over depraved children',[64] and it was these individuals who were best employed in workhouse schools. He claimed that there were many talented teachers in his area of jurisdiction, which included Worcestershire. Similar opinions about workhouse teachers were held nationally, as the comments of Sir James Graham, the Home Secretary, illustrated. He stated that: 'The evidence through the reports of Inspectors of Workhouses is this: that in every school the child principally depends upon the [school] master, and in a workhouse school it depends on the [school] master more, because the children see scarcely anyone else.'[65] Interestingly he also thought that capitation allowances, introduced in workhouse schools in 1856 and later applied to elementary schools in general in 1861, were detrimental, because they drove out talented teachers, particularly where workhouse school pupil numbers fluctuated wildly. In this way the capitation system was most unfair, because it was an inequitable way of distributing salary according to merit. Before 1856, attaining a standard of certificate resulted in a particular amount of government grant, irrespective of the number of children present, but after this date the number of children present at the school inspection was now taken into account, which unfairly caused government grants to fluctuate wildly. The salary initially offered to the workhouse schoolteacher was usually the amount of the government grant attracted by their predecessor and if a higher grant was attracted by the newcomer, they received the higher amount.

Inflated salaries were sometimes offered in an attempt to attract better-qualified workhouse school staff, an approach which the Poor Law Board objected to and which proved wholly unsuccessful. This ploy was used at Droitwich in 1856[66] where potential replacement schoolmistresses were offered £5 more than the previous female teacher had received. In spite of the Poor Law Board's objections to this, the Guardians there would not relent, although the inducement offered proved unsuccessful in attracting a more suitable teacher. The replacement schoolmistress, appointed 'pro tempore', was not well qualified, so she was paid the same salary as her predecessor,[67] although it appeared possible that the Droitwich Guardians had no intention of paying the inflated salary offered anyway. They alone, among the thirteen Worcestershire Poor Law unions, had attempted to reduce all officers' salaries by 20 per cent in 1850[68] and if this mercenary attitude was typical they were unlikely to pay higher salaries to school staff than were absolutely necessary. In spite of this, the Poor Law Board had not allowed the Guardians to reduce the salaries below the nationally agreed norms.[69] Good teachers were always in short supply in the Poor Law system, but Boards of Guardians were reluctant to pay higher salaries to hard-pressed school staff, as they saw their major responsibility was to minimise the cost of the Poor Law locally. For this reason, when the schoolmistress at King's Norton workhouse in 1858[70] asked for a pay rise, because there were forty-six children in the workhouse school, an assistant teacher was appointed instead at a cost of £1 per week, who was then dismissed when the school numbers fell. Such penny-pinching approaches continued and in as late as 1869, at Kidderminster,[71] the Guardians told the schoolmistress there that they would not agree to a pay rise, but instead they would remove the boys from her care and make them the responsibility of the workhouse master.[72]

Workhouse schoolteachers' salary levels were clearly very important in deciding whether a teacher would enter the Poor Law education system, with all of the privations that were implied by doing so and indeed whether they stayed there once appointed. In elementary schools in the period from 1840, the inspectorate distributed the government grant and determined the level of certificate given to the teacher, but some school authorities chose not to be inspected. This obviously created two categories of schools; those inspected and those not inspected, which in turn influenced the schoolteacher's status. Those in inspected schools were perceived as superior to their uninspected contemporaries and in this context those teaching in workhouses, all of whom were inspected annually, had a slight advantage over teachers employed in uninspected elementary schools. However, this slight advantage was eroded by the fact that the workhouse teachers' certificate was not transferable to non-workhouse schools before 1862, when schools in both systems came under the 'Revised Code'. A comparison of the salaries paid in the two types of school, made by S.P. Oberman, revealed the extent of the differences between the Poor Law and elementary systems. In 1847, £70 per annum was the best salary paid to an elementary schoolmaster nationally,[73] but the average salary paid in most of these schools at this date was much less than this. By comparison the salaries paid to workhouse schoolmasters in Worcestershire were even lower still, but when allowances for lodgings and victuals, put at £13 8s 8d by Assistant Commissioner Alfred Austin,[74] were added to this basic salary, workhouse school salaries in the county were broadly comparable.

A comparison of the attributes of applicants for schoolteaching posts in both systems was also revealing, as there were as many critical remarks about the quality and characteristics of those applying to work in both elementary and Poor Law education systems. It has been suggested, by Asher Tropp, that the majority of male applicants for posts in elementary schools 'were men who had tried other trades and failed, having been semi-skilled craftsmen, shopkeepers, clerks, and superior domestic servants'.[75] The quality of entrants to the two parallel schooling systems was thus comparable. In spite of this, teaching in a workhouse school was less attractive than work in a school outside the Poor Law system. This was probably inevitable, not because the salary offered was lower, but because such work lacked social prestige. To work with children was bad enough, but to work with pauperised children was even worse. For this reason Michael Hefford suggests that all women entrants to elementary teaching from Hockerill Teacher Training College between 1852 and 1855,[76] rejected a career in the Poor Law education system at the conclusion of their course. The majority of these women came from artisan origins and while they may have found the salaries offered in workhouses quite attractive, they were deterred by the low prestige of the work and the possibility of being tainted by pauperism. In spite of this, by 1862 HMI T.G. Bowyer felt able to describe workhouse teachers as 'a very respectable, hard working and conscientious class of persons, who make up by diligence and dedication to their duties, for deficiencies under which many of them labour in regard to ability and instruction'.[77] By now, there were a few teachers willing to tolerate the privations and conditions of the workhouse and they could justifiably be described as 'dedicated'. Generally, however, Worcestershire's workhouse teachers did not stay in office for long, although in spite of this Guardians continued to lay down stringent requirements for the applicants for workhouse teaching posts, in line with the continuing policy of the Central Poor Law Authority. Sometimes other demands were made of applicants for workhouse schoolteaching posts by Boards of Guardians. Thus at Kidderminster in 1847,[78] it was required that applicants for the vacant teaching post there must be acquainted with the 'National System of Education', which effectively meant that only trained teachers, or teachers experienced in a National school who had probably been pupil-teachers there, could apply. Such stringency meant that there were no suitable applicants for the post, which hindered rather than helped the cause of education in the union and went some way to explain the fact that according to S.P. Oberman, there were more vacancies for schoolmistresses at Kidderminster than in any other union in the country.[79] There were fourteen schoolmistresses appointed between 1835 and 1847, all of whom eventually resigned.

When trained or experienced applicants did apply for a workhouse teaching post they tended to be appointed, as at Droitwich union in

1850, after advertisements were placed in *The Times*, *The Midland Counties Herald* and rather surprisingly in *The Gardener's Chronicle*,[80] which specified that an experienced schoolmistress, over twenty-five years old, was sought. King's Norton Guardians were even more specific than this; they asked that only widows over twenty-five years old should apply, but unusually they were willing to accept a woman with dependent children,[81] although they did not specify where such children would live. This level of care, allied to a willingness to be flexible in their negotiations, meant that suitably qualified applicants were appointed in both of these cases. It was more often the case that Guardians were stringent about their requirements for teachers and unwilling to be flexible. This was the case at Droitwich in 1850[82] where the Guardians were particularly awkward in attempting to impose conditions on the appointment of a schoolmistress there. They insisted that the appointee pass her inspection by HMI before they would appoint her permanently, although at this point the Poor Law Board intervened and decided that this stipulation was illegal. This schoolmistress resigned immediately, stating that: 'In consequence of your not appointing a schoolmaster',[83] that had been promised at interview,[84] she saw no alternative to resignation. The Guardians now tacitly accepted the justice of her case by giving her a good testimonial and her rail fare to London. What this case illustrated was that it was unrealistic to expect workhouse teachers to be trained and/or experienced, although this was a preoccupation that persisted in as late as 1865,[85] when the Bromsgrove Guardians still regretted that no experienced or trained applicants offered themselves for appointment.

In most cases there were only very young applicants for teaching posts, with the youngest person being appointed permanently at Droitwich in 1866.[86] She was only sixteen years old, but in spite of this it would be unfair to suggest that all workhouse teachers were young and of very poor quality, because there were efficient teachers in workhouse schools, including some in Worcestershire. Noticeably, however, the least adequate Poor Law teachers tended to work in rural workhouse schools with small numbers of pupils, which were often in very isolated areas and serving small communities. This heightened the feeling of claustrophobia in such workhouses and made living conditions even more institutional for the staff as well as the inmates. Indeed, Assistant Commissioner Ruddock suggested that the living conditions of workhouse schoolmistresses were poor. He stated that in the period from 1834 to 1844, 'they are generally pent up in a small closet boarded off from the common sleeping apartment of the children'.[87] Although in some Poor Law unions in England and Wales the living conditions of such workhouse school staff were to be marginally improved, in Worcestershire, which still had a large number of isolated workhouse schools, there were few improvements before 1871. In such circumstances a diversity in the quality of Poor Law education appeared inevitable and it was no surprise that Thomas B. Browne, the HMI for workhouse schools, commented in 1850: 'It [the diversity] is impossible to evaluate because in general terms . . . the difference between them is as great as the difference between black and white.'[88] It was the pressures that these conditions caused on workhouse teachers that led Robert Weale, the Assistant Poor Law Commissioner for the Worcestershire area, to refer to workhouse teachers in his evidence to the Select Committee on the Education of Pauper Children in 1862. He said of them: 'I think that we have very competent teachers indeed. I am sorry to say that we very often lose such teachers, the competition being so great.'[89] The talented workhouse teacher was easily lured away from the unconducive atmosphere of the Poor Law school. They were also afraid of the danger of being tainted by the paupers who existed there, which would make it difficult to obtain employment elsewhere.

Inevitably, some teachers left Poor Law schools and moved to elementary day schools run by the voluntary school societies, while others stayed in the Poor Law system and attempted to gain promotion, sometimes as teachers, but also in non-teaching posts. However, some applications for such promotions were unsuccessful, for example when the schoolmaster from Kidderminster union applied to become the master of Wolverhampton workhouse in 1856,[90] he was unsuccessful and remained in his existing post until he retired. Soon after his retirement he suffered a paralytic seizure[91] which meant that he became an inmate of the Strand workhouse in London, but the Kidderminster Guardians refused to accept any responsibility for him,[92] which illustrated well the lack of care shown by Boards of Guardians for their erstwhile good and loyal servants. Some other workhouse teachers faired better in gaining alternative Poor Law posts – a male teacher at Evesham in 1860 was appointed schoolmaster at Worcester gaol, which was definitely a promotion and meant an increased salary.[93] Elsewhere workhouse schoolmasters were even more successful, as at Worcester in 1863, where a man gained promotion to become relieving officer at Edgeware union.[94] Clearly proven ability was the key to success, as the most efficient of all Worcestershire's workhouse schoolmasters, who gained a level II certificate of efficiency in 1865[95] and again in 1866[96] at Stourbridge workhouse, was rewarded by being appointed master of Ledbury workhouse in 1867.[97] Sometimes successes were attained by being appointed to other Poor Law schools, the schoolmaster at Kidderminster union was appointed to a similar post at the very much larger school at Wolverhampton workhouse.[98] However, it was another schoolmaster from Kidderminster who was most successful in gaining promotion within the workhouse schooling system, when he was appointed to Quatt industrial school in 1867.[99] This farm school, established by Mr Wycliffe-Wilson, was regarded as a model by the Poor Law Board, because pauper children were trained in agriculture and the institution made a profit at the same time. Indeed, such an institution came closest to attaining Jeremy Bentham's utilitarian aims for the Poor Law proposed in *Pauper Management Improved*, published in 1785. His suggested organisation for a new Poor Law went further and envisaged a National Charity Company set up to make a huge profit from pauper labour, to the extent that it would pay for the entire Poor Law system, but this proposal was never adopted. The workhouse school staff discussed so far all gained posts that were a definite promotion, but some others did not fair so well. The schoolmaster at Evesham in 1866 was appointed to the smaller workhouse at Willerton,[100] which was a definite demotion. Of workhouse schoolteachers moving out of Poor Law education system, the schoolmaster at Stourbridge in 1852[101] was most unusual. He used his experience in workhouse schools to start his own private school, but there was no indication of the success of this venture. Occasionally other male teachers became schoolmasters in elementary schools,[102] but these successes only represented a small minority of male teachers in county workhouses. For most male workhouse teachers the status of workhouse schoolmaster was the highest rank they attained in their lives.

Workhouse schoolmistresses were in a somewhat different position from their male contemporaries, as they were sometimes promoted either to be matron of a workhouse or as a teacher in a larger workhouse. However, such women were unusual, as most workhouse schoolmistresses left teaching, got married or sought other occupations. Whilst the schoolmistress at Shipston on Stour in 1849[103] gained a post as schoolmistress in a similar sized school at Headington, Oxfordshire, which was 'more to her liking', and perhaps more significantly at an increased salary, it was the physical conditions in workhouses that often influenced other women teachers to leave their school posts. Other schoolmistresses 'gained (an)other position(s) at more salary and less confinement',[104] while others left just for an increased salary at very much larger workhouses.[105] In other cases promotions were within the same union, as when the schoolteacher at Martley in 1861[106] became matron there, having been schoolmistress 'until the matron's position fell vacant'. Her husband had already been master there for three years, with another woman already occupying the position of mistress of the house. However, the confinement of the workhouse sometimes led a schoolmistress to leave her post without obtaining another.[107] This may have been an excuse, which appeared to be the case at Evesham union again in 1870, where the replacement schoolmistress also left within seven months.[108] Like workhouse schoolmasters, Poor Law schoolmistresses, who usually came from marginally higher social origins than their male contemporaries, did not generally move into higher social status groups when they left employment in the workhouse, although their propensity to marry meant that the pattern among females was not as apparent as among their male contemporaries.

As suggested earlier, the workhouse was an inhospitable place to work anyway, partly because of the living conditions teachers had to endure in the closed workhouse community, and partly because of the taint of the poor. It was believed that this would be carried by anyone who worked in a workhouse school, making them unacceptable for employment in schools outside the Poor Law system. Indeed as very few county workhouse schoolteachers were ever appointed to such elementary schools, this fear may have been justified. The unattractive nature of the workhouse schoolteachers' duties, which have aptly been referred to by M.A. Crowther as being 'really those of full time attendants, as in most unions they supervise the children constantly',[109] together with the very low salaries offered, did not encourage applicants and explained the poor quality of those who did apply in rural Worcestershire – here there was no pool of experienced teachers to draw upon. Most applicants in the county were local. Thus, in spite of Poor Law Commission's suggestion in the 1830s and 1840s that experienced teachers were necessary in workhouse schools, the staff of the Worcestershire Poor Law union schools tended to be young and inexperienced, so they inevitably had problems in disciplining the children, even in a coercive institutional atmosphere.

The belief, expressed soon after the Poor Law Amendment Act was implemented in 1834, that the character of the school staff was important was constantly re-emphasised by the Poor Law Central Authority throughout the period to 1871 [110] in the hope that the beneficial influence of teachers would counterbalance the presumed insidious effects of the workhouse. For this reason workhouse teachers had to be carefully selected, preferably being trained and thus more able to fulfil the 'exacting task of teaching such [pauper] pupils'.[111] However, as has already been suggested, such qualified individuals were not appointed locally, and even nationally this need was ignored, as no qualifications were required to become a workhouse schoolteacher, even after the Poor Law Board came to office in 1847. After this date, workhouse teachers appointed in the county were often patently unsuitable, so that it was said of schoolmasters that they 'have often been dependent on parochial relief, and are generally ignorant and unskilled'.[112] The schoolmistress at Stourbridge union in 1847, was probably thought more suitable, but HMI still thought that '. . . [while] it is likely that she will do well' he still had 'some doubts as to her temper',[113] a sentiment with which the Assistant Commissioner agreed. He commented: 'There is a young schoolmistress who is very young, but in acquirements she seems not deficient. I think she will do though her character is scarcely formed.'[114] This schoolmistress was 'satisfactory' when inspected in 1848, but even then it was said, apparently in mitigation, that the children were 'very young and frequently change'[115] and that they undoubtedly caused some problems.

It was the character of the teacher that was thought all important, with his or her teaching ability apparently secondary to this. Thus testimonials were given as a reference of character rather than of teaching efficiency, so that the Guardians at Worcester in 1857 were delighted when they appointed a schoolmaster said to be 'of high character',[116] who had also been trained at Worcester Diocesan Training College at Saltley for six months. He had also taught at Spilsby, Lincolnshire for one year and he had good testimonials from this post. However, within three months, this man was forced to resign, having been found guilty at Gloucester Assizes of fraudulently falsifying his baptismal certificate. He had not been baptised an Anglican and was therefore not eligible to attend the training college,[117] which invalidated his teacher's certificate. In spite of this unfortunate experience, other Guardians were more fortunate when they appointed such qualified teachers.[118] Although the Poor Law Central Authority's regulations demanded competent teachers, there were doubts in the 1830s and 1840s whether those employed were competent and the parsimony exhibited by Boards of Guardians only accentuated this problem. This situation was clearly known to the Poor Law Commission, because in a circular, distributed in 1838,[119] they included a questionnaire intended to probe the nature of education offered in workhouse schools, the sort of individuals employed as teachers, their background, whether they themselves had been pauperised and whether they were formally qualified to teach. In spite of this, problems persisted, because in 1848 the Poor Law Board[120] again insisted that there was a need to examine the qualifications of school staff. This followed an adverse annual report in 1847, in which it was stated: 'The proper education and training of children in the workhouse is essential to the improvement of their condition, as well as being highly important with reference to the social condition of the working class generally, and the increased efficiency of workhouse schools must always be an object of much solicitude with the Board.' It went on to ask whether teachers were trained to 'fulfil the exacting task of teaching such pupils'.[121]

As suggested earlier, the staff of the workhouse schools in Worcestershire were usually young and untrained and, according to Pamela Horn, most of them came fresh to teaching, an inevitable situation given the lack of opportunities for teacher training[122] and the low salary offered to Poor Law teachers. Indeed, according to S.P. Oberman, in as late as 1859, at a time when there were only thirty-four training colleges in the country, out of the 2,192 graduates from Battersea Training College in the twenty-three years from 1840,[123] only thirty-five individuals went to teach in Poor Law establishments. In spite of the unattractiveness of workhouse schools, there were still some very good teachers appointed to them, so that Assistant Poor Law Commissioner W.H.T. Hawley was able to assert, of his south-western region, in 1862[124] 'most of them . . . have been to training schools and they have certificates', although this did not appear to be the case in Worcestershire. Hawley also insisted that: 'They were from all quarters, many of them from the Kneller Hall Institute',[125] which had been set up specifically to train workhouse schoolteachers, which he clearly saw as an advantage. However, another Assistant Commissioner, Andrew Doyle, questioned the worth of Kneller Hall, which existed between 1850 and 1855, referring to it as 'a complete failure . . . [and] . . . an enormous waste of public money'.[126] In contemporary literature, Kneller Hall was said to train teachers for district schools, but when such schools were not created in large numbers, 'its scholars . . . [thought themselves] . . . too good to accept or retain the ill paid and irksome office of workhouse schoolmasters'.[127] Doyle disputed this purpose, stating that 'Kneller Hall was instituted for the special purpose of training masters for [all] workhouse schools',[128] although an investigation of extant evidence suggests that while this was the intended purpose, it was impossible to ensure that these teachers obtained posts in such schools.

Teacher training developed during the nineteenth century and training colleges became more plentiful, but still few college-trained teachers applied for workhouse school posts in Worcestershire and there was no increase in appointments of teachers trained as pupil-teachers either. Whilst this was not an acceptable situation, HMI Thomas B. Browne placed the blame for this on Boards of Guardians, who were unwilling to offer attractive salaries or improved conditions of employment. He suggested in 1861 that teachers of good moral influence could be secured: 'By vesting the powers to appoint teachers in fewer hands',[129] who should select 'any man or woman possessed of a fair degree of intelligence and Christian principle whose heart is in his work'.[130] Thomas B. Browne clearly also believed in the concept of a 'born teacher', because he believed that 'they (teaching skills) can be acquired to a certain extent. I think that the art of teaching is a gift, although it may be developed.'[131] He made no suggestion about how such 'born teachers' might be attracted to workhouse education. Clearly, if a sufficiency of suitably qualified workhouse teachers were to be provided, some initiative by the Poor Law Central Authority was required. It was to this purpose that James P. Kay had experimented with a pupil-teacher system at Gressenhall workhouse in East Anglia, when he was Assistant Poor Law Commissioner for that region. He selected suitably talented inmate children who were trained as pupil-teachers, although his experiment ended when he moved to become secretary to the Privy Council Committee on Education. This system was not adopted in workhouse schools elsewhere and certainly not in Worcestershire. However, there were some trials with the system in district schools and it was introduced in the elementary schooling system after 1846.

The shortage of sufficiently trained workhouse teachers continued, which proved a problem in most of England and Wales, particularly in rural areas like Worcestershire. Clearly, in a free market, workhouse schools were not attractive, but this situation did slowly improve, so that by 1871 applicants for schoolteaching posts in county workhouses were more likely than not to be trained and/or experienced. The problem was not obtaining applicants for workhouse schoolteaching posts, it was getting suitably qualified individuals to apply. A workhouse schoolmistress leaving her post was usually replaced within one month, but often the new incumbent to the post proved totally inadequate. In such circumstances an inmate was sometimes appointed and it was often said that this was an interim arrangement, to placate the Poor Law Central Authority, who disapproved of this practice, as adult paupers were thought to taint the children, no matter how carefully they were selected. Thus in most places the appointment of inmates ceased by 1840. However, the small Tenbury Wells union made such an appointment in 1842,[132] when an inmate was permanently appointed as schoolmistress and also to 'help the matron', although this experiment failed within a month, with the woman dismissed as 'unsuitable'.[133] Even when faced with this mass of evidence about the poor quality of workhouse schoolteachers, one must still question the assumption, made by Norman Longmate, that: 'In many workhouse schools at this time [the 1840s] the pupils were, in any case, in little danger of learning anything, for often the Guardians economised by using other inmates as teachers'.[134] This belief was no doubt based on evidence given to the Privy Council Committee on Education in 1847, that 'an inspection of forty-one schools in the northern counties found that teachers in twenty-five schools were themselves paupers', but the northern counties were far from typical and many of the workhouse teachers employed in Worcestershire were regarded by HMI and other workhouse inspectors as at least satisfactory. Indeed, Guardians usually attempted to ensure this, but there were rare exceptions. For instance at Kidderminster in 1844,[135] a temporary appointment of a personal acquaintance was made 'by the master'. This was for six weeks, until the full-time appointee could take up their post. Normally however, county Boards of Guardians were scrupulous in their care over school appointments.

In the whole of England and Wales where the New Poor Law was implemented, Boards of Guardians sometimes remained vehement about Less Eligibility as a determinant of what education was offered in workhouses. However, there were exceptions to this among Worcestershire unions. For instance, Evesham Guardians were reported in 1846,[136] because they had made no provision for the education of children in the workhouse, which had over thirty child inmates at that time and where it was stated that 'the children are placed under the care of a man and a woman, who are paupers and themselves ignorant of what the children at least might learn'.[137] Whilst the minimal education offered, in most other places, may have conformed to the Guardians' perception of Less Eligibility, that at Evesham still did not satisfy the Poor Law central administration, because even two years later it was reported that the inmate children 'ought to be taught to read and write and to know the 4 rules of arithmetic'.[138] Whilst workhouse inspectors drew attention to this problem, there was no satisfactory solution attempted, so that HMI was still able to state: 'No children can, in my opinion be more neglected as regards education, than the children of Evesham workhouse, and it is apparent that [the school] master has much more on his hands than he can possibly attend to.'[139] The need for a teacher, who had to be a good model, was re-emphasised and the Guardians now acted immediately to appoint a schoolmaster-porter,[140] about whom the Assistant Poor Law Commissioner expressed satisfaction.[141] He had apparently abandoned his attempt to improve education at Evesham workhouse because he now chose to ignore the man's portering duties, which the schoolmaster still performed.

What was reported as the worst case of an unsuitable workhouse schoolteacher being appointed in Worcestershire was at Upton upon Severn in 1847, where a land-surveyor called Whiteside, apparently with seventeen years successful teaching experience, was appointed. His appointment was approved immediately by HMI, probably because he was regarded as a very suitable appointee. However, within a year, HMI described him as 'a man of inferior acquirements, but he takes great pains'[142] and indeed the school had initially improved under his care, to the extent that he was given a certificate of 'probation' Grade III, with a government grant of £25.[143] However, by early 1851, the Assistant Poor Law Commissioner was expressing his concern about the quality of the schoolmaster, although in spite of this HMI confirmed his previous certificate and again gave a government grant of £25. This situation was reconfirmed in the next two years, after which there was a clear deterioration in the school. This was first noted in 1855 when another HMI, who visited the Upton on Severn workhouse school because the regular inspector was unavailable, refused to award a certificate and paid no government grant. Logically, the reason for this was that either the schoolmaster had deteriorated in health and efficiency or the criteria used by various HMI to judge teachers differed. However, this latter explanation appeared unlikely, because this was not the only place in the county, where a teacher was seen by different HMI at subsequent inspections. Usually in such cases, there was a concurrence of opinion about a teacher's performance, but here there was a profound disagreement. Indeed, so poor was the second HMI's opinion of this schoolmaster that the inspector stated: 'It is obviously useless to examine the schoolmaster, whose school is in a most unsatisfactory state, who is both by age, (he was fifty-five years old) and infirmity totally incapacitated for the discharge of his duties. He was unable to preserve discipline or draft classes in my presence.'[144] This statement suggested that it was a deterioration in the teacher's health that caused these adverse criticisms and when this HMI returned to the school, he was again critical. He stated that 'this poor man is wholly unfit for his post, and I may say that he is retained because he is infirm and deaf and would be a pauper if not maintained in his present situation, to the sacrifice of the children'.[145] No certificate or grant was given, but the Guardians did not dismiss him, presumably because they wanted to avoid this man's pauperisation. They continued to employ him until late 1855. At this time, the Guardians contemplated sending the workhouse children to the local National School,[146] but the Assistant Commissioner, responsible for the union, indicated that the children sent there would still need superintending at the workhouse, so that someone would have to be employed to do this. In answer to this, the HMI for the elementary school in Upton upon Severn was critical of that school. He stated that it was 'inferior', but in spite of this the local Assistant Poor Law Commissioner, in a marginal comment on the Poor Law Central Authority's copy of the minute, favoured the children's attendance at that school. He believed that this arrangement would 'break the monotony of the workhouse . . . [and] . . . it would rid them [the children] of the badge of the degraded caste'.[147] In spite of HMI's advice about the inferior quality of the local elementary school, the Guardians still decided to send the pauper children out of the workhouse to school, with the agreement of both the Poor Law Central Authority and officials of the Privy Council Committee on Education, who certainly knew of the adverse opinions about Upton on Severn elementary school. This also meant that the workhouse schoolmaster would be dismissed, which would probably have meant that he became a pauper, such was his state of health. However, for the children to get to their new school, they had to walk one-eighth of a mile and they clearly needed to be supervised to do this.

The now redundant schoolmaster was employed to supervise this walk as well as to be an industrial training instructor,[148] to fulfil the Poor Law Board's requirement that the workhouse children be given this training, which was not available at the elementary school. With hindsight, this may have been a prevarication designed to avoid the pauperisation of this infirm old man, although the arrangement was rather surprisingly immediately approved by the Assistant Poor Law Commissioner, who had previously made adverse comments about Whiteside – he now insisted that he was 'able to cope' with his new responsibilities.[149] In spite of this, he did wonder what trade Whiteside would teach. Whilst the level of care taken over this appointment was suspect, it did illustrate that an Assistant Poor Law Commissioner's opinions were important in the decision to proceed with an appointment. In spite of this scheme being sanctioned, Assistant Poor Law Commissioner Sir J. Walsham had previously made adverse comments about this sort of arrangement. He had stated: 'I am quite satisfied that the extension of similar arrangements, except when unavoidable would produce educational results inferior to those attained in the workhouse schools.'[150] Furthermore, he thought that boys under eight years old could be placed with the girls and a schoolmistress appointed to teach them, which would avoid the evil of sending inmate children out of the workhouse.

In the county, a few of the workhouse schoolmistresses appointed were trained teachers, as at Worcester in 1841 where the schoolmistress appointed there had been 'employed as a schoolmistress at St George's National School, in Kidderminster'.[151] Similarly the woman teacher at Stourbridge in 1846 was described as 'a trained teacher', who had been employed as a 'Governess at Napton National School'.[152] In other unions appointees had taught as pupil-teachers in day schools.[153] However, the status of most teachers appointed was less certain, as it was not stated whether these teachers were qualified.[154] Most female school staff appointed were untrained, excepting that some had been Sunday schoolteachers. In several cases 'joint appointments' were made to county workhouse schools, with the husband employed as the schoolmaster or porter and the wife as schoolmistress. It was the male in such partnerships who was most likely to be unsatisfactory, so that in four cases a husband was dismissed for indiscipline or cruelty, but no schoolmistress 'joint appointee' was ever found guilty of any misdemeanour. In other cases couples did resign because of the injurious effect of the workhouse atmosphere on their health, particularly that of the wife.[155]

In the county between 1834 and 1871, 102 schoolmistresses were appointed, but one resigned without taking up her post because she felt it would be 'too much for her'. All of the schoolmistresses appointed were Protestant and most were inevitably Anglican, because this creed was favoured by Guardians. In terms of age, most schoolmistresses appointed were between twenty and forty years old, with only four under twenty and four over forty years old. The oldest appointee was fifty-one years old. Older schoolmistresses, over twenty-five years old, were favoured by some Guardians, because younger women were considered unreliable, particularly as they had difficulty in disciplining workhouse children. Thus, when Kidderminster Guardians successfully advertised for: 'A respectable middle-aged lady to act as schoolmistress for the union workhouse' in 1839, such a person was appointed.[156] More often, very young schoolmistresses were appointed[157] and such appointments were clearly acceptable to the Poor Law Commission, because they usually sanctioned them immediately, although sometimes such teachers were criticised for showing 'too much severity towards the children'.[158] One such young teacher, aged sixteen, remained in office for over seven and a half years,[159] which was the longest period spent as a workhouse schoolmistress in Worcestershire between 1834 to 1871. More usually, woman teachers were in office for less than two years, often leaving because they found the task too much for them. Others were advised to resign even more quickly after only a month's trial, usually because they had difficulty in dealing with classroom indiscipline, but sometimes because they resorted to severe punishment in an effort to control the children.

The ability to discipline workhouse children was inevitably considered very important for any teacher employed in a Poor Law school, so that even if teachers were very competent in instructing the children if they lacked control, they were liable to be dismissed. Thus at Worcester in 1847,[160] the schoolmaster and schoolmistress were criticised, not because they were unable to teach, but because they were unable to control the children. Indeed in 1848, the same schoolmaster was said to be 'competent to teach but defective in systems of power and command – the boys have been rebellious, but they are at present orderly'.[161] This emphasis on discipline was well demonstrated by the use of the word 'subordination', used in workhouse orders and regulations, which unequivocally implied the social control expected of workhouses by the Poor Law central authority. Nevertheless, workhouse officers also wanted control over the children, but this was for another reason. They desired to maintain their pauper charges in a compliant mood, because this produced individuals who were manageable and hence less threatening. Inevitably, some workhouse children were indisciplined and indeed this was sometimes why the child was an inmate, but such a lack of discipline seldom proved a problem. But the effect of workhouse discipline was so insidious that inmate children gained a veneer of respectability, which became seen as desirable by the middle classes. Basically, such children had respect for their social superiors, which made them very acceptable as servants, the only ex-workhouse inmates likely to be encountered by respectable middle-class citizens. However, this sort of control was not unique to workhouses and indeed it has been suggested by M.A. Crowther, that, 'it is difficult to discover any system of formal education that does not inculcate a respect for the values of the social leaders',[162] so that perhaps workhouse education was no different from any other form of institutionalised education. King's Norton union, contiguous with Birmingham, had grown at a prodigious rate in the period from 1834 to 1871[163] and as early as in 1838[164] the Guardians there had discussed the nature of punishments and rewards used by schoolteachers to maintain discipline. Some teachers there adopted 'reward books' as prizes for good behaviour, but other schoolmistresses punished children by 'setting them stand on a stool in one corner of the room and having a dunce's cap on their heads', for no more than thirty minutes for those over six years old, and for no more than fifteen minutes for those under six years old.[165] Other female teachers were tempted to use corporal punishment, which under Poor Law Board regulations could not be used on girls,[166] and sometimes schoolmistresses were warned by the Board of Guardians not to use corporal punishment on girls who misbehaved.[167]

In spite of this disapprobation, corporal punishment could be legitimately used on inmate boys, but not by the schoolmistress, although there was a way round this regulation. The schoolmistress maintained 'subordination in the school' by getting the porter to chastise the boys where this was necessary,[168] but sometimes miscreant boys were chastised by the workhouse master or the schoolmaster. In spite of this some schoolmistresses (and schoolmasters) could not control the children even using the range of legal punishments available. One schoolmistress at King's Norton in 1858 was 'directed . . . in the case of her inflicting corporal punishment to use a birch and not a cane or stick, and suggested the priority in cases of corporal punishment being required to hand the offender over to the master',[169] although the medical officer later requested that this schoolmistress, 'refrain from unusual modes of punishment' and that she should be 'provided with a birch rod to use in case of corporal punishment being resorted to'.[170] She presumably complied as there was no further comment.

Making an example of a miscreant pupil was another approach to punishment used in workhouses. At Bromsgrove in 1863 the schoolmistress had two boys beaten for disobedience and general bad behaviour with: 'The whole of the children . . . [being] . . . brought into the room reasoned with and cautioned and the master was instructed that if the boys did not behave well, to birch them with a rod that was produced.'[171] Such a punishment could not be used on girls and there was an obvious inequality here. The most extreme punishment for girl inmates over the age of twelve years, without sending them before the magistrates, was to commit them to the refractory ward, if one existed, for a specified period of time. This happened at Bromsgrove in 1856[172] when a twelve-year-old girl, who was disobedient, 'was . . . confined in the refractory ward for twenty-four hours with a change of diet – Remit to twelve hours if she apologised'. If this extreme treatment failed, the child could be removed from the children's ward and placed with able-bodied adult paupers of the same sex, breaching the inviolable classification of the workhouse, which was an action not liked by Guardians who were conditioned to believe in the importance of absolute segregation. Sometimes children who behaved very badly and 'set a bad example . . . to the rest of the school' were dealt with in this way.[173]

Generally workhouse punishments were carefully regulated, but illegal punishments were undoubtedly used, with girls and boys sometimes improperly severely beaten, although such cases invariably went unrecorded and it was only in cases reported to Boards of Guardians that they were apparent. At Kidderminster in 1848[174] the Assistant Poor Law Commissioner reported a complaint about the schoolmaster there, who had improperly punished a boy under his charge. When the inspector talked with the schoolmaster, he found him 'unacquainted with the provisions of article 140 of the general order of 24th June 1847, respecting the punishment of children in the workhouse'.[175] Ironically had the punishment administered been entered in the punishment book, the schoolmaster would have escaped admonishment. In other cases maltreatment was extreme and this led to much more severe outcomes for the teacher. At Stourbridge in

1852[176] a pauper complained that her child, and another, had been beaten. No marks were found on the inmate's son, but there were red marks on the other boy's shoulders. On investigation, many more cases of beatings by this schoolmaster became known, which included striking three boys with his hand and beating others with sticks. Indeed at this time, three boys 'had black ears' occasioned 'by fillips given by the fingers, and in the case of Micawdie by a box with the open hand', so that when he was questioned this boy said that the schoolmaster had given him twelve 'custards' – or blows on the open palm of the hand with a piece of wood – 'because he could not tell what S–A–L–M–O–N spelt'. While these charges were denied by the schoolmaster, they were corroborated by the monitor, who also said that the teacher had hit another boy for not writing properly. Again this was denied and the schoolmaster suggested that the whole thing was 'a trumped up charge altogether'. In spite of this the evidence against the teacher was convincing, as two other boys had bruised thighs, having been hit with a round ruler for not sitting properly, and the legs of a six-year-old boy were bruised where he had been hit with a piece of deal wood, for being unable to say his letters. Another six-year-old had been hit with a stick for climbing on the wall, but the schoolmaster claimed that these injuries were sustained 'when the boys had fallen while climbing a rope, and had tumbled about'. Finally and conclusively, the head of one boy was bruised to an extent that demonstrated that the schoolmaster 'used violence that would bespeak inordinate passion and a cruel and malignant disposition'. In spite of the severity of these injuries, the workhouse master only reported these facts because the Poor Law Board regulations had not been followed, so that these punishments went unrecorded. Had they been recorded there would probably have been no charge to answer, but in these circumstances the schoolmaster, who was thirty-nine years old and had twenty years teaching experience, but who was new to the workhouse office, was regarded as blameworthy. Whilst he denied all charges he still offered to resign, but this was not allowed. Instead, when all of these cases of maltreatment were proved, he was forced to resign for infringing regulations rather than for beating children. His enforced resignation was recorded, along with the details of his maltreatment of children, which ensured that he would never be employed in the Poor Law education system again.

Sometimes even corporal punishment failed as a deterrent. At Worcester in 1853 the boys were considered, 'not in quite so good a state of discipline as the Guardians could wish'.[177] The Guardians there resolved to erect a room to deter intransigent boys which, 'will have a beneficial effect and be the means of preventing disorderly and insubordinate conduct and tend very much to improve the boys' behaviour'. This was the only such room used in the county. Methods used to maintain discipline varied, with illegal methods sometimes being used. At Worcester in 1859 the schoolmistress was criticised for being 'cross in her manner to the children',[178] having been previously cautioned for using corporal punishment on girls. She continued to administer taps on the hand with a small stick as 'part of her ordinary discipline', claiming that 'she scarcely considered such correction to be corporal punishment'.[179] Within four months the Assistant Poor Law Commissioner reported: 'I have visited the girls' school at 9.17 a.m. today. I found it entirely disorderly and the schoolmistress absent. I consider her utterly unfit for her office.'[180] The schoolmistress, who resigned within two days,[181] had attended Borough Road Training School, had eighteen years teaching experience and had received very good reports in her five years at the workhouse. Ironically, she was exactly the type of teacher demanded by the Poor Law Board but she could not cope without resorting to corporal punishment. How then did others cope? Illegal methods were undoubtedly used to control the children, a fact normally hidden from the Assistant Poor Law Commissioner, HMI and Guardians, because officers superior to the teacher were unlikely to pass on complaints as they had overall responsibility for discipline and they did not wish to be implicated. It was only where excessive punishment methods were used or where a parent complained, that these illicit methods become apparent.

The resignation of a schoolmistress sometimes caused problems; at Kidderminster in 1841, a schoolmistress there resigned[182] and she was not replaced for over a year. Indeed, her replacement did not settle into her post easily, having great difficulty in controlling the children, which led[183] to an investigation of her capabilities in 1842, although schoolmistresses in this union seldom stayed in office for more than a year, with inquiries of this type quite common, so that on this occasion although the teacher was found 'competent', discipline problems were soon to recur. Sometimes such problems became a major preoccupation for the Guardians, but few cases of indiscipline were serious. In any case, discipline was probably overstated as a cause for concern by both the Poor Law Central Authority and the Guardians, as it was thought to be one facet lacking in paupers and therefore any failure of the schoolteacher to control the children was thought important. An adverse report on discipline from HMI caused the teacher's certificate to be withheld and no government grant was paid. In this circumstance the teacher was usually dismissed. Sometimes, however, there were extenuating circumstances, as at Stourbridge in 1853; 'A wholly inexperienced schoolmistress'[184] resigned within two months of her appointment, but the Assistant Poor Law Commissioner admitted 'the school is peculiar and requires an experienced and efficient teacher'.[185] The girls at the workhouse he described as 'unusually insubordinate and difficult'. The problems of finding competent teachers were many, as has already been discussed. At Evesham, the schoolmistress appointed in 1867 was given fair reports in her first three years, but when seen for the first time by HMI Browne in 1870,[186] she was described as incompetent and the discipline of the school as 'bad'. Thomas B. Browne recommended that she be replaced, but HMI's presence in the room may have caused discipline problems and no allowance was apparently made for this. Good discipline was occasionally commented on,[187] for example at Shipston on Stour in 1862, where HMI stated: 'The children passed a good examination and their attainment and discipline are creditable to the teacher, who could not accomplish what she has done without exercise of a rare degree of industry and intelligence.'[188] Indeed this outstanding schoolmistress had been a successful pupil-teacher at Kirkdale Industrial School, Liverpool. She came with excellent testimonials and was eventually appointed to the West Derby workhouse at Liverpool,[189] the largest workhouse school in the country.

Discipline problems were sometimes perceived as caused by a lack of essential equipment in schoolrooms, such as desks, forms, slates and even books. The Guardians at Worcester in 1852 stated that they were, 'desirous that the school should be supplied with everything necessary to keep them [the children] in a proper state of discipline, order and efficiency'.[190] They then listed a large number of items considered necessary to do this, but HMI commented[191] that Guardians should be vigilant when spending public money, so that they could not make all of the alterations that were desirable. However, the frequent change of children was, undoubtedly, the major cause of discipline problems in workhouse schools. At Stourbridge in 1848 it was said: 'The girls are very backward. They are young and change frequently'[192] and at the same union in as late as 1868 recently admitted children still caused problems. This concerned HMI who sometimes took such matters into account when examining children, as at Bromsgrove in 1866 when

HMI stated: 'The children have passed a fair examination according to their age, and the time they have been in the school.'[193] Discipline problems were reported at Pershore in 1848,[194] but on investigation there was no cause for concern, although it was suggested that 'in future the bell in the morning will be rung twice instead of once as henceforth at an interval of 15 minutes, and the children kept upstairs till the time after the adults, so that the schoolmistress may better be able to meet them coming down'. Clearly, the presence of adult paupers in the same room as the children was still considered threatening, so that this problem was solved by altering the routine that was considered all important when dealing with pauper children.

There were some cases of dismissal of school staff for maltreatment of children, for drunkenness, for other misdemeanours and for supposedly sending an obscene letter. This involved the schoolmaster at Stourbridge in 1845,[195] who was accused of sending an obscene letter to a serving girl in the town. The offending letter was sent to a handwriting expert, who could not prove who had written it. In spite of this, the sexually explicit nature of the letter required that a person even suspected of writing it must be dismissed. The Stourbridge Guardians were told to demand the schoolmaster's resignation, although he refused to resign. He wrote to the Poor Law Commission stating that he had only a 'speaking acquaintance with the girl'. The investigating inspector disputed this, as 'he (the schoolmaster) took walks with her'.[196] The inspector again insisted that the schoolmaster must resign. At this stage the Guardians became impatient to appoint a replacement schoolmaster, so they banned the supposed offender from the workhouse premises, but he still refused to resign, invoking the support of a minority of Guardians in doing this. He was eventually dismissed in 1846,[197] in spite of the case against him not being proved. Whilst one can appreciate that the Poor Law Commission wanted no scandal, this dismissal decision appeared unjust because there was no substantive evidence against the schoolmaster.

Sometimes workhouse schoolteachers were dismissed for illegal and immoral acts. The schoolmistress of Upton upon Severn was dismissed in 1847[198] for stealing 10 lbs of coal from the workhouse, while the schoolmistress at Pershore in 1848,[199] was charged with unspecified misconduct by the matron. She resigned,[200] but later[201] she asked the Guardians to make an investigation about 'recent reports circulating in Pershore while she held that office'. The Guardians refused this, saying that she was offered the chance of an enquiry at the time of her resignation, which she had refused. Another schoolmistress, at Droitwich in 1853,[202] inevitably resigned having suffered a miscarriage and the workhouse master was said to be the father of the child,[203] so that he (and his wife) resigned later. When the schoolmistress applied for a testimonial, 'in spite of my not deserving one, as to the respectability of my family and also to the competency of my teaching',[204] she was surprisingly supplied with one, although the post she was applying for was not as a teacher. This letter also asked that no reporters be allowed into the room for the enquiry, 'as being an orphan and having my bread to seek, this might be the means of doing me harm',[205] which was apparently complied with. The schoolmaster and schoolmistress at Worcester in 1855, were charged by the master and matron of the workhouse with 'familiarity';[206] a charge that both denied. They countercharged the matron with a trivial offence and that the master used bad language and was of ill temper. The charges against the teachers and against the master were investigated, with the master being censured and the schoolmaster and schoolmistress being told to 'avoid familiarity in future'.[207]

Given the context of the workhouse, unfounded charges were brought against schoolteachers, because inmates were inevitably vindictive about workhouse staff. Thus, the new schoolmistress at Shipston on Stour in 1851[208] was said to have arrived back at the workhouse with the master when both were drunk, although a subsequent inquiry found this claim to be malicious. At Bromsgrove in 1856, the matron 'infringed the schoolmistress's character', but no fault was found in this case,[209] but as the school staff had to be beyond reproach, the matron was thanked for bringing the matter to the attention of the Guardians. At Droitwich in 1864,[210] the schoolmistress was inevitably dismissed when found guilty of improper behaviour with the porter. Elsewhere male workhouse staff had sexual relations with inmate women. This happened at Kidderminster in 1869 where the schoolmaster, who was the nephew of the master, became 'pro tempore' master when his uncle died, but when he returned to his duties as schoolmaster in early 1869 he was 'accused by an inmate, near confinement, of having connexion with her'.[211] He admitted the offence and was dismissed,[212] but meanwhile he had applied for a post as master at Pershore union. The Guardians there were informed of his offence, which debarred him from that post. His name was then automatically added to a central register of dismissals, kept to ensure that offenders were not employed in the Poor Law system again. Such schoolteachers were obviously not regarded as suitable models of moral rectitude for inmate pauper children.

As has already been suggested, there was a consensus among the Guardians, the public at large and among workhouse staff that education was beneficial for inmate children. The Guardians and the general public regarded education as curative of pauperism, while the workhouse officers probably considered it beneficial because it occupied children's time while they were in the workhouse, preventing them from becoming nuisances. For this reason, this aspect of the treatment of inmate children was very carefully monitored and controlled. Workhouse schoolteachers were also continually scrutinised by the Poor Law inspector, who was responsible for ensuring persons appointed to teaching posts were suitable and that they performed their duties in accordance with centrally written rules and regulations – this ensured that National Uniformity was maintained. However, the workhouse inspectors' visits were irregular and were seldom more than quarterly, so that there must be doubt about the quality of workhouse education and its supervision.

The appointment of a school inspector specific to workhouse schools was undoubtedly seen as an advance, but he attended the workhouse only annually. The problems of monitoring were solved, in the eyes of the Central Poor Law Authority, by the creation of a bureaucratic hierarchy among workhouse officers, so that one officer inspected his subordinates. In this hierarchy, because of his superior social position, the workhouse chaplain was dominant. He had oversight of the school and because of his middle-class status he was trusted by the Central Poor Law Authority. It was believed that he would accept utilitarian orthodoxy and hence ensure compliance to national rules and regulations. This was usually the case, but there were instances where a particularly forceful chaplain overruled the workhouse inspector. In spite of his lack of expertise in elementary education the workhouse chaplain ensured that the workhouse was a 'total institution' dominated by Anglicanism. After about 1838 workhouse teachers were given certificates of competency, which was long before a similar system was adopted for non-Poor Law elementary schools. In spite of this, there was continuing evidence of low standards of teaching and attainment in workhouse schools, although the use of regular inspection gradually raised standards. The lowest standards of all existed in small rural unions, where the salary offered to the workhouse schoolteachers was very low indeed, so that no qualified teacher would take up such an appointment. In these workhouses, education was at a very minimal standard. Rural unions also tended to attract schoolmistresses, with schoolmasters found only in urban workhouses in Worcestershire, throughout the period to 1871. In most cases the post of workhouse schoolteacher appears to have been unattractive and those appointed did not stay for long. Only for five years after the 1862 'Revised Code' were workhouse schools directly comparable with elementary schools, at the time when capitation allowances were added to the basic salaries of workhouse teachers. Outside Poor Law schools the result of the 'Revised Code' was to reduce education costs, deleteriously affecting the school curriculum, but this does not appear to have happened in Worcestershire workhouse schools. The gradual improvement in all aspects of standards continued. The salaries offered to workhouse school staff became marginally more competitive as salaries in non Poor Law schools worsened, but they were still insufficient to attract and maintain the right sort of teacher to county workhouse schools.

The lifestyle of a teacher in a workhouse, virtually incarcerated in a closed total institution with attendant privations, caused them to become institutionalised and tainted by association with the poor, so that these posts remained an unattractive prospect. It appeared that once appointed to a workhouse post a schoolteacher remained in the Poor Law education system with little chance of promotion. Thus, few Worcestershire workhouse teachers moved to better posts. The vast majority of schoolmasters left for other occupations, while many schoolmistresses married and left the teaching profession. For these reasons, problems of attracting applicants for the school posts in workhouses continued and were further enhanced by the demands of Guardians for what were regarded as suitable applicants. This meant that the highest moral standards were expected of applicants, because the schoolteacher was expected to counterbalance the insidious adverse influence of the workhouse on pauper children. The result of all this, together with the low salary offered and the unattractive nature of the work and living conditions, was that few suitable applicants came forward and in many cases there where no applications resulting from advertisements, so an adult inmate was sometimes put in charge of the workhouse school, a practice wholly disapproved of by the central Poor Law authority. An attempt, by James Kay-Shuttleworth, to solve the problem of a supply of workhouse teachers was to take able pauper children as apprentice teachers or pupil-teachers. At the end of a period of apprenticeship these individuals were then to be sent for training at a college. However, this did not happen within the county, but elsewhere the graduates of such colleges found workhouse schools less conducive than the elementary schools, to whom they were most attractive applicants. Once appointed, having passed through the very exacting selection procedure, workhouse schoolteachers were under constant scrutiny and this, together with the problems of controlling unruly inmate children, particularly those constantly coming and going from the workhouses, led to problems. Thus quite often, such teachers over-punished children and encountered the wrath of the Poor Law authorities for doing this. In cases such as these, they were often dismissed or forced to resign. However, many others left their posts of their own volition, because they found their work unpleasant and unconducive to health. For these reasons, only rarely did a workhouse schoolteacher stay in a post for a prolonged period of time.

The rules and regulations applied to workhouse schoolteachers were uniform, but the manner of interpretation was not. Faced with the problem of having no applicants for teaching posts, Guardians would appoint unsuitable people and attempt to cover this up. However, the contrast between rural and urban unions within Worcestershire, regarding the quality of schoolteachers, was apparent. In rural unions the salary that could be offered remained low and this restricted the quality of the applicant. It was also the case that no rural union appointed a schoolmaster or an industrial trainer and the quality of education offered in these places must therefore have been influenced. The implication of this was that rural workhouse schools were often co-educational, in contrast to most contemporary rural elementary schools. Ironically, in spite of evidence that schoolmistresses were from superior social status positions to their male contemporaries, schoolmasters were obviously preferred because they were presumed to be able to cope better than women, although this probably merely indicated contemporary gender bias.

In spite of the Principle of National Uniformity, the educational provision in Worcestershire workhouses varied considerably. The transitory inmate child, who belonged to a section of the working class continually existing on the margins of pauperism, was unlikely to regularly attend elementary school outside the workhouse and an analysis of relative eligibility would have to be tempered with this realisation. In spite of the provision of industrial training – not available in elementary schools – the teaching offered in the workhouse was probably less eligible, because these institutions remained unattractive to work in and few good teachers were attracted to them. However, the workhouse school was likely to be more eligible for its individual inmate scholars, who would probably have received no education outside the workhouse. This type of analysis would however have been difficult to sustain had Alec Ross's[213] or S.P. Oberman's[214] perspective, based on national Poor Law authority sources, been used. In stark contrast, Anne Digby[215] and others,[216] who based their work on local sources, drew similar conclusions to those presented here.

As Gertrude Himmelfarb suggests, the definition of poverty and the way it was regarded altered between 1834 and 1871, with the changed attitudes and methods of workhouse teachers demonstrating this well. The children were, after about 1840, regarded as different from adult paupers and they were treated accordingly by the workhouse officers. However, education became relatively quickly regarded as an essential in the treatment of children in workhouses to ensure that they did not become lifelong paupers. These developments and those that followed led to workhouse education being comparable with elementary education, once again indicating the altered attitude to poverty described by Gertrude Himmelfarb.[217] Regarding the workhouse conforming to Erving Goffman's analysis as a 'total institution', there is unique evidence available for considering workhouse teachers in this aspect. Such teachers were concerned that they would become institutionalised and hence marked by their workhouse experience for life. The teachers, like their pauper charges, were incarcerated in the workhouse for a prolonged period. Their life style there was contingent on the same rules and regulations as the inmates, so that logically they must have been institutionalised in a manner very similar to the paupers. In these circumstances they were probably unemployable in other than an institutional context if they had spent a prolonged period employed in workhouses. It was arguably this realisation that made such teachers transitory, with few of them willing to spend a whole working life in a Poor Law institution. Regarding the institutionalisation of the staff, the workhouse conformed exactly to the model of the 'total institution' suggested by Erving Goffman in *Asylums*.[218] It remains to examine the implications of this for the methods, organisation and the curriculum of the county's workhouse schools.

6

THE WORKHOUSE SCHOOL

The Central Poor Law Authority continued to emphasise the importance of education in the treatment of indoor pauper children throughout the nineteenth century, a level of interference which Anne Digby has aptly called 'the state's incursion . . . [into the lives of the working classes] . . . which was most fully developed in workhouse schooling in the mid-nineteenth century'.[1] Contemporaneously, this was clearly indicated by the huge quantity of administrative literature produced, which related to workhouse education and by contemporary opinions, such as those of George Godwin,[2] who suggested that such interference was for the good of the children. Retrospective analysis by A.J. Donajgrodski[3] suggests a 'social police' function for the Poor Law,[4] with the social control of paupers and mendicants the major motive for Poor Law policy. Indeed, James P. Kay (later Kay-Shuttleworth) suggested as much in 1862, when he referred to 'the preservation of internal peace . . . [depending] . . . on the education of the working classes'[5] which were revealing sentiments, because as well as being first Secretary of the Privy Council Committee on Education, Kay also had experience of the Poor Law as an Assistant Commissioner in East Anglia, where he had been actively involved in developing the first workhouse schools. However, from Brian Simon's perspective[6] and from a Marxist point of view, workhouse education did not create opportunities for inmate children, rather it created a false consciousness, which was functional because it calmed potential social disorder. This was welcomed by Guardians and workhouse officers alike, because it created an atmosphere in which the inmates were compliant and in which they created no discipline problems. Therefore, it appeared logical that this was the motive for national Poor Law policy.

In England and Wales between 1834 and 1871 there was an overt connection between workhouse education and elementary education, although this relationship may have been more fundamental than was previously believed. Indeed, A. Middleton and S. Weitzman have suggested that: 'Although the Poor Law never had control over [all] education, the tenets of the period, influenced by the doctrine of *laissez faire*, and a mandate of complete parental responsibility for children, ensured that the elementary school remained in many minds a type of poor relief.'[7] Thus, all elementary education had a social control function, although it was in Poor Law educational institutions that this function was most developed, so that an investigation of the pedagogy, organisation and management of these schools, together with their curriculum, appeared essential to illuminate the nature of social control in nineteenth-century society and particularly under the New Poor Law.

The nature of Poor Law education in Worcestershire Poor Law unions inevitably varied. All pauper education in the county took place in individual workhouse schools, because district and separate Poor Law schools were inappropriate in an essentially rural county, with an urban fringe only around Birmingham and the Black Country. Previously under the Old Poor Law, schooling had not generally been provided in poorhouses. However, when James P. Kay became a Poor Law Assistant Commissioner in East Anglia, he soon saw such education as 'one of the most important means of eradicating the germ of pauperism from the rising generation'.[8] In spite of this, there was no consensus between Poor Law officials on this matter and another Assistant Commissioner, W.H.T. Hawley, thought that youth in the poorhouses under the Old Poor Law were 'languishing in idleness and ignorance'[9] and he thought there was little immediate improvement after 1834, even in places influenced by Kay.

Apparently, from 1834 onwards, the Poor Law Commission did want to provide education in workhouses, in spite of the Principle of Less Eligibility, so they encouraged Boards of Guardians to provide schools. Many county Guardians favoured Less Eligibility and were resistant to the idea of even minimal education for indoor child paupers, although the Central Poor Law Authority were unabashed. Among Worcestershire Guardians there was a profound disinterest in workhouse education, to the extent that the county's Boards of Guardians were said by Alec Ross to be 'lacking vigour in their support'[10] of workhouse schooling. However, within five years,[11] Kidderminster workhouse school was working for more than the three hours per day demanded by the Poor

Law Commission. It operated from 9.00 a.m. to 12.00 p.m. and from 2.00 p.m. to 4.00 p.m. in winter and 2.00 p.m. to 5.00 p.m. in summer, which were similar hours to those quoted for Westhampnett union in 1837;[12] regarded as a 'good example'. However, Kidderminster union was not typical of county unions, as it was the only Worcestershire union to provide even rudimentary workhouse schooling at this date.

Kidderminster was probably the most active Worcestershire Poor Law union regarding education, because it had one of the largest, most threatening urban populations, together with a large number of inmate children, including orphans and foundlings. In such circumstances, education was an obvious way of occupying children's time and the situation could be improved further by including industrial training. For this reason, W.E. Hickson, a self-professed expert on Poor Law matters, suggested that workhouse schools were 'as bad as is possible to be imagined',[13] but contemporaneously, others claimed that in some areas of the country, including parts of Worcestershire, elementary schools were inferior to those in workhouses. Inevitably, proponents of Poor Law education publicised good examples, such as the workhouse school at Petworth in Sussex,[14] where it was said: 'The girls are taught everything that can be taught for the purpose of making them useful servants, cleaning the house and mending clothes' and 'the boys are taught to read and write'.[15] However, such education was unusual, as according to Kay in 1837, indoor pauper children were likely to become 'for a time, and probably a long period . . . dependent upon the ratepayers' and they were 'infested with vermin' and 'often covered with itch'. In such circumstances they became 'brutish . . . ignorant, vicious and disorderly' because they received 'no sort of education in letters, or a general training in habits of industry'.[16] In such circumstances some action was surely necessary.

Boards of Guardians were elected to represent the interests of local Poor Rate payers and thus whether education was offered in the local workhouse was determined by an interaction between the demands of the Central Poor Law Authority and the needs of the local community, as perceived by these Guardians. Hence, while the national guidelines were unequivocal in their support of workhouse education, the ideology of local Boards of Guardians differed and workhouse education provision varied considerably. However, so too did the elementary education provided outside the workhouse, which was sometimes seen as a mere extension of Poor Relief and given equally low priority. For this reason some Poor Law unions, who provided a workhouse school, had no elementary school for non-pauper children.

Whilst there was no public comment about this in Worcestershire, elsewhere this situation was highlighted. For instance, at Westhampnett in Sussex in 1837, the clerk to the Guardians there suggested that education in areas of the union, where no National school existed, was inferior to the education of the pauper children in the workhouse.[17] He assured the Select Committee on the Poor Law Amendment Act in 1837 that, workhouse children 'were growing up . . . being able to read and write'.[18] Arithmetic was also taught in the morning, while in the afternoon they were 'classed as tailors, shoemakers and straw platters',[19] with the girls taught 'the general duties of household servants'.[20] In Petworth union,[21] also in Sussex, reading was taught but not writing or arithmetic, a situation not merely countenanced by the Guardians, but positively welcomed by them.[22] In other Sussex unions, no workhouse education was offered until well after the passing of the Poor Law Amendment Act in 1834.

Clearly, as the workhouse education available to pauper children varied from union to union, some inmate children were more eligible than others in this respect, which was in direct contravention of the basic Principles of Poor Relief, Less Eligibility and National Uniformity. Ironically therefore, workhouse education was often superior to the elementary education available in large tracts of the country, particularly in burgeoning urban areas, where immigrants were crowded into densely packed poor quality housing, with no schools available. This was certainly the case in the poorest areas of urban Worcestershire, the very areas from which many child paupers came, so that these individuals were definitely more eligible than their non-pauper contemporaries from their home parishes, regarding education. In spite of this obvious contravention of its guiding Principles, the Poor Law Commission insisted that they wanted to attain and maintain Less Eligibility, a quest that Edwin Chadwick alluded to in 1837, when he stated that 'the Commissioners wished to make no distinction between a pauper child's education, and [that of] an independent labourer's child'.[23] The benefits of workhouse education to the Poor Law Central Authority, in terms of the resultant compliance of inmate pauper children, clearly outweighed the erosion of the basic principles of Poor Law administration and indeed the Bishop of London, a self-appointed expert on such matters, also approved of these effects. He stated in 1834 that, 'improvement had taken place, where education has been imparted to the labouring classes' and he cited evidence from the 1832 Poor Law Inquiry in his support. He suggested that 'the superiority of the educated over the uneducated labourer', who he said were 'most dangerous',[24] was well illustrated by comparing workmen from Stockport and Oldham. He concluded that the rate of instruction in the elementary schools determined the quality of these workers. Educated and literate paupers were seen by the Bishop as less threatening than their illiterate contemporaries, so that education for pauper children was obviously desirable.

The poor state of some elementary education was well demonstrated by school inspection after 1839, which revealed that many elementary schools, where they existed, were in a worse state than schools in workhouses. Thus, many Poor Law schools were superior to those provided for non-paupers outside workhouses and this was regarded as desirable, even though it made pauper children more eligible than their non-pauper contemporaries. One of the Assistant Poor Law Commissioners, Edward Gulson, was so certain of the efficacy of workhouse education that he suggested that the instruction given would 'enable them [pauper children] to provide for themselves independently'.[25] However, the estimated 40 per cent of workhouse school pupils who were transient did cause problems. Indeed, this was the case at Tenbury Wells workhouse in 1851, where 61.1 per cent of the child inmates were 'ins and outs', the largest proportion of transient child inmates anywhere in England, who caused persistent problems throughout the period from 1834 to 1871. Such children were clearly relatively unaffected by the short periods of workhouse education they received.

The relative ineffectiveness of workhouse education for short-stay inmate children was recognised by the Newcastle Commission Report in 1861, which criticised the mixing of transient pupils with the more permanent ones, which was said to be a 'fatal error', because such children 'bring in with them evil enough to undo all the good that the teachers have been labouring to instil into their scholars'.[26] This effect was recognised by teachers and one schoolmistress was so depressed that she 'felt she was training up girls for a life of vice and depravity'. This claim was countered by an Assistant Poor Law Commissioner, Robert Weale, who suggested that children outside workhouses were 'subject to the worst external influences', so that they 'formed[ed] a most dangerous class to be let loose among orphan and deserted children'.[27] In this circumstance, the rehabilitation – or rescue – of such transient children as well as their long-stay contemporaries was vital, which was a priority that outweighed the violation of the Principle of Less Eligibility. Indeed in 1836, the Poor Law Commission suggested that children were to be treated as a 'special case' to whom the normal tenets of Poor Law administration need not be applied.[28]

The opinions of James P. Kay, who was initially active in administering the New Poor Law and who became the leading administrator for elementary education in the mid-nineteenth century, were revealing. In 1838 he wanted to 'combine sound religious education with a careful industrial training, and such an amount of secular instruction, as shall invigorate the children, and thereby increase their chances of maintaining themselves in after life',[29] because he saw this as 'securing the cessation of their dependence, by elevating their moral condition'.[30] This, he thought, would ameliorate the children's condition by raising 'the moral and intellectual atmosphere of the workhouse to the highest pitch'.[31] This was in spite of the fact that the Principle of Less Eligibility,[32] a major theoretical underpinning of the New Poor Law, was infringed by doing this. This opinion, supporting workhouse schools, was shared by many of the other Assistant Poor Law Commissioners, who had been selected because of their adherence to the utilitarian principles of the New Poor Law. Thus, one of these workhouse inspectors, Edward Gulson, argued in favour of giving advantages to pauper children because, 'that evil is very much less than the evil of allowing children to be brought up in such a way that they must remain paupers',[33] but the implementation of these principles was inevitably problematical. Basically, the workhouse was seen as an unsuitable environment for children. For these reasons, Kay saw the workhouse school 'presenting . . . formidable difficulties',[34] because while the education offered in workhouses was, according to a contemporary opinion, 'sufficient and satisfactory . . . they [the pauper children] are always taught to read, and generally to write; in most cases they are taught a little ciphering, and in general . . . the girls to sew and knit; and a variety of employment for the boys'.[35] This education took place in the uninspiring claustrophobic atmosphere of the workhouse, which was regarded by most commentators as a damaging environment for a child.

In many unions attempts were made to compensate for the uninspiring atmosphere of the general workhouse in an effort to improve matters and religion was seen as important in this respect. This led the chaplain at Kidderminster, in 1839, to state that 'suitable prayers are read at the commencement and termination of school hours' and 'the children have made considerable progress in reading, and most often can say the catechism and can answer questions from it. They are learning the parables, and can answer questions from those they know tolerably well.'[36] Here the religious curriculum was clearly seen as having a beneficial effect, but writing was not taught, so that accusations that workhouse children were indoctrinated rather than educated may be sustainable. Elsewhere, there was disagreement about teaching writing to the lower orders, so that George Bartley in his book *The People's Schools*, suggested retrospectively that 'such skills might make the young restless, or facilitate forgeries'.[37] By the time the 1895 edition of his book was published, he had removed this reference, presumably because it now sounded anachronistic. In fact, Gertrude Himmelfarb in her book *The Idea of Poverty*, has suggested that religious education formed a major part of the nineteenth-century workhouse school curriculum, which she saw as an 'imposed morality' produced in the closed atmosphere of the total institution, which inculcated this middle-class morality.

An Act of Parliament of 1828 repealed the Test Acts and stipulated that a child was not to be educated in any school in a creed other than that of his parents, or if orphaned in a creed 'to which his godparents may object'[38] – this requirement was included in the 1834 Poor Law Amendment Act. Thus, Anglicanism came to dominate workhouses, but in spite of their overt religious atmosphere, they were still considered no place for children, as they were thought to manufacture paupers. Even more importantly, it was said 'there is no provision for any exercise or mental facility',[39] as the child's workhouse timetable left little time for even the youngest child to play. In spite of this, Assistant Commissioner Hall still suggested[40] that a garden for play was necessary in all workhouses, even though in most institutions, not even a yard was provided. However, this may not have been so in all parts of England and Wales, because while Kay did suggest that pauper children gained exercise from work, he thought that there should be facilities for 'gymnastic exercise' on a 'circular swing',[41] which had apparently been provided in Norfolk workhouses. In a few other places children were allowed to leave the workhouse for exercise, although according to Assistant Poor Law Commissioner Edward Gulson,[42] in most cases there was a total lack of facilities for incarcerated children to use for exercise. In spite of such adverse comments, contemporary opinion was that workhouse children were 'healthy, decidedly so'.[43]

From the evidence available, it appeared that Poor Law education was in a satisfactory state, an opinion canvassed by Edwin Chadwick who asked the Assistant Poor Law Commissioners, in the 1840s, to respond to a questionnaire, 'at as early a period as may suffice for the collection of accurate information' about the state of the workhouse schools. [44] The issues raised were:

1. The state of pauper education prior to the passing of the Poor Law Amendment Act.
2. Improvements that had been introduced into the pauper schools since the passing of the Poor Law Amendment Act.
3. The further improvements that might be introduced into pauper schools, and the obstacles to further improvement.

What was unclear in the responses to the questionnaire was how these issues were to be answered. Indeed, this was a matter of conjecture, as no detailed knowledge of the education in workhouse schools prior to 1834 existed and thus any retrospective analysis was extremely suspect.

The intellectual diet offered in workhouses was severely limited and must have been unsatisfying to many children, but in part this inadequacy was worsened by the relative youth and inexperience of the workhouse schoolteachers, a deficiency that made improvement difficult, because there were no adequate teachers available to take the place of the inadequate ones already in the workhouse schools. However, there was another restraint on progress in that the Bible, the Prayer Book and various religious tracts were usually the only reading material available, although this situation was gradually to change. At Kidderminster union in July 1845, one pound was spent on 'a few books of instructive, moral and amusing character',[45] but even here the choice of books was still the chaplain's and it was probably religious books that were purchased. After 1844, HMI reduced the chaplain's influence in this respect by recommending books and refusing to pay the government grant until HMI's official suggestions were implemented, thus creating the first opportunity for non-scriptural books to be regularly introduced into workhouse schools.

The Poor Law central administration continually interfered with workhouse education, which they clearly regarded as too important to be left to local Guardians, who could not be trusted to implement central policy. Thus the Poor Law Commission decided in 1835, that, children were to be given 'such other instructions . . . as are calculated to train them to habits of usefulness and virtue',[46] a decision they amplified in 1838 by stating the purpose of workhouse education was to fit 'the children for obtaining the situation of independent labourers and performing their duties in after life'.[47] But in spite of such decisions made by the Central Poor Law Authority, there was no consensus about workhouse education among Boards of Guardians, whose members were sometimes in continual disagreement with one another about this matter.

Attitudes to workhouse education differed and this provided a marked contrast between Guardians representing rural as opposed to urban parishes. The Select Committee of 1838 recognised this, when they referred to 'farmers . . . not aware of the necessity of education',[48] who refused to increase the teacher's salary to attract able teachers. Indeed, according to S.E. Finer, Edwin Chadwick went further, suggesting that rural Guardians resisted such expenditure, as they did not appreciate the importance of education, having received little instruction themselves,[49] but Robert Weale, the Assistant Poor Law Commissioner for Worcestershire, did not fully agree with this opinion. He suggested, in 1837, that county Guardians would support workhouse schooling if they were certain of the sort of education that was necessary, although Robert Weale himself was far from certain about this matter. He later expressed the opinion that some workhouse education violated the Principle of Less Eligibility, a matter that was further complicated, because 'the education of the peasantry and the lower order of artisans . . . is in such a degraded state, that it is impossible to devise a system for a workhouse which will not be more attractive and useful'.[50] However, he was certain that children should be taught a trade and he insisted that such education must be in a workhouse school.

The Newcastle Royal Commission agreed with the Poor Law Central Authority about Guardians' attitudes. They commented that 'in all but the largest towns . . . [Guardians] . . . are taken from a class generally indifferent to education, often hostile to it'.[51] Thus, the ambivalence of some Guardians was explicable, because while some unions were composed exclusively of urban parishes, or exclusively of rural ones, where Guardians agreed about education, others consisted of a mixture of urban and rural parishes, where a consensus was impossible. For instance, at Pershore in 1839, the visiting committee there proposed that 'a quantity of pens, ink, paper and other necessary articles' to teach writing be purchased. However, the whole Board of Guardians changed this decision when they met, because the consensus was that 'it is quite unnecessary to teach the children in the union workhouse the accomplishment of writing'.[52] The visiting committee, which was composed of individuals who lived in the urban area close to this workhouse, was untypical, whereas the majority of Guardians were from more distant rural parishes and they opposed writing being taught. Ironically, the 1844 Parish Apprentices Act soon overturned this decision, because this legislation required that pauper apprentices be able 'to read and write their own names unaided'.[53] Thus, the

Pershore Guardians' attention was drawn to the need for writing to be taught and they ordered the teaching of writing in 1845.[54]

Of the county Poor Law unions, only Martley gained national renown for its stand on workhouse education. The Guardians there decided to resist the Poor Law Commission's many demands to teach writing and by doing this they broke the Law, which initially led to disciplinary action against the workhouse master, who was appointed in 1843.[55] His appointment had been in spite of Poor Law Commission disquiet, as at this time he was described as 'insolvent' and thus not officially eligible for the post. Indeed, such concerns continued and later, he was charged with inefficiency, but the chairman of the Guardians defended him at the enquiry, where the matter of workhouse education was discussed. Ironically this enquiry was minuted and the opinions expressed were open to public scrutiny, so that it emerged that while there had been schoolmistresses employed at Martley workhouse since 1839,[56] none of them had stayed long and indeed two women had resigned during 1845, after which time the school was left unattended for almost a year. It also appeared that while education was initially neglected by default, rather than by intent, the Guardians became reluctant to appoint another workhouse schoolmistress. They decided instead to cease teaching writing, a decision they justified to the Poor Law Commission, because 'pauper child inmates of the workhouse received as good an education as that generally given in the country and they do not feel themselves justified in going to any expense whereby they [inmate pauper children] might receive advantages that are not attainable by the children of those who support their families without parochial relief'.[57] These reasons were regarded as 'insufficient' by the Poor Law Commission, who threatened the Guardians with a writ of mandamus. Clearly, a precedent resisting the teaching of writing was not to be allowed at any cost. The Poor Law Central Authority now stated that the children 'ought to receive such an amount of instruction as will fit them for good situations in after life',[58] a desire that the lack of instruction in writing, arithmetic and reading put at risk, particularly as the reading taught at Martley was said to have been 'totally scriptural'. The Poor Law Commission again demanded that a schoolmaster be appointed, which ran contrary to an order, made in 1837,[59] that small unions need only appoint a schoolmaster, or a schoolmistress, but not both. It thus appeared that the Commission wished to make an example of this recalcitrant union, as they now accused the Guardians of having 'both boys and girls under the care of the schoolmistress' and they demanded that an 'efficient schoolmaster' be appointed contrary to their own rules and regulations. However, in spite of this, the Guardians still refused to appoint a schoolmaster,[60] but the Assistant Poor Law Commissioner Edward Gulson, persisted by insisting that 'a well qualified schoolmaster's appointment should be enforced',[61] because he was still 'far from satisfied with the state of the house or school'.

The Guardians were clearly concerned about this official displeasure, because they did appoint a new schoolmistress and she began to teach writing, but when the Assistant Poor Law Commissioner revisited, some seven months later, he reported: 'I found no improvement in arrangements had been effected by the Guardians for the education of children in the school.' At this time he cited the case of a girl, aged sixteen years, who had been an inmate of the workhouse for six and a half years, who he described as 'nice looking' and 'intelligent', but when offered for apprenticing she 'did not know how to write a word; nor does she know the use of a single figure',[62] which made her officially ineligible for apprenticing. The inspector also stated that other children were in a similar state, but the chairman of the Guardians still insisted that the workhouse education offered was 'sufficient'. Nevertheless, Assistant Commissioner Gulson stated in a marginal comment on the minutes,[63] that he had the support of a clergyman, an ex-officio Guardian, who was possibly the chaplain.

The new schoolmistress was clearly seen by the Central Poor Law Authority as a welcome development and she was allowed to stay, but they still demanded a schoolmaster in addition and it was suggested that if one was not appointed the Guardians would be issued with a 'special order', which would also mean that the government grant would be withheld. This certainly perturbed the Guardians, but still they resolved to leave the matter for further consideration. This prevarication lasted over a month, but they eventually again refused to comply,[64] possibly because they thought that a delay would mean that the Poor Law Board, the successor organisation to the Commission, would be in existence and that they would interpret the rules in Martley union's favour. They were mistaken in this belief, as there was continuity in official thinking and indeed Assistant Poor Law Commissioner Gulson appended another note to the minutes.[65] He was clearly losing patience, because he demanded that a 'special order' be issued compelling the appointment of a schoolmaster. The Guardians still refused to comply, but this time their concern was even greater, because they stated that they would only allow educational change if they were ordered to do so. Whilst Assistant Poor

Law Commissioner Gulson clearly wanted a direct order to be issued,[66] the matter was still left in abeyance. The constant pressure from the central authority began to have an effect on Martley Guardians, because they now offered to appoint another schoolmistress to replace the existing one, who they said was 'temporary',[67] although she had been in office twenty months, with her appointment sanctioned in the normal way as a 'permanent appointment'[68] and she had satisfactorily completed a three month trial. In this case, the Guardians pressure was grossly unfair, but it clearly affected her, because she resigned.[69] Even now the Guardians were adamant that they would neither appoint a schoolmaster nor teach writing or arithmetic. They appointed another schoolmistress early in 1847, but HMI almost immediately commented that this schoolmistress refused to teach writing, because 'she is probably supposing that she is acting in accordance with the members of the Board'.[70] He again asked that the Guardians be ordered to comply with the Poor Law Board's directive, suggesting that there was some support among the Guardians for educational changes and he reported: 'A clergyman expressed to me a strong desire that such an order be sent.'[71] Instead, the Poor Law Board withheld the schoolmistress's salary, apparently preferring an oblique approach, placing the defenceless schoolmistress in an untenable position, to a direct confrontation with the Guardians.

The central authority now drew the schoolmistress's attention to the provisions of the Poor Law Amendment Act regarding education, but also to the legal penalties she faced if she ignored regulations and the Guardians were also informed of this.[72] These warnings clearly caused concern, but still the Guardians were unwilling to relent, which led the Poor Law Board to state, in July 1848, that the Board of Guardians have no discretion in interpreting the Law. It was said that the original intention of pauper education was to reduce reliance on 'eleemosynary relief'[73] and that children in workhouses were not blameworthy for their own plight. This was a principle considered important enough to be repeated in a letter to the Privy Council Committee on Education. This pressure was to no avail as, in July 1848,[74] HMI still reported that the Guardians had again ordered the schoolmistress not to teach writing or arithmetic, but in spite of this he was able to assert that her efficiency had improved. He clearly thought that the Guardians were to blame for the unsatisfactory situation and felt able to issue a 'certificate of probation'. However, the Guardians now denied that they had forbidden writing and arithmetic to be taught,[75] stating that they had 'only refused to give her [the schoolmistress] facilities' to teach these skills. They further suggested that the fault was hers, which was a questionable assertion that marked the Guardians' capitulation over workhouse education, as they now agreed that writing and arithmetic would be taught at the workhouse school in future.

The Poor Law Board had gained compliance after this long wrangle over workhouse education, but their approach of applying pressure on a defenceless and innocent employee, instead of using a special order to compel the Guardians to comply with the regulations, was worrying and revealing. The central administration were clearly satisfied with this strategy and the principle underlying their concerns was considered so important that the case was publicised in the *Official Circular*, without Martley union being named.[76] In spite of this, the Guardians wrote to the Poor Law Board[77] asking why their correspondence had been publicised and they received this reply: 'It was done to demonstrate the Poor Law Board's thinking on the matter.'[78] Obviously, Martley union was to provide a cautionary example for other unions, so that when the Annual Report of 1850 revealed an apparently similar situation to that at Martley, in Upton upon Severn, where it was said: 'There are about 30 children (boys and girls) in the school who were not taught to read and write or to understand the nature of figures though (when I visited) some of them were 12 or 14 years old',[79] it was the schoolmistress who was immediately blamed for these circumstances. This was in spite of a suspicion that the Guardians did not want these basic skills taught. This teacher was said to be 'unable to cope' and was speedily replaced.

It appeared to be the personal opinions of Guardians about the value of the education of pauper children that influenced their readiness to create schools in workhouses. Thus, the tardiness of Worcestershire unions to provide workhouse education was arguably because only a minority of county Guardians wholly agreed with the opinion, held by the Poor Law Commission, that workhouse education had a curative influence over mendicancy, while many others were very sceptical about such claims. This meant that even by the late 1830s and early 1840s some Boards of Guardians maintained the Principle of Less Eligibility at all costs, because they believed implicitly in the Benthamite ideology underpinning the New Law, although this orthodoxy inevitably led them to infringe other major tenets of Poor Law administration – particularly the Principle of National Uniformity. These basic principles of administration now proved impossible to maintain, even in the most fundamentalist unions.

Martley was the most orthodox of county unions, as indicated by its dogged resistance to teaching writing. While its resistance to this innovation was unique, the opinions of the Martley Guardians were probably held by a sizeable minority of Guardians in most Worcestershire unions. However, this was the only real resistance in Worcestershire to the abandonment of the utilitarian principles of Poor Law administration for children before 1847, when the Poor Law Commission was replaced by the Poor Law Board. It now appeared that it was vociferous and socially influential Guardians, with high personal status, who gathered a caucus of support around them and dominated Board meetings. Thus, it was the views of these men that were conveyed to the Poor Law Commission in the minutes of meetings and any minority view – expressed in Guardians' meetings – remained masked, so that Boards of Guardians' minutes invariably only represented dominant sectional interests.

Workhouse education in Worcestershire was not provided uniformly, in spite of the Principle of National Uniformity. What was provided depended on the whim and fancy of the Guardians. By 1836,[80] while schooling was theoretically for a minimum of three hours per day, many schools met for much less time. In many cases, it was contemporaneously suggested that 'reading writing and the principles of the Christian religion' were taught, together with instruction 'calculated to train them (the children) in the habits of usefulness, industry and virtue', although this decision appeared unpopular with some unions, particularly where parishes were tardy to form a Poor Law union, which was generally a problem in the north of England. Pershore, Shipston on Stour, Stourbridge and Worcester unions operated workhouse schools from as early as 1836,[81] although some of them were in very unsuitable premises. Kidderminster Guardians began to provide workhouse education in 1837, but there was no schoolroom in the children's section of the workhouse there,[82] although the problems created must have been pressing, because one was built by 1838,[83] with additional furniture added later.

Of the county's Poor Law unions Worcester's was unique, as it had been formed under Gilbert's Act in 1782, when it had built and opened a house of industry. Thus by 1848, this union had a sixty-five year tradition of providing education to paupers, when HMI told the Worcester Guardians that it was 'the desire of the Government to secure for the pauper children sound and useful education together, with such moral and industrial training as may prepare them for a course of honest industry and independent livelihood in after life'.[84] Whilst, arguably, this was Worcester Guardians' intention from the outset, in 1782 the inspector thought it necessary to state that: 'In some unions the education of pauper children had gained great excellence.'[85] He clearly believed that the education provided by such unions was often superior to that offered to the children of independent labourers, so that many long-term indoor pauper children were more eligible regarding education than their non-pauper contemporaries.

It was this same preoccupation with the education of pauper children that led W.E. Hickson,[86] a self-professed expert on the Poor Laws, to suggest that education and training 'are absolutely essential to the final extinction of pauperism in this country'. This was in 1836, two years after the passing of the Poor Law Amendment Act, when Hickson believed that the education received in workhouses was still 'merely nominal',[87] so that the notion of workhouse education as a cure for pauperism was questionable. Instead, it was regarded merely as a preventative measure, for crime as well as pauperism. This, Hickson believed, meant that the Poor Law Commissioners were responsible for 'whether 100,000 children at least, shall be raised to the ranks of moral intelligent beings, or remain all their lives the pariahs of English Society – a burthen and a disgrace to the community'. Implicitly, Hickson rejected the idea that the Principle of Less Eligibility should prevent pauper children from being supplied with education, because it was only orphaned and deserted children who were found alone in the workhouse, which meant that it was impossible for parents to gain education for their children without making their whole family dependent on the parish. This they were reluctant to do, which thus ensured little abuse of the system. This meant that Hickson had demonstrated that workhouses were merely asylums for orphaned and deserted children, that were totally inappropriate for this purpose. The workhouse was seen as 'a contaminated environment' in which a pauper child would spend five or ten years of their early life, so that separate children's establishments were essential, which was an analysis with which the Newcastle Royal Commission agreed.[88]

There were many critics of the workhouse schools, including a group of 'voluntary helpers' influenced by Louisa Twining, who was regarded by many as an expert on workhouse children and workhouse education. Such people founded the Workhouse Visiting Society, an offshoot of the National Association for the Promotion of Social Science, in 1858. This society, which only operated until 1865, coordinated workhouse visiting by laymen, and particularly laywomen, but its influence became great, partly because of its journal,[89] which contained extremely paternalistic articles, most with a very particular view of the plight of the workhouse child. It was this work that led Elizabeth Twining, Louisa's sister, to give evidence on workhouse education to the Newcastle Royal Commission, in which she asserted that such children were 'unfit for any kind of service', at an age when children outside the workhouse were fit for such work. Thus, such children were often returned to the workhouse as unsuitable, because of 'a want of life and action, a want of internal inspection and visitation by voluntary friends; a want of devoted zeal and love of teachers; a want of family life and care'. This caused her to also question the worth of intellectual education to such children,[90] about whom Miss Twining claimed to know so much. Such so-called experts, like the Misses Twining, who doubted the insight of others, including the Poor Law professionals, prescribed paternalistic remedies for the workhouse schools. These usually involved making 'an appointment of a superior class of person' to oversee each school. However, by 1858, Poor Law Board staff had become more professional and exhibited more skill and expertise in their work, so much so that they saw the intervention of the experts of the Workhouse Visiting Society as unhelpful and unwelcome. Thus, one Assistant Poor Law Commissioner, Sir John Walsham, believed that Miss Louisa Twining 'manifested her repugnance for workhouse establishments', a distaste that 'appears . . . to pervade and colour all her evidence'[91] which he claimed was not supported by facts. Another of the Assistant Poor Law Commissioners, Robert Weale, the man with responsibility for the Worcestershire unions, went on to indicate that there was 'conclusive evidence that the statements of Miss Louisa Twining . . . [and Mr Patrick Cumin] . . . so far as my district is concerned are unfounded'.[92] This caused a debate about this issue to begin.

The perceived need for schools where pauper children could be dealt with within a separate institution from their adult contemporaries, who were seen as dangerous and likely to infect youngsters with mendicancy, led to discussions of the district school idea. This type of institution was first discussed by the Select Committee on the Working of the Poor Law Amendment Act in 1838, when it was suggested that: 'The strict confinement of children in the workhouse would be likely to prove injurious to their health . . . and if district schools, to which they shall have presently occasion to allude should be generally established all difficulties on this point would be removed.'[93] Six years later in 1844, an Act of Parliament[94] allowed separate schools to be formed, but not specifically district schools. While Parliament saw this scheme as potentially a vast improvement in Poor Law education, it was not welcomed by the Poor Law Commission, who were made responsible for funding such institutions.[95] Under the 1844 Act, unions within a fifteen mile radius could combine forming school districts, to be funded with up to 20 per cent of the combined Poor Rates.

Separate schools were to be large, with each containing between 800 and 1,000 children, so that they were only viable in more populous areas. Worcestershire had no such areas and therefore no separate schools were formed, but in spite of this, discussions did continue about the idea of separate schools. The industrial school, which taught industrial trades, was the most favoured type of separate school, with both the Poor Law Commission and HMI, so that Jellinger C. Symons, the workhouse schools' inspector responsible for Worcestershire, wrote a pamphlet in 1848, strongly supporting such schools.[96] However, even his influence could not persuade the county's Boards of Guardians that such schools were practicable within Worcestershire.

It was ironical that such discussions appeared to hamper the development of individual workhouse schools, because at Bromsgrove in 1838, when there was a vacancy for a schoolmaster, the Assistant Poor Law Commissioner was 'not at present disposed to appoint a schoolmaster and would wish to learn the intentions of the Government regards the establishment of industrial schools before expressing an opinion'.[97] In spite of this, the Guardians proceeded to appoint a schoolmaster, but HMI persisted in his doubts whether a teacher was essential, as the 'boys were too young for industrial training'.[98] This sort of opinion remained and as late as 1851 at Pershore union, it was said 'the smallness of the numbers make it likely that the children will be removed elsewhere'.[99] On this occasion, they were recommended to go to the local National Society school and not to an industrial school.[100] They commenced attendance at the National school in 1852,[101] which was coincidental with the death of the workhouse schoolmistress. The issue of separate schools was not resolved, because Assistant Commissioner Edward Gulson told the Poor Law Board, in 1854, that there was no district school in the county,[102] and he repeated this comment in 1855.[103] He mentioned it again in the Poor Law Board Annual Report in 1857[104] when he reported no progress in establishing district schools.

The only possibility of founding such schools in a rural county, like Worcestershire, was by adopting the suggestion that such schools should be open to outdoor pauper children and indeed to some non-pauper pupils as well.[105] However, Assistant Poor Law Commissioner Gulson, among others, saw such an arrangement as potentially causing harm to the inmate child by introducing infections both moral and physical. Even more importantly, it was thought that this arrangement would make the non-pauper child more liable to be pauperised in after life, an eventuality that could not be countenanced. For such reasons, the idea was not mentioned again in the county and no local county Poor Law authority proceeded with plans for district schools on this basis. Indeed, comments by an official at Upton upon Severn union, cited by S.P. Oberman,[106] may have been pertinent to this decision. He suggested that Catholic parents would resist sending their children to separate schools, open to non-paupers, because they believed that proselytism would occur. At about the same time, Assistant Commissioner Gulson also responded without enthusiasm to the idea of opening such schools, even to children in receipt of outdoor relief. However, when Kidderminster workhouse school was 'overcrowded and unsatisfactory'[107] in 1857, the HMI blamed the schoolmistress for this situation and she was charged with neglect, while he also attempted to promote an industrial school. He thought that the removal of all children under five years old into an infant school would enable the existing school to be transformed into an industrial school.[108] Although the Kidderminster Guardians to some extent agreed with this assessment, they also blamed the schoolmistress for some of the inadequacies in the school, so that she was forced to resign. Therefore in spite of the tacit support of a small group of Guardians, the idea of a separate school was never adopted.

In spite of a reduced emphasis on the endemic nature of pauperism among both experts and laypeople from the 1840s onwards, the Poor Law Board, which was created in 1847, continued to have a preoccupation with the deleterious effects of child inmates associating with adult paupers. Thus in 1849 they stated that two-thirds of workhouses were defective because of imperfect separation of the classes of paupers and pressure for complete separation continued. These demands were accentuated as the size of the indoor child-pauper population grew. In these circumstances, separate schools remained the preferred solution to this problem but there were some experts who demurred from this opinion. George Coode, assistant secretary to the Central Poor Law Authority, stated in 1849 that he would 'be much more inclined to recommend separate establishments for this degraded class (able-bodied adults) than I should separate establishments for children',[109] so that he suggested the logical approach of removing the cause of the contamination. However, this apparently sensible idea was not seriously investigated. The debate about separate schools continued and in 1858

163

evidence to the Newcastle Royal Commission again commented unfavourably on the standard of education in workhouse schools.[110] This gave Nassau Senior, the classical economist and government adviser on the Poor Laws, an opportunity to insist that separate institutions for children were essential. Despite advice from such an influential source, Worcestershire Guardians, like those in most other rural unions, resisted establishing such institutions on financial grounds, using the fact that it would militate against Less Eligibility as a justification. Although pauper children in the mid-nineteenth century generally came to be regarded as blameless for their plight, historians of this period of Poor Law administration, such as Sidney and Beatrice Webb, writing in the early twentieth century long after these events, suggested that such children were unworthy individuals of 'small social value'.[111] This, they suggested, was the reason why separate children's institutions were of such low priority for Guardians, but of such high priority for central Poor Law administrators. It does appear more likely that Worcestershire Guardians' failure to build separate schools was because of insufficient pauper children in the area, rather than because of the perceived social worth of the clientele of these institutions. The Poor Law Board were unabashed by such opinions and in 1861 they suggested that: 'Although some difficulties may occasionally arise in the management of separate establishments for children their maintenance and education in schools removed from the association of the workhouse are so manifestly advantageous, that it appears highly desirable to promote the foundation of such schools in all practicable cases.' However, George Coode, who retired as secretary of the Poor Law Board in 1848, still disagreed. He believed that enforcing the building of separate schools would 'take away from the Guardians, who represented the poor-rate payers, their right to determine whether a certain enormous expenditure shall or shall not be incurred', which he thought was 'virtual despotism'.[112]

George Coode had calculated the total cost of a scheme for separate schools for pauper children as £10,357, 960 and he was very critical of this cost. He clearly believed that a 'very lofty standard . . . completely inapplicable to the condition of life of very poor children' had been used in assessing workhouse schools, which had therefore been shown to be worse than they were. The standards obtained from normal workhouse education was, he thought, completely appropriate to the needs of pauper youngsters, whereas the expectations of education for pauper children in separate schools were unrealistic. This opinion was bolstered by another belief, that children in workhouses were not as liable to contact evil as they 'would be if they were at large in their own homes'[113] and indeed Coode thought: 'They were not subjected [in the workhouse] to the same amount of moral contamination as the poor generally.'[114] Thus, he thought, the Privy Council Committee on Education's expectations of elementary education were too high, so that he fully supported Guardians who, 'are willing to provide for such (children) a humble plain education as fits them to serve in their locality, but have no inclination to educate paupers' children so much above their own'.[115] These opinions were shared by a fair proportion of Guardians, including many in Worcestershire, and indeed some Assistant Poor Law Commissioners, probably in unguarded moments, admitted support for workhouse schools. These opinions, however, had little impact on the three Poor Law Commissioners, on Poor Law Board officials, and on influential politicians. Amongst these people the idea of separate schools for pauper children continued to be attractive, probably indicating the perceived continuing threat of the more populous areas of England and Wales, where separate schools were practicable.

Generally, the education offered in rural workhouses in the country as a whole, was regarded as 'exceeding in solid useful plain excellence that of the average school under the control of the Privy Council',[116] which caused some people to question whether this break with the Principle of Less Eligibility was appropriate. This feeling about the standard of workhouse education on offer was certainly accepted in Worcestershire, but it was also accepted by some Central Poor Law Authority's officials, all of whom clearly favoured enhanced educational opportunity for workhouse children, although they did not always support separate schools, which was the system of pauper education favoured by the Poor Law Board. Thus, Assistant Poor Law Commissioner Edward Gulson, one of the county's inspectors of workhouses, applauded the Poor Law Board's decision, made in 1863, not to 'coerce Guardians'[117] into accepting district schools. He believed that the improvement in workhouse schools, already achieved, had been underrated, while the superiority of other schools over those in workhouses had been exaggerated. He later reacted very strongly to what he regarded as the 'palliatives' recommended by the Privy Council Committee on Education, as a solution of what they saw as 'inadequacies' in workhouse schooling. These criticisms followed the Newcastle Royal Commission, which Gulson thought had unjustly castigated the standard of workhouse schooling. He was particularly upset by the suggestion that the 'Revised Code' of 1861, which he regarded as inappropriate to the needs of workhouse schools, should be uncritically applied, simply to bring the Poor Law schools in line with elementary education outside the workhouses.

In spite of the opposition of its officers in the field, the Poor Law Board continued to attempt to promote the idea of district schools. In 1866, an Act of Parliament allowed 'the cost of sending and keeping a child at [district] schools'[118] to be paid, providing costs were no greater than a workhouse school. A questionnaire was issued by the Poor Law Board at this time, which raised the following:

1. Whether in the event of a school for girls being established in the county under the Act on the principles and under the management of which they could approve, they will be likely to send occasionally suitable girls from their workhouse lists.
2. About how many in the course of a year they might send.
3. The actual cost as charged to the parish of a girl in your workhouse.[119]

However, Kidderminster union, one of the most populous and urban unions in the county, was swift to reply to this enquiry. They stated that 'this Board believes that the female children in the workhouse . . . receive therein a sufficiently moral, religious, industrial and useful education from the schoolmistress',[120] so that they were satisfied with the education offered to the girls. Sixty-one girls had left Kidderminster workhouse, aged between two and sixteen years, between June 1863 and January 1865. They went 'to situations of various kinds' and only one female had returned to the workhouse, for an undisclosed reason probably known to the Guardians, but which went unrecorded in the minutes. These Guardians were thus able to claim that while they approved of the principle of a district school, they could not pledge themselves to use such an institution,[121] which was apparently the case in all county unions, although the reasons for opposing such an institution certainly differed. The district school idea was rejected by all county unions.

In spite of their complacency, Kidderminster union determined in 1849 to do something about child paupers in the union. It attempted to persuade Bridgnorth union to take orphan boys into Quatt industrial school, a unique profit-making agricultural training school founded by Mr Wycliffe Wilson at Quatford, mid-way between Bridgnorth and Kidderminster.[122] Droitwich Guardians made a similar approach about a year later,[123] but both requests were unsuccessful, although Stourbridge Guardians applied successfully to send boys to the Quatt school in 1862.[124] On this occasion thirty-two orphan boys were sent, although the number fell steadily as boys gained employment. This agreement was not renewed after 1866.[125]

Most Assistant Poor Law Commissioners, like Edward Gulson, condemned the Newcastle Royal Commission Report's conclusion that overtly promoted the idea of separate schools for pauper children on the basis of their advocacy by people like the Misses Twining, self-appointed experts on the treatment of Poor Law children. This indignation was typical of the Assistant Poor Law Commissioners, so that another inspector, W.H.T. Hawley, described conclusions based on such evidence as 'ignorant of and indifferent to the evidence of the Poor Law Board' and guilty of '. . . rejecting the testimony of practical and influential witnesses'.[126] He also suggested that the evidence of 'partial' witnesses unreasonably meant that: 'Parliament is called upon to suppress all existing workhouse schools, as being nurseries of crime and vice, and to substitute for them an enormously expensive system of centralised compulsory education.' Thus, the education offered in workhouses provided a 'quality of mental instruction . . . [of] . . . too high a standard for the condition of life of the children to whom it applied', which made the workhouse 'children of quicker intellect . . . aspire to a position of life far beyond the sphere in which their lot is cast',[127] whereas children of lesser ability 'forgot all with which they have been crammed as soon as they quit school'. The opinions of men like Assistant Commissioner, Sir John Walsham, had favoured district schools before the advent of the Poor Law Board in 1847, at a time when 'the workhouse schools were more or less open to criticism'. However, by the 1860s he had changed his mind, as the workhouse schools had considerably improved. By 1861, at the time when the Newcastle Royal Commission was so critical of individual workhouse schools, he had decided to support such individual institutions.[128] He stated: 'I (now) dissent entirely from that sweeping condemnation of the moral and intellectual results effected by the workhouse schools.'[129]

Another of the Assistant Poor Law Commissioners, Andrew Doyle, agreed that the Newcastle Royal Commission Report was biased. He suggested that 'the inquiry as conducted . . . was unfairly restricted; that the evidence invited was partial; [and] that the evidence is not even impartially presented in the report'[130] and '[the] attempt was not even made to ascertain the facts one way or the other'.[131] The Report was also said to resurrect old evidence. For instance there was a letter from Nassau Senior, written in 1850, from which, according to Edward

Doyle, 'large passages had been omitted'.[132] There was also a critical letter, written in 1851 to one of the Poor Law Commissioners, E.C. Tufnell, by an ex-workhouse inmate who had complained about the condition of workhouse schools. The contemporary opinion was that this was because of 'a lack of better evidence',[133] so that the Newcastle Royal Commission had as one of its predetermined purposes the discrediting of workhouse education. This conclusion appeared to be likely as the anti-workhouse school lobby, which consisted of socially influential people, was certainly in the ascendancy.

The HMI for workhouse schools, Thomas B. Browne, summed up most Poor Law officials' opinions on this matter later in 1861, when he gave evidence to the Select Committee, arguably set up to balance the Report of the Newcastle Royal Commission. He stated: 'I have long felt that good schools are quite practicable in well-managed workhouses . . . and there is no doubt that many children have left such schools, who have turned out well.'[134] By 1860, most Poor Law officials had changed their earlier opinions in support of separate schools and they now favoured individual workhouse schools. They clearly saw the whole tenor of the Newcastle Royal Commission's questioning as biased, as was its choice of witnesses, their response to evidence and the style of their final report. Such central officials now believed that the aim of neutralising the contamination of pauper children by adult mendicants, which was so strongly supported by the Workhouse Visiting Society, was impossible and that separate schools were not the way forward. This favoured solution among Poor Law amateur helpers was said by them to provide 'better education for less expenditure'. However, in 1862, E.C. Tufnell cited a cost of £23 18s 6d per annum for maintaining a child in a district school,[135] a sum that compared very unfavourably with the £2 13s 2d per annum cited in 1857. In spite of this huge unexplained discrepancy in estimated costs, any expenditure on separate schools continued to be seen as worthwhile, so that enthusiastic proponents of these relatively untried institutions claimed that they were superior to individual workhouse schools, no matter what the cost. Thomas B. Browne, the HMI for Poor Law schools in Worcestershire, had been consistent in his support of individual workhouse schools, as he was convinced that if these schools were efficiently administered they were very satisfactory indeed and more likely to prepare the pauper child for the sort of employment they obtained when they left the workhouse. As obtaining employment for inmate children, at the earliest moment, remained a priority in

Browne's opinion, this probably explained why no district schools were ever built in the relatively rural county of Worcestershire.

After 1847, the Poor Law Board demanded to know more about workhouse children's classifications and a more accurate picture of the extent of the child pauper problem. In spite of this, the Central Poor Law Authority appeared unwilling, or unable, to act to alleviate this problem and the emphasis on separate schools for Poor Law children continued. Thus, locally, the Guardians at Worcester in 1848 were advised to control the 'constant intercourse between the children and the grown up paupers of both sexes',[136] which the Poor Law Board used as a pretext to again demand a district school. This belief informed comments in the Poor Law Board Annual Report of 1850[137] by Frederick Temple, Principal of Kneller Hall Training School, who stated that the boys would 'never be depauperised; they mix with the men, most of them gaol birds'.[138] Thus, given such facts which had been supplied by socially influential witnesses to the Newcastle Royal Commission on Popular Education in 1858, it was logically concluded that education in the workhouse was impossible. This was partly because 'the influence of the workhouse . . . [was] . . . itself pernicious', but also because 'proper leaders . . . [could] . . . not be induced to take charge of the schools'.[139] Indeed the situation was so bad that Patrick Cumin's evidence to the Royal Commission was that 'children [were not only] most inefficiently trained, but [also] actually nurtured in vice and that a large proportion of them turn out thieves, or prostitutes, or paupers, or something of that sort'.[140] For this reason the fact that the workhouse at Evesham at about this time was described as 'barely adequate because of communication'[141] between children and adult paupers and that at Shipston on Stour to be 'ill arranged . . . [so that] . . . the children are not completely separated from the adult inmates, with whom I believe they work'[142] was a cause for great concern. Some other experts, employed in a professional capacity in Poor Law administration, disagreed with this, so that, for instance, Assistant Commissioner Robert Weale considered that it was contact with other children, rather than with adults, that was the major danger facing inmate pauper youngsters. To illustrate this, he cited an example where a prostitute of 'almost incredible juvenility . . . [had been] . . . admitted to a workhouse school and permitted to associate with the other children'.[143] This was a decision taken unconsciously, despite the fact that to Robert Weale the dangers were obvious and continuing. Therefore, he considered it to be control over who entered the workhouse rather than how inmates were segregated when they were in the institution, that was most important.

Thomas B. Browne, who was HMI for the area, was a strong supporter of schools within workhouses. He was very influential regarding the treatment of inmate children in the county and was not completely convinced by Robert Weale's theories. He believed that 'they [workhouse children] may even have less evil . . . in the workhouse . . . than falls their lot in the daily walk to a National School or a British School through the streets of a populous town',[144] which was an opinion with which Assistant Commissioners Henry G. Bowyer and Andrew Doyle came to agree. Both of these men had supported separate schools in the 1840s, but by the 1860s they too felt that the threat of the general workhouse had been overstated,[145] so that the inmate child was in greater danger in its environment outside the workhouse than inside the institution. It was also their opinion that a district school was unnecessary, as such schools did not give a more suitable education than a workhouse school. Assistant Poor Law Commissioner Henley disagreed. He gave evidence to the Newcastle Royal Commission suggesting that contamination of children in workhouses was inevitable, given that 22.9 per cent of males and 39.5 per cent of females, who had been educated in workhouses in Worcestershire, were returned from service as unsuitable.[146] He went on to suggest that, when these returnees eventually left the workhouse, at the age of sixteen years, they generally did return to the institution. This, he thought, demonstrated something about workhouse education, although it was probably the unsuitability of the employment found for these youthful inmate paupers that was at fault and which explained their return to the workhouse. However, contemporaneously, another Assistant Commissioner, John T. Graves, sought to question the figures Henley cited. His alternative statistics[147] showed that only Martley, of the county's unions, had more than 5 per cent of its inmates who had spent at least part of their childhood in workhouse schools. This direct contradiction of evidence was difficult to explain, but the situation described by J.T. Graves appeared more common than that cited by Assistant Poor Law Commissioner Henley.

While opinions among Poor Law officials about the importance of separate Poor Law schools differed, there was a consensus about the importance of a good workhouse schoolteacher, who was universally assumed to have a beneficial influence. There was one group, however, who sometimes disagreed about the nature of workhouse schoolteachers. These were the inmates of the workhouse, who knew from personal experience what the institution and its staff were like. Inevitably, they had different opinions about the workhouse and its staff, about the Poor Law Central Authority and its staff, the local administrators, the Guardians and non-pauperised citizens in general. HMI at Droitwich suggested in 1853: 'The elder children are already improving and I expect will make some further advance this year under Miss Smith who has excellent methods of imparting knowledge and I think will train the children morally and industrially and exercises a kindly influence over them.'[148] While Miss Smith certainly impressed both HMI and the Guardians, the inmates were clearly not so impressed, because when HMI inspected the school later he 'felt it right to mention that I am told . . . that several female inmates . . . told the children to answer none of my questions in order that the schoolmistress might therefore be dismissed'.[149] Evidence of this sort was rare, particularly as it clearly demonstrated that communication between the inmate adults and children was possible. In spite of this, HMI stated that he 'imputed no blame [for this situation] to the officers', and he begged 'to earnestly call the attention of the Board of Guardians to . . . [the] . . . grave injury to the children and injustice to the schoolmistress' that these circumstances caused. He also insisted that he could not make an objective assessment, but he was critical of 'a deficiency in practical usefulness' among the children on his next visit.[150] He later insisted that some allowance be made for the 'youth of the children and the interruption of their attendance'. Separation was again at fault at Droitwich in 1857,[151] where HMI complained that girls were allowed to nurse patients in the female adult wards, which seriously infringed segregation. However, this situation was not resolved, as Assistant Commissioner W.H.T. Hawley referred to this same point again in 1861, when he described 'moves to relax . . . classification, and to permit them [the girls] to be employed as nurses in the sick wards, and to take charge of the infants of able bodied-women'.[152] He commented 'I have not encouraged it' in spite of a regulation allowing it. Girls continued to be allowed to nurse patients in the female adult wards, which continued to seriously infringe segregation.

It was suggested by the Poor Law Central Authority that in schools attached to workhouses, well-qualified staff were required to improve discipline and moral training. While this was the ideal, parsimony led some county unions to continue to use the services of the porter, the matron or a pauper as schoolmaster or schoolmistress. Indeed, in 1838,[153] it was even suggested that some Guardians showed favour, by appointing people known to them, rather than better qualified applicants from further afield and there was some suggestion that irregularities in such appointments may have occurred. Whilst Assistant Commissioner Edward Gulson agreed that this may have happened, he saw the low salary offered as the major reason why 'fit and proper persons' did not apply for these posts. In this circumstance the advantage of employing paupers as schoolteachers was enhanced as they were also removed from the relief lists, saving the Poor Rate payers even more money. In 1842 the Poor Law Commission legitimated this practice, when they restated that: 'A schoolmaster or schoolmistress need only be appointed if the Guardians think fit',[154] which was taken by some Guardians to mean that the post could be filled by a pauper with no qualifications, if the Board of Guardians saw fit.

The two-tiered Poor Law administration created in 1834 helped to promote education in workhouses, with the most active enthusiasm for instruction for pauper children coming from the permanent staff of the Poor Law Central Authority. However, the provision of workhouse schools was dependent on the retrospective decisions of auditors, who could disallow expenditure after the event, which made the implementation of some educational ideas, some of them innovations, problematical. This situation was further compounded by the local financing of the Poor Law, which inevitably led to parsimony and caused the Poor Law Commission problems in getting its policies implemented. Persuasion and cajoling were sometimes necessary in some unions, although only rarely did intransigent unions resist introducing education altogether. However, education policy had to be applied flexibly, because to have done otherwise would have led to insuperable problems.

Locally elected and accountable Boards of Guardians, who were cognisant of the local situation, implemented the central educational policy and in most cases the system within Worcestershire worked increasingly well, with administrative problems continually diminishing between 1834 and 1871. In part this was because the system became more efficient, but undoubtedly the increased efficiency of workhouse staff was another factor. Thus, the efficiency of the school staff at Kidderminster workhouse was carefully monitored by the Guardians,[155] because the plan on which the school was run was considered very important. The Poor Law Commission had enquired in 1838[156] whether the 'National System of Education' was in use in the county's workhouses, which caused the Guardians' interest to focus on this aspect. Indeed, by 1840 Kidderminster required its schoolmistress to be acquainted with that system and the chaplain assessed her efficiency in that respect.[157] He assured the Guardians she was efficient,[158] although the Assistant Poor Law Commissioner was clearly not satisfied, particularly with the way the schoolmistress taught writing,[159] because of a lack of slates. The Guardians at this workhouse school had converted a stable into a schoolroom, so that 'the National System of Education of the children can be fully carried out', although this was not a success, probably because the room was totally unsuited to its new purpose. Another new schoolroom was commissioned here in 1840.[160] A dozen oak boards were now purchased, on which the lessons were pasted, which was indicative of the National System, although there continued to be great difficulty in finding efficient teachers, according to the Select Committee in 1837–8, 'there was no place to look for a master or mistress who could give the children a good course of instruction'.[161]

The need for efficient workhouse teachers led to suggestions that a training school should be founded to which 'the Guardians should be forced to go to . . . find such teachers', but this idea was not immediately proceeded with.[162] Instead unions adopted different approaches, as at King's Norton in 1850, where the Board of Guardians asked that a copy of their advertisement for a schoolmistress be sent to 'each lady principal of [the] training institutions at Whitelands, Salisbury and Exeter'.[163] Usually, such approaches proved futile because the 'graduates' of these colleges did not want to enter the workhouse teaching profession. For this reason, Worcester Guardians must have been delighted when they recruited a schoolmaster from Kneller Hall Training School in 1853,[164] who was recommended by the Revd Frederick Temple, the Principal of the College. However, within a week he resigned, so that Temple wrote to apologise 'for the annoyance that has been caused by my recommendation of Mr Prellin, and his subsequent conduct in quitting his situation on grounds which in my opinion were quite insufficient'. Frederick Temple was clearly incensed by Prellin's behaviour. He was told that he would not be recommended again. In 1858[165] Kidderminster Guardians tried another approach, when they advertised for school staff in *The National Society Monthly*, but this proved unsuccessful and trained teachers in workhouse schools remained unusual. Some teachers attempted to take advantage of this situation, so that at King's Norton in 1850,[166] the schoolmistress there asked if her fees would be paid for her to attend training school, but this was refused. The Poor Law Board did offer three months leave of absence, if the schoolmistress paid for her own training, but she declined their offer.

As the Poor Law Commission grew in size and complexity, more permanent central office staff were appointed and the numbers of local union and workhouse staff also increased. The Assistant Poor Law Commissioners, who were at the interface between the central and local administrations, now became more aware that pauper education was at its most effective where suitable facilities existed. Thus, in the 1840s, the central authority sought to promote the provision of efficient workhouse education and Edwin Chadwick, the secretary to the Commission, referred to workhouse discipline being 'to a considerable extent dependent on convenient schoolrooms' and the way in which they were arranged and organised. In spite of this, some county workhouse schoolrooms were still inadequate long after this time and discipline problems inevitably persisted. For example, the standard of workhouse discipline was thought to be in danger at Kidderminster in 1848, where the schoolroom was criticised because it was impossible 'to give such directions . . . for accustoming the children to habits of industry'. The chapel at this workhouse was also used as a schoolroom, for which it was clearly unsuited and which led to 'desecration',[167] which created further problems.

The general workhouse accommodation at Kidderminster was continually criticised in the 1830s and 1840s, because it was thought to threaten institutional discipline. Such criticisms reached a peak in 1848[168] when a formal complaint was made, but nothing was done at this time to solve these problems. This was partly because the Guardians attempted to deflect criticism, by claiming that they were 'bound to exercise great care in the expenditure of money, as district schools may be created in the area'. This was a clear prevarication, as no such school was ever planned or created. Similarly, at Worcester in 1850,[169] when there was criticism of the workhouse schoolroom there, which was seen as a threat to discipline, the Guardians suggested a new one, although the Poor Law Board were dissatisfied with the site suggested, as they regarded it as 'too close to the burial ground'. The Poor Law Board now suggested a new and entirely separate school,[170] but the Guardians now stated that they could not afford to finance such a school, again indicating the insincerity of their original offer of a new schoolroom. Problems continued and a year later the classroom at Worcester was again criticised, this time because it was accessible from many parts of the workhouse, which enabled schoolchildren to contact adult paupers.[171] No change was ever made to prevent this and thus a moral danger to the inmate children continued.

Another workhouse schoolroom criticised by a central authority official was at Upton upon Severn union in 1853,[172] where the Guardians had been self-congratulatory about their schoolroom that they considered 'sufficiently large, well-ventilated and freshly whitewashed'.[173] However, Assistant Poor Law Commissioner J.T. Graves disagreed. He asked the size of the room,[174] which he clearly regarded as too small for the number of inmate children, but when the Guardians replied,[175] it was obvious that Graves had made an error of judgement and he had to apologise. The schoolroom was of adequate size, but he had been unaware that only half of the children occupied the room at any one time. In spite of this official's error, this case did indicate a continuing vigilance about the physical conditions in which pauper children were educated in workhouse schools.

Cases such as this clearly indicated that the number of children resident in a workhouse was crucial in determining whether or not a schoolroom was considered suitable, so that some rooms were totally inadequate in winter when the workhouse was full, but adequate in the summer months, when there were fewer inmate children. For this reason, expenditure by Guardians on new schoolrooms, to be used for only the four or five winter months, was thought extravagant and not a priority. The school staff were expected to cope. The schoolroom at Shipston on Stour was criticised as 'inadequate' in 1861,[176] as was the one at Evesham in 1864,[177] and new schoolrooms were demanded by the Poor Law Central Authority. The existing schoolroom at Evesham was enlarged in 1865,[178] while the facilities at Shipston on Stour remained unaltered.

Elsewhere, at Bromsgrove in 1868, HMI found fault when he stated: 'I find the numbers much increased and the schoolroom rather crowded, and it must have been quite insufficient for attendance in the winter . . . [he was] . . . quite sure that the schoolmistress has done all that is in her power in the crowded state of the school.'[179] In spite of comments such as this, Guardians were reticent to spend money on replacement schoolrooms, which meant that decisions by King's Norton Guardians to raise a loan of £600 in 1850[180] and of Stourbridge Guardians to borrow £1,500 in 1868,[181] to replace 'totally unsuitable' existing schoolrooms, were unusual. Stourbridge Guardians' decision was forced by the threatened resignation of the schoolmistress, who was a most effective teacher and whose health had suffered because of 'the closeness of the schoolroom which [was said to be] barely sufficient in size'.[182] The Guardian's anxiety to retain her services explained their eagerness to build a new schoolroom,[183] although their efforts came too late and the schoolmistress resigned.[184] In spite of this, the new schoolroom was said to be 'in use' in 1871.[185] A new schoolroom was also built at Bromsgrove in 1869.[186]

In other places schoolrooms needed improvement, particularly because they were too dark, so that at Shipston on Stour union in 1869, HMI stated: 'It would be a material improvement if the schoolroom was made light.' However, no improvement was made here, because the inspector criticised this room again in 1871,[187] stating: 'It is very low and narrow and not properly constructed for a schoolroom and also too small considering the number of children receiving instruction in it.'[188] This clearly concerned the Guardians, who now wrote to the Poor Law Board asking what size a schoolroom to accommodate eighty children should be.[189] The central authority replied '25 ft × 18 ft × 12 ft'[190] and added that a grant would be available if a new schoolroom was built which demonstrated an inferior standard expected of workhouse schooling compared with elementary schooling in general, as this recommendation was less than the size contemporaneously required by the National Society if schoolrooms were to receive a building grant from that source. In a few cases schoolrooms were said to be injurious to the health of the children, so that, at Kidderminster in 1860, the schoolroom was said to be 'ill constructed and ill ventilated, so as to cause sickness among the children who occupied it'.[191] Initially these premises were reroofed,[192] but three years later in 1865, these new roofs were blamed as they were 'unhealthy . . . and . . . they generate heat'.[193] Elsewhere, schoolroom equipment was at fault, so that at Stourbridge in 1852, 'the books and apparatus in use in the school, as well as the desks and furniture are imperfect',[194] a fault solved by refurnishing the room.[195] This worked, as HMI now made favourable comments about this school. At Droitwich in 1848, the detached vagrants' wards were converted into two day rooms, one for boys and one for girls, with further space provided in a shed in the girls' yard,[196] which considerably increased the space available for education. This solution had already been used at Pershore union in 1839,[197] and was also adopted at King's Norton in 1868,[198] where the woman tramps' ward was converted to accommodate children during the day time. In spite of such measures, the provision of adequate accommodation for education in workhouses continued to be a problem.

The continued development of Poor Law education was ensured by adopting advances in pedagogy and methods from elementary education outside workhouses. The gallery, which was very popular in elementary school classrooms during the 1840s, particularly as a means of presenting object lessons, was suggested as a useful additional piece of schoolroom equipment by the teacher at the boys' school at Worcester in 1848,[199] which was a development approved of by HMI.[200] This same inspector decided that a gallery was 'desirable in the girls' schoolroom, though it is not I think quite as desirable as in the boys' school. No doubt they will provide one.'[201] This apparatus was provided in 1852 and by 1863 Kidderminster workhouse school also had a gallery and desks were added to the schoolroom there at a cost of £6 5s 0d.[202] However, in some places, particularly before 1850, workhouse schools still lacked basic equipment, such as blackboards. Indeed, at Worcester in 1840,[203] there were no slates in the whole school and as such equipment was thought crucial to the teaching of writing this was a vital criticism. In spite of this, Assistant Poor Law Commissioner Hall,[204] responsible for inspecting workhouses in the south-eastern region, still told the Newcastle Royal Commission, in 1861, that some unions were extravagant in their expenditure on workhouse education, which clearly demonstrated the ignorance of some Poor Law central officials of the more rural unions outside the south-east, as Worcestershire unions certainly could not be accused of such extravagance.

These inadequacies in workhouse education were well known, but still some influential people believed that it was wrong for pauper children to be given advantages over their non-pauper contemporaries. For this reason, Droitwich union attempted to influence the Poor Law Board regarding workhouse education and Less Eligibility in 1848.[205] Sir John S. Pakington,[206] a founder member of the Board of Guardians and resident of Westwood Park, on the outskirts of the town, attempted to use his social influence to convey the opinion to the Poor Law Board that: 'The education . . . afforded to the children in the workhouse is sufficient for children in their situation in life and that it is more ample than the education which the children of the independent labourer receives.' It was suggested that an independent labourer could neither afford education for his child, nor forego the wages of his child being educated, but the Privy Council Committee on Education disagreed. In 1852, they described the instruction given in workhouse schools as of 'the most meagre kind',[207] which was possibly Sidney and Beatrice Webb's source for a comment in their retrospective book on the New Poor Law, published in 1909, which stated that, during this period, 'the workhouse schools continued to improve very slowly in educational efficiency'.[208] What they did not say was how this efficiency was measured.

Before 1863, workhouse schools had been the responsibility of the Privy Council Committee on Education, with the rules they applied to elementary schools also applied to workhouse schools, so that, for instance, an attendance register had been kept at Bromsgrove, after 1850.[209] HMI Jellinger C. Symons,[210] who visited workhouse schools in Worcestershire, reported direct to the Privy Council Committee and then to the Poor Law Central Authority. This system operated from the inception of the inspection of workhouse schools in the early 1840s. Sir William Joliffe, one of the first workhouse school inspectors, told the Select Committee in 1861: 'I received my appointment [in 1840] and Mr E.C. Tufnell commenced about six months before I did',[211] before that date 'the schools were not under regular and constant inspection'.[212] Therefore, evidence existed about the quality of Poor Law education, which enabled Patrick Cumin, a self-professed expert, to report to the Newcastle Royal Commission that regularity of attendance and the length of time spent at school 'readily accounted for the improved knowledge of the workhouse child'.[213] It was inevitable that workhouse children attended school more regularly than their contemporaries outside the workhouse, because their incarceration in the institution meant that they had no choice about attending school.

According to Anne Digby, by the 1850s the relationship between the Poor Law Board and the Privy Council Committee on Education was fraught, particularly as the HMI of workhouse schools appeared to have more power than his contemporaries responsible for inspecting elementary schools.[214] This power was possibly misused, however, so that in 1855, Assistant Poor Law Commissioner Edward Gulson commented that the Poor Law Board must 'possess and continue to possess the superior control of the arrangement of education in workhouses'. He regarded 'the education of pauper children as . . . but one portion of Poor Law Economy . . . [which] . . . ought to be treated in connection with the general policy of Poor Law administration'. He linked this to the duality of inspection by Assistant Poor Law Commissioners and HMIs, and went on to accuse HMIs of directing their word 'exclusively, or nearly so to the improvement of education in the workhouses'. This meant, he thought, that their plans were 'not always . . . subordinated to the economy and peculiarities of workhouse administration'. Often HMIs communicated opinions about individual workhouse schools directly to Guardians, before they had discussed these with the Assistant Poor Law

Commissioners. This, Edward Gulson thought, tended 'to impair the superior control of the Poor Law Board',[215] which he clearly thought was undesirable. This situation was resolved in 1863 when inspection was transferred to the Poor Law Board.[216]

The five HMIs employed by the Privy Council Committee on Education were now transferred to the Poor Law Board, in a successful attempt to ensure continuity, as suggested in a report from the Privy Council Committee, after the Newcastle Royal Commission Report in 1861.[217] This Royal Commission Report also led Sidney and Beatrice Webb to make critical comment in their work on Poor Law history published in 1909. They suggested that HMI's 'criticisms [were] all in favour of large district schools as compared with the single union schools',[218] but this was at least an overstatement. Contemporaneously, HMI Thomas B. Browne, who was Jellinger C. Symons successor, supported individual schools, as he was convinced that the schools attached to workhouses in his district, which included Worcestershire, were more than satisfactory. He went further, as he had 'reason to believe that pauper children generally become emancipated from pauperism when they leave [such] school[s]',[219] although he did regret that: 'In the workhouse school, as in other schools, the children are often not allowed to remain a sufficient time to receive proper instruction.'[220] He also recognised that some Guardians, apparently representing rural parishes, were too ready 'to remove children from school and place them at profitable work'.[221] Thus, it followed that workhouse schoolteachers were of the greatest importance and that efficient teachers needed to be encouraged to stay in the workhouse school system. One way of doing this was to improve their conditions of employment, by giving an annual vacation, which Browne saw as giving 'Some respite from school work . . . [which] . . . is good for both teachers and children . . . [as] . . . they are likely to work afterwards the better in consequence.'[222]

In spite of these sentiments in the opinion of many contemporary social observers, the workhouse remained no place for children because it inflicted great damage on them, which was a situation enhanced by the unsuitability of the workhouse master to control pauper children. This criticism was probably unfair to the local officials, who became much more competent with experience. This was commented on by central Poor Law Board professionals, the Assistant Poor Law Commissioners and HMI for workhouse schools, who profoundly disagreed with such adverse comments about workhouse schools and their effects. The numbers of inmate children resident in most workhouses were usually small and in many cases this prevented an attractive salary being offered to trained and talented teachers, who were in scarce supply anyway. This meant that where the teacher was inadequate, the workhouse master had no choice but to take personal responsibility for workhouse schools. However, by the 1860s, HMI Thomas B. Browne was able to assert that 'there are many schools in this district [including Worcestershire] of a very creditable character where the children are as well managed and taught as can reasonably be expected'.[223] In spite of this, 'good schools' were not common according to Sidney and Beatrice Webb, and Worcester union workhouse school was the only good example in the county, cited by HMI Thomas B. Browne.[224]

Reports by HMIs referred to inadequacies of the workhouse school curriculum, with the three 'r's' considered most inadequately taught of all. When the inspectors asked the pupils questions they found that the children did not understand what they were learning. Thus at Shipston on Stour in 1847,[225] where spelling was taught by copying, the schoolmistress was criticised for the state of the copies she gave the children. The HMI reported: 'One of these was the word FACENATE [intended I suppose for FASCINATE].' The HMI was not impressed here, but the chaplain disagreed and passed a favourable comment on this schoolmistress. There were six serious complaints made about the teaching of spelling by schoolmistresses in the county between 1834 and 1871, but only two against schoolmasters. Details of misspellings by the schoolmistress at Stourbridge were given in 1853.[226] There, HMI reported, in 'spelling from dictation PRETENTION, PHYSICIAN, SOPHISM, APPORTION, PETITION, OPOSM and POSSESSION were misspelt, and written in the exam paper, OCCURED, MANUFACTURY AND MANUFACTURY'S were misspelt'. Here, spelling books were recommended to improve the teaching of spelling. Similarly, at Worcester in 1861,[227] in spite of a tolerable performance, the HMI was to state: 'The [schoolchildren] are deficient in spelling and required to be closely questioned on the subject matter of their lessons', but no recommendation was made here as to how the problem might be overcome.[228]

It was very unusual for the teaching of spelling to be commended and only at Droitwich, in 1856, was this done.[229] Criticisms of the teaching of spelling continued until 1871, as at Bromsgrove, where the last recorded criticism before the replacement of the Poor Law Board by the Local Government Board, was made in 1870. For this reason, the comments of Assistant Commissioner Robert Weale to the Newcastle Royal Commission, in which he described the education offered in the workhouse as 'not ambitious in its range, but thoroughly sound of its kind',[230] appeared reasonably appropriate. Writing was usually said to be 'good', when apparently this usually referred to penmanship, which implied calligraphy – an approach clearly not mastered by some workhouse schoolteachers. However, within Worcestershire, only at Shipston on Stour union in 1847,[231] was the teaching of writing heavily criticised, but the importance of the schoolteacher as a model in using copybooks was continually emphasised, as at Droitwich in 1861.[232] The teaching of reading was a cause for concern at Stourbridge in 1864, where the children were said to 'read too slowly and monotonously . . . [and they] . . . do not understand the words in their books, that they are in the habit of using themselves and hearing'.[233] In spite of such comments, HMI and Assistant Poor Law Commissioners were generally sympathetic to workhouse teachers, as they came to recognise the task of teaching pauper inmates effectively as difficult. For instance at Bromsgrove in 1867, HMI explained deficiencies in reading, writing and arithmetic on 'account . . . [of] . . . the fact of their [the children] being recently admitted, or naturally dull'.[234] Similarly, HMIs were often understanding about the inadequacies in teaching arithmetic, which was often criticised because of a lack of understanding of elementary concepts by the teachers. Indeed in some cases teachers were incapable of teaching arithmetic and for this reason it was not taught in some workhouse schools, which was the case at Upton on Severn in 1847,[235] and at Stourbridge in 1853,[236] where this subject was 'the most deficient of all subjects'.

Whilst it is possible to portray HMIs and Assistant Poor Law Commissioners as understanding of the plight of workhouse schoolteachers, more probably they felt powerless to replace the ineffective teacher with an alternative one. The lack of suitable recruits to workhouse education meant that a workhouse was usually better to retain an inefficient teacher than to dismiss them without replacement. However, some teachers refused to be helped by the advice of Central Poor Law Authority officials, which happened at Stourbridge in 1859 where, in spite of being severely criticised, the schoolmaster refused HMI's advice. On his next visit the inspector reported that the schoolmaster had previously been given hints about arithmetic which had been ignored. A similar situation prevailed at the girls' school of the same union where: 'Even in orderly and elementary theory . . . they were wholly deficient', but no improvement occurred. HMI eventually reported in a marginal comment: 'The girls could not write even a simple addition sum',[237] so the schoolmistress resigned. Elsewhere, at

Droitwich in 1861, arithmetic was described as 'backward',[238] but at Shipston on Stour union in 1847, a more specific criticism had been made: 'None have got further than subtraction, and few could do subtraction sums – They are also imperfect in tables.'[239] Such problems with the workhouse school's curriculum and with the Poor Law schooling system's pedagogy, persisted until after the replacement of the Poor Law Board by the Local Government Board, in 1871.

Very occasionally, teachers were praised for their teaching methods, with HMIs and Assistant Poor Law Commissioners appearing to desire to spread good practice. Unusually, at Droitwich in 1856,[240] and at Evesham in 1859, the male teachers were said to be 'most effective' in their 'teaching of singing',[241] while at Shipston on Stour in 1859,[242] geography was well taught and drill and singing were praised at Evesham in 1864. Drill, a subject borrowed from military establishments, was considered good training for children, particularly those with parents who lacked discipline. The subject was thought 'desirable' at Droitwich in 1866,[243] where it was apparently not previously taught, so as to instil discipline into the boys. This development exactly mirrored innovations in the contemporary elementary school curriculum. Another development was the teaching of sport in workhouse schools. In 1861, James Kay-Shuttleworth[244] referred to sport being taught, but there was no indication of this happening in Worcestershire.

Poor Law inspectors had great power over all aspects of the workhouse school and arguably they had influence over how education was regarded by Guardians. However, it appeared to be threats rather than the wisdom of the inspector's advice that was crucial in the adoption of improved methods. This was indicated, at Pershore in 1839, when the visiting committee there ordered 'that the books recommended by Jellinger C. Symons, [the HMI] for the use of the school be purchased'.[245] The inspector's other advice, to purchase other equipment, was only followed when he threatened to withhold the government grant if the books were not purchased. These books were ordered, but more materials, where the grant was not threatened, were not requisitioned. Generally, there was a commonality in the approaches used in teaching various subjects in the workhouse school curriculum, so that in 1848, writing was taught using copybooks and alphabet cards, at both Bromsgrove[246] and Droitwich,[247] which appeared to represent the normal approach elsewhere. However, all was not well at Kidderminster in 1848,[248] and at Droitwich in 1851,[249] where the reading books were found to be inadequate. HMI ordered that more books be obtained, but even such simple solutions sometimes caused disputes, as some Guardians resented central authority interference. For instance, when Worcester Guardians in 1852[250] were told to order new reading books by HMI, who had criticised the existing ones, the Poor Law Board claimed that they had received no such order. In this case, it was possible that the order for books had been lost, but more likely that the Guardians had used a convenient prevarication to avoid allowing the central authority to dictate policy for their workhouse school. It was certainly the case that school books were rarer in some unions than others and that sometimes they were provided from private sources. This was done at Bromsgrove in 1852,[251] where Lord Lyttelton[252] gave books to be lent to inmates and at Kidderminster in the same year,[253] where Bibles were given to children whose conduct had been good while they were in the workhouse – providing, of course, they could read. Later, in the same union, the *Village Lesson Book*[254] was given as a gift. This was endorsed by the HMI and a similar scheme was adopted at Dudley in 1857,[255] when the Bibles there were paid for by Sir Horace St. Paul, Bart – the workhouse chaplain.

Inevitably, differences between schools enabled HMIs to compare workhouse schools, sometimes in the same workhouse. This was done at Worcester in 1863, when HMI stated that 'the girls are more lively and intelligent and more correct than the boys',[256] but later[257] the same HMI was critical of both schools. In other cases workhouse schools in the same locality were compared, as at Martley in 1863, where it was reported: 'I think that most children ought to be affected [by the school] and find the children are much more advanced in other workhouses under similar circumstance . . . [Martley was] . . . not in an advanced state.'[258] However, illogically, comparisons were sometimes made with workhouse schools not known to Guardians. At Droitwich in 1861, HMI stated: 'The difference between one workhouse and another is really astonishing as any Guardian would find who might happen to visit Ripon workhouse, where 18 or 20 children are instructed by a schoolmistress under similar circumstances',[259] although the Droitwich Guardians were not offered an opportunity to visit this distant workhouse. Most commonly, the same school at different times was compared, as for instance at Stourbridge in 1858, where the HMI stated: 'The instruction was next to none in May and indeed not to say that its state [even if improved] in August is not the slightest proof that I had made any mistake when I inspected it.'[260] He commented on the same school in 1864: 'The boys' school is in a very low state at present owing I think to the recent discharge of the more forward pupils, but when I remember it as it was in 1861, I cannot help, but suspect that there may have been some neglect on behalf of the previous schoolmaster.'[261] In spite of the central Poor Law officials diligence, the improvement of workhouse education, between 1834 and 1871, was slow.

Comments on the state of the children's learning, or lack of it, were commonly made. Thus at Shipston on Stour in 1847, HMI stated: 'The children are numerous in proportion to the number of adult inmates. They are taught by a young schoolmistress who was appointed about 6 weeks ago and is on trial. They are very backward.'[262] While at Worcester in the same year it was said, 'the girls are well behaved, but backward in learning'.[263] In fact, once an adverse criticism had been made, others often followed, so that four months after this initial comment, HMI stated: 'I found the girls so ignorant that in my opinion the schoolmistress must be incompetent.'[264] A summation of the comments of workhouse inspectors, including HMIs and Assistant Commissioners, provide a comment on workhouse schools generally. In the 1860s, they were described as 'below the reasonable standard of elementary schools' by Assistant Poor Law Commissioner Ruddock, although in 1859 he had been certain that there was 'a gratifying improvement . . . with greater amounts of general intelligence, and generally speaking, with better religious instruction'.[265] The confusing signals given by Poor Law officials about workhouse schools continued and appeared to be contingent on the audience for which the reports were intended. Thus an HMI, or an Assistant Commissioner, reporting to Poor Law officials would favour workhouse schools, while to outside audiences, such as the Newcastle Royal Commission, they tended to be lukewarm in their support for such schools, or in some cases they opposed them.

Reports to Boards of Guardians, which were also sent to the Poor Law Central Authority, were usually critical in detail, but were generally supportive of individual workhouse schools. However, sometimes mixed criticisms were included in HMIs' reports on workhouse schools, as at Worcester in 1864, where the children there were described as 'heedless'[266] in their answers. Elsewhere workhouse schooling was of a much better standard according to workhouse inspectors' reports. This variation summed up the dilemma of the inspectors, who had to judge teaching from the effective answering of questions, as they had little else to base their assessment on. Given that the teacher's salary depended on the response of their pupils at the inspection, particularly after the introduction of the 'Revised Code' in 1862, the understandable response of some teachers was to prepare their pupils to answer the inspector's questions, by teaching approaches involving rote learning. Thus, pupils basically barked back answers as a response to the inspector asking a question. Indeed, when pupils at Evesham union in 1866 had not learned this skill, the inspector thought that 'the children have not learned to attend to what they are about',[267] and at Droitwich in 1867: 'The children . . . [were thought] . . . dull and required to be clearly questioned as to the meaning of their lessons to be led to think and to exercise their minds.'[268] The implication of such comments for the teacher was a loss of salary and for the Board of Guardians, a reduction in the government grant available to run the workhouse school.

In 1847, the Privy Council Committee on Education described workhouse schools as being 'wretchedly supplied with books and apparatus',[269] which led to a Poor Law Board circular in 1849, 'extending to the workhouse schools the privilege of getting at low cost the school books of which they [the Privy Council Committee on Education] had arranged the publication for elementary schools'.[270] Savings of between 32 per cent and 55 per cent on the cost of these books were available, with an average saving of 43 per cent. The Poor Law Board were now 'desirous of promoting the introduction of suitable books into workhouse schools' and they 'succeeded in making arrangements with several publishers to supply, for the use of the schools, the books and maps in question, on the same terms as they are furnished to their Lordships [the Privy Council Committee on Education] for the use of other schools'.[271] Thus, 'Books for the use of scholars' and 'Books for the use of teachers' were to be made available in workhouse schools, which were exactly similar to those recommended for elementary schools outside the Poor Law system. There were 72 scholars' books and 55 teachers' books listed, together with 115 maps.[272] The publication of these lists, by the Poor Law Board, now meant that workhouse school children could be treated in a similar way to their non-pauper contemporaries, but this only happened if these books were purchased and this was in the hands of individual Boards of Guardians. Only a minority of unions ordered such books. The book orders placed differed from union to union, so that uniformity, where it existed, was fortuitous and constantly eroded. However, Worcestershire's Boards of Guardians appeared reticent to commit themselves to expenditure on the books recommended.

Workhouse school books were now ordered from 'the Poor Law

Board's publisher – Mr Charles King' and full details of these books was given. The rules specified that once purchased, these books were to be 'devoted solely to the use of the said school, and that the name of the union shall be written or stamped in each book as soon as received'. Details of the numbers of children and teachers at the school were also required with the order, possibly because it was thought that this would control both parsimony and extravagance, although experience suggested that parsimony was more likely, but this procedure may also have been a check on Less Eligibility.

The books on offer varied in price from ½d for *The Child's First Reading Book* to 7s 6d for *Reading Disentangled*, being a series of elementary reading lessons on sheets, which were pasted to millboard, and maps; from 1s 9d, for a map of the British Isles and one of Palestine, to £3 10s 0d, for a set of ten maps in a wooden case, although there was no reduction for bulk purchases. Twenty-three book publishers were represented in the lists,[273] with larger publishing houses clearly considering this a profitable market. Unusually the Government, through the Education Department, published *A Box of Singing Tables for Elementary Schools*. One obvious advantage of this system of purchasing books was that HMI could now recommend books from these lists, and their decisions could be enforced by threatening to withhold government grant payments.[274]

At Droitwich in 1867, comment was passed on religious knowledge, when the HMI said that 'their answers were satisfactory' and 'They have evidently been well and carefully taught by the . . . schoolmistress'.[275] As the chaplain, who had a vested interest in religious education, was in constant contact with the workhouse school, he ensured effective teaching of religious matters, although this may not have been the case everywhere. At Worcester in 1848, the reports say that 'insufficient means have been taken to make them understand what they have learned'[276] regarding Bible studies and such criticisms were repeated at Kidderminster in 1848 where it was stated 'out of 16 girls only 3 can read tolerably in the New Testament, none appear to understand even the simple truths of the Gospels'.[277] Schoolmistresses, rather than schoolmasters, were most criticised in this respect, with only the schoolmaster at Bromsgrove in 1854,[278] criticised about his religious teaching. He was said to have neglected the Catechism; which was a charge he strongly denied.

Another facet of social control by the chaplain was his censorship of the literature coming into the workhouse, a duty much influenced by his restrictive choice, which was referred to at Westhampnett union in the Report of the Select Committee on the Poor Law Amendment Act in 1837.[279] Books, principally those recommended by the National Society – the Anglican Church's Voluntary Elementary Education Society – which were almost automatically acceptable to the chaplain, and those which he saw as proper, were adopted.[280] This situation was clearly acceptable to the Poor Law central administration, as James Kay, then an Assistant Poor Law Commissioner, suggested 'if any other books than these [the Bible Testaments, Books of Common Prayer, and the Church Catechism] are employed, they are submitted to the chaplain . . . [and] . . . we think it is right that differences of opinion be referred to the Diocese'.[281] The control of the workhouse community by the Anglican Church was thus ensured, while it was believed that the interests of paupers from other faiths was protected by a conscience clause.[282] The protection of the interests of Jews in the workhouses of the East End of London is the most often cited example of this sort of protection in operation.

Locally, the chaplain at Kidderminster workhouse in 1841, was asked if a lady might send *The Saturday Magazine* and *The Penny Magazine* into the workhouse 'for the amusement of the poor'.[283] However, her request was refused by the chaplain, who thought 'it is not desirable that any book other than those used by the children, the Bible, prayer book and religious tracts be allowed'. At Droitwich in 1841, the chaplain there declared 'a tract of very objectionable character'[284] should be destroyed rather than be allowed into the workhouse, although no details of what this tract was were recorded. Once the censorship system had been set up, Guardians regularly asked the chaplain's advice on other matters of moral, religious and educational importance and sometimes his advice was at variance with that given by workhouse inspectors. The chaplain's advice on the whole variety of matters referred to him was invariably coloured by his ideology and his Anglicanism, which inevitably enhanced the influence of the established church over workhouse communities. Thus, cheap material published by the Society for the Promotion of Christian Knowledge (SPCK), another Anglican Education Society, was purchased by many unions on the advice of the chaplain. Such books and pamphlets were offered to the unions at concessionary rates, with 25 per cent reductions available in 1847,[285] a cheapness that was very attractive, which made them liable to be purchased, again reinforcing the Anglican influence in the workhouse. In 1844, SPCK went still further, when they offered free Bibles and Prayer Books to all county unions, an offer that was unanimously accepted, so that this material became the staple source for teaching in many workhouse schools and these books were often replaced by other SPCK publications when copies wore out. In 1847, Kidderminster Guardians[286] ordered ten Testaments and twenty Collects from the SPCK, probably because they were cheap and recommended by the chaplain. Elsewhere, the schoolroom at Upton upon Severn union in 1853, was also said to be 'well provided with bibles and secular reading material'.[287] Between 1834 and 1844, literature other than cheap or free SPCK books were of low priority with Guardians, particularly when auditors determined retrospectively whether such texts were necessary, and whether Guardians' purchases could be disallowed after the event. Thus, few Guardians took the risk of ordering more than Bibles and Prayer Books from the SPCK. In this early period of Poor Law development, there was a distinct lack of enthusiasm among Guardians for providing more than rudimentary equipment for workhouse education, such that the Poor Law Commission's obvious desire to promote education was held back.

It was proselytism, which was feared by most religious denominations, that often led to controversy regarding religious education in workhouses. Thus, the Hon Charles Langdale,[288] a Roman Catholic, who gave evidence to the Newcastle Royal Commission on Popular Education in 1861, deplored the 'system equally evil to the parent and the child, utterly alienating the latter from any feeling of affection towards those whom the laws both of nature and of God command them to love and reverence . . . a violation of every human feeling and I may add, too generally of every principle of the rights and conscience'.[289]

The fear of proselytism was constantly emphasised by non-Anglican Guardians and ministers, but a recent investigation of religious education in workhouses, in the period 1834 to 1871 by S.P. Oberman,[290] suggests that educational innovation often originated with these non-Anglican Guardians and that the suppression of their views made the emergence of educational innovations, particularly relating to religious matters, difficult. On most Boards of Guardians there was a reactionary rump of Anglicans, who prevented fresh thinking on religious matters. This certainly appeared to be the case at Dudley in 1858,[291] where a Roman Catholic Guardian proposed a motion to ensure that Roman Catholic children were not proselytised. The reaction to this was forthright as the majority of Dudley's Guardians, who were Anglicans, reacted immediately and strongly, proposing an amendment that the motion was 'in direct antagonism with the principles of the Glorious Protestant Constitution of this Kingdom'. The motion was said to be: 'The result of popish influence . . . [and] . . . a step in the determined effort now made by Romanists to undermine the principles of the glorious Protestant constitution in church and state – As protestant subjects of our beloved Queen, we firmly and positively decline to give any direction to the master of our workhouse to enable him to act under it [the motion].' This amendment was inevitably strongly supported by most Guardians who were professed Anglicans and a letter was sent to the Poor Law Board restating the resolution, and describing 'Popish education'.[292] Religion continued to impose a morality acceptable to the ruling élite of society on the pauperised poor, one of the most vulnerable groups in society. Thus schoolteachers, even those who were not Anglicans, were expected to teach the Church Catechism to ensure the dominance of Anglicanism. Thus, at Evesham in 1859,[293] a 'strict Baptist' was appointed as teacher, who had agreed to teach the Catechism, with his appointment sanctioned on this basis.[294] It was by laying down explicit rules, which were rigorously applied, that social control was maintained, so that the experiences of the pauper child in the workhouse were ruthlessly manipulated to maintain acceptable influences, which David Roberts suggests was of advantage to the 'ruling élite', thus clearly demonstrating paternalistic motives.[295]

In Worcestershire, workhouse schools were thought appropriate for most pauper children, but some children posed continual problems. For instance, non-Anglican children were a problem, because the workhouses were Anglican dominated. Orphaned, deserted, blind, deaf and dumb children were another group with special needs difficult to satisfy in ordinary workhouses, so that special institutions were often set up to cope with such individuals. These were usually set up by philanthropic groups, because the Poor Law central authority were opposed to involvement in such special provisions. These specialist institutions accepted workhouse children, although the paying of fees at these institutions was illegal and against central authority rules and regulations. Such fees had been made illegal under the Certified Schools' Act of 1862,[296] so that only if an institution was certified under that Act could payments be made. No local institutions were certified, so when county unions attempted to rid themselves of problem children to these institutions they had to pay a fee and they thus broke the Law. This happened at Bromsgrove in 1862,[297] where payment was made for a boy to attend Birmingham Blind Asylum, with the expenditure questioned by the auditors, because the asylum was not recognised under the Certified Schools' Act. The payment of this fee was eventually 'disallowed'.[298]

The improved efficiency of the workhouse schools, between 1834 and 1871, was accounted for by George Coode, the Assistant Secretary of the Poor Law Board, who stated that it was due to:

1. The regularity of attendance of the children.
2. The adequacy of the teaching powers.
3. The unambitious nature of the education given which gives time for what is taught to be taught properly.
4. The mixture of industrial and mental work taught to the children. They rarely receive more than three hours mental culture a day.
5. The constant intercourse between children and their teacher, they being out of reach of (what are often the vulgar and demoralising) influences of home.[299]

Coode concluded that 'if improvements are required, they will be introduced, but not from the fine dictates of empiricism'. Thus, to ensure future success he suggested they:

1. Keep the standards of mental education.
2. Extend the means of industrial training as far as is practicable.
3. Provide that the classification be strictly adhered to and that the children on no account be allowed to come into contact with adults.
4. Impress on the Boards of Guardians the necessity of using great caution in selecting the employers with whom they are to place children as servants.
5. Exercise a strict supervision of them through the agency of their officers, for some time after they have left the workhouse to enter their service.[300]

It would be an overstatement to claim class conspiracy as the only determinant of the provision of workhouse education between 1834 and 1871, but the interaction of the central authority's influence with that of the local Guardians, and with that of the chaplain, gave a commonality to the type of religious teaching offered in the workhouse and to the general education provided there. The Central Poor Law Authority was apparently not concerned when this commonality evolved, providing the religious and general education offered within the workhouse initially conformed to the Principle of National Uniformity. This situation theoretically created uniformity and hindered social change, so that the paupers were subjugated by a bureaucratic organisation designed and manipulated by one social grouping, the ruling élite. The worst excesses of this system were cautioned against by Assistant Commissioner W.H.T. Hawley, when he said it was 'contrary to prudence and justice to permit unauthorised experimentalists . . . ignorant of the nature of those regulations as they are of their scope and necessity, to tamper with a measure of vast social reform'.[301] Undoubtedly, workhouse children gained something from the education they received and as has been suggested by Chesney Kellow, 'workhouses and reformatories really could confer a benefit . . . for in a fast evolving industrial society the analphabetic was at an even graver disadvantage . . . and the unemployed man who could not write was doubly likely to be reduced to beggary'.[302] Advantage there certainly was, but at what cost? One would thus disagree with M.A. Crowther's statement that: 'As educational institutions the Poor Law schools seem never to have succeeded.'[303]

In Worcestershire such institutions were relatively successful, given the generally primitive nature of elementary education available in much of the county prior to the 1870 Education Act.[304] Workhouse schools also consciously attempted to prepare their pupils for an occupation in a way that elementary schools in the county could not do, so that while one must agree with Francis Duke's judgement, that the major function of the curriculum of the workhouse school was to 'inculcate habits of industry and docility',[305] some workhouse children undoubtedly gained much more than this from their experience in the institution. However, this was an unintended outcome, as the workhouse régime was certainly seen as moral training by most contemporary advocates of the New Poor Law, be they ideologues, churchmen or enthusiastic 'expert laypeople'. It can thus be argued that this was exactly how elementary education was perceived, as this too was poor relief and hence the needs of workhouse children were no different from the needs of their non-pauper contemporaries. Thus, a commonality of approach would be expected, and indeed this was present in both workhouse schools and elementary schools. In both schooling systems the Anglican Church was particularly active in organising the education provided, although in the case of workhouse schools they lacked the fiscal control they had within National Society schools. However, the requirement that the workhouse chaplain be an Anglican compensated for this and was a potent force in making the workhouse school overtly Anglican. This greatly concerned representatives of other religious denominations, who often claimed proselytism. Thus, most aspects of the workhouse child's life were determined by the chaplain and influenced by that officer's personal religious ideology and commitment, even if this was sometimes unconsciously.

Workhouse education was considered of such great importance that its improvement appeared inevitable, in spite of the problems of appointing good school staff. Such improvement was aided by two important measures: school inspection and a government grant in support of workhouse schools. In spite of these improvements the workhouse continued to be no place for children and there was continuous concern among Poor Law officials about the workhouse children's plight. In spite of the current opinion, that the workhouse school was the equal of elementary schools outside the workhouse, many contemporary social commentators remained suspicious about this view.

Most Poor Law Guardians could subscribe to the opinion that the workhouse should maintain a moral environment and there was a consensus about this, so that the staff, with whom workhouse children came into contact, had to be beyond reproach and pauper inmates as teachers were soon rejected as unsuitable. Guardians were always assiduous in their adherence to rules and regulations regarding the separation of pauper children from adult inmates which were seen as essential, although some Guardians were noticeably less enthusiastic regarding workhouse education, than about other aspects of the workhouse régime. Anne Digby,[306] in her comprehensive study of Norfolk, described how Guardians in that county were willing to accept the recommendations of James Kay (later Kay-Shuttleworth) regarding the setting up of workhouse schools. Such enlightened attitudes were almost completely lacking in Worcestershire and it appeared likely that the lack of an analogue to Kay's influence, so far from East Anglia, was the cause of this.

Boards of Guardians were elected by Poor Rate payers and saw it as in their supporters' interest to be as parsimonious as possible regarding Poor Law spending. For this reason, given that they had to provide education, they would only support individual workhouse schools, as these were the cheapest form of workhouse education available. However, most rural Guardians were blinkered and could see little purpose in intellectual education for what they regarded as future agricultural labourers. In this respect they differed from some urban Guardians, who saw some utility in educating prospective employees. Thus, generally speaking, there was less resistance to workhouse education in urban unions than in rural ones. What clearly differed was the perception of the education necessary for an individual to fulfil his station in life. In spite of the central Poor Law authorities attempts to enforce a workhouse school curriculum, locally, opinions differed as to what should be included in the union workhouse schools' curriculum, so that some rural Guardians resisted teaching writing, while urban Guardians were more expansive in their thinking. This argument was a reprise of the Blagdon Injunction, in which Hannah More had been forbidden to teach writing at a Sunday school in a rural Somerset village, in the early nineteenth century. But even when the curriculum was decided, matters such as the number and type of books and other equipment available, the state of the schoolroom and the quality of the schoolteachers were important. Insufficient books and equipment were sometimes remedied by the intervention of HMI, who threatened to withhold the government grant until the central authority's wishes were carried out. Few Guardians resisted the determined Assistant Poor Law Commissioner or HMI, who eventually got his way, but a few rural Boards of Guardians in Worcestershire, notably at Martley union, did exactly this. Thus, determined Guardians delayed innovation, using a variety of tactics and they often claimed continued adherence to the Principles of Less Eligibility and National Uniformity for all classes of pauper, as a justification for this. These principles, which this sort of Guardian continued to see as inviolable, had been rejected as inappropriate for children by Poor Law officials soon after 1834, when more enlightened urban Guardians had accepted a wide view of the purposes and structure of workhouse education. Divergences of opinion did not just occur between the Poor Law central authority and Guardians. What have been referred to as 'expert laypeople', who spent much energy and time in becoming experienced regarding the pauper class, also disagreed with emerging policy. These individuals formed the Workhouse Visiting Society, in the late 1850s, as an offshoot of the National Association for the Promotion of Social Science, but they were seen as meddling amateurs by central Poor Law administrators. However, they did form a vociferous opposition to altered policy and the basis of much adverse criticism to the Newcastle Royal Commission about workhouse schooling. Ironically this criticism unified Poor Law Board officials thinking about workhouse schools. Evidence from Poor Law Board officials to a Select Committee on the Education of Destitute Children, set up in 1861 as a result of the adverse criticisms made in the Newcastle Royal Commission Report, was positive about the developments that had occurred in individual workhouse schools. They suggested that if a distinction was made between transient and long-stay inmate children, then individual workhouse schools were successful, as they prevented return to the workhouse of many long-term child inmates, who had been in the institution for a sufficient time for the schooling provided to be effective. Similarly, this also settled the debate about district and separate schools, which had been set up in the metropolis and elsewhere in the urban south-east to the acclaim of influential partisan individuals within the headquarters of the Poor Law Board. However, these were an irrelevance in most non-Metropolitan areas of the country, including Worcestershire.

Although literature published from the mid-1840s to the late 1850s promoted district schools and denigrated workhouse schools, according to Alec Ross, the separate school idea proved unworkable in most urban and all rural unions. However, studies based on central authority sources[307] inevitably overstate the importance of the district school idea and while, in Worcestershire, Guardians were forced to consider the idea because of Poor Law Board insistence, they were realistic enough to recognise it as unworkable, even before the District School Act demonstrated this to be the case. School districts, as proposed, were impossible to form in rural areas. The HMI responsible for Worcestershire workhouse schools, Thomas B. Browne, unlike his predecessor Jellinger C. Symons, strongly supported individual schools within workhouses, both nationally and locally, but as with James P. Kay's influence in Norfolk,[308] Browne's influence was mainly felt regionally, on the west side of England, where he was HMI. Thus statements made by Sidney and Beatrice Webb[309] and others, that district schools were supported by all Poor Law education officials, must be questioned.

What occurred in the Poor Law schooling system was probably inevitable, given its organisation, size and the fact that it became bureaucratised soon after its inception, which led to an increased expertise among officials. A dual system was created with a national upper tier and a local lower one, essentially a prototype of the system adopted in elementary education, after the 1870 Education Act.[310] The Worcestershire workhouse schools undoubtedly improved under this influence, in spite of continuing criticism about the premises in which schooling took place, because schoolrooms were inadequate between October and March, when the workhouses were full to capacity, but adequate in the spring and summer when the workhouse emptied.

Gradually, however, school premises improved and innovations were apparent between 1834 and 1871, with many ideas adopted from National schools, such as the gallery, which was in use in some county workhouse schools.

Rural unions tended to have more conservative Guardians than urban ones and in most urban places the major tenets of the Poor Law, National Uniformity and Less Eligibility were abandoned without concern. In rural places Guardians often adhered rigidly to these tenets, in part due to their parsimony on behalf of the farming communities they largely represented, so that rural schools undoubtedly differed from urban ones, partly as a function of size, but also because of Guardians' attitudes. Nevertheless, the perspective obtained from national sources, by historians such as Alec Ross,[311] largely misses this difference, whereas Anne Digby,[312] using similar distinctions between rural and urban places in Norfolk and significantly using Guardians' minute books as her prime source, comes to similar conclusions to these. This book reveals that the education offered to children in Worcestershire workhouses, as 'total institutions', influenced the changing definition and nature of poverty between 1834 and 1871 in line with Gertrude Himmelfarb's conclusions in *The Idea of Poverty*.[313]

7

EMPLOYMENT AND THE WORKHOUSE CHILD

It was the Poor Law Commission's belief, from its inception in 1834, that the general workhouse was no place for children. Instead, the central authority believed this most vulnerable group of paupers, who were liable to spend much of their childhood in Poor Law institutions, should be kept in specialist workhouses. These institutions were to be staffed by carefully trained officers, who were intended to protect such youngsters from life-long pauperism, which was thought endemic in general workhouses. Whilst most Poor Law Guardians, including those in Worcestershire, apparently subscribed to such theories, practicalities of organisation and finance made specialist institutions to deal with such child paupers impossible to create. Usually, workhouses created immediately after the Poor Law Amendment Act were adaptations of Old Poor Law institutions, which had been designed to accommodate fewer paupers of a very different character to those they now housed. Only at Dudley was there a separate children's department, created in the old workhouse at Sedgley. Although this facility proved inappropriate, it remained in use until 1858, when a new general workhouse was built. Elsewhere, inmate children were accommodated in general workhouses, where segregation was incomplete and imperfect, and where the staff were untrained to deal with youngsters. In spite of this, education and training became the normal means of ameliorating the plight of such children, at least until they could be sent from the workhouse as apprentices or servants, which was usually done at the earliest possible opportunity. This was ironical, as one might argue that it was the long-term child inmate who suffered most from the Poor Law Commission's orthodoxy regarding apprenticeship.

Apprenticeship had been used under the Old Poor Law to rid parishes of destitute, orphaned and deserted children, which gained clear advantages for the parish and usually some benefits for the child. Under the New Poor Law, the central authority sought to dissuade Guardians from apprenticing inmate children, because it wished to maintain the Principle of Less Eligibility. They believed that a continuation of the old system of apprenticeship would place pauper children at an unacceptable advantage over their non-pauper contemporaries. However, to local Boards of Guardians, this was an unconvincing rationale. In urban unions the problem of inmate children was particularly pressing and getting worse, so that the Guardians demanded a restart to apprenticing immediately, which they believed would solve the problems of segregating and educating such children. These arguments were clearly convincing, because the Poor Law Commission soon tacitly allowed apprenticing and saved face by attempting to dissuade Guardians from paying premiums with apprentices, thus preventing a complete breach of the Principle of Less Eligibility. This chapter investigates some of the issues relating to pauper apprenticeship between 1834 and 1871. It examines the notion that the Principles of Less Eligibility and National Uniformity were maintained in spite of the widespread use of apprenticeship and service as a means of dealing with the child pauper problem. It also attempts to evaluate the utility of apprenticeship to the pauper child and examines the Central Poor Law Authority's ideological shift, from determined opposition to pauper apprenticing to the tacit acceptance of such schemes.

At the root of the central authority's problems was the ambivalence of the middle and upper classes towards the system of apprenticing pauper children under the Old Poor Law. This unease had been reflected in the Poor Law Inquiry Commission report of 1834,[1] that saw virtue in potential life-long paupers being removed from their parish of origin to be apprenticed, because at the termination of the period of apprenticeship such children altered their parish of settlement and ceased to be a burden on their home parish. However, the middle and upper classes did not like enforced apprenticeships under the Old Poor Law. In these cases, poor children were allocated to the next ratepayer on the rota to receive an apprentice. The allotment of apprentices was used in Worcestershire, only in Powick parish, between 1780 and 1834, where it had caused great resentment, particularly as there was no cognisance of the ability of the ratepayer to support the apprentice or of the worth of the apprenticeship to the child.

The Poor Law Inquiry Commission's report recommended that the relief of pauper apprentices be excepted from the general abolition of outdoor relief for the able-bodied. It suggested that the new central Poor Law administration make new regulations for apprenticing, but that it abandoned compulsory apprenticing. This advice was based on evidence of 'the practice in different parishes for apprenticing poor children' given to the Inquiry Commission, who eventually reported: 'We have less information on this subject than on any other subject'.[2] Thus, because the evidence was scant and contradictory it proved impossible to draw conclusions, so that the Commission asked for a period of 'experimentation' and appraisal before apprenticeship regulations were rewritten. Thus, the Poor Law Amendment Act of 1834 did not repeal existing regulations relating to apprenticeship, which would not have pleased utilitarian ideologues, still influenced by Bentham's ideas, including Edwin Chadwick, secretary to the Poor Law Commission. The need for the continuing relief of needy children meant that parish apprenticeship had been retained, although the Poor Law Commission did not encourage this, because they 'certainly entertain[ed] opinions unfavourable to that state of servitude which is created by apprenticing pauper children'.[3] This opinion, based on orthodox utilitarianism, undoubtedly coloured their attitude until 1847, when the Commission was replaced by the Poor Law Board and they continued attempts to maintain the Principle of Less Eligibility, although Boards of Guardians, formed to administer the Poor Law locally who were generally not orthodox utilitarians, often held very different opinions. For such Boards, parish apprenticeships were functional in getting rid of the problem of unwanted destitute children. This was particularly so, because many of these Guardians had administered apprenticeship under the Old Poor Law and they continued to believe that these old solutions were still credible.

Conflict between central and local administrations over this matter appeared inevitable. In its first ten years of operation the Poor Law Commission issued no rules and regulations for apprenticeship, in spite of the passing of a Parish Apprentices' Act in 1842.[4] Disagreement about parish apprenticing continued after Edwin Chadwick's final departure from the Poor Law Commission in 1842. The Parish Apprentices' Act of 1844[5] was more effective in promoting change and it forced the central authority to issue regulations for apprenticeship, but still the Commission expressed doubts. They enclosed a letter with their regulations making clear that the central administrators' collective opinion opposed parish apprenticeship. It stated that they hoped 'that the regulations imposed by us tend gradually to diminish the number of children thus dealt with'.[6] This duplicity about pauper apprenticing continued, with the Commission now wanting to prohibit the payment of premiums with apprentices, unless they were infirm. Parish authorities under the Old Poor Law had often paid premiums, believing that suitable masters would only be found if incentives were offered. In spite of the Poor Law Commission's continued opposition, urban Poor Law unions continually demanded to recommence parish apprenticings, with the practicalities of local administration inevitably being more important to them than the ideology of central administrators and it appeared likely that some pauper children were unofficially sent as apprentices and servants. In 1845 apprenticeship regulations were finally written, allowing the payment of premiums with apprentices, although this document was again clearly produced with ill grace, because with it went another letter stating that apprenticeship was still not part of official policy, so that the system of apprenticing 'doubtless [will] continue to be practised in those districts where it has hitherto prevailed'.[7] However, the central authority admitted no desire to promote the introduction of parish apprenticeship, where it had not existed previously.

The numbers of pauper children named in Board of Guardians' Minute Books as being bound apprentice, in Worcestershire unions between 1837 and 1871, was investigated and it was found that of the county unions, Bromsgrove and Kidderminster unions restarted apprenticing soonest in September 1837, although the Poor Law Commission clearly disapproved of this development, as they continued to discourage parish apprenticeships. Thus, Assistant Poor Law Commissioners became generally obstructive when parish apprenticeships were suggested. This strategy was clearly ineffective, as apprenticings were relatively common in 1838, 1839 and 1840, particularly for boys. Sixty-five of the seventy children apprenticed during this period were males, possibly demonstrating the relative ease with which girls could still be found employment in domestic service at this date, so there was little need to apprentice them. The Poor Law Commission's obstructiveness probably also explained the Parish Apprentices' Act of 1842, which had arguably been written to dissuade unions from apprenticing pauper children. There was a ban on pauper apprenticings until the central authority produced new apprenticeship regulations, so that parish apprenticings were rare in 1841 and 1842. This moratorium on parish apprenticeships continued until after the 1844 Parish Apprentices' Act was passed, after which there was a steady increase in apprentice numbers, probably encouraged by premiums that could now be offered.

Eleven of the thirteen Worcestershire Poor Law unions apprenticed pauper children between 1837 and 1871, with only Evesham and Martley unions failing to apprentice any pauper children at all. Evesham had apprenticed no pauper children under the Old Poor Law, whereas Martley, a relatively sparsely populated rural union, where it continued to be possible to find agricultural employment, had previously apprenticed many pauper children. In contrast, usually the most urban unions in the county took most pauper apprentices. Although parts of the Black Country regularly accepted pauper apprentices, the town of Dudley did not. It apprenticed only one boy, between 1837 to 1871, which was probably because it was very easy to obtain employment for pauper children in this burgeoning industrial town without resorting to apprenticing. This explanation also probably partly accounted for the relative scarcity of pauper apprenticeships in the Stourbridge and Worcester unions. However, Bromsgrove, Droitwich, Kidderminster and King's Norton unions accepted substantial numbers of pauper children as apprentices, including some from outside the home union. Pershore, at the centre of a market gardening area in the valley of the River Avon, was not a typical rural union. Its employment was even more seasonal and casual than in other country places and there were difficulties here in finding permanent employment for young children, so that the need for parish apprenticeships was great. The result was that there were equal numbers of boys and girls apprenticed here, probably demonstrating the relative lack of suitable employment for girls in the area. This meant that they had to be found suitable apprenticeships. In other unions, where substantial numbers of pauper children were apprenticed, a large majority of those bound were boys, who were usually sent outside the union, which had the advantage of shifting their settlement to beyond the home union at the end of the apprenticeship period. Bromsgrove, Kidderminster and King's Norton unions each apprenticed over 100 pauper children in the period between 1837 and 1871. They all recommenced apprenticing between 1837 and 1840 and reduced their use of parish apprenticeships around the time of the 1844 Parish Apprentices' Act, in line with the Poor Law Commissions moratorium. At this time Assistant Poor Law Commissioners insisted that unions await the outcome of the Act before apprenticing more children. They then allowed apprenticing to recommence after the Act, but now each union showed a different distribution of apprenticing, probably because of differences in their local economies. Interestingly, however, the reintroduction of apprentice premiums in 1845, did not greatly increase overall pauper apprenticeship numbers, although many unions continued to favour apprenticing children outside their home area.

Bromsgrove and Kidderminster unions apprenticed children in the Black Country, apart from in Dudley, in an area relatively close to the home union, where apprentices were constantly demanded as cheap labour. In the case of King's Norton union, contiguous with Birmingham, apprentices were also in great demand. Here, the 'experimentation' demanded by the Poor Law Inquiry Commission, in 1834, was undertaken with enthusiasm, contrary to the Poor Law Commission's wishes. Worcester union recommenced apprenticing as soon as it could after 1837, when the Guardians there wrote to the Poor Law Commission stating that there were 'healthy boys and girls suitable for apprenticing'.[8] This was in a union where previously, before the 1834 Act, the Guardians would have simply found suitable masters and immediately proceeded to apprentice children under the 1814 legislation[9] and they would certainly have paid apprenticing premiums, which the Poor Law Commission now saw as iniquitous. The Commission's letter about this referred to 'the evils attending apprenticing', particularly with the 'paying of premiums from the poor rates'[10] and suggested that apprenticing might only be adopted for orphan children and others dependent on the parish, providing no premium apart from clothes was paid. This must have seemed odd to the Guardians, particularly as the Commission went further and explained that their opposition was because such apprenticings infringed the Principle of Less Eligibility. They asserted that: 'It rarely happens that the labouring classes who support their families by their own exertions are in a position to give a premium with their child, a premium with a pauper child then, is a better situation than the children of the independent labourer, which would obviously be open to serious objection.' In the 1830s and early 1840s, in the opinion of the central administration, the Principle of Less Eligibility was still essential to the administration of the New Poor Law.

When parish apprenticings restarted after the 1834 Poor Law Amendment Act, a backlog of apprenticeships had to be cleared and the boys apprenticed then were, on average, older than they had been between 1781 and 1834, when children as young as seven or eight years of age had sometimes been apprenticed. Between 1796 and 1800, the annual average age of apprentices had been as low as 9.1 years and it was never higher than 11.5 years. However, between 1837 to 1871, the annual average age of apprenticing was much higher. It varied between 11.8 and 14.1 years, partly because of legislation outlawing the employment of very young children, but also because the prevailing economic circumstances, which had generally improved. This made the apprenticing of very young children unnecessary, which was demonstrated when the relationship between the average age of apprenticing and the average real wage index was calculated. This proved to be fairly strong. It gave a Spearman Rank Order Correlation Coefficient of +0.64, which demonstrated a relatively strong relationship between the increased cost of living and the tendency for pauper children to be apprenticed at younger ages. The connection between personal economic circumstances and the tendency to apprentice young pauper children was obvious, because the cost of living appeared critical in determining which individuals became destitute. Logically, as real wage indices increased, the cost of living fell and the need to apprentice young children was reduced. The same was true for the relationship between the number of nine, ten and eleven year olds apprenticed and the Cost of Living Index, which gave a Spearman Rank Order Correlation Coefficient of +0.72, which again demonstrated a fairly strong relationship here too.

The Worcester Guardians contemplated reintroducing pauper apprenticeship in 1838, but because of the climate of opinion about pauper apprenticeship among central authority officials, they were extremely wary. Thus, when they wrote to the Poor Law Commission asking if they had 'rules for apprenticing',[11] there was a swift reply, stating that no such rules yet existed, as they were still being written, but in the interim 'only orphans, bastards and deserted children should be apprenticed', although an exception could be made for individuals 'prevented by bodily and mental infirmity from providing their own livelihood'.[12] In the event, the Worcester Guardians' interest in apprenticing was taken as a signal that the union intended to reintroduce apprenticing and the Commission demanded that they be kept informed of the amount of premium the Guardians intended to pay with each apprentice. Thus, while the Poor Law Commission could do little to prevent pauper apprenticing, it did attempt to dissuade Guardians from paying premiums, an approach that was doomed to fail, unless the central authority specifically banned these payments and monitored the ban assiduously. This proved impossible to do, as premiums were not illegal and because potential masters were well aware of the previous practice of paying premiums with pauper apprentices under the Old Poor Law. Employers had come to regard these payments as a transfer fee for the apprentice's settlement at the end of an apprenticeship.

Once the Worcester Guardians had asked for advice, they felt obliged to adhere to it, so that in 1838 they sent details of all children sent as apprentices at parish expense to the Commission.[13] Only four boys were apprenticed during the year and all were deserted, orphaned, or from a family where the mother was a widow. All were sent to masters of known good character and no premiums were paid with them. This satisfied the Poor Law Commission, who ratified these apprenticings within four days.[14] Worcester union's next attempt at apprenticing came about a year later,[15] when they decided to apprentice six boys to carpet weavers in Bridgnorth, but this time they did not ask the Poor Law Commission's advice or seek its approval. However, when the minutes of the Board of Guardians' meeting, which detailed these apprenticeships, were received at Somerset House – the Offices of the Poor Law Commission in London – Assistant Poor Law Commissioner Robert Weale was immediately sent to investigate.[16] He expressed himself against the intended apprenticings, because he believed they did not conform to the Commission's expectations about apprenticeship, as the intended masters were unsuitable, but this did not dissuade the Guardians from apprenticing these boys. Robert Weale did not take direct action to interfere with the Guardians' decisions, but instead he adopted an alternative and intermediate strategy. He laid down the following rules:

> The character of the intended masters were to be investigated; only orphans or bastards were to be sent on a month's trial and these children were to be given a free choice of whether they wished to be apprenticed or not, so that there was to be no coercion; and no premium apart from clothes was offered as an incentive to the master. Finally, a careful check was to be kept on the boys, who were to be produced to the Assistant Poor Law Commissioner, or his agent, at least every three months, if demanded.

The Worcester Guardians agreed to apply these rules in future. Rules and regulations were produced by the Poor Law Commission in 1845, which had much in common with the temporary rules produced by Robert Weale.[17] Under these official rules, pauper children had to be above nine years old before they could be sent to a master, who had to be in trade or business on their own account. These apprenticeships were for a period of no more than eight years, with no premium apart from clothes given, 'unless the person [the apprentice] was maimed, deformed, or suffering from permanent bodily infirmity'. In such cases a premium was to be paid in two instalments, half at the outset and half after one year of the apprenticeship, to ensure the continuance of that apprenticeship. Now any child to be sent as a parish apprentice was to be able to read and write their names unaided and permission from the parent had to be sought if a child was be sent more than thirty miles from its home. Children were not normally sent this distance from home to be apprenticed unless particularly good prospects were available or where a relative living in a distant area asked for a child as an apprentice. This stipulation was made to ensure continuing contact with parents, which it was thought would protect the child from maltreatment. There was one innovation in the official regulations not envisaged by Robert Weale's earlier regulations. This was medical inspection, which meant that a child had to be certified fit to be apprenticed, a new duty for the workhouse medical officer, who could also certify apprentices eligible for a premium to be paid to them because they were infirm or deformed.

The suitability of an applicant to take an apprentice or servant was also determined by the potential master's social status, so that when Jellinger C. Symons, HMI for workhouse schools, applied to Kidderminster Guardians for a boy as a servant in 1852,[18] this apprenticing was allowed immediately, with no time limit specified on the apprenticeship indenture – a clear contravention of a new legal requirement that a time limit be declared. However, within four months,[19] the boy was sent back as unsuitable and he was returned in a very sorry state, such that the Guardians successfully demanded he be reclothed at Jellinger C. Symons's expense. Indeed, it appeared possible that this matter may have been taken further had the person responsible for this ill treatment not been a senior Poor Law Board official. This case was in stark contrast to that of Mrs Hedley, the wife of the landlord of the Black Cross inn, at Bromsgrove. When she applied for a servant in 1864,[20] she was told that this could not be allowed and it appeared that the only reason for refusal was the applicant's relatively low social status. This reason was masked because, when Mrs Hedley complained to the Guardians about their refusal to grant her a servant, they replied that they were sorry and that 'they had not wished to cause offence or insult to her'. In spite of this, this lady was never allowed a servant, although there appeared to be no consistency in the way such applications were dealt with. The unofficial rules, used in such cases were applied differently from union to union, so that pauper children in other places in Worcestershire were often sent as servants to publicans.

The Parish Apprentices' Act of 1844[21] had abolished the allotment of apprentices and allowed premiums to be paid, which had been the practice under the Old Poor Law. This led some county unions to ask to start apprenticing immediately, but the Poor Law Commission resisted being rushed, so that in November 1844,[22] when Bromsgrove Guardians asked the amount of a premium that might be offered with an apprentice, the Commission refused to be drawn. Whilst they refused to state a fee, they did not say that a premium could not be paid. They gave a similar reply to Droitwich Guardians a month or so later,[23] when a carpet weaver from Kidderminster, asked for clothes for a boy sent on trial, but the Poor Law Commission insisted that they had no rules regarding apprenticeship premiums, including the giving of clothes. New apprenticeship rules allowing a premium to be paid were received by Boards of Guardians in January 1845, although a circular letter, sent with these new rules, still attempted to dissuade Guardians from paying premiums. Thus, Droitwich Guardians realised immediately that the apprenticeship they had in mind, while 'not directly opposed to the wording of the Act (regarding the occupational status of the master) would at least be contrary to the spirit of the provision'.[24] They decided not to confront the Central Poor Law Authority, and they successfully demanded that this apprentice be returned to the workhouse.[25]

The new apprenticeship regulations of 1845 were an attempt by the Poor Law Commission to regulate 'proceedings to be taken in relation to apprenticing pauper children'.[26] After this date, any union not cognisant of the new apprenticeship regulations came into dispute with the Assistant Poor Law Commissioner for the area, who used financial sanctions to force compliance with the regulations. Whereas between 1834 and 1838 individual unions' accounts were audited annually, from 1838 audit districts were created, so that if accounts were not agreed, an investigation drew attention to illegal expenditure, which could then be disallowed. This meant that between 1838 and 1845, illegal apprenticeship fees were identified in this way and those deemed illegal disallowed, which meant that all unions apparently came to comply with the Poor Law Commission's opinions on this matter.

In a relatively unusual case in 1845,[27] immediately before the issuing of national parish apprenticeship regulations, Bromsgrove Guardians decided to apprentice a boy aged ten years old to a fish-hook manufacturer in Redditch and they agreed a premium of two suits of clothes and £15. This was an inducement that was deemed illegal at the annual audit,[28] because this apprenticeship had been arranged before the payment of premiums was legalised. For this reason, the central Poor Law authority demanded that the Guardians reclaim the illegal apprenticeship fee. However, when this was done, this master very surprisingly did not return the apprentice, who completed his craft training. In fact, between 1781 to 1834, premiums with apprentices were relatively common and indeed in some parishes they were even expected, but the situation was to change and after 1834 Guardians were specifically dissuaded from making such payments, unless the child to be apprenticed was disabled. The justification for this was the utilitarian principles that informed the New Poor Law, which specifically forbade an able-bodied pauper child being placed at an advantage over its non-pauper contemporaries, thus contravening the Principle of Less Eligibility. Paying premiums fell into this category and the practice became much less common for a decade after 1834. Thus, only three of the seventy-four apprenticings between 1837 and 1844 attracted premiums and the Commission's advice was that only clothing could be offered as an incentive for a master to take an apprentice, even though for the fifty years before 1834 local apprentice masters expected to receive fees, not clothing, with apprentices.

The 1845 national rules for apprenticing allowed a premium to be paid, but only 40 of the 363 apprenticeships arranged in the county between 1845 and 1871 involved a fee. The policy of the Poor Law Commission between 1834 and 1844 was to discourage the paying of money with children sent for craft training, which broke the local custom of paying apprenticeship fees that had been common for at least fifty years prior to 1834. However, after the passing of the New Poor Law in 1834, most pauper children were sent to masters without a premium being paid, although some unions ignored the central authority's rules. For instance, Pershore union paid a premium with sixteen out of the twenty-two children it bound apprentice between 1837 and 1845, although only one of these children was described as infirm. Indeed, a very large fee of £10 was paid with an apparently able-bodied boy from Strensham in 1839,[29] and no mention was made of his fitness, possibly in the hope that the Poor Law Commission would not notice. There were six cases of a premium being paid with infirm pauper child during this period, but the case of a deaf and dumb boy being apprenticed at Bromsgrove was unique. Here a premium of £7 0s 0d was paid for him to be apprenticed to a bootmaker in 1851.[30] In the other five cases, lameness was the reason for a fee being offered, but perhaps significantly all of the fees paid were less than the premium offered with the mute child. Premiums offered with able-bodied pauper apprentices, in Worcestershire between 1834 and 1871, varied between £1 and £15 for boys and from 10s to £2 for girls, with the average paid for boys being £5 0s 6d and £1 8s 5d the mean fee for girls. County Guardians probably arranged apprenticeships for as little money as possible, a principle that undoubtedly met with the approval of both local Poor Rate payers and central Poor Law officials alike. For this reason, the Guardians usually agreed with Central Poor Law Authority and offered no apprenticeship fees at all. However, in a minority of cases, they felt that a craft training opportunity for a pauper child was worth a fee, even for an able-bodied child. In spite of this, no discernible connection was apparent between the size of the premium paid and the level of skill involved in the apprenticing trade.

Some county unions adopted a principle of apprentice at all cost, so that children were apprenticed to masters considered unsuitable by the Central Poor Law Authority. Mining apprenticeships in the Black Country and carpet weaving ones in Kidderminster were much criticised on this basis, although such cases were relatively unusual. The bulk of such cases were from Worcester union where, of twenty-six apprenticeships arranged in the period from June 1840 to June 1845, fifteen were to carpet weavers, and in Kidderminster union, where eight of the fifteen apprentices were to miners in the Black Country, the most hazardous and unhealthy of all apprenticing occupations. These dangers were well illustrated by the early reports of the Factory Inspectorate,[31] who described mining accidents sometimes involving apprentices. For instance, in 1838, the death of a pauper apprentice was reported to Droitwich Guardians by his master, who stated that the boy had been involved in an accident that had 'deprived him of life', so that he asked for an 'allowance towards the expenses he had been put to in burying him'.[32] The Guardians refused to allow this, a decision with which the Poor Law Commission later agreed. Another pauper apprentice, from Grafton Flyford in Pershore union, was killed in a mine at Old Hill by a fall of coal in 1850.[33] However, while mining was the most dangerous of all industries accepting apprentices, other trades had poor working conditions and harsh treatment for apprentices, which sometimes caused apprentices to abscond. Thus, in 1866,[34] a boy from Kidderminster union, who was apprenticed to a chainmaker at Cradley Heath, absconded because he said that he had been 'ill treated', although significantly he voluntarily returned to the workhouse instead of running away. This action, which suggested that he had strong evidence of maltreatment, led the Guardians to investigate and it was discovered that the boy had malformed ankles and feet that made it impossible for him to work as a chainmaker. Indeed this boy should never have been certified medically fit for apprenticing, so that in this case the medical inspection was apparently regarded as a mere formality. However, the medical officer was not reprimanded for inattention and nor was the case of maltreatment investigated. The Guardians simply sent the boy to an aunt, who was paid outdoor relief to care for him.

The apprenticing regulations of 1845, laid down by the Poor Law Commission, required that 'no child shall be bound to a person who is not a householder, or assessed to the poor rate in his own name, or is a journeyman, or is a person not carrying on trade or business on his own account'.[35] For this reason carpet weavers were confirmed as unacceptable as masters, because from about 1820 onwards they were employed by carpet manufacturers in the carpet factories of Kidderminster and were no longer in business on their own account, whereas before this date, these men had employed pauper boys and girls as drawboys (or girls). Now, in 1846[36] when Bromsgrove Guardians apprenticed a boy to a carpet weaver in Kidderminster, they did not report the facts to the Poor Commission, but the apprenticeship was recorded in the Guardians' minutes. Had this been noticed by the Commission, the Guardians would have been reprimanded for ignoring regulations, but whether this was done appeared a matter of chance, which questions the efficiency of the Poor Law Commission's administration. Only in a few cases were such illegal apprenticeships ever questioned. Kidderminster Guardians were unlucky, because when they attempted to apprentice a boy to a carpet weaver in the town, they were told 'the apprenticing of boys to carpet weavers is not allowed',[37] although whether illegal actions were noticed by the Poor Law Central Authority continued to be a matter of chance.

Coal miners, including butties – men who subcontracted work from the pit owners – like carpet weavers, were also regarded as unsuitable as apprentice masters after 1845. Both Bromsgrove and King's Norton unions in 1845,[38] soon after the new apprenticeship regulations were published, successfully evaded the rules by apprenticing boys to coal miners in the Black Country. In spite of this, the Poor Law Board reaffirmed their opinion, in 1849, that 'miners were not carrying on trade in their own right and that they were not eligible to take apprentices'.[39] However, within a few months, Bromsgrove Guardians again apprenticed two boys to miners[40] after the medical officer had certified them fit. No questions were asked by the Poor Law Board on this occasion, but within two years, in 1851, West Bromwich Guardians objected to Bromsgrove's apprenticing of a boy in contravention of the Commission's regulation.[41] This objection received the swift response from Bromsgrove Guardians that: 'If the Poor Law Board do not allow boys to miners, it will lead to serious inconvenience and difficulty'.[42] In spite of this, the Poor Law Board had no choice but to support West Bromwich Guardians' objection, although they later changed their opinion, after Lord Lyttelton, an influential lobbyist who lived at Hagley, near Stourbridge, had visited Somerset House to argue Bromsgrove Guardians' case.[43] He argued that Black Country colliers had their own capital and were thus suitable masters, an opinion with which the Poor Law Board now agreed. They now asserted that this was indeed a special case and that Bromsgrove union could continue to apprentice boys as miners in the Black Country, a judgement that appeared doubtful under the regulations. However, the intervention of an influential upper-class individual caused the central Poor Law Authorities to reconsider their decision in spite of their earlier opposition. The Poor Law Board now suggested that 'much discrimination and careful enquiry are required before apprenticing to colliers can safely take place',[44] but the county Boards of Guardians now fell into two distinct groups; those with upper-class individuals as members (as at Bromsgrove, Droitwich and Shipston on Stour) and those without such members. Thus, when the central Poor Law administration enforced their regulations, they sometimes deferred to the status of these upper-class individuals, making the treatment of unions by the Central Authority inconsistent, so that little uniformity in the process of apprenticing was possible, because of the manner of applying regulations that was more dependent on local factors, which was a clear contravention of the Principle of National Uniformity. The Law of Settlement of 1662 still applied after the 1834 Poor Law Amendment Act, thus placing a burden on the parish (union) accepting the apprentice and thus giving sufficient reason for unions accepting apprentices to be asked for their permission before an apprenticing took place, although this had not happened in the case cited earlier at West Bromwich. Usually Guardians who were asked agreed to these requests to allow apprenticings in their area as a matter of routine. The practice of asking the permission of the Board of Guardians of the union in which the child was bound apprentice was confirmed in the 1845 rules for apprenticeship, when new responsibilities were also conferred on apprentice masters.

These new responsibilities meant that a boy apprenticed by Bromsgrove Guardians in 1846, who was described as infirm and was apprenticed to the same fish-hook manufacturer who had earlier been forced to return an apprenticeship premium, and who was also sent with a premium of £15, was treated very differently. His apprenticeship indenture, which was unique in the county, specified the wages the boy was to be paid. These were to be: '9d per week for the first year, 11d per week for the second year, and 18d per week for the third and last year'.[45] This wording was in compliance with the 1845 rules for apprenticing, which required that wages were to be specified on the apprenticeship indenture. However, this case also illustrated that such rules were ignored, as no other Boards of Guardians complied with this regulation and none were censured for their omission.

One influence of the new regulations was that a common form of apprenticeship indenture was now used which specified the master's duties, thus satisfying one of the central Poor Law authority's disquiets about apprenticing. Their intentions were clearly stated in a circular letter in February 1845, when they said that: 'The object of the Commissioners has been to secure a careful attention on the part of the persons who bind children out to the fitness and propriety of the step which is to affect permanently the future condition of these children.'[46] The old system was clearly faulty, because it allowed too much freedom to apprentice masters, so that the new regulations of 1845,[47] which limited the place of work and the place of residence of the apprentice which were to be clearly stated on the indentures, were a clear improvement. Whereas, previously, apprentices could sometimes not be found to be inspected by the relieving officer because they had moved their address or even changed masters, they were theoretically now traceable. It was the new educational clauses in the 1845 regulation, that caused most problems for county unions. For instance at Bromsgrove, Guardians were worried about apprentices being required to 'read and write their names without assistance' before being apprenticed,[48] apparently because they were unconvinced that children from their union would be able to do this. They asked the visiting committee, who were responsible for the workhouse school, to investigate and they found that there was indeed a problem, which led to the schoolteachers there being told to improve their teaching of reading and writing. Such inadequacy in literacy skills appeared quite usual in rural unions, so that somewhat typically the education at Martley union was at fault, when a girl from there was sent to service who was 'utterly ignorant'.[49]

In 1847[50] and 1848[51] it was reported by the Poor Law Central Authority that the 1844 Act was 'working well', so that there was no need for the Poor Law Board to produce new rules and regulations regarding apprenticeship. However, according to Sidney and Beatrice Webb[52] by 1850 there was questioning of the desirability of apprenticeship in its existing form. This, it has been suggested by J.H. Stallard,[53] was because there was no pauper apprenticing other than of workhouse children, which caused disquiet as outdoor pauper children were considered as worthy of the opportunities provided by apprenticeship as were indoor pauper children, to whom such opportunities were exclusively available.

Other seemingly attractive ways of dealing with the pauper child problem included sending boys into the armed forces, to the merchant marine or to the fishing industry. However, when a circular was sent in March 1844, asking for a return of 'those children removed from the union workhouses into the army, and into the navy'[54] there was a nil return from all county unions, which suggested that this apparently simple and attractive solution to the child pauper problem was not a viable one. There was a similar negative response by Shipston on Stour union in 1845,[55] when they were asked to return a form showing those children apprenticed to the sea service in the period from 1834 to 1845. Five weeks earlier, these Guardians had apparently been keen to use seafaring apprenticeships, when they corresponded with the Poor Law Commission about five boys who wished to be apprenticed at sea, asking that 'the lads be placed on board one of HM ships'.[56] In this case the Poor Law Commission had replied[57] that inexperienced people were not wanted in the navy at that time. This reticence may have been explicable, because an Act of Parliament, passed later in 1845,[58] eventually completely prevented apprenticing on board ships, because of the conditions found there. Another Act of Parliament of 1850,[59] created opportunities for pauper boys to be apprenticed at sea, if the shipping company taking them was licensed to accept such trainees. The Poor Law Board now encouraged Guardians[60] to consider merchant marine apprenticeships and a letter was enclosed listing suitable marine masters to be approached to take pauper apprentices. There was no response from any county union at this time, although in 1854[61] Evesham Guardians again asked the Poor Law Board about enlistment in the Royal Navy. The response given was a repeat of the negative reply to Shipston on Stour Guardians in 1845. Ten years after this the Evesham Guardians asked about apprenticeships in the fishing trade,[62] which caused an immediate prevarication by the Poor Law Board, which completely missed the point. They replied that such an arrangement was difficult because Poor Law unions had been illegally canvassed for suitable apprentices, which was probably a reference to a circular sent direct to Droitwich Guardians at about this time from T. Waites and Co.[63] This fishing boat company was not licensed to receive pauper apprentices and had been successfully prosecuted for illegal approaches to Guardians, which led to the company being fined 40s for a breach of Poor Law Board regulations. In spite of this, Droitwich Guardians were still interested in these apprenticeships and the Poor Law Board suggested another company,

Holbeg and Bowen Co., a shipping company, who were licensed to take apprentices.[64] However, there were no vacancies at this time. Two years later[65] Bromsgrove Guardians were approached by J. Surdin and Co. of Liverpool, a shipper licensed to take apprentices, but ironically there were no boys suitable for apprenticing and their offer was refused. Thus, it appeared that the demand for apprentices often did not coincide with the presence of suitable pauper children in the workhouses, which was probably inevitable given that the destitution of children available for apprenticing was caused by the same economic circumstances that led potential employers to delay taking on additional labour.

After 1847, when the Poor Law Commission was replaced by the Poor Law Board, the central authority slowly began to change its attitude and began to encourage apprenticeship as a convenient way of ridding unions of the troublesome problem of dependent pauper children. The Central Poor Law Authority now gradually reacted positively to Poor Law unions' demands to apprentice children, so that county Guardians, who had always favoured apprenticeship, were now officially encouraged to use it. At about this time, Bromsgrove Guardians stated that 'much good might be effected by forming a society of ratepayers having for its object the apprenticing of poor children', a sentiment which now gained official approval, although the Guardians real disquiet was about the tendency of pauper children in Bromsgrove to learn nailmaking, a trade with few skills, because:

> as soon as they [the children] can learn sufficient means to support themselves they begin to work on their own account, allowing their parents a portion of their earnings inadequate for their support instead of giving up the whole to their parents at a time when such help would be most useful in enabling them to economise their united means to improve their condition, besides at this period, just as children are emerging from infancy, by remaining under the control of their parents, they are likely to acquire provident habits and become members of society.[66]

These Guardians demonstrated an uncharacteristic confidence in the providence of the working classes, in believing that the joint income of the family would ever be applied to supporting the whole family, thus reducing the need for poor relief. More usually, the working classes were regarded as wholly improvident and to blame for their own parlous state. For instance, on this occasion, a young nailmaker was cited, because once he had gained rudimentary skills, he did not add to the joint income of the family, thus reducing its propensity to become pauperised. Thus, he was regarded as blameworthy and a threat to Bromsgrove society and for this reason the Board of Guardians considered it preferable if these boys be apprenticed and efficiently controlled by their apprentice master, presumably outside the Bromsgrove union. In this way the threat to the local society was reduced. However, when a public meeting was called to discuss the idea and to provide a means of defraying the costs, the idea was rejected, in spite of the schemes' supposed attractions.

Apprenticeship remained the most common way for permanent inmate pauper children to leave county workhouses between 1847 to 1871, but occasionally pauper children were removed by relatives or were sent to orphanages or adopted. The children who were apprenticed were usually orphaned, deserted or bastards, who had been in the workhouse for prolonged periods of time and who had no one outside the institution to care for them. They formed a large minority of workhouse child inmates and were the sole responsibility of the Guardians. For the majority of pauper children in the workhouse the institution was a short-term expediency sought by parents in times of severe economic conditions or when inclement weather forced them out of work in their outdoor occupations, which meant that many of these children returned to the workhouse regularly. Few of these children were apprenticed by the union, because their parents did not ask for help in doing this, so that most such children drifted into employment, but there are no records of this and it is difficult to be specific about the outcome. Of orphaned, deserted and illegitimate pauper apprentices we know more, as great care was taken in dealing with these inmates, because it was realised that the 'taint of the workhouse' was on them and they were thus believed to have a greater propensity to return to the workhouse in later life than other poor children, including the 'ins and outs', who returned to the institution at regular intervals. A child's length of stay in the workhouse thus appeared imperative in determining the lasting effects of incarceration there.

From the very beginning of the county Poor Law unions in 1836, attempts were made to distance pauper apprentices from their workhouse origins. Thus, in 1839, Kidderminster Guardians ordered that the clothes of children to be apprenticed were 'not to be pauper clothing' or to have 'pauper buttons'.[67] This was so that the new apprentice was not identifiable as a workhouse child. This potential harm to the pauper apprentice was also considered important by Pershore Guardians in 1839, when they expressed the belief that 'boys of twelve or fourteen should as early as possible be placed in a situation where they can obtain their own livelihood, as continuance in the workhouse under any circumstances cannot fail to be injurious to them'.[68] Such attempts to distance pauper children from their institutional origins continued throughout the period to 1871. The same reasoning lay behind a decision to give girls sums of money for clothing when they were sent to service, so that the chance of them being recognised as from the workhouse was reduced. Thus, a girl sent to service from Tenbury Wells union in 1838,[69] was allowed 16s 4d to purchase clothing.

If an apprenticeship failed, the blame sometimes lay with the person taking the apprentice, with some such children neglected once they were with their master (or mistress). For instance in 1838,[70] Tenbury Wells' Guardians demanded to know why some apprentices were not being supported by their masters. One girl servant was returned to the workhouse having been unofficially rejected by the lady to whom she was sent, but the Guardians successfully demanded that she be returned to her mistress in this case. Pressure on Guardians to ensure that pauper children were satisfactorily placed in apprenticeship or service was increased after the 1844, when the Parish Apprentices' Act was passed. Now, a request from farm labourers at Chaddesley Corbett, in Kidderminster union in 1845, for two girls out of the workhouse 'to nurse their children'[71] during the harvest months was refused, whereas previously such a request would have been acceded to. After the 1844 Act a great deal more care was taken regarding the character and situation of potential masters and by 1846 the apprenticing of children from the workhouse was largely regularised. It now had the character and function envisaged by the Poor Law Inquiry Commission in 1834, in providing a sound base from which a pauper child could begin an independent life. Potential apprentice masters were now carefully vetted to ensure they were suitable individuals to receive apprentices, who were now medically inspected to ensure their capability to work and tested to ensure that they were literate.

The medical officer of Bromsgrove union workhouse examined seven children in August 1846 and proclaimed them 'fit for apprenticing'.[72] However, in other cases, the medical officer certified children infirm, so that suitable apprenticeships, backed by the assurance of an apprenticeship premium, could be ensured. At Bromsgrove in 1847, a boy aged fourteen years with 'a dislocation of the knee',[73] was given a premium of £6 0s 0d and clothing to the value of £1 0s 0d. Premiums paid with infirm apprentices were usually greater than those for able-bodied apprentices, although medical inspection sometimes appeared a mere formality, with only a small unrepresentative minority of inspected pauper children declared unfit. Uniquely, at Droitwich in 1847,[74] the medical officer declared an eleven-year-old boy 'too weak to be apprenticed' to a cordwainer, so that the apprenticeship was abandoned. However, there must have been other infirm pauper children offered for apprenticeship who were simply passed medically fit and sent away anyway.

Children were sometimes apprenticed in their home union, but more often they were sent to industrial centres such as Birmingham and the Black Country, where apprenticeship opportunities were more plentiful. Black Country places, such as Bilston, Bloxwich, Darlaston, Sedgley, Wednesbury, West Bromwich, and to some extent Wolverhampton, offered mining apprenticeships, while Kidderminster took pauper apprentices in a variety of trades, but not in the carpet-weaving trade. Glass-making and glass-cutting in the area around Brierley Hill also attracted pauper apprentices, while other boys continued to be sent to shoemakers and tailors, but these apprentices tended to be younger than others, because these trades were regarded as not strenuous, so that it was thought that youngsters could cope with the work.

There were 344 boys and 93 girls apprenticed between 1837 and 1871, a smaller number per year, on average, than in the period 1781 to 1834. However, what was more important was that the nature of these apprenticeships had altered. Whereas, previously, outdoor pauper children were sometimes apprenticed, now those apprenticed were exclusively indoor paupers and there were significant differences in the trades to which children were now apprenticed. The major change regarding the apprenticing of boys occurred in rural places, where apprenticing to agricultural labouring was now much less common than before 1834. This was probably because work for boys on the land was now found without the need to apprentice them. Generally boys were now apprenticed to trades with increased skill levels, although eleven boys were still sent to carpet weavers, probably to be employed as drawboys, setting up the carpet looms, which was unskilled work. Most skilled workers in the carpet trade continued to be recruited by internal recruitment, from families already employed in the trade, which ensured a maintenance of their monopoly over this sort of work. Most pauper carpet-weaving apprentices came from Worcester union, although such apprenticing ceased after 1847, when carpet weavers were declared unsuitable masters. Likewise, little or no skill was apparently taught to boys sent to the coal and mineral mining industries based in the Black

Country, but in spite of this ninety-one boys were sent there between 1837 and 1871, mainly from Bromsgrove and Droitwich unions. Skilled occupations attracted most of the remaining male apprentices.

Of ninety-three girls apprenticed between 1837 and 1871, seventy-two went to domestic service, while there were nine girls with no description entered on their indentures, who probably also became domestic servants. However, given the employment market for females in the nineteenth century, these low numbers were no surprise. Analysis of domestic service apprenticeships in Bromsgrove, Droitwich, Kidderminster, King's Norton and Pershore unions revealed that between 75 per cent and 91 per cent of girls apprenticed were as domestic servants. Droitwich and Pershore unions apprenticed a larger percentage of girls to household work than did the other three more urban unions investigated, which was probably explained by the fact that unskilled female employment was more easily available in urban unions, close to the Black Country and to Birmingham, than elsewhere in rural Worcestershire. There was probably less need to apprentice girls in these urban unions.

Perhaps significantly, some unions sent children further afield to be apprenticed than others, with the geographical location of the union, and its nature, appearing important in determining this. Bromsgrove and Kidderminster unions, which were conveniently placed to send children to the Black Country and King's Norton union, contiguous with the fast-developing industrial town of Birmingham, found apprenticeships for many pauper children. Even in these large urban unions the supply of suitable apprenticeships was sometimes scarce, so that Guardians had to advertise for suitable masters. King's Norton first advertised for apprentice opportunities in 1856,[75] when three apprenticings for boys resulted and they advertised again in 1862, this time stating that the Guardians 'would be pleased to hear of places for them [girls of thirteen to fifteen years old] and would permit a reasonable trial for respectable applicants',[76] but no girls were apprenticed on this occasion. Another attempt was made, in 1868, when two advertisements were placed announcing that girls were 'available for service',[77] and on this occasion local clergymen were asked to vouch for the respectability of all applicants. The girls fit for service were listed by the medical officer and four were sent to service following this publicity, a success that caused the same union to advertise again in 1870.[78] Droitwich union were less successful in its advertising for apprenticeship places at about this time,[79] but most other unions did not bother to advertise at all, apparently because they found sufficient places for apprentices and servants without publicity. Indeed, sometimes enquiries for apprentices and servants came from neighbouring unions, with potential masters considering a distance between the apprentice and his home union desirable, a principle of which most Guardians approved, because this also ensured resettlement of the child at the end of its apprenticeship. Thus, when a Worcester hairdresser asked Droitwich Guardians for a suitable apprentice in 1848, this apprenticeship was allowed immediately,[80] as was an apprenticeship to a chemist and druggist from Darlaston in 1854.[81] In other cases the numbers of apprentices requested was higher, as when Baldwin and Co., iron founders of Stourport, offered to take a number of boys over twelve years old from Kidderminster workhouse in 1869, 'giving them employment coupled with careful oversight under competent workmen'.[82] This was an opportunity that was accepted, so that two boys were sent on two months' trial and eventually apprenticed.[83]

The distance migrated by pauper apprentices also revealed some interesting patterns. Of 346 male pauper apprentices, 253 (73.1 per cent) moved away from their parish (union) of origin, so that their settlement was altered at the end of their craft training. The average distance migrated by these boys was 9.8 miles, in contrast to 91 female apprentices, 67 (76.3 per cent) of whom moved from their place of birth to be apprenticed. The average distance migrated by these girls was only 5.15 miles, which again probably illustrated that apprenticeships for the smaller numbers of pauper girls involved were more easily found locally. These findings contrasted with the period from 1781 to 1834, when fewer apprentices of both sexes migrated shorter distances, although this was in a situation where an apprentice only had to move out of its parish of birth to alter its settlement. In contrast, after 1834, an apprentice had to move out of their union of birth to attain a new place of settlement, which involved moving much greater distances. However, in rural unions, the problems of child pauperism had become less severe and apprenticing thus became less common.

There were differences between unions that apprenticed small numbers of inmate pauper children and unions that apprenticed more than 100 children in the period from 1834 to 1871. In unions apprenticing large numbers of pauper children, a lower percentage of females than males migrated from their birthplaces when apprenticed, which probably again reflected the relative ease with which apprenticeships for girls could be obtained. Such girls moved shorter average distances than did their male contemporaries, but the geographical location of the unions was inevitably very important in determining the nature of this migration. Those unions furthest from the industrial centres of the Black Country and Birmingham now sent their apprentices greater distances to obtain employment than did less isolated unions. Few children were sent over 30 miles from their birthplace, a temptation that was resisted because those sent further afield invoked special inspection arrangements, under the 1845 apprenticeship regulations.

An Act of Parliament in 1851[84] enabled Guardians to claim expenses for sending a relieving officer to report on pauper children apprenticed up to five miles from the home union, but not for those sent further away, which undoubtedly acted as a disincentive to such long distance apprenticeships. Pauper child apprentices now had to be inspected by the relieving officer of the union who accepted them. The relieving officer of the receiving union now reported what he found to the apprentice's home union, which was an arrangement thought to safeguard the accepting union as well as the apprentice itself. Thus, King's Norton inspected a boy from Warwick union, who had been apprenticed to a man in Northfield in 1854.[85] He was visited by the King's Norton union relieving officer, who reported satisfactorily to Warwick Guardians, as well as to his own Board of Guardians. Such reports were usually reasonable and King's Norton Guardians retrospective comment of 1870 reflected this, when they stated 'their (the apprentices) employers have scarcely a fault to find with their general behaviour and habits of industry'.[86] In spite of this, the employer's perception was considered crucial, while the opinion of the relieving officer was seldom used and the opinion of the apprentice was never quoted – in spite of regulations produced after the Act, in 1851,[87] that required that this be done.

Very occasionally adverse reports on apprentices were made by relieving officers. This was the case when George Smith, of Blockley in Shipston on Stour union, took twelve girls from the Bristol union workhouse in 1859[88] to train as silk throwsters. The basic problem here was that Mr Smith took the girls 'under contract', instead of apprenticing them, in a scheme approximating to batch apprenticing. Almost inevitably the local Guardians objected to this as the arrangement was outmoded and had received much adverse criticism at the time of the Poor Law report in 1834. The chairman of Shipston on Stour Board of Guardians, Lord Rederdale, was so exercised by this that he instituted an enquiry and made a personal visit to the Poor Law Board in London to discuss the matter.[89] Again, the chairman was a man of influence, who probably intended to use his status to persuade the Central Poor Law Authority of the justice of the local Guardian's case. In the event, all that happened was that Assistant Poor Law Commissioner J.T. Graves was sent to investigate the way that the girls were treated and housed. Graves found the lodgings, bedding, clothing and food of the girls satisfactory, but he was worried about the religious education offered. This was particularly because one Roman Catholic girl had been sent to Anglican services while in the workhouse and to the local Baptist Church by the silk manufacturer, so that a charge of proselytism could be justly levelled equally at the workhouse administrators and at the apprentice master. However, the Assistant Poor Law Commissioner insisted that generally great care had been taken over religious instruction. He considered the girls equipped to do well, being able to earn wages of five shillings a week at the end of their agreement, which was just sufficient for a single woman to subsist on. He stated that the Poor Law Board could be assured that 'there are no temptations, and that prostitution does not exist in the town',[90] so that the Commissioners could be satisfied about employment arrangements. This satisfied the Poor Law Board, who made no further comment and matters were allowed to rest. Thus, Lord Rederdale's influence was clearly insufficient to take the matter further, whereas a more influential contemporary might have been able to do more. However, Rederdale had obtained a hearing for the Shipston on Stour Guardian's complaint. Some similar warnings about the possible outcome of apprenticeships received even less attention, as when Bromsgrove Guardians wanted to send a boy as an apprentice to a hairdresser in Birmingham in 1867. In this case, the Birmingham Guardians drew attention to the fact that the master, 'carried on trade on a Sunday',[91] which they clearly regarded as morally suspect, but the Bromsgrove Guardians were undaunted and proceeded with the apprenticeship anyway.

Apprenticeships were sometimes unsuccessful and a master returned an apprentice, or servant, who proved unsatisfactory. This happened at Droitwich in 1840,[92] when a girl servant was returned to the workhouse for dishonesty and the Guardians wrote to the Poor Law Commission for advice as to how this girl might be punished. The central authority suggested that the girl, aged fourteen years old, be placed in the adult women's ward, so that she would not taint other girls,[93] but the Guardians found this punishment unacceptable. This reaction illustrated well the deteriorating relationships that had evolved between central and local Poor Law administrations, which were now sometimes acrimonious. The Central Poor Law Authority was an advisory body, but their advice sometimes caused resentment. Such tensions in relationships were first apparent at Worcester, in 1841, when the Guardians sent a resolution to the Poor Law Commission that stated that: 'the powers of the Assistant Poor Law Commissioner relative to parish apprenticeship would be more suitably left to the discretion of the Guardians'.[94] This situation was created and accentuated by the action of Assistant Commissioner Robert Weale in writing unofficial local apprenticeship regulations, which caused some resentment. The Guardians saw official regulations as unnecessary and they still adhered to Robert Weale's unofficial rules, although this situation was to improve, as greater agreement developed between local and central Poor Law administrations regarding apprenticeship, so that by 1871 there was usually a concordance between these two groups regarding pauper apprenticeship.

Inevitably, some children refused to work once they were apprenticed. Thus, an outdoor pauper child from Stourbridge, who had unusually been apprenticed at his father's request to an engineer at Brierley Hill,[95] refused to work and conducted himself badly, so that the Guardians cancelled his indentures and he was returned to the workhouse. However, King's Norton Guardians in 1863,[96] refused to apply such sanctions – as they pointed out to the master, he could summons his apprentice before the magistrates and force him to work. They gave similar advice again in 1864,[97] but elsewhere apprentices were returned to the workhouse having been dealt with by the magistrates, in some cases having been convicted of criminal offences. At Bromsgrove in 1852,[98] the indentures of a button-maker's apprentice were cancelled after four months, when he was found guilty of theft and was sent to prison for ten days. Similarly, at Kidderminster in 1854,[99] another boy was returned to the workhouse for dishonesty. However, in other cases a longer period elapsed before a criminal offence was committed. Thus, a boy apprenticed by Droitwich union in 1857,[100] was convicted of stealing from his master and was imprisoned with his indentures cancelled, in spite of the fact that seven years of his apprenticeship had elapsed.[101] He was returned to the workhouse on his release from prison and later he refused to be apprenticed again.[102] Servants were the group most commonly returned to the workhouse for indiscipline, as in 1858[103] when a baker brought his servant back to King's Norton Guardians demanding she be disciplined. He said he was unable to keep her owing to her 'misconduct' (the word 'dishonesty' had been scored out in the minutes), so that her apprenticeship was cancelled and she was re-admitted to the workhouse.

In other cases, apprentices sometimes complained about their masters, as when a shoemaker's apprentice at Bromsgrove, in 1851,[104] complained about not being taught to make shoes, merely to repair them. However, his master appeared before the Guardians and produced a pair of shoes made by the boy, which caused the Guardians to express their satisfaction with the training given. The boy now alleged that he had not been given clothes promised to him when he was apprenticed, but the master retorted that the boy's parents had offered to supply clothes, but this was contrary to the Guardian's recollection and they demanded that the master supply his apprentice with clothes. Occasionally apprenticing arrangements were unsatisfactory from the outset and pauper children refused to be apprenticed. This happened at King's Norton in 1851,[105] when a girl refused to go as a domestic servant to a man in Northfield. The Guardians were relatively powerless in this situation, although they did punish this girl, but elsewhere a boy from Bromsgrove, who refused to be apprenticed to a miner at Darlaston in 1853, because 'he had objections to coal pits and would not work in them',[106] was allowed to stay in the workhouse.

Cases of maltreatment of apprentices and servants were worrying to both the Guardians and the central administration. For instance, at Droitwich in 1852,[107] a girl was sent as a servant to a woman in Barbourne Lane, Worcester, but after a short time she returned to the workhouse complaining about being ill-treated. This complaint was sustained and her mistress was fined £2 11s 0d for unlawful assault. However, not all cases were regarded as seriously as this, as at Droitwich in 1853, when a man who 'treated an apprentice in a harsh and improper manner', was not prosecuted; instead he was told to 'use all correction in future more modestly' and his apprentice was advised to be 'more industrious in future and more obedient'.[108] There was only one case of severe maltreatment of an apprentice in the county between 1837 and 1871, at Cleobury Mortimer in 1861,[109] where a girl from Kidderminster workhouse, who was originally sent as a servant to Chaddesley Corbett in 1859, had moved with the agreement of the Kidderminster Guardians. When this girl returned to Kidderminster workhouse in 1861 the girl was in 'a deplorable state, suffering from ill-usage to a considerable extent . . . the poor girl had been shamefully and cruelly treated [and was in] a most emaciated and wretched state'.[110] The maltreatment was so bad that the mistress and her husband were prosecuted at Shrewsbury Crown Court. Whilst the husband was found not guilty of any offence, his wife was found guilty of ill-treating the girl and was sentenced to six month's imprisonment. The costs of the case (£23 10s 0d) were paid by Cleobury Mortimer Guardians, who were reimbursed by Kidderminster union. In a less severe case, in 1870, Kidderminster Guardians investigated the complaints of a boy, who said he was being overworked and ill-treated,[111] but while the Guardians found some cause for his complaints, these were insufficient to prosecute the master, so instead they released the boy from his apprenticeship agreement.

The situation of apprentices improved during the period 1834 to 1871, as conditions became more regulated and both the central authority and local Boards of Guardians investigated complaints about ill-treatment and prosecuted errant masters in gross cases. Now there was apparently an effort made to ensure equitable treatment for all pauper apprentices and common attitudes towards apprenticeship were encouraged. The rules and regulations produced in 1844 and 1845[112] began this process by legitimating the good practices instigated by Assistant Poor Law Commissioner Robert Weale's temporary regulations.[113] This undoubtedly influenced the Poor Law Commission in formulating their own rules in 1845, although there were some innovations in these. For instance medical inspection was introduced, as were the educational clauses demanding apprentices be able to read and write their own name unaided before being eligible to be apprenticed. However, the most influential of all the innovations was that specifying the duties of the master.

When, prior to 1845, apprentices were treated badly they were seldom removed from their masters, so that Guardians had been relatively ineffective in dealing with such situations. Now, however, complainants were invariably withdrawn from their apprenticeships and their indentures cancelled, which removed them from any further potential danger. Apprentices' living conditions were also better regulated under the new code of practice and it was ensured that their wages were paid regularly. Relieving officers did this by diligently monitoring conditions, including the apprentice's rights to religious freedom and to education (albeit only on Sunday). Whilst the 1834 Poor Law Amendment Act had been beneficial to parish apprentices, outlawing the allotment system of apprenticing, the 1844 Act and the regulations that followed it, in 1845, were even more effective in improving matters. The Act and these regulations remained in force until after 1871, because the central administration found it unnecessary to issue many amending orders and regulations on this topic between 1845 and 1871. Instead, they relied on the enforcement of existing rules and regulations by the Assistant Poor Law Commissioners, aided by union relieving officers. This illustrated the success of the Poor Law central administration in writing water-tight apprenticeship rules this early in their history.

The diligence of Poor Law officials, both at a local and a national level, ensured that conditions for pauper apprentices improved drastically between 1834 and 1871, with the most remarkable transformation of the Central Poor Law Authority's opinion towards pauper apprenticing occurring between 1834 and 1844. Where initially there was a refusal to encourage such apprenticeship, this was replaced by a period of reluctant acceptance of apprenticeship, around the time of the creation of the Poor Law Board in 1847, following the first regulations for apprenticing. This was followed by a rapid conversion to an acceptance of the apprenticeship system, which was now thought to aid workhouse children in getting a start in life, thus avoiding life-long pauperism. Whilst pauper apprentices gained in employment prospects one might argue that this was at the expense of the children of the independent poor, which was a stark contravention of the Principle of Less Eligibility.

It was apparent that the orthodoxy of the central Poor Law authority towards apprenticeship before 1844 and its adherence to the utilitarian principles, on which the administration of poor relief was based, was to be eroded. However, this was probably inevitable given the nature of the problem posed to Boards of Guardians, particularly in urban unions, by the large numbers of destitute children alone in the workhouses. Inevitably, urban unions continued to use pauper apprenticeship as a solution to these problems as they had done under the Old Poor Law prior to 1834. Whilst the Poor Law Board, after 1847, initially tacitly sanctioned apprenticeship, it soon came to actively support its use, with a changed attitude coinciding with the related joint demise of the influence of utilitarian ideologues and of Edwin Chadwick at the Central Poor Law Authority.

Between about 1850 and 1871 apprenticeship rates settled at a constant level and while one might argue that it was functional for unions to rid themselves of the problems posed by long-term pauper child inmates, it was apparent that most Guardians used apprenticeship with more care and humanity than previously, so that children were placed in appropriate positions and increasingly their conditions were monitored. The Principle of Less Eligibility was eroded and eventually ignored, so that the administration of apprenticeship became pragmatic, which also meant that any notion of uniformity of treatment in this aspect of Poor Law administration was impossible. Thus, the Principle of National Uniformity was also eroded. Apprenticeship and service had utility not only to the Poor Law unions, but increasingly its usefulness to the child was also recognised and it can be seen as one element in the rescue of permanent child pauper inmates from life-long pauperism adopted by Poor Law administrators and public alike.

A distinction between rural and urban unions was apparent, as after 1834 rural unions virtually ceased apprenticeships, whereas prior to the Poor Law Amendment Act[114] they had apprenticed the largest numbers of parish poor children, using the now discredited and illegal allotment system of apprenticing. After 1834, urban Poor Law unions continued to apprentice pauper children, although at a lower rate than previously, which possibly demonstrated that the attempt to supplant apprenticeship by education as a means of solving the problem caused by the pauper child, suggested by Francis Duke,[115] must therefore have been partly successful. Again this conclusion can only be reached from local studies that use the supposedly biased evidence of Boards of Guardian's Minute Books, that had been rejected as sources by administrative historians like Alec Ross.[116] Obviously apprenticeship continued to provide the only legitimate escape from the workhouse for the deserted or orphaned destitute child, for whom the alternative was continued residence in the workhouse with the continued threat of life-long pauperism thought to be endemic there. This was the very eventuality the New Poor Law had been intended to avoid. Parish apprenticeships were seldom available to transient child inmates of the workhouses, and then one is left with the unfortunate impression that the New Poor Law cared less for these equally vulnerable individuals than for their destitute peers in the workhouse.

CONCLUSION

This book on the condition and treatment of indoor pauper children in the thirteen Worcestershire Poor Law unions, between 1834 and 1871, adds to the stock of studies about the New Poor Law. There have been over thirty detailed studies produced during the last four decades, which fall into two distinct categories: social histories and administrative histories, with the methodology employed by the historians writing them largely determining the nature of the outcome of the research. Social histories are written using local sources, such as Boards of Guardians' Minute Books, whilst administrative histories of the New Poor Law use central Poor Law administration sources, such as printed annual reports or the quarterly reports presented by Poor Law inspectors. This book has used Boards of Guardians' Minute Books as its prime sources, which were then elucidated, where necessary, from central administration papers such as orders and circulars. It is a social history intended to describe the conditions endured by the largest group of all indoor paupers – the children. Social histories tend also to relate to a specific geographical locality and are thus also local histories, whereas administrative histories relate to the national scene, although typically they illustrate points of procedure by reference to local documents, such as Guardians' Minute Books. Other social histories of the New Poor Law[1] provide useful comparisons with this book, particularly as some of them relate to rural counties. However, many other social histories of the Poor Law relate to towns or cities.[2] Most of these works also relate to all categories of pauper, including children. There are a few studies[3] relating to the treatment of child paupers that were useful for comparison. All of these were clearly social histories. Other work[4] has investigated the national administration of the New Poor Law, while a few administrative historians[5] have studied the national administration of the Poor Law relating to child paupers. Still more historians have studied aspects such as workhouse architecture[6] or specific workhouse and union offices.[7] This book is more detailed than most other work on the New Poor Law, deliberately so, as it is an attempt to reconstruct the situation of the workhouse child between 1834 and 1871. It has been organised to consider general treatment, medical treatment, education and training. This conclusion attempts a synoptic appraisal in relation to the treatment of such children.

Administrative historians[8] are clearly mindful of the methodological distinction between the two categories of Poor Law history and specifically reject Boards of Guardians' Minutes as biased sources, choosing instead what they regard as objective sources; the central administration's annual reports. These documents were produced by the Poor Law Commission, and after 1847 by the Poor Law Board, and consisted of collations of material produced during the year, including copies of all administrative orders and circulars, inspectors' reports and detailed reports of specific incidents occurring in various Poor Law unions. It would thus be possible to argue that these documents were just as biased, perhaps even consistently biased. This was not the case with locally generated minutes, which varied from union to union, and indeed from time to time, as the membership of Boards of Guardians altered. While the consistency of national Poor Law papers lent themselves to the administrative historian's purpose, any criticism of local sources is an overstatement, for the very biases objected to are important in this book, a major aim of which was to describe in detail the life of a child inmate in Worcestershire, between 1834 and 1871. Administrative literature published with the particular purpose of informing and convincing parliamentarians, and others, of the smooth running of the Poor Law machine, was not useful in achieving the prime aim of this book. Whilst recognising that the Board of Guardians' Minutes will have been the edited version of happenings in the workhouse, together with the Guardians' opinions on those events, it was likely that they were a more realistic view than the expurgated version offered by national Poor Law papers, which had been passed through a filter of orthodoxy within Somerset House, the headquarters of the central administration. The present book is thus a local social history of the New Poor Law in Worcestershire.

Implicit in many studies, and in literature about the history of the New Poor Law, was a belief in the existence of a rural and an urban version of the law. Whilst this was a useful device for contrasting, say, Tenbury Wells union, the most rural Worcestershire union, with Dudley, the most urban one, these places were extremes and comparisons may be misleading. In fact, there was probably a continuum of unions arrayed between these extremes, according to their rurality or urbanity, which was related not only to the size of population of the union, but also to population density and indeed to the nature of the union. As suggested, in nineteenth-century literature, it was urban, industrialised and hence densely populated areas that were threatening to the middle and upper classes, because of the social problems that were found there. Whilst this was a cause for concern to the social élite, it was not a cause for concern to Poor Law institutions. They simply provided workhouse facilities, whatever the nature of paupers using them. It was the numbers of paupers in the workhouses that created problems, particularly for inmate children, many of whom were permanently in the workhouse, so that although the cause of an individual seeking relief in an urban union was different to that in a rural place, the nature of the pauper's needs and the relief given did not vary. Indeed, the Principle of National Uniformity was intended to preclude such variation. Essentially, therefore, variations in the treatment received by indoor child paupers was explicable in terms of the size of the problem, with the size of population likely to become pauperised being one important element and thus the urban or rural nature of the union was, in some senses, unimportant.

Within broad bounds, the treatment provided in the Worcestershire Poor Law union with the largest indoor child pauper population was similar to that where there were the smallest numbers of pauper children, although within the county there were difficulties relating to finance that clouded this issue. Larger unions spent more on workhouse officers' salaries, while central administration rules and regulations specifically precluded the appointment of some types of officer in small unions. For instance, industrial training was provided in all unions, but it was only in larger unions that a specific officer responsible for such training was appointed and the provision of nursing staff was similarly circumscribed. For such reasons, whilst all unions did provide the same range of services to pauper inmates, it depended on the size of union how these services were organised and variation between large and small unions within the county thus appeared inevitable. The division of the Poor Law into urban and rural sectors was therefore inappropriate, rather there was a continuum of treatment of pauper children that appeared to be related to the amount of usage of workhouse facilities, rather than to the urban or rural nature of the union.

The Poor Law continued to be a social control measure, with local

Poor Law officials acting as 'social police', as described by A.P. Donajgrodski.[9] What certainly differed was the local inhabitants' perception of whether the destitute (or near destitute) poor were threatening, although the evidence amassed in this study does not suggest that within the county the poor were seen as that threatening. This was apparent from Guardians' minute books, which contained no indication of such a threat and this was in stark contrast to Metropolitan and other large urban areas, where the destitute poor were certainly seen as threatening. Within the county there appeared to be an acceptance that workhouses must be provided, although some unions were slow in forming and some areas were without a workhouse for up to three years after the Poor Law Amendment Act in 1834.

The different dates of the formation of Poor Law unions also indicated the relative enthusiasm of the inhabitants of a locality for the New Poor Law. However, there was no pattern to this and thus some rural unions, as well as urban ones, were slow to form. Setting up a local Poor Law union and opening a workhouse was a procedure prescribed by statute and circumscribed by rules and regulations from the outset. The Assistant Poor Law Commissioners, initially employed because of their orthodoxy towards the utilitarian ideology of the New Poor Law, had oversight of the creation of unions and the setting up of workhouses. All union workhouses were set up to conform to the same rules and regulations and all were uniformly staffed according to the central authority's edicts regarding staff: pauper ratios. The workhouse staff were also remunerated according to fixed salary scales that were unattractive, given the privations implicit in their workhouse life. The implication of this was that the Poor Law was a social control mechanism, although the nature of the threat posed by destitute individuals determined how overt this mechanism was. The Principle of Less Eligibility, a major tenet of the New Poor Law, was the product of Jeremy Bentham's utilitarian ideas in *Pauper Management Improved*, published in 1785. This suggested that there should be a 'workhouse test' in which the destitute should make a conscious decision to enter the workhouse, thus accepting the privations implied. The workhouse was to be an environment that was not attractive to potential inmates. The conditions there were to be no better than the conditions enjoyed (or more properly endured) by the lowest level of independent labourer outside the workhouse. Given that the condition of this class was parlous anyway, which resulted in their homes invariably being squalid, their diet wholly inadequate and their health, at best, indifferent, this was difficult. This situation was made even more complex by an insistence that the treatment of inmates should be humane, that they be kept in sanitary conditions, fed an adequate, if monotonous, diet and that their conditions be well regulated. Thus requirements that the workhouse provide Less Eligibility and consistent, effective, humane and regulated conditions were at first sight contradictory.

Inevitably, education and training were soon used as a solution to coping with the problems created by workhouse children and eventually the Poor Law central authority began to demand that such education must be provided. They then prescribed its type, but the different nature of the county's unions began to cause problems. Generally, rural unions were more resistant to demands for thorough intellectual, industrial and moral training than were urban ones. The case of Martley union's resistance to teaching writing, between 1839 and 1848, was the most extreme case nationally of such resistance. Problems stemmed from the nature of rural Guardians, who tended to be elected by farmers and rural craftsmen, who saw little use in the workhouse education offered. They saw it as infringing the Principle of Less Eligibility. On the other hand, urban Guardians saw the education offered as having utility for them, as they were the employers of labour, and contemporaneously the virtues of a trained and educated workforce was emerging. They saw workhouse education as beneficial to child paupers and were quite willing to accept less rigid definitions of Less Eligibility. Guardians in intermediate places, that were neither rural nor urban, such as Pershore, where the Boards of Guardians were drawn from both rural and urban parishes, disagreed. The Guardians representing urban parishes within Pershore union, differed profoundly in their opinions from those representing rural places. The resolution of this favoured the rural Guardians, who were in a slight majority on the Board. Education in union workhouses thus often differed because of variations in the dominant ideology of the Board of Guardians. Any notion of uniformity of treatment between unions must therefore be questioned, particularly when the financing of the Poor Law was also considered, because unions with a small potential pauper population had less Poor Rate support. The New Poor Law initially rigidly maintained Less Eligibility for all classes of pauper, including children, although within ten years changed attitudes towards the culpability of child inmates for their plight, meant that Less Eligibility was rejected as a principle for the treatment of child paupers.

National Uniformity, another major tenet of the New Poor Law, was thus to be ensured by adherence to rigid regulations, but because the size of the potentially pauperised population varied, this did not imply uniformity of treatment. The greatest problems with inmate children in Worcestershire unions arose when large numbers of children were crowded into the workhouses. By 1840 it was apparent that more than one-third of all county workhouse inmates were children (those under sixteen years old). This problem was exacerbated because children were in the workhouse for the longest periods of time of any pauper, theoretically, in some cases for up to sixteen years. Children, although not specifically mentioned in the Poor Law Amendment Act, were present in the county's workhouses from the outset in 1834. This was inevitable, given that the traditional means of ridding parishes of destitute and orphaned children, that of parish apprenticeship, was now officially disapproved of and had ceased, between 1834 and 1844.

National Uniformity was initially a simplistic concept, which presumed common treatment of all pauper classes, although, as suggested, the needs of many classes of pauper differed considerably from those for whom the workhouse régime had originally been designed. However, the workhouse was a wholly segregated place, with all inmates meeting only at meal times, when they were assiduously controlled. In this circumstance, to talk of a unitary 'total institution' was misleading. Rather, the workhouse was an agglomeration of several different total institutions, each with a different purpose. The children's wards could thus operate in a different way from adult and aged persons' wards without infringing the Principle of National Uniformity. This meant that the Principle could be said to be maintained between similar wards in workhouses nationally. The earliest rules and regulations produced were intended to be applied universally, but gradually specific rules relating to the conduct of specific classes of pauper evolved. After 1847, when the Poor Law Board came into existence, there were few rules and regulations that applied across the whole spectrum of paupers. The exceptions to this related to such matters as admissions and discharge procedures.

For this reason the apparent violation of the Principle of Less Eligibility, according to its strict utilitarian definition, can be explained. The creation of the Poor Law Board, to replace the Poor Law Commission in 1847, was a watershed, because before this date there was relatively strict adherence to the basic Principles of Poor Law administration, yet later differential treatment of the various classes of pauper in their separate workhouse departments was officially countenanced. Thus, there was indeed an attempt to programme the workhouse child, so that it did not become a life-long pauper and the findings of this study suggest that the workhouse was relatively effective in doing this.

Initially, soon after 1834, unions attempted to provide an illusion of equal treatment, although after 1847 this pretence was dropped. Nowhere was this more apparent than in the treatment of child paupers, who, together with the aged, were treated as special cases. This probably happened unofficially within the first two or three years of the introduction of the New Poor Law, although this was masked from the central authority until after 1847. To some extent the demise of Edwin Chadwick's utilitarian influence, towards the end of the 1830s, allowed a more fluid interpretation of rules and regulations, but rigidities within the administrative structure of the Poor Law Commission caused old attitudes to prevail. National Uniformity as a principle of poor relief was probably inappropriate from the outset. It proved unworkable within Worcestershire and was rejected, in most places, by 1847.

The New Poor Law was seen as essentially preventative, intended to 'rescue' children from life-long pauperism, although they continued to be considered as tainted stock both on the grounds of their parentage and their experience. In the county, they were placed in workhouses considered to have mendancy endemic in them, so that the need for separation was obvious. The nationally prescribed separation of children into district schools or separate schools was seen as inappropriate and unworkable in a rural area. For this reason, in county workhouses, children were rigidly and completely separated in their own wards, so that different rules and regulations could be applied to them. They were treated and hence institutionalised very differently from other classes of inmate. Increasingly, Less Eligibility was not seen as an inviolable principle with regard to the rescue of children from life-long pauperism.

To the casual observer a more, rather than less, eligible treatment of pauper inmates in workhouses was apparent. They lived in adequate workhouse accommodation, which was regularly cleaned, although sometimes overcrowded. They were given plentiful but uninteresting food, which was cooked in sanitary conditions and their health was regularly monitored, with illness and injuries promptly treated by trained medical staff. This more eligible treatment may have appeared particularly so for child paupers, who were also provided with an intellectual, moral and industrial training superior to that offered to most of their non-pauper contemporaries, at least for the first couple of decades after 1834. Long stay, orphaned and deserted child inmates were also provided with pauper apprenticeships, sometimes at union expense, and once apprenticed greater care was taken of these children than that of non-pauper apprentices.

The theory behind the workhouse differed from the practice. This was because once opened, the workhouses filled not with able-bodied adult mendicants but with large numbers of aged and young individuals. The single deterrent purpose of the workhouse was thus inappropriate to these classes of pauper. The aged were to be 'reset' for a future life, although many of them came to the workhouse to die, and the young were there to be set, rather than reset, on a non-pauper future. The Principles of Less Eligibility and of National Uniformity – the major Benthamite tenets of the New Poor Law – thus caused problems from the outset, particularly regarding children. However, some Worcestershire Guardians continued to adhere to these outmoded ideas, so that Less Eligibility differed from place to place, particularly in relation to child paupers. Some Guardians, such as those at Martley, over a long period of time resisted innovation in the treatment of child paupers for this reason. By 1847, when the Poor Law Board was created, children were treated as a special case in some unions, but elsewhere the twin principles of treatment were still adhered to. Most markedly, Dudley union was willing to offer far more to paupers, particularly children, than a strict adherence to Less Eligibility allowed, whereas some rural unions, such as Martley, continued to apply the principles rigidly. The practices initially adopted in Worcestershire workhouses were based on Poor Law Central Authority advice, but the approach of union Guardians and local officers differed from place to place, dependent on local circumstances, on previous experience under the Old Poor Law and on the interactions of the various personalities involved.

Erving Goffman suggested: 'Total institutions frequently claim to be concerned with rehabilitation, that is, with resetting the inmates self-regulatory mechanism so that after he leaves he will maintain the standards of the establishment of his own accord.'[10] This was the description he gave in his classical sociological study *Asylums* of the effects of a 'total institution' on its inmates. It exactly described the purpose of the workhouses set up under the Poor Law Amendment Act in 1834. Initially, the intention had been to reset all pauper inmates in the same way, so that they were rescued from life-long pauperism. This was to be done by a single system in which all paupers, no matter what their age or sex, were to be treated exactly similarly in the workhouse, a total institution, initially designed to be as efficient as possible at re-programming individuals. The whole régime of the workhouse had this as its aim. However, the obligation of the staff to maintain certain humane standards of treatment for inmates presented problems in itself, but a further set of characteristic problems was found in the constant conflict between humane standards on the one hand and institutional efficiency on the other.

Erving Goffman described the conflicts between the caring and the efficiency role of the staff in an institution – the same conflicts highlighted in this study. This analysis was particularly appropriate with regard to workhouse schoolteachers, who were in general caring individuals, whose status improved between 1834 and 1871, partly because of their improved efficiency. This development was possibly related to the influence of a more rigid school inspection, although this caused them to adopt coping strategies, such as children barking at school inspector's questions, in an attempt to demonstrate improvement. Unfortunately, this caused their humane approach to be eroded. The whole tenor of the workhouse was aimed at improved efficiency of treatment and any impediment to this was dealt with. As schoolteachers, and other workhouse officers who dealt with inmate children, became more efficient, workhouse education undoubtedly improved in measurable quality (as determined by inspection). However, this was at a cost because it appeared likely that the interpersonal relationship between the workhouse pupil and its teacher was worsened by the process. The prime aim of the workhouse, which was a 'total institution', as defined by Erving Goffman, was to prevent children becoming hereditary paupers, although the staff were not unscathed by their own institutional experience. Confinement of workhouse staff ensured that they too became institutionalised and from the present study of Worcestershire it appeared that this was recognised by staff members who talked in terms of the workhouse being 'too confined'. Indeed, many such officers chose not to make a career of their Poor Law offices, thus escaping being tainted by the pauperism that was regarded as extremely contagious and disease-like. Workhouse officers were certainly not considered immune from it. They, like the children in the workhouse, would succumb if they remained there for too long. For this reason, doctors, who were generally middle-class individuals, were particularly reluctant to take up Poor Law medical officers' posts, because they recognised that this prejudiced their private patients against them.

While suggesting that inmate pauper children were more eligible than their non-pauper poor contemporaries, this judgement may be an illusion, because such advantages had to be balanced against the distinct disadvantages of workhouse life. These were most marked for permanent child inmates, who, unlike adults and dependent children, could not leave the workhouse at three hours' notice. Once such individuals had reached a level of destitution where they countenanced entry to the workhouse, gaining the epithet 'pauper', they were considered tainted for life, so that subsequent entry to the workhouse did not have the same impact on them again. Some individuals were undoubtedly not deterred by the workhouse, although some people preferred to starve rather than enter it. Other people coming to the workhouse for the first time were so influenced by their experience there that they would never return, yet others undoubtedly became habitual users of these facilities, accepting it as a solution to distress, such as unemployment, illness, or in the case of women, confinement at childbirth. Destitute or orphaned children had no choice, as they remained in the workhouse for as long as the union authorities deemed they should and the workhouse's effectiveness depended on the length of their stay there. Institutionalisation was most effective of all with this group, so that while they gained the advantages suggested, they suffered disadvantages of an institutional life devoid of personal fulfilment and individuality. Initially it was presumed that the same environment meant to deter adult paupers was appropriate to the needs of the developing child. However, it was difficult to equate negative freedoms such as from hunger, disease and unemployment, with positive freedoms of speech and action and most importantly the freedoms of choice and individuality. Given these circumstances, the workhouse was designed as a total institution intended to attain its prime aim; to deter individuals from becoming a life-long burden on the Poor Rates.

The initial structure of the central Poor Law administration was simple. It had a directorate, consisting of the three Poor Law Commissioners, together with a permanent secretary and a number of Assistant Poor Law Commissioners, each with a regional responsibility. Almost immediately, however, it became apparent that the regions given to Assistant Commissioners were too large. These regions were now re-drawn and more Assistant Commissioners were appointed. In spite of this, the task was still seen as too great and this time additional specialised inspectors were appointed. These were of lower status than Assistant Poor Law Commissioners and included workhouse inspectors, school inspectors, and later still inspectors of medical and culinary provisions. Inevitably, finance still had to be controlled. This was initially done by a system where a single auditor was appointed for each union, who then sent his accounts to a central auditor. This soon proved impractical and district auditors were now appointed by an expanded audit department at Somerset House, the headquarters of the Central Poor Law Authority. These two examples of specialisation were symptomatic of bureaucratisation, the process that created a changed national administrative structure, but which also caused a change in the nature of the Board of Guardians' Minutes.

The bulk of communication between central and local Poor Law officials (or vice versa) was continually reducing between 1834 and 1871 and its nature also altered, with individually drafted hand-written letters no longer being sent in both directions. These were now replaced by a printed *pro forma*. Thus the administration now became habitual, with correspondence, after 1847, becoming less revealing and increasingly emanating from specialist officials. This approach was distinctive, so that the auditors' department, the school inspector and other departments increasingly used special pro forma letters in their communication with local Poor Law unions. Whilst this process was inevitable it did alter the previously subjective nature of correspondence, so that comments became more guarded, which militated against one major purpose of this study, to describe the condition and treatment of individual child paupers.

As the central Poor Law administration became more bureaucratic, so too did the local administration. This consisted of an elected Board of Guardians, a clerk – who was usually a local solicitor – a relieving officer, responsible for determining who received poor relief and the nature of the aid given, together with a medical officer responsible for a district of the union. The workhouse was staffed by a master and matron, often a husband and wife, who were helped by a porter. Soon after 1834 it became apparent that this local structure was inadequate for the task set, which had been grossly underestimated. The problems the master and matron encountered in running the workhouse, even with the porter's help, were great. Whilst rules and regulations allowed the appointment of school staff and a chaplain, at this stage these appointments were not yet compulsory, so that few county unions went to the trouble of appointing such staff. Soon, however, when problems with indiscipline in workhouses became apparent and pressing, school staff were appointed, as was a chaplain, who had to be of the Anglican faith. The Poor Law authorities believed that the chaplain would have a controlling influence, because, invariably, he was the person with the highest social status in the local Poor Law hierarchy. Thus, it was presumed he would be orthodox in his adherence to the ideology of utilitarian Poor Law administration. His controlling influence was apparent amongst Boards of Guardians in the county.

Gradually, between 1847 and 1871, other staff such as nurses, cooks, industrial trainers, bakers, millers, shoemakers and tailors were added to workhouse staffs in larger unions, which had more finance available to appoint such officers. However, small unions, such as

Tenbury Wells and Upton upon Severn, were unable even to continue to employ a schoolmistress because there were too few children, again illustrating the contrast between large and small unions.

Locally, bureaucratisation much influenced clerks to Boards of Guardians, who had initially spent up to one day a week on their Poor Law duties. Gradually the time they spent on their Poor Law duties increased, as they became responsible for more correspondence with the central authority, and inevitably this meant increasing their expertise in Poor Law matters. They were now consulted by the Guardians on interpretations of the Poor Law. In larger unions they also now became Poor Law professionals, causing the quality of their correspondence with the central authority to change, because it now contained implicit understandings about Poor Law interpretation. This book on the Poor Law in Worcestershire has attempted to regain such interpretations, although any understanding is inevitably incomplete. What developed very quickly in the Poor Law administration of Worcestershire was a bureaucracy, which in part improved the efficiency of administration, but it did also cause problems for individual inmate children.

The Poor Law had originated as a punitive measure, intended to 'sanitise' society against the dangers of pauperism. It became changed in the case of children, because they were now to be given advantages, as they were regarded as blameless social unfortunates. The definition of poverty for this group had thus been radically altered and indeed this conformed to Gertrude Himmelfarb's expectations outlined in her book, *The Idea of Poverty*.[11] She suggested that while the New Poor Law continued to be the imposition of an alien élite moral code on the destitute working classes, the definition of poverty and the ascription of its causes had altered. In turn this caused the perceived nature of poverty to also alter, together with the philosophical underpinning of the Poor Law. In Worcestershire, as elsewhere, whilst adult paupers continued to be regarded as a social danger, afflicted as they were with the contagious disease of pauperism, society became more discriminating. Within the closed institution of the workhouse, differential treatment was possible, although there was variation between workhouses. In part this was due to the attitude of Guardians, but the size of the pauper child population was also imperative, as was the character of workhouse officers. Impressions gleaned from Guardians' Minute Books will tend to be misleading, because most interaction between pauper children and the workhouse officers went unrecorded. In spite of this, there was some changes in attitude towards child paupers detectable from Guardians'

Minute Books in county unions. They ceased to be treated less eligibly and were given superior treatment to that afforded to the children of the lowest level of independent labourer outside the workhouse, which provided the normal definition of Less Eligibility. However, what was impossible to calculate was the value of freedom foregone by such children. Thus, whilst the New Poor Law in Worcestershire did impose a middle-class morality on working-class pauper children, as suggested by Gertrude Himmelfarb, some children will have found this functional, as it improved their employment prospects.

The findings of this study are in broad agreement with those of many social histories of the New Poor Law produced in the last four decades. However, these are at variance with some of the findings of administrative histories of the Law, such as those by Alec Ross[12] and S.P. Obermann,[13] whose purposes were very different to those of this study. The prime sources used also differed, as did the modes of exploiting them. Perhaps inevitably, the greatest congruence was between the findings of Anne Digby,[14] in her investigation of the New Poor Law in Norfolk. The great similarity between Norfolk and Worcestershire, between 1834 to 1871, with regard to the size and nature of the population, the distribution of that population in a rural setting and the local economy was probably the reason for this. Worcestershire was not as directly influenced by James P. Kay (later Kay-Shuttleworth), who had introduced a pupil-teacher system at Gressenhall workhouse, as was Norfolk. However, it was much influenced by Thomas B. Browne, the HMI for workhouse schools in the area, who, after 1860, opposed the setting up of district schools in the county. This approach to educating and training workhouse children was singularly inappropriate in a rural area, where there were too few children to sustain such a school, but Thomas B. Browne's influence, against such schools, made the resistance of Guardians to these schools even more acceptable.

. The initial purpose of this study was to increase the author's understanding of why the workhouse was so feared by his grandparents. It has attained this aim, for what they clearly feared was institutionalisation, which once completed might blight their lives. However, it has done more than this, because it has developed a measure of empathy with working-class people in the past. Whilst this can never be complete, it is worth striving for, because this is essential to any real understanding of the past. The study has also raised some interesting issues, some of which mark Worcestershire off as different from other areas. There were, however, inevitably many similarities between the findings of this study and those of other social histories of the New Poor Law between 1834 and 1871. It adds to our understanding of the development and working of systematic institutional solutions to the problems of the pauperised poor in England and Wales in the middle third of the nineteenth century. Hopefully, it will also provoke others to investigate the New Poor Law in other geographical localities and for other classes of pauper. For instance there is a clear need for someone to study the mode of treatment of aged paupers, those who were sick and indeed those who were mentally ill. Without continued study, a complete understanding of a vital part in the development of the Welfare State in England will be impossible.

The mass of detail collated in this study enabled a clearer impression to be gained of the everyday life of pauper children under the New Poor Law and it approximates to 'history from below'. It focuses on a single class of pauper in thirteen different unions over eighty-seven years and is thus unusual in the narrowness of its focus and the breadth of its geographical and temporal span. It illustrates well the methodological distinction between social and administrative histories of the New Poor Law in an English county, which although essentially rural, contained some very urban unions. This enabled a new perspective, questioning the belief in a separate rural and urban Poor Law to be developed. Thus, there was a continuum between these two 'ideal types' of local administration, with the level of usage, rather than the urban or rural nature of the union, determining how overt was the social control function of the workhouse. In all cases it was clearly a total institution which altered its nature over time, as perceptions of the causes and treatment of pauperism changed. The purpose of the workhouse throughout the period 1834 to 1871 continued to be as a deterrent, imposing an alien middle-class morality and culture on working-class children. Arguably, such deterrence endures as a feature of modern welfare policy.

NOTES

ABBREVIATIONS

BOD – Bodleian Library, Oxford; BML – Barnes' Medical Library, University of Birmingham; BPL – Birmingham Public Library; BUL – Birmingham University Library; DPL – Dudley Public Library, Local Studies Department; HCRO – Hereford County Record Office, Harold Street, Hereford; HLL. – House of Lords' Library; PRO – Public Record Office, Kew, Surrey; WCRO – Worcester County Record Office, County Hall, Worcester. At the PRO: MH12 – Ministry of Health Records, ZHC1 – Library Reference. At WCRO: Loc – Location, Acc – Accession Number, Par – Parcel. MSS Guardians' Minutes: Bro – Bromsgrove, Dro – Droitwich, Dud – Dudley, Eve – Evesham, Kid – Kidderminster, Kin – King's Norton, Mar – Martley, Per – Pershore, Shi – Shipston on Stour, Sto – Stourbridge, Ten – Tenbury Wells, Upt – Upton upon Severn, Wor – Worcester. APLC – Assistant Poor Law Commissioner; MSS – Manuscripts, NRC – Newcastle Royal Commission; PCCE – Privy Council Committee on Education; PLB – Poor Law Board; PLC – Poor Law Commission; SC – Select Committee.
N.B. All references to Acts of Parliament in this chapter use PROTHEROE, G.W., *Select Statutes and Constitutional Documents* reference numbers.

INTRODUCTION

1. S.G. and E.O.A. Checkland, (eds.), *The Poor Law Report of 1834* (Penguin, 1974), p. 395.
2. Ibid., pp. 396–7.
3. 22 Geo, III c.83 (1782).
4. A.M. Ross, 'The Care and Education of Pauper Children in England and Wales 1834 to 1896' (Unpub. Ph.D. Thesis, University of London, 1955).
5. S.P. Obermann, 'The Education of Children in Poor Law Institutions in England and Wales during the Period 1834 to 1870'

(Unpub. Ph.D. Thesis, Queen's University, Belfast, 1982).
6. A. Digby, *Pauper Palaces*, (RKP, 1978).
7. G. Himmelfarb, *The Idea of Poverty in the Early Industrial Revolution* (Faber, 1984).
8. E. Goffman, *Asylums* (Penguin, 1970).

CHAPTER 1

1. 25 Edw. III s.2 (1350).
2. M. McKisack, *The Fourteenth Century 1307–1399* (Oxford, OUP, 1959), pp. 335–6.
3. 5 Eliz. I c.4. (1563) Section I.
4. 14 Eliz. I c.5. (1572).
5. 39 & 40 Eliz. I c.3. (1597–8).
6. 43 & 44 Eliz. I c.2. (1601).
7. 13 & 14 Car. II c.12. (1662).
8. 9 Will. III c.30. (1697–8).
9. 9 Geo. I, c.7. (1722).
10. Sometimes a class of managers who came between employers and employees altering the relationships of these two groups. Face to face relationships between employers and employees became difficult.
11. A. Redford, *Labour Migration in England 1800 to 1850* (Revised and edited by W.H. Challoner, Manchester, Manchester University Press, 1976) and developed by W.T.R. Pryce. Cited in M. Anderson, *Urban Migration in Nineteenth Century Lancashire* (Milton Keynes, Open University Press, 1974).
12. Small hamlets like Eastham, Rochford and Great Witley in the extreme west of the county depopulated by about 10 per cent between 1801 and 1831. Source: *1851 Census Report*.
13. In an extended family several generations lived together in the same geographical locality and were able to provide mutual support. This support may have been financial or practical. For instance older relatives could be relied on to look after children

14. whilst their parents worked in agriculture.
2 Geo. III. c.39. (1762).
15. Jonas Hanway, *An Earnest Appeal for Mercy to the Children of the Poor* (1766). [Hanway (1712–86) was born in Portsmouth and sent to school in London. He was apprenticed to a merchant in Lisbon and he became a merchant in St Petersburg. He became Governor of the Foundlings' Hospital in 1758 where he worked ceaselessly for poor children.]
16. 7 Geo. III. c.39. (1767).
17. Hanway, *An Earnest Appeal for Mercy to the Children of the Poor* (1766).
18. Ibid.
19. Ibid.
20. 2 Geo. III. c.22. (1762).
21. 7 Geo. III. c.39. (1767).
22. 9 Geo I. c7. (1723)
23. 22 Geo. III. c.83. (1782).
24. Ibid.
25. Ibid.
26. Ibid.
27. Ibid.
28. Ibid.
29. Sir G. Nicholls, *History of the English Poor Law*, (1854), p. 99.
30. 22 Geo. III. c.83. (1782).
31. 23 Geo. III. c.56. (1783).
32. 26 Geo. III. c.58. (1786).
33. Revd J. Townsend, *Dissertation on the Poor Laws* (1785). Cited by S & B. Webb, *English Poor Law History* (Part II. Vol. I. Longman Green, 1929), pp. 11–12.
34. Thomas Malthus, *First Essay on Population* (1798, republished by Penguin, 1970), p. 97.
35. Ibid.
36. Ibid.
37. Ibid.
38. As suggested by N.C. Edsall in *The Anti-Poor Law Movement* (Manchester University Press, 1971).
39. 35 Geo. III. c.101. (1795).
40. 49 Geo. III. c.124. (1809).
41. 50 Geo. III. c.51. (1810).
42. 58 Geo. III. c.69. (1818) usually known as Sturges-Bournes Act. [This was sponsored by William Sturges-Bourne, 1769 to 1845. Educated at Winchester and Christ Church Oxford MA (1793) and DCL (1831). He was MP for Hornsea 1798 to 1831. Senior Secretary to the Treasury 1804–6, Lord of Treasury 1807–9, Home Secretary 1827, Commissioner for Woods and Forests 1827, Lord Warden of the New Forest 1828–31. P.C. 1814. He also sponsored 59' Geo. III. c.18. (1819).]
43. 13 & 14 Car. II. c.12. (1662).
44. Ibid.
45. 59 Geo. III. c.18 (1819).
46. 60 Geo. III & Geo. IV. c.5. (1820).
47. Poem by George Crabbe, quoted by Webb, *English Poor Law History*, Part II. Vol. I, p. 419.
48. S. & B. Webb, *English Poor Law Policy* (Cass, 1910), p. 34.
49. 5 Geo. IV. c.83. (1824).
50. William Hale, Letter to Patrick Colquhoun, 21 October 1800.
51. 42 Geo. III. c.46. (1802).
52. Ibid.
53. Ibid.
54. Select Committee on the State of Children Employed in Manufactures, 1816. *Children's Employment* (Irish Universities Press, 1972), Vol. 1, pp. 178–185. P.P. 1816. (397) III.
55. Ibid.
56. 42 Geo. III. c.46. (1802).
57. SC on the State of Children Employed in Manufactures, Vol. 1, pp. 178–85.
58. Geo. III. c.46. (1802).
59. 59 Geo. III. c.18. (1819).
60. Ibid.
61. Geo. III & Geo. IV. c.5. (1820).
62. 1 and 2 Will. IV. c.39. (1831).
63. Ibid.
64. 3 and 4 Will. IV. c.103. (1833).
65. Ibid.
66. Ibid.
67. Ibid.
68. Ibid.
69. 7 and 8 Vict. c.101 (1844).

CHAPTER 2

1. Geoffrey Oxley, *Poor Relief in England and Wales 1601–1834* (Newton Abbot, David & Charles, 1974), p. 76.
2. 22 Geo. III c.83 (1782).
3. 7 Geo. III. c.39 (1767).
4. 9 & 10 Will. III c.14 (1698).
5. Webb, *English Poor Law History*, Part I, p. 210.
6. Evidence of C.P. Villiers to the Poor Law Inquiry Commissioners, Appendix A, p. 8.
7. In villages in the Severn Valley to the north-west of Kidderminster such as Arley, Hampton and Highley.
8. Webb, *English Poor Law History*, Part I, p. 203.
9. The population of Kidderminster Borough was:

DATE	1801	1811	1821	1831	1841	1851
MALES	3,020	3,848	5,280	7,433	7,156	8,517
FEMALES	3,090	4,190	5,429	7,548	7,243	8,516
TOTAL	6,110	8,038	10,709	14,981	14,399	17,023

Source: The 1851 Census, P.P. [1631] LXXXIX.

10. From an interview with Walter Bunch in June 1984. He was retired and in charge of the

Muniment's Room at Brinton's Carpets Limited, Kidderminster.

11. Peter Mathias, *The First Industrial Nation* (Harper and Row, 1969), p. 365.

12. J.H. Bettey, *Rural Life in Wessex* (Moonraker, 1977), p. 56.

13. Evidence of Samuel Makin to the SC on Silk Ribbon Weavers, Report, IX (1818), 36, p. 126. Cited by Michael E. Rose, *The English Poor Law 1780–1830* (Newton Abbot, David & Charles, 1971), pp. 54–5.

14. 7 & 8 Will. III. c.32 (1696).

15. C.P. Villiers Report, to the Poor Law Inquiry Commissioners, Appendix A, p. 8.

16. A. Redford, *Labour Migration in England 1800–1850* (Revised and edited by W.H. Challover, Manchester, Manchester University Press, 1976), pp. 182–90.

17. Rufus S. Tucker, 'Real Wages of Artisans in London 1729–1835', in Arthur J. Taylor (ed.), *The Standard of Living in Britain in the Industrial Revolution* (Methuen, 1975), pp. 21–35.

18. 9 & 10 Will. III. c.14 (1698).

19. 5 Eliz. I. c.3 (1563).

20. 'Service' was the urban equivalent of 'Housewifery' in rural areas.

21. 4 & 5 Will.IV. c.76 (1834).

CHAPTER 3

1. 4 & 5 Will.IV. c.76 (1834).

2. E. Halevy, *The Age of Peel and Cobden* (Benn, 1970), p. 145.

3. Unions were not created in parts of Lancashire and Yorkshire.

4. N. Gash, *Aristocracy and People* (Arnold, 1979), p. 195.

5. Introduced in G. Himmelfarb, *The Idea of Poverty in England in the Early Industrial Revolution* (Faber, 1984).

6. PLC Order, 10 December 1852 theoretically abolished outdoor relief. This occurred in 396 of the 538 unions.

7. Webb, *English Poor Law Policy*, p. 7.

8. Checkland, *The Poor Law Report of 1834*, p. 430.

9. Ibid.

10. Dudley union was formed by the amalgamation of four parishes each with its own workhouse.

11. Checkland, *The Poor Law Report of 1834*, p. 335.

12. Ibid., p. 336.

13. Himmelfarb, *The Idea of Poverty in England in the Early Industrial Revolution*.

14. Hansard, 6 August 1848. Vol. 100. p. 1,217. Speech by Charles Butler.

15. S.E. Finer, *The Life and Times of Sir Edwin Chadwick* (Methuen, 1952), p. 193.

16. Ibid., p. 193. Tenniel's reference was to Bismarck.

17. Chadwick had been Bentham's Secretary and was much influenced by him.

18. Finer, *The Life and Times of Sir Edwin Chadwick*, p. 207.

19. Ibid., pp. 274–91.

20. 10 & 11 Vict. c.110 (1847).

21. Mar 19 January 1846, PRO MH12\14081. This case is cited at greater length in Chapter 6 on education.

22. Webb, *English Poor Law Policy*, p. 88.

23. G.D.H. Cole, and R. Postgate, *The British Common People* (Methuen, 1961) p. 277.

24. PLC, Consolidated Order, 7 March 1836. 2nd Annual Report, 1836. HLL.

25. Dro 5 April 1837, PRO MH12\13930. WCRO Loc b251\Acc 401\Par 1(i).

26. PLC, Consolidated Order, 1838. 5th Annual Report, 1839, PRO ZHC1/1249/1295.

27. Wor 29 December 1840. PRO MH12\14203.

28. Per. 15 May 1837. PRO MH12\14104. WCRO Loc b251\Acc 409\Par 1.

29. Kid 2 July 1846. PRO MH12\14018. WCRO Loc b251. Acc.403\Par 6.

30. PLC, 13th Annual Report, 1847. PRO ZHC1/1748.

31. PLC, General Order, 5 February 1842. 8th Annual Report, 1842. PRO ZHC1/1386.

32. PLC, Consolidated Order, 24 July 1847. 13th Annual Report, 1847. PRO ZHC1/1748.

33. Sir George Nicholls. Quoted in Cole and Postgate, *The British Common People*, p. 274.

34. PLB, Order 1848. 1st Annual Report, 1849. PRO ZHC1/1806.

35. Ibid.

36. Letter from Lord George Cornewall-Lewis (Poor Law Commissioner) to Sir Edmund Head, 6 November 1851. Sir Edmund Head was Secretary to the PLB. Cited by Webb, *English Poor Law Policy*, p. 86.

37. Dud 13 May 1858. PRO MH12\13964. DPL/A251.

38. PLB, Circular, 6 July 1868. 21st Annual Report, 1869. PRO MH12\3303.

39. PLC, Consolidated Order, 24 July 1847. 13th Annual Report, 1847. PRO ZHC1/1748.

40. Dro 19 July 1848. PRO MH12\13933. WCRO Loc b251\Acc 401\Par 4.

41. Dro 2 August 1848, PRO MH12\13933. WCRO Loc b251\Acc 401\Par 4.

42. Dro 4 October 1848. PRO MH12\13933. WCRO Loc b251\Acc 401\Par 4.

43. Dro 17 October 1849. PRO MH12\13934. WCRO Loc b251\Acc 401\Par 4.

44. Ibid.

45. Wor 6 August 1855. PRO MH12\14208.

46. Wor 3 September 1855. PRO MH12\14208.

47. Shi 15 December 1862. PRO MH12\14122.

48. Shi 23 January 1863. PRO MH12\14122.

49. Wor 9 February 1869. PRO MH12\14211.

50. Kid 25 May 1847. PRO MH12\14019.

WCRO Loc b251\Acc 403\Par 6.

51. Mar 20 May 1865. PRO MH12\14089. WCRO Loc b251\Acc 406\Par 2. The Guardians wanted to send her to a home at West Wanstead, run by 'The London Society for the Protection of Young Females and the Prevention of Juvenile Prostitution'.

52. Mar 9 June 1865. PRO MH12\14089. WCRO Loc b251\Acc 406\Par 2.

53. Mar 17 June 1865. PRO MH12\14089. WCRO Loc b251\Acc 406\Par 2. The home was not certified under the Certified Schools' Act of 1862 – 25 & 26 Vict. c.43.

54. Mar 23 June 1865. PRO MH12\14089. WCRO Loc b251\Acc 406\Par 2.

55. Upt 2 April 1861. PRO MH12\14187. WCRO Loc 251\Acc 414\Par 7.

56. Shi 16 November 1859. PRO MH12\14121.

57. She went to the London Penitentiary for the Reform of Unfortunate Women.

58. See Note 43. Kid 25 May 1847. PRO MH12\14019. WCRO Loc b251\Acc 403\Par 6.

59. Kid 25 May 1857. PRO MH12\14019. WCRO Loc b251\Acc 403\Par 11.

60. This title must have been incorrect. She was probably the Hon. Mrs. Way.

61. Mar 8 July 1863. PRO MH12\14088. WCRO Loc b251\Acc 406\Par 1.

62. SC on Poor Relief, 1861, Reprints of British Parliamentary Papers, Irish Universities Press, 1970. Vol. 25, *Poor Law*. pp. 662–71.

63. *Workhouse Visiting Society Journal* (1859 to 1865). BOD.

64. Ibid., respectively: January 1859, Vol. i, pp. 25–73, November 1861, Vol. xvi, pp. 518–20, and October 1863, Vol. xxvii, pp. 128–9.

65. Bro 13 July 1858. PRO MH12\13911. WCRO Loc b251\Acc 400\Par 6.

66. Bro 27 December 1859. PRO MH12\13911. WCRO Loc b251\Acc 400\Par 6.

67. Bro 20 August 1861. PRO MH12\13911. WCRO Loc b251\Acc 400\Par 6.

68. Bro 10 October 1865. PRO MH12\13912. WCRO Loc b251\Acc 400\Par 7. The visit took place on 29 October 1865.

69. PLC Special Report on the Further Amendment of the Poor Laws, 1836, HLL.

70. Ten 15 October 1844. PRO MH12\14170. WCRO Loc b251\Acc 413\Par 3.

71. Wor 8 July 1841. PRO MH12\14203.

72. Sto 12 May 1842. PRO MH12\14135.

73. Wor 26 September 1842. PRO MH12\14203.

74. Wor 10 June 1845. PRO MH12\14204.

75. Wor 20 March 1847. PRO MH12\14205.

76. The wearing of these yellow and black striped dresses was discontinued in 1840.

77. PLC, Consolidated Order, 7 March 1836. 2nd Annual Report, 1836. HLL.

78. PLC, General Order, 5 February 1842. 8th Annual Report, 1842. PRO ZHC1/1386.

79. PLC, Consolidated Order, 24 July 1847. 13th Annual Report, 1847. PRO ZHC1/1748.

80. PLC, General Order, 5 February 1842. 8th Annual Report, 1842. PRO ZHC1/1386.

81. Bed sharing by mothers and infants appeared to have only been practised in overcrowded workhouses.

82. King's Norton, Kidderminster, Pershore, Shipston on Stour and Worcester unions allowed adoptions.

83. Shi 23 September 1850. PRO MH12\14119.

84. Wor 30 January 1852. PRO MH12\14207.

85. Shi 28 July 1863. PRO MH12\14122.

86. Kid 6 September 1864. PRO MH12\14023. WCRO Loc b251\Acc 403\Par 16.

87. Per 26 July 1860. PRO MH12\14108. WCRO Loc b251\Acc 409\Par 8.

88. Per 9 February 1860. PRO MH12\14108. WCRO Loc b251\Acc 409\Par 8.

89. Kid 6 January 1857. PRO MH12\14021. WCRO Loc b251\Acc 403\Par 11.

90. This was after the Parish Apprentices' Act (7 & 8 Vict. c.101) was passed in 1844.

91. Kid 15 September 1865. PRO MH12\14024. WCRO Loc b251\Acc 403\Par 17.

92. Per 7 April 1868. PRO MH12\14109. WCRO Loc b251\Acc 409\Par 9.

93. Dro 15 March 1871. PRO MH12\13941. WCRO Loc b251\Acc 401\Par 13.

94. Kin 4 September 1867. PRO MH12\14044. BPL File F1.

95. Set up under 22 Geo. III c.83 (1782).

96. PLC Order, 2 March 1835. 2nd Annual Report, 1836. HLL.

97. Kid 8 November 1837. PRO MH12\14016. WCRO Loc b251\Acc 403\Par 1.

98. Kin 24 June 1844. PRO MH12\14040. BPL File F1.

99. Dro 10 April 1844. PRO MH12\14018. WCRO Acc. 401\Par 2.

100. Kin 3 June 1838. PRO MH12\14039. BPL File F1.

101. Kin 3 May 1839. PRO MH12\14039. BPL File F1.

102. Kid 8 June 1839. PRO MH12\14017. WCRO Loc b251\Acc 403\Par 2.

103. Bro 2 August 1841. PRO MH12\13905. WCRO Loc b251\Acc 403\Par 3.

104. Dro 19 November 1845. PRO MH12\13932. WCRO Loc b251\Acc 401\Par 3.

105. 'Farina' referred to potato starch.

106. Dro 31 December 1845. PRO MH12\13932. WCRO Loc b251\Acc 401\Par 3.

107. Bro 15 March 1839. PRO MH12\13904. WCRO Loc 251\Acc 400\Par 1(ii).

108. PLC, Consolidated Order, 7 March 1836. 2nd Annual Report, 1836. HLL.

109. PLC, General Order, 5 February 1842. 8th Annual Report, 1842. PRO ZHC1/1386.

110. Dro 8 April 1840. PRO MH12\13931. WCRO Loc b251\Acc 401\Par 2.

111. Dro 15 April 1840. Letter from the PLC.

PRO MH12\13931. WCRO Loc b251\Acc 401\Par 2.

112. Dro 24 February 1847. PRO MH12\13933. WCRO Loc b251\Acc 401\Par 3.

113. Evesham Guardians, MSS Minutes, 17 August 1869. PRO MH12\14003. WCRO Loc b251\Acc 402\Par 20.

114. Sto 2 November 1870. PRO MH12\14145.

115. 12 & 13 Vict. c.103 (1849).

116. Dro 5 August 1868. PRO MH12\13940. WCRO Loc b251\Acc 401\Par 12.

117. Kid 15 December 1868, PRO MH12\14024. WCRO Loc b251\Acc 403\Par 19.

118. Dro 18 October 1848. PRO MH12\13933. WCRO Loc b251\Acc 401\Par 4.

119. Per 10 December 1850, 3 February 1852, 16 March 1852 and 30 March 1852. PRO MH12\14106. WCRO Loc b251\Acc 409\Par 7.

120. Upt 12 December 1862. PRO MH12\14187.

121. Shi 4 February 1856. PRO MH12\14120.

122. Sto 15 May 1855. PRO MH12\14141.

123. 22 Geo. III. c.83 (1782).

124. Dud 9 November 1849, PRO MH12\13961. DPL/A251.

125. Dud 26 August 1853. PRO MH12\13963. DPL/A251.

126. Dud 23 September, 1853. PRO MH12\13963. DPL/A251.

127. Dud 19 May 1854. PRO MH12\13963. DPL/A251.

128. Dud 13 May 1858. PRO MH12\13964. DPL/A251.

129. Mar 30 July 1859. PRO MH12\14086.

130. Mar 30 September 1859. PROMH12\14086.

131. Mar 4 November 1859. PRO MH12\14086.

132. Upt 23 May 1868. PRO MH12\14189.

133. Upt 2 November 1868. PRO MH12\14189.

134. Upt 7 January 1858. PRO MH12\14186. WCRO Loc b251\Acc 414\Par 8.

135. Kin 5 August 1868. PRO MH12\14045. BPL File F1.

136. The PLB was replaced by the Local Government Board in 1871.

137. Bro 20 June 1855. PRO MH12\13910. WCRO Loc b251\Acc 400\Par 5.

138. Per 12 September 1856. PRO MH12\14107. WCRO Loc b251\Acc 409\Par 7.

139. Kid 1 July 1856. PRO MH12\14021. WCRO Loc b251\Acc 403\Par 10.

140. G. Kitson-Clark, *The Making of Victorian England* (Methuen, 1962), p. 140.

141. Kin 12 February 1851, PRO MH12\14042. BPL File F1.

142. Kin 9 April 1851. PRO MH12\14042. BPL File F1.

143. Per 15 February 1853. PRO MH12\14106. WCRO Loc b251\Acc 409\Par 7.

144. Bro 12 November 1861. PRO MH12\13911. WCRO Loc b251\Acc 400\Par 6.

145. Bro 12 May 1863. PRO MH12\13912. WCRO Loc b251\Acc 400\Par 6.

146. PLC, Consolidated Order, 7 March 1836. 2nd Annual Report, 1836. HLL.

147. Dro 22 May 1839. PRO MH12\13930. WCRO Loc b251\Acc 401\Par 1(ii).

148. Wor 24 November 1840. PRO MH12\14203.
Hours of labour were: 25 March to 29 September: Hour of rising, 5.00 a.m.; work, 6.00 a.m. to 8.00 a.m.; breakfast and prayers, 8.00 a.m. to 9.00 a.m.; work, 9.00 a.m. to 1.00 p.m.; dinner, 1.00 p.m. to 2.00 p.m.; work, 2.00 p.m. to 7.30 p.m.; supper, 7.30 p.m. to 8.30 p.m.; bed, 9.00 p.m. 29 September to 25 March: Hour of rising, 6.30 a.m.; work, 7.00 a.m. to 8.00 a.m.; breakfast and prayers, 8.00 a.m. to 9.00 a.m.; work, 9.00 a.m. to 1.00 p.m.; dinner, 1.00 p.m. to 2.00 p.m.; work, 2.00 p.m. to 7.30 p.m.; supper, 7.30 p.m. to 8.30 p.m.; bed, 8.30 p.m.

149. Bro 1 August 1842. PRO MH12\13905. WCRO Loc 251\Acc 400\Par 2(i).

150. PLC, General Order, 5 February 1842. 8th Annual Report, 1842. PRO ZHC1/1386.

151. Wor 24 November 1840, PRO MH12\14203.

152. 4 & 5 Will. IV. c.76 (1834).

153. PLC, General Order, 28 July 1837. 4th Annual Report, 1838. PRO ZHC1/1295.

154. PLC, General Order, 5 February 1842. 8th Annual Report, 1842. PRO ZHC1/1386.

155. Kid 25 April 1843. PRO MH12\14018. WCRO Loc b251\Acc 403\Par 4.

156. PLC, General Order, 5 February 1842. 8th Annual Report, 1842. PRO ZHC1/1386.

157. As defined by E. Goffman in *Asylums* (Penguin, 1977).

158. PLC, General Order, 28 July 1837. 4th Annual Report, 1838. PRO ZHC1/1295.

159. Kin 20 April 1838. PRO MH12\14039. BPL File F1.

160. Dro 27 January 1841. PRO MH12\13931. WCRO Loc b251\Acc 401\Par 2.

161. PLC, Order, 17 December 1841. 8th Annual Report, 1842. PRO ZHC1/1386.

162. Dro 7 November 1838. PRO MH12\13930. WCRO Loc b251\Acc 401\Par 1(ii).

163. Kid 8 December 1840. PRO MH12\14017. WCRO Loc b251\Acc 403\Par 3.

164. PLC, Circular, 17 December 1841. 8th Annual Report, 1842. PRO ZHC1/1386.

165. Ibid.

166. PLC, Instructional Letter, 17 December 1841. 8th Annual Report, 1842. PRO ZHC1/1386.

167. Kid 2 August 1842. PRO MH12\14017. WCRO Loc b251\Acc 403\Par 4.

168. Kin 24 April 1850, PRO MH12\14041. BPL File F1.

169. PLC, Instructional Letter, in Order, 17 December 1841. 8th Annual Report, 1842. PRO ZHC1/1386. Instructional Letter.

170. PLC, Consolidated Order, 24 July 1847. 13th

Annual Report, 1847. PRO ZHC1/1748.

171. Wor 18 May 1853. PRO MH12\14207.

172. Wor 8 July 1853. Letter from the PLB. PRO MH12\14207.

173. Bro 6 December 1847. PRO MH12\13908. WCRO Loc b251\Acc 400\Par 4.

174. Dro 13 December 1856. PRO MH12\13936. WCRO Loc b251\Acc 401\Par 7.

175. Dro 6 November 1861. PRO MH12\13938. WCRO Loc b251\Acc 401\Par 9.

176. Dro 4 20 November 1861. PRO MH12\13938. WCRO Loc b251\Acc 401\Par 9.

177. Dro 4 March 1863. PRO MH12\13938. WCRO Loc b251\Acc 401\Par 10.

178. Dro 12 December 1849. PRO MH12\13934. WCRO Loc b251\Acc 401\Par 4.

179. Bro 5 July 1864. PRO MH12\13912. WCRO Loc b251\Acc 400\Par 6.

180. Per 6 December 1853. PRO MH12\14106. WCRO Loc b251\Acc 409\Par 7.

181. Dro 13 August 1856. PRO MH12\13936. WCRO Loc b251\Acc 401\Par 7.

182. Bro 13 July 1853. PRO MH12\13910. WCRO Loc b251\Acc 400\Par 5.

183. Dro 28 August 1861. PRO MH12\13938. WCRO Loc b251\Acc 401\Par 9.

184. Dro 27 November 1861. PRO MH12\13938. WCRO Loc b251\Acc 401\Par 9.

185. Dro 3 September 1862. PRO MH12\13938. WCRO Loc b251\Acc 401\Par 9.

186. Kin 17 March 1850. PRO MH12\14041. BPL File F1.

187. Shi 29 March 1858. PRO MH12\14121.

188. Dro 28 August 1861. PRO MH12\13938. WCRO Loc b251\Acc 401\Par 9.

189. Referred to in note 166. Kin 24 April 1850, PRO MH12\14041. BPL File F1. The boy attempted to abscond on three occasions.

190. Fearnhill Heath was five miles from the workhouse.

191. Bro 5 July 1864. PRO MH12\13911. WCRO Loc b251\Acc 400\Par 6.

192. Dro 19 August 1868. PRO MH12\13940. WCRO Loc b251\Acc 401\Par 12.

193. Dro 2 March 1870. PRO MH12\13941. WCRO Loc b251\Acc 401\Par 13.

194. Referred to in note 180.

195. Dro 20 February 1856. PRO MH12\13936. WCRO Loc b251\Acc 401\Par 7.

196. Dro 17 August 1863. PRO MH12\13938. WCRO Loc b251\Acc 401\Par 10.

197. Kid 19 July 1870. PRO MH12\14024. WCRO Loc b251\Acc 403\Par 20.

198. M.A. Crowther, *The Workhouse System 1834–1929* (Methuen, 1981), p. 218.

199. Per 10 December 1835. PRO MH12\14103. WCRO Loc b251. Acc.409\Par 1.

200. Super Diet was the computer program used. It was written by the University of Surrey Computer Service and adapted by Worcester College of Higher Education Computer Service.

201. The diet used for comparison was what would be regarded today as a balanced diet.

202. Ruth G. Hodgkinson, *The Origins of the National Health Service* (Wellcome, 1967), p. 48.

203. Dud 8 July 1838. PRO MH12\13958. DPL/A251.

204. Bro 8 November 1841. PRO MH12\13905. WCRO Loc 251\Acc 400\Par 2(i).

205. Bro 18 October 1843. PRO MH12\13906. WCRO Loc 251\Acc 400\Par 2(ii).

206. Dro 4 November 1846. PRO MH12\13932. WCRO Loc b251\Acc 401\Par 3.

207. It provided about 100 additional calories per day.

208. Dro 4 November 1846. PRO MH12\13932. WCRO Loc b251\Acc 401\Par 3.

209. Kin 12 April 1839. PRO MH12\14039. BPL File F1.

210. Kin 1 January 1841. PRO MH12\14039. BPL File F1.

211. Ibid.

212. Crowther, *The Workhouse System 1834–1929*, p. 215.

213. K. Chesney, *The Victorian Underworld* (Penguin, 1972), p. 18.

214. PLC, Circular. 2 March 1835. 11th Annual Report, 1835. HLL.

215. Per 25 April 1837. PRO MH12\14104. WCRO Loc b251\Acc 409\Par 2.

216. PLC, Instructional Letter, 4 February 1836. 2nd Annual Report, 1836. HLL.

217. PLC, Order, 7 March 1836. 2nd Annual Report, 1836. HLL.

218. PLC, Circular Letter, 12 March 1838. 4th Annual Report, 1838. PRO ZHC1/1295.

219. Wor 25 May 1837. PRO MH12\14202.

220. Only Anglicans tended to be appointed to officers' posts.

221. Kid 12 March 1838. Letter from the PLC. PRO MH12\14016. WCRO Loc b251\Acc 403\Par 2.

222. PLC, Instructional Letter, 5 February 1842. 8th Annual Report, 1842. PRO ZHC1/1386.

223. PLC Consolidated Order, 19 April 1836, in 3rd Annual Report, 1837. PRO ZHC1/1150.

224. PLC Letter, 14 June 1838, in 5th Annual Report, (1839), PRO ZHC1, 1249/1295.

225. PLC Regulation, 5 February 1842, in 8th Annual Report (1842) PRO. ZHC1/1386.

226. Himmelfarb, *The Idea of Poverty in England in the Early Industrial Revolution.*

227. As discussed by A. D'Entreves, 'Negative Liberty', in D101 Social Science Foundation Course Team *Understanding Society* (Open University Press, 1970), pp. 30–5.

CHAPTER 4

1. Geoffrey Crossick, *An Artisan Elite in Victorian Society*, (Croom-Helm, 1978). Crossick based this on E. Hobsbawm, 'The Labour Aristocracy in the Nineteenth Century', article in *Labouring Men*, (Methuen, 1964), pp. 272–315.
2. Hodgkinson, *The Origins of the National Health Service*, pp. 315–16.
3. SC on Poor Law Medical Relief, P.P. 1844, (312) IX. Question 9832.
4. 4 & 5 Will. IV. c.76 (1834).
5. Sir L. Woodward, *The Age of Reform*, (OUP 1979), p. 99.
6. 48 & 49 Vict. c.46 (1885).
7. 4 & 5 Will. IV. c.76 (1834).
8. *Lancet*, Leading article, 2 April 1842 p. 16. BUL (BML).
9. Hodgkinson, *The Origins of the National Health Service*, p. 10.
10. Letter from Major General M. Marriott, Chairman of Pershore Guardians, 1836. Cited by Hodgkinson, *The Origins of the National Health Service*, p. 10.
11. PLC General Order, 5 February 1842. 8th Annual Report, 1842. PRO ZHC1/1386.
12. Mar 31 August 1852. PRO MH12\14083.
13. Hodgkinson, *The Origins of the National Health Service*, p. 77.
14. Edward Baines – Speech to the House of Commons, *Hansard*, 12 July 1853. Vol. 129, c.138.
15. Webb, *English Poor Law History*, Part II. Vol. 1, p. 118.
16. PLB – Circular, 12 April 1865. In 18th Annual Report, 1866. PRO ZHC1/3039.
17. 30 Vict. c.6 (1867).
18. *Lancet*, Leading Article, 12 September 1835. p. 786. BUL (BML).
19. PLC General Order, 5 February 1842. 8th Annual Report, 1842. PRO ZHC1/1386.
20. Hodgkinson, *The Origins of the National Health Service*, p. 8.
21. Cited by F.B. Smith, *The Peoples' Health 1830–1910* (Croom-Helm, 1979), p. 360.
22. *Lancet*, Leading Article, 3 October 1835, p. 49. BUL (BML).
23. Smith, *The People's Health 1830–1910*, p. 355.
24. Hodgkinson, *The Origins of the National Health Service*, p. 373.
25. PLC, 2nd Annual Report, 1836. HLL.
26. Cited by Hodgkinson, *The Origins of the National Health Service*, p. 386.
27. *Lancet*, Leading Article, 26 December 1835. pp. 508–10. BUL (BML).
28. PLC Consolidated Order, 24 July 1847, in 13th Annual Report, 1847, PRO ZHC1/1748.
29. PLC Order, 4 January 1844. 10th Annual Report, 1844. PRO ZHC1 1493.
30. 7 & 8 Vict. c.101 (1845).
31. PLB Circular, 16 November 1849, Art. 138. p. 13. 2nd Annual Report, 1850. PRO ZHC1/1866.
    Discharge Register – 1844 to 1865. DPL.
33. Bromyard Poor Law Union (Herefordshire) – Admissions and Discharge Register in Hereford County Record Office. Ref. K42.
34. Kid 25 February 1840.PRO MH12\14017. WCRO Loc b251\Acc 403\Par 3.
35. Kid 3 March 1840. PRO MH12\14017. WCRO Loc b251\Acc 403\Par 3.
36. PLC, 10th Annual Report 1844, ZHC1/1493.
37. 8 & 9 Vict. c.101 (1845).
38. 8 & 9 Vict. c.83 (1845).
39. 8 & 9 Vict. c.101 (1845), sections 3 to 5.
40. 8 & 9 Vict. c.83 (1845).
41. D.J. Mellett, 'Bureaucracy and Mental Illness: The Commissioners on Lunacy 1845–90', *Journal of Medical History*, 25, (1981) p. 236.
42. Hodgkinson, *The Origins of the National Health Service*, p. 575.
43. 25 & 26 Vict. c. 111 (1862).
44. Mellett, 'Bureaucracy and Mental Illness: The Commissioners on Lunacy 1845–90', p. 243.
45. Wor 14 January 1847. PRO MH12\14205.
46. Mellett, 'Bureaucracy and Mental Illness: The Commissioners on Lunacy 1845–90', p. 236.
47. Mar 24 January 1851. PRO MH12\14083.
48. Gloucestershire County Lunatic Asylum was at Fairford.
49. Shi 24 January 1851. PRO MH12\14119.
50. Upt 7 January 1858. PRO MH12\14186. WCRO Loc 251\Acc 414\Par 6.
51. Webb, *English Poor Law History*, Part II. Vol. 1., p. 341.
52. Upt 19 January 1858. PRO MH12\14119. WCRO Loc 251\Acc 414\Par 6.
53. Upt 25 July 1858. PRO MH12\14186. WCRO Loc 251\Acc 414\Par 6.
54. For instance Masters, A., *Bedlam* (R.K.P., 1977) and Mellett A., 'Bureaucracy and Mental Illness: The Commissioners on Lunacy 1845–90', p. 236.
55. Shi 13 October 1863. PRO MH12\14122.
56. PLC, Circular, January 1844. In the 10th Annual Report, 1844. ZHC1/1493.
57. Kin 28 December 1853. PRO MH12\14042. BPL File F1.
58. Poor Law Act 1860 referred to by Hodgkinson, *The Origins of the National Health Service*, p. 362.
59. *Lancet*, anonymous letter, 4 February 1871. p. 181, BUL (BML)
60. Bro 25 January 1859. PRO MH12\13911. WCRO Loc b251\Acc 400\Par 6.
61. Report on the Sanitary Condition of the Labouring Population of Great Britain, July 1842. P.P. 1842 (HL-) XXVI.

62. Bro 19 March 1861. PRO MH12\13911. WCRO Loc b251\Acc 400\Par 6.
63. Smith, *The People's Health 1830–1910*, p. 65.
64. Henry Butler, *What is the Harm?* (1864). Quoted by Smith, *The People's Health 1830–1910*, p. 70.
65. Kid 3 October 1848. PRO MH12\14019. WCRO Loc b251\Acc 403\Par 7.
66. Kid 7 November 1848. PRO MH12\14019. WCRO Loc b251\Acc 403\Par 7.
67. Per 12 November 1854. PRO MH12\14107. WCRO Loc b251\Acc 409\Par 7.
68. Webb, *English Poor Law Policy*, p. 116.
69. Bro 14 August 1866. PRO MH12\13912. WCRO Loc b251\Acc 400. Par 7.
70. Dro 30 July 1866. PRO MH12\13939. WCRO Loc b251\Acc 401. Par 11.
71. Dro 29 January 1840. PRO MH12\13931. WCRO Loc b251\Acc 401\Par 2.
72. PLB, Official Circular 14 & 15, April and May 1848. 1st Annual Report, 1849. PRO ZHC1/1806.
73. Wor 18 June, 1847. PRO MH12\14205.
74. Bro 27 May 1862. PRO MH12\13912. WCRO Loc b251\Acc 400. Par 6.
75. Bro 1 April 1862. PRO MH12\13912. WCRO Loc b251\Acc 400\Par 6.
76. Smith, *The People's Health 1830–1910*, p. 143.
77. Dro 22 June 1859, PRO MH12\13937. WCRO Loc b251\Acc 401. Par 8 and 6 January 1869. PRO MH12\13941. WCRO Loc b251\Acc 401\Par 12.
78. Sto 8 June 1859. PRO MH12\14137.
79. Sto 25 May 1859. PRO MH12\14137.
80. Bro 8 May 1866. PRO MH12\13912. WCRO Loc b251\Acc 400\Par 7.
81. Kirby, Letter, *Lancet*, 31 October 1835, p. 178, BUL (BML).
82. *Lancet*, 18 March 1837, p. 896, BUL (BML).
83. Statistics cited by Smith, *The People's Health 1830–1910*, p. 105.
84. Dro 8 July 1868. PRO MH12\13940. WCRO Loc b251\Acc 401\Par 12.
85. Kid 25 April 1865. PRO MH12\14023. WCRO Loc b251\Acc 403\Par 17.
86. Bro 28 June 1870. PRO MH12\13913. WCRO Loc b251\Acc 400\Par 7.
87. Nineteenth-century spelling of debility.
88. Which was done at Worcester and cited by Wor 21 October 1869. PRO MH12\14211.
89. F. McGendie, 'Physical Conditions of the Tissues of the Human Body', *Lancet*, November 8 1834. p. 229. BUL (BML).
90. R.H. Crisp, Letter, *Lancet*, 7 March 1835, p. 810, BUL (BML).
91. *Lancet*, 11 November 1871, p. 675, BUL (BML).
92. Dro 17 April 1861. PRO MH12\13938. WCRO Loc b251\Acc 401\Par 9.
93. Bro 21 April 1868.PRO MH12\13913. WCRO Loc b251\Acc 400\Par 7.
94. Bro 27 October 1868. The expert was George E. Hyde the medical officer of Worcester Gaol. PRO MH12\13913. WCRO Loc b251\Acc 400\Par 7.
95. Reported in Dro 24 March 1868. PRO MH12\13940. WCRO Loc b251\Acc 401\Par 12.
96. Kid 15 July 1856. PRO MH12\14021. WCRO Loc b251\Acc 403\Par 11.
97. PLC, 13th Annual Report, 1847. PRO ZHC1/1748.
98. Mar 26 December 1857. PRO MH12\14085.
99. Mar 8 February 1858. PRO MH12\14086.
100. Bro 14 April 1862. PRO MH12\13912. WCRO Loc 251\Acc 400\Par 6.
101. Dro 16 January 1839. PRO MH12\13930. WCRO Loc b251\Acc 401\Par 1(ii).
102. Bro 7 January 1839. PRO MH12\13904. WCRO Loc 251\Acc 400\Par 1(ii).
103. Kid 4 February 1862. PRO MH12\14023. WCRO Loc b251\Acc 403\Par 15.
104. *Lancet*, 31 December 1836. p. 507. BUL (BML).
105. Dro 15 April 1857. PRO MH12\13936. WCRO Loc b251\Acc 401\Par 8.
106. Kid 26 November 1861 to 4 March 1862. PRO MH12\14023. WCRO Loc b251\Acc 403\Par 14.
107. Kin 26 May 1862. PRO MH12\14044. BPL File F1.
108. Dro 16 September 1868. PRO MH12\13940. WCRO Loc b251\Acc 401\Par 12.
109. Dro 14 and 27 October 1868. PRO MH12\13940. WCRO Loc b251\Acc 401\Par 12.
110. Dro 27 October 1868. PRO MH12\13940. WCRO Loc b251\Acc 401\Par 12.
111. Dro 5 January 1870. PRO MH12\13941. WCRO Loc b251\Acc 401\Par 13.
112. Bro 31 January 1842. PRO MH12\13905. WCRO Loc 251\Acc 400\Par 2(i).
113. Kid 3 March 1863. PRO MH12\14023. WCRO Loc b251\Acc 403\Par 15.
114. Dro 24 March 1868, PRO MH12\13913, WCRO Loc b251\Acc 401\Par 12.
115. Moss, William, letter, *Lancet*, 4 April 1835, Vol. II. p. 13. BUL (BML).
116. Kid 12 October 1841. PRO MH12\WCRO Loc b251\Acc 403\Par 3.
117. Kin 22 May 1840. PRO MH12\14039. BPL File F1.
118. A. Thompson, 'Lecture', *Lancet*, 9 May 1835, p. 189, BUL (BML).
119. Bro 31 January 1842. PRO MH12\13905. WCRO Loc 251\Acc 400\Par 2(i).
120. L. Stewart, *Lancet*, 28 November 1835, pp. 337–8, BUL (BML).
121. Ibid. Author Clifton.
122. Ibid. Author Headland.
123. Kid 26 February 1861. PRO MH12\14023. WCRO Loc b251\Acc 403\Par 14.
124. Mar 18 March 1847. PRO MH12\14082.

125. L. Wardrop, 'Clinical Observations on Various Diseases', *Lancet*, 3 January 1835, p. 515, BUL (BML).
126. S. Liveings, 'A Nineteenth Century Teacher', (Author Dr J.H. Brydges) 1928, Quoted by Webb, *English Poor Law History*, Part II, Vol. 1, p. 284.
127. Kin 17 October 1855. PRO MH12\14042. BPL File F1.
128. Mar 10 March 1857. PRO MH12\14085.
129. Mar 19 July 1859. PRO MH12\14086.
130. Kid 27 September 1864 and 12 September 1865. PRO MH12\14023. WCRO Loc b251\Acc 403\Par 17.
131. Kid 31 January 1865. PRO MH12\14023. WCRO Loc b251\Acc 403\Par 17.
132. Kid 14 November 1865. PRO MH12\14023. WCRO Loc b251\Acc 403\Par 17.
133. *Lancet*, 'Observations on Epidemic Ophthalmia', 3 May 1851, p. 489, BUL (BML).
134. PLC, Order, 4 January 1844. 9th Annual Report, 1844. PRO ZHC1/1434.
135. Cited by Hodgkinson, *The Origins of the National Health Service*, p. 125.
136. These statistics included all children given medical relief, either as 'Indoor' or 'Outdoor Relief'.
137. Sto 20 May 1841. PRO MH12\14135.
138. T.R. Edmonds, 'Mortality of Infants in England', *Lancet*, 30 July 1836, p. 691, BUL (BML).
139. As suggested by Smith, *The People's Health 1830–1910*, p. 65.
140. M. Armstrong, *Stability and Change in an English County Town 1841–51*, (CUP, 1974), p. 57.
141. Smith, *The People's Health 1830–1910*, pp. 47–55.
142. SC on the Poor Laws, 1844. Evidence of George Cornewall-Lewis. Quoted by Hodgkinson, *The Origins of the National Health Service*, p. 132.
143. Mar 28 April 1846. PRO MH12\14081.
144. Mar 19 May 1846. PRO MH12\14081.
145. Per 21 January 1851. PRO MH12\14106. WCRO Loc b251\Acc 409\Par 7.
146. Shi 13 May 1851. PRO MH12\14119.
147. Shi 4 April 1856. PRO MH12\14120.
148. Dro 16 December 1857. PRO MH12\13936. WCRO Loc b251\Acc 401\Par 7.
149. Dro 11 September 1870. PRO MH12\13941. WCRO Loc b251\Acc 401\Par 13.
150. Discussed in *Lancet*, Leading Article, 1 April 1871, p. 457, BUL (BML).
151. Wor 8 April 1871. PRO MH12\14212.
152. PLC, Order, 1846. 13th Annual Report. PRO ZHC1/1748.
153. T. Laffan, *The Medical Profession* (Dublin, 1887), p. 76, BUL (BML).
154. Sto 2 February 1855. PRO MH12\14141.
155. Kid 29 June 1858 and 10 August 1858. PRO MH12\14141. WCRO Loc b251\Acc 403\Par 11.
156. PLB, Circular, 2 April 1868, in 20th Annual Report, PRO ZHC1/3222.
157. *Worcester Herald*, 13 May 1865, 31 May 1865 and 31 August 1867. WPL (Microfilm), Berrow's Newspapers Archive.
158. A. Hodgkinson, *The Origins of the National Health Service*, p. 420.
159. Dro 26 October 1853. PRO MH12\13935. WCRO Loc b251\Acc 401\Par 6.
160. Kid 1 August 1854. PRO MH12\14021. WCRO Loc b251\Acc 403\Par 10.
161. Per 1854. PRO MH12\14107. WCRO Loc b251\Acc 409\Par 7.
162. Per 11 October 1865. PRO MH12\14108. WCRO Loc b251\Acc 409\Par 8.
163. Diseases and complaints treated by the Medical Officer of Droitwich Union. January 1865 to December 1870. PRO MH12\18939. Abscess. Diseased Ankle. Nechrous. Aphonia. Ecynema. Peritonitis. Biliousness (Hepatic). Erysipelas. Pneumonia. Bronchitis. Febris. Rheumatic Fever. Cardiac Condition. Fits. Rheumatism. Cervical Abscess. Fracture. Scabies. Cold. Glandular Swelling. Simple Fever. Cold Abscess. Hip Joint Disease. Skin Eruption. Congestion and Cold. Hydrocephalus. Spina Bifida. Constipation. Manition. Strumous Wrist. Cough and Cold. Low Fever. Tonsilitis. Diarrhoea. Worms.
164. Dud 19 December 1856. PRO MH12\13964. DPL.
165. Kin 1 September 1869. PRO MH12\14045. BPL File F1.
166. Upt 18 February 1868. PRO MH12\14189.
167. Kid 19 May 1868. PRO MH12\14024. Loc b251\Acc 403\Par 19.
168. Kid 13 August 1839. PRO MH12\14017. WCRO Loc b251\Acc 403\Par 2.
169. Kid 3 September 1839. PRO MH12\14017. WCRO Loc b251\Acc 403\Par 2.
170. Dro 5 April 1868. PRO MH12\13940. WCRO Loc b251\Acc 401\Par 12.
171. Webb, *English Poor Law History*, Vol. I, Part II, p. 319.
172. PLB, 17th Annual Report 1866–7. PRO ZHC1/2962.
173. Hansard, 1867, Vol. clxxxv. c. 163.
174. The PLB was replaced by the Local Government Board in 1871.
175. G. Himmelfarb, *The Idea of Poverty in England in the Early Industrial Revolution*.
176. E. Goffman, *Asylums*.

CHAPTER 5

1. R. Johnson, 'Education Policy and Social Control in Early Victorian England', *Past and Present*, Vol. 49, 1970, p. 10.

2. G. Himmelfarb, *The Idea of Poverty in England in the Early Industrial Revolution.*
3. D. Roberts, *Paternalism in Early Victorian England*, (Croom-Helm, 1979), pp. 61–2.
4. B. Simon, *Two Nations and the Educational Structure 1780–1870* (Lawrence and Wishart, 1974), p. 223.
5. A.J. Donajgrodski, "Social Police" and the Bureaucratic Elite' in *Social Control in Nineteenth-Century Britain* (Croom-Helm, 1977), pp. 51–77.
6. Jeremy Bentham, 'Panopticon or Inspection House', in *Works*, (1840), Vol. IV, p. 39, BUL.
7. Goffman, *Asylums*, introduction.
8. M.A. Crowther, *The Workhouse System 1834–1929* (Methuen, 1981), p. 38. Citing S. Jackman, *Galloping Head* (1958), p. 63.
9. Ibid., p. 127.
10. Ibid., p. 128.
11. PLC, Order, 2 March 1835. PLC 1st Annual Report. (1) 1835, HLL.
12. Ibid. PLC Order, 2 March 1835. Art. XXXVI.
13. PLC, Order, 4 January 1844. PLC 10th Annual Report. 1844. PRO ZHC1/1493. Art. 77.
14. Kid 2nd. December 1848. PRO MH12\14017. WCRO Loc b251\Acc 403\Par 7.
15. Ibid.
16. Kid 27 August 1849. PRO MH12\14019. WCRO Loc b251\Acc 403\Par 7.
17. PLC, Consolidated Order, 19 December 1836. PLC 3rd Annual Report. 1837. PRO ZHC1/1150.
18. PLC, Order, 2 March 1835. 11th Annual Report. 1838. HLL.
19. PLC, Order, 2 December 1837. PLC 4th Annual Report. 1838. PRO ZHC1/1295.
20. A. Digby, *Pauper Palaces* (RKP, 1978), p. 184.
21. Ibid.
22. PLC, Order. 2 December 1837. 4th Annual Report. 1838. PRO ZHC1/1295.
23. Kid 22 October 1839. PRO MH12\14017. WCRO Loc b251\Acc 403\Par 2.
24. Wor 13 July 1840. PRO MH12\14203.
25. Ten 7 April 1840. PRO MH12\14169. WCRO Loc b251\Acc 413\Par 3.
26. Kid 16 October 1838. PRO MH12\14016. WCRO Loc b251\Acc 403\Par 2.
27. Kid 9 July 1844. PRO MH12\14018. WCRO Loc b251\Acc 403\Par 5.
28. Kid 1 October 1844. PRO MH12\14018. WCRO Loc b251\Acc 403\Par 5.
29. Per 23 September 1848. PRO MH12\14106. WCRO Loc b251\Acc 409\Par 4.
30. Per 13 March 1849. PRO MH12\14106. WCRO Loc b251\Acc 409\Par 4.
31. Bro 8 September 1852. PRO MH12\13910. WCRO Loc b251\Acc 400\Par 5.
32. Bro 13 October 1852. PRO MH12\13910.

33. Bro 10 November 1852. PRO MH12\13910. WCRO Loc b251\Acc 400\Par 5.
34. Bro 24 August 1853. PRO MH12\13910. WCRO Loc b251\Acc 400\Par 5.
35. Bro 6 November 1853. PRO MH12\13910. WCRO Loc b251\Acc 400\Par 5.
36. Bro 3 November 1857. PRO MH12\13911. WCRO Loc b251\Acc 400\Par 6.
37. Bro 23 August 1859. PRO MH12\13911. WCRO Loc b251\Acc 400\Par 6.
38. Dro 20 August 1862. PRO MH12\13938. WCRO Loc b251\Acc 401\Par 10.
39. Dro 8 October 1862. PRO MH12\13938. WCRO Loc b251\Acc 401\Par 10.
40. Dro 25 February 1863. PRO MH12\13938. WCRO Loc b251\Acc 401\Par 10.
41. Dro 9 March 1864. PRO MH12\13939. WCRO Loc b251\Acc 401\Par 10.
42. Bro 23 November 1852. PRO MH12\13910. WCRO Loc b251\Acc 400\Par 5.
43. Kid 12 October 1869. PRO MH12\14024. WCRO Loc b251\Acc 403\Par 20.
44. Dro 23 April 1851. PRO MH12\13934. WCRO Loc b251\Acc 401\Par 5.
45. Sto 27 July 1860. PRO MH12\14143.
46. Dud 1 January 1857. PRO MH12\13964. DPL/G/DU/1.4.
47. Per 4 March 1851. PRO MH12\14106. WCRO Loc b251\Acc 409\Par 5.
48. Per 18 March 1851. PRO MH12\14106. WCRO Loc b251\Acc 409\Par 5.
49. Sto 9 October 1848. PRO MH12\14138.
50. Sto 26 April 1844. PRO MH12\14136.
51. PLB, 1st Annual Report, 1849, PRO ZHC1/1806.
52. Wor 13 September 1843, PRO MH12\14204.
53. Sto 31 October 1843. PRO MH12\14136.
54. Cited by Crowther, *The Workhouse System 1834 to 1929*, p. 127.
55. Digby, *Pauper Palaces*, p. 187.
56. Obermann, 'The Education of Children in the Poor Law Institutions of England and Wales during the Period 1834 to 1870', p. 135.
57. SC on the Education of Pauper Children 1861–2. Brown's Evidence. Question 12439. P.P. (519) XLIX.
58. Eve 27 July 1847. PRO MH12\13999.
59. Crowther, *The Workhouse System 1834–1929*, p. 127.
60. Obermann, 'The Education of Children in the Poor Law Institutions of England and Wales during the Period 1834 to 1870', p. 135.
61. PCCE Minutes 1857–8, P.P. (2386) XLV, p. 60.
62. Per 20 February 1838. PRO MH12\14105. WCRO Loc b251\Acc 409\Par 2.
63. *Education Census 1851*, [P.P. 1692] XC.
64. SC on the Education of Pauper Children 1861–2, P.P. (519) XLIX, Question 12348.

65. Ibid. Question 6518.
66. Dro 20 February 1856. PRO MH12\13936. WCRO Loc b251\Acc 401\Par 7.
67. Dro 21 May 1856. PRO MH12\13936. WCRO Loc b251\Acc 401\Par 7.
68. Dro 27 February 1850. PRO MH12\13934. WCRO Loc b251\Acc 401\Par 5.
69. Dro 27 March 1850. PRO MH12\13934. WCRO Loc b251\Acc 401\Par 5.
70. Kin 20 January 1858. PRO MH12\14043. BPL F1.
71. Kid 9 November 1869. PRO MH12\14024. WCRO Loc b251\Acc 403\Par 20.
72. Ibid.
73. Obermann, 'The Education of Children in the Poor Law Institutions of England and Wales during the Period 1834 to 1870', p. 138. Citing P.P. 1847-8. (998) p. 28.
74. APLC A. Austin's Report, 3 February 1848. PRO MH32/74.
75. Asher, Tropp, *The Schoolteachers*, (London, RKP), 1957, p. 10.
76. Michael, Heafford, 'Women Entrants to a Teacher Training College 1852-1860', *History of Education Society Bulletin* (No. 23. Spring 1979), pp. 14-21.
77. H.G. Bowyers evidence to SC 1861-2, Question 3007. PRO MH12\13934. WCRO Loc b251\Acc 401\Par 5.
78. Kid 20 April 1847. PRO MH12\14019. WCRO Loc b251\Acc 403\Par 6.
79. Obermann, 'The Education of Children in the Poor Law Institutions of England and Wales during the Period 1834 to 1870', p. 161.
80. Dro 25 September 1850. PRO MH12\13934. WCRO Loc b251\Acc 401\Par 5.
81. Kin 12 January 1853. PRO MH12\14042. BPL F1.
82. Dro 30 October 1850. PRO MH12\13934. WCRO Loc b251\Acc 401\Par 5.
83. Dro 6 November 1850. PRO MH12\13934. WCRO Loc b251\Acc 401\Par 5.
84. Dro 18 December 1850. PRO MH12\13934. WCRO Loc b251\Acc 401\Par 5.
85. Bro 9 May 1865. PRO MH12\13912. WCRO Loc b251\Acc 400\Par 7.
86. Dro 3 October 1866. PRO MH12\13939. WCRO Loc b251\Acc 401\Par 11.
87. PCCE Minutes August 9 1847. Cited by SC on the Education of Pauper Children, 1861-2, P.P. (519) XLIX.
88. SC on the Education of Pauper Children, 1861-2, P.P. (519) XLIX, Q12448.
89. Ibid. Q4773.
90. Kid 29 April 1856. PRO MH12\14021. WCRO Loc b251\Acc 403\Par 10.
91. Kid 12 July 1859. PRO MH12\14022. WCRO Loc b251\Acc 403\Par 13.
92. Kid 25 November 1859. PRO MH12\14022. WCRO Loc b251\Acc 403\Par 13.
93. Eve 19 July 1860. PRO MH12\14001.
94. Wor 5 March 1863, PRO MH12\14210.
95. Sto 3 October 1865. PRO MH12\14143.
96. Sto 3 January 1866. PRO MH12\14143.
97. Sto 28 June 1867. PRO MH12\14144.
98. Kid 6 December 1864. PRO MH12\14023. WCRO Loc b251\Acc 403\Par 17.
99. Kid 7 May 1867. PRO MH12\14024. WCRO Loc b251\Acc 403\Par 19.
100. Eve 17 July 1866. PRO MH12\14001.
101. Sto 26 May 1850. PRO MH12\14139.
102. This happened at Worcester in Wor 23 March 1857, PRO MH12\14208 and at Evesham in Eve 5 November 1861. PRO MH12\14001.
103. Shi 23 July 1849, PRO MH12\14118.
104. Sto 27 April 1853. PRO MH12\14140.
105. Sto 22 March 1869. PRO MH12\14144.
106. Mar 2 May 1861. PRO MH12\14087.
107. Eve 13 May 1870. PRO MH12\14003.
108. Eve 11 January 1871. PRO MH12\14003.
109. Crowther, *The Workhouse System 1834-1929*, p. 38, citing Jackman, *Galloping Head*.
110. As highlighted in SC on the Education of Pauper Children 1861-2, P.P. (519) XLIX. Question 12501.
111. Ibid. Doyles's evidence.Question 4277.
112. Ibid. Lambert's evidence Question 5063.
113. Sto 14 June 1847, PRO MH12\14137.
114. Sto 25 May 1847, PRO MH12\14137.
115. Sto 18 February 1848, PRO MH12\14138.
116. Wor 28 May 1857, PRO MH12\14208.
117. Wor 28 May 1857, PRO MH12\14208.
118. As at Martley in Mar 16 August 1858, PRO MH12\14090.
119. PLC Circular, 22 June 1838. PLC 5th Annual Report. 1839. PRO ZHC1/1249/1295.
120. Mentioned in PCCE Minutes 1847 August 9, p. iv.
121. PLC 13th Annual Report, 1847, PRO, ZHC1/1348.
122. P. Horn, *Education in Rural England* (Methuen, 1976), p. 87.
123. Obermann, 'The Education of Children in Poor Law Institutions in England and Wales during the Period 1834 to 1871', p. 152.
124. SC on Poor Relief, 1862, P.P. (321) Question 5660.
125. Ibid. Question 5559.
126. SC on the Education of Pauper Children, 1862, A. Doyle, P.P. (510) XLIX, p. 81.
127. Ibid.
128. Ibid.
129. T.B. Browne's evidence to SC on Poor Relief 1861, P.P. (474-I), p. 671, Question 12374.
130. Ibid. Question 12375.
131. Ibid. P.P. 671-2, Question 12376.
132. Ten 12 July 1842. PRO MH12\14169. WCRO Loc b251\Acc 413\Par 3.
133. Ten 9 August 1842. PRO MH12\14169. WCRO Loc b251\Acc 413\Par 3.
134. N. Longmate, *The Workhouse*, (Temple Smith, 1974), p. 168.

135. Kid 29 October 44, PRO MH12\14018. WCRO Loc b251\Acc 403\Par 5.
136. Eve 6 June 1846. (Letter to Guardians from PLC) PRO MH12\13999.
137. Eve 6 July 1846. PRO MH12\13999.
138. Ibid.
139. Eve 26 July 1847. PRO MH12\13999.
140. Ibid.
141. Ibid.
142. Upt 20 July 1848. PRO MH12\14183. WCRO Loc 251\Acc 414\Par 5.
143. Upt 28 February 1850. PRO MH12\14184. WCRO Loc 251\Acc 414\Par 5.
144. Upt 29 September 1855. PRO MH12\14185. WCRO Loc 251\Acc 414\Par 6.
145. Ibid.
146. Ibid. (Appended by APLC).
147. Upt 14 December 1855. PRO MH12\1418. WCRO Loc 251\Acc 414\Par 6.
148. Upt 15 January 1856. PRO MH12\14186. WCRO Loc 251\Acc 414\Par 7.
149. Ibid.
150. SC on the Education of Pauper Children, 1861–2. P.P. (519) XLIX. Sir J. Walsham's Evidence. p. 43.
151. Wor 22 May 1841. PRO MH12\14203.
152. Sto 23 January 1846. PRO MH12\14137.
153. Mar 16 March 1844. PRO MH12\14081.
154. For instance the teachers at Worcester, Wor 17 January 1845. PRO MH12\14204, and at Shipston on Stour, Ship 18 April 1846. PRO MH12\14117.
155. For instance at Droitwich in Dro 27 May 1866. H.M.I.'s Report. PRO MH12\13939. WCRO Loc b251\Acc 401\Par 11.
156. Kid 2 July 1839. PRO MH12\14017. WCRO Loc b251\Acc 403\Par 2.
157. For instance at Bro 11 March 1839. PRO MH12\13904. WCRO Loc b251\Acc 400\Par 1(ii).
158. Bro 3 June 1839. PRO MH12\13904. WCRO Loc b251\Acc 400\Par 1(ii).
159. Bro 1 November 1847. PRO MH12\13908. WCRO Loc b251\Acc 400\Par 4.
160. Wor 30 September 1847. PRO MH12\14205.
161. Wor 3 June 1848. PRO MH12\14205.
161. Bro 1 November 1847. PRO MH12\13908. WCRO Loc b251\Acc 400\Par 4.
162. Crowther, The Workhouse System 1834 to 1929.
161. The Population Growth of King's Norton.

DATE 1801 1811 1821 1831 1841 1851 1861 1871

POP/N 2,807 3,068 3,651 3,977 5,550 7,759 13,364 21,845

Source: 1851 Census Report. (1852) P.P. (1631) LXXXV, p. 78. 1871 Census Report. (1873) P.P. (676–I) LXVI, p. 315.
164. Kin 8 June 1838. PRO MH12\14039. BPL F1.
165. Ibid.
166. Cited in Kin 24 June 1847. PRO MH12\14041. BPL F1.
167. As at Pershore in Per 24 June 1848. PRO MH12\14106. WCRO Loc b251\Acc 409\Par 4.
168. As at Droitwich in Dro 29 March 1848. PRO MH12\13933. WCRO Loc b251\Acc 401\Par 3.
169. Kin 3 February 1858. PRO MH12\14043. BPL F1.
170. Kin 14 April 1858. PRO MH12\14043. BPL F1.
171. Bro 27 October 1863. PRO MH12\13912. WCRO Loc b251\Acc 400\Par 6.
172. Bro 13 February 1856. PRO MH12\13911. WCRO Loc b251\Acc 400\Par 7.
173. As at King's Norton in Kin 25 September 1861. PRO MH12\14044. BPL F1.
174. Kid 6 May 1848. PRO MH12\14019. WCRO Loc b251\Acc 403\Par 7.
175. PLB Order, 24 June 1847, PLB, 1st Annual Report, 1849, PRO ZHC1/1806.
176. Sto 20 August 1852. PRO MH12\14139.
177. Wor 18 May 1853. PRO MH12\14207.
178. Wor 28 May 1859. PRO MH12\14208.
179. Wor 3 June 1854. (Reported), 24 June 1859. (Investigated) PRO MH12\14208.
180. Wor 6 September 1859. PRO MH12\14208. Board.
181. Wor 8 September 1859. PRO MH12\14208.
182. Kid 27 July 1841. PRO MH12\14017. WCRO Loc b251\Acc 403\Par 3.
183. Kid 2 August 1842. PRO MH12\14017. WCRO Loc b251\Acc 403\Par 4.
184. Sto 12 January 1853. PRO MH12\14140.
185. Sto 6 January 1854. PRO MH12\14140.
186. Eve 31 January 1870. PRO MH12\14003.
187. As at Mar 23 November 1861. PRO MH12\14087.
188. Shi 27 May 1862. PRO MH12\14122. (Citing H.M.I.'s Report of 6 August 1861, PRO MH12\14121.)
189. Shi 4 February 1863. PRO MH12\14122.
190. Wor 11 October 1852. PRO MH12\14207.
191. Ibid.
192. Sto 18 February 1848. PRO MH12\14138.
193. Bro 6 November 1866. PRO MH12\13912. WCRO Loc b251\Acc 400\Par 7.
194. Per 18 January 1848. PRO MH12\14106. WCRO Loc b251\Acc 409\Par 4.
195. Sto 3 January 1846, PRO MH12\14137.
196. Sto 5 February 1846, PRO MH12\14137.
197. Sto 21 February 1846, PRO MH12\14137.
198. Upt 1 June 1847, PRO MH12\14182, WCRO Loc 251\Acc 414\Par 4.
199. Per 24 June 1848, PRO MH12\14106, WCRO Loc 251\Acc 409\Par 5.
200. Ibid.
201. Per 23 December 1848, PRO MH12\14106, WCRO Loc 251\Acc 409\Par 5.
202. Dro 9 March 1853, PRO MH12\13935, WCRO Loc b251\Acc 401\Par 6.

203. Dro 16 March 1853, PRO MH12\13935, WCRO Loc b251\Acc 401, Par 6.
204. Dro 20 April 1853, PRO MH12\13953, WCRO Loc b251\Acc 401, Par 6.
205. Ibid.
206. Wor 1 January 1855, PRO MH12\14208.
207. Wor 31 January 1855, PRO MH12\14208.
208. Shi 24 February 1851, PRO MH12\14119.
209. Bro 10 September 1856, PRO MH12\13911, WCRO Loc b251\Acc 400 Par 6.
210. Dro 23 March 1864, PRO MH12\13966, WCRO Loc b251\Acc 401\Par 10.
211. Kid 19 January 1869, PRO MH12\14024, WCRO Loc b251\Acc 403\Par 19.
212. Kid 2 February 1869, PRO MH12\14204, WCRO Loc b251\Acc 403, Par 19.
213. Ross, 'The Care and Education of Pauper Children in England and Wales 1834 to 1896'.
214. Obermann, 'The Education of Children in Poor Law Institutions in England and Wales during the Period 1834 to 1870'.
215. Digby, *Pauper Palaces*, 1978.
216. Such as D.B. Hughes, 'The Education of Pauper Children in Monmouthshire 1834 to 1929' (Unpub. M.A. Dissertation, University of Cardiff, 1967).
217. G. Himmelfarb, *The Idea of Poverty in England in the Early Industrial Revolution*.
218. E. Goffman., *Asylums*, introduction.

CHAPTER 6

1. Digby, *Pauper Palaces*, p. 188.
2. George Godwin, *Town Swamps and Social Bridges*, (London, 1859). (Reprinted. A. King (ed.) Leicester University Press, 1972), p. 26. Godwin was an urban/social reformer and architect. He was editor of *The Builder*.
3. Donajgrodski, '"Social Police" and the Bureaucratic Elite', in Donajgrodski, *Social Control in Nineteenth-Century Britain* or R. Johnson 'Educating the Educators: "Experts" and the State 1833–9', in Donajgrodski, *Social Control in Nineteenth-Century Britain*.
4. Ibid. pp. 186–7.
5. James Kay-Shuttleworth, *Four Periods of Public Education* (London, 1862), p. 61.
6. B. Simon, *Two Nations and the Education Structure*, p. 168.
7. A. Middleton and S. Weitzman, *A Place for Everyone*, (Gollancz), 1976, p. 58.
8. J.P. Kay, 'On the Establishing of Pauper Schools', *Journal of the Royal Statistical Society*, 1838, Vol. 1, p. 23. Cited by A. Digby, *Pauper Palaces*, p. 180.
9. SC on the Education of Pauper Children, 1861–2. P.P. (510) XLIX, p. 22.
10. Ross, 'The Care and Education of Pauper Children in England and Wales 1834–96', p. 71.
11. Kid 20 August 1839. PRO MH12\14017. WCRO Loc b251\Acc 403\Par 2.
12. SC on the Poor Law Amendment Act, 1837. P.P. (131) XVII. Part 1. 2nd Report. p. 48. Question.3666.
13. SC on the Poor Law Amendment Act, P.P. 1837–8 (202) XVIII. Part 1. Questionnaire. Question 13185.
14. SC on the Poor Law Amendment Act, 1837. P.P. (131) XVII. Part 1. Report. Question 969.
15. Ibid. 2nd. Question 971.
16. SC on the Poor Law Amendment Act, 1838. P.P. (202) XVIII. Part 1. 14 Report. Question 4403.
17. SC on the Poor Law Amendment Act, 1837. P.P. (131) XVII. Part 1. 2nd Report. Question 3683.
18. Ibid. Question 3675.
19. Ibid. Question 3670.
20. Ibid. Question 3686.
21. SC on the Poor Law Amendment Act, 1837. P.P. (481) XVII. Part 1. 1 Report. Question 1833.
22. Ibid.
23. SC on the Poor Law Amendment Act, 1837. P.P. (350) XVII. Part II. 12 Report. Question 12611.
24. SC on Education 1834, P.P. (572) IX. Question 2488.
25. SC on the Poor Law Amendment Act, 1837 (140) XVIII. Part 1. 1 Report. Question 987.
26. Newcastle Royal Commission, 1861. P.P. (2794–1) XXI. Vol. I. Part I. p. 355.
27. SC on the Education of Pauper Children, 1861–2. P.P. (510) XLIX. p. 4.
28. PLC 2nd Annual Report, 1836, HLL.
29. SC on the Education of the Poorer Classes, 1837–8. P.P. (589) VII. Question 122.
30. SC on the Poor Law Amendment Act, 1838. P.P. (220) XVIII. Part I. 16 Report. Question 4799.
31. SC on the Education of the Poorer Classes, 1837–8. P.P. (202) XVIII. Part 1. Question 124.
32. Ibid. Question 125.
33. Ibid. Question 992.
34. Ibid. 13 Report. Question 4402.
35. SC on the Poor Law Amendment Act, 1837–8. P.P. (161) XVIII, Part I. 6 and 7 Report. Question 2529.
36. Kid 26 March 1839. PRO MH12\14017. WCRO Loc b251\Acc 403\Par 2.
37. G.C.T. Bartley, *The People's Schools*, (London, 1885), p. 372. Comparison with 1895 Edition.
38. 9 Geo. IV. c.17 (1828).
39. 4 & 5 Will. IV. c.78. s.15 (1834).
40. SC on the Poor Law Amendment Act, 1837–8. 6 and 7 P.P. (161) XVIII, Part I. Report. Question 2552.
41. SC on the Poor Law Amendment Act, 1838.

P.P. (220) XVIII. Part I. 16 Report. Question 4507.

42. SC on the Poor Law Amendment Act, 1837–8. P.P. (140) XVIII. Part 1. 3rd Report. Question 951.

43. Ibid. Question 956.

44. Letter from the Marquis of Normanby, Home Secretary, to Edwin Chadwick, 3 February 1840. Letter to Guardians – same date. PLC 6th Annual Report. 1840. PRO ZHC1/1295.

45. Kid 8 July 1845. PRO MH12\14018. WCRO Loc b251\Acc 403\Par 5.

46. PLC Order, 2 March 1835. WCRO Loc b251\Acc 403\Par 65.

47. PLC Circular, 22 June 1838, WCRO Loc b251\Acc 403\Par 65.

48. SC on the Poor Law Amendment Act, 1837–8. P.P. (202) XVIII. Part 1, Question 986.

49. Finer, The Life and Times of Sir Edwin Chadwick, pp. 152–3.

50. APLC R. Weale's Report. 12–9–37. PRO MH32/85.

51. NRC, 1861 P.P. (2794–1) XXI. Part I, p. 359.

52. Per 13 August 1839. PRO MH12\14105. WCRO Loc b251\Acc 409\Par 2.

53. 8 & 9 Vict. c.83 (1844).

54. Per 11 February 1845. WCRO Loc b251\Acc 409\Par 3.

55. Mar 15 February 1843. PRO MH12\14081.

56. Mar 7 March 1839. PRO MH12\14080.

57. Mar 19 January 1846. PRO MH12\14081.

58. Ibid. Letter to Martley Guardians.

59. PLC Order 21 January 1837. WCRO Loc b251\Acc 403\Par 65.

60. Mar 9 February 1846. Letter to PLC. PRO MH12\14081.

61. Ibid. Letter to Martley Guardians.

62. Mar 23 September 1846. Report of APLC E. Gulson. PRO MH12\14081.

63. Ibid. Appended to PLC copy of MSS Minutes.

64. Mar 5 November 1846. Letter to PLC PRO MH12\14081.

65. Mar 12 November 1846. Appended to letter to Martley Guardians. PRO MH12\14081.

66. Mar 4 December 1846. Letter to PLC PRO MH12\14081.

67. Mar 18 March 1847. PRO MH12\14082.

68. Mar 21 June 1845. PRO MH12\14081.

69. Mar 29 July 1847. PRO MH12\14082.

70. Mar 18 August 1847. Report of H.M.I. PRO MH12\14082.

71. Mar 8 May 1848. PRO MH12\14082.

72. Mar 17 May 1848. Letter to PLB. PRO MH12\14082.

73. 'Eleemosynary' – this meant Poor Law relief likely to increase and prolong dependence on the Poor Rates.

74. PLB letter to PCCE Minutes 10 July 1848. PRO MH32/87.

75. Mar 21 August 1848. PRO MH12\14082.

76. Mar 28 August 1848. 'Official Circular', July and August 1848, enclosed, PRO MH12\14082.

77. Mar 9 September 1848. Letter to PLB. PRO MH12\14082.

78. Mar 16 September 1848. Letter to PLB. PRO MH12\14082.

79. Cited by PLB 2nd Annual Report. 1850. p. 8. PRO ZHC1/1866.

80. PLC Consolidated Order for the Relief of Town Unions, 5 February 1836. WCRO Loc b251\Acc 403\Par 65.

81. Dates of formation of Poor Law unions. The dates of the first minutes are given in brackets. Bromsgrove. 8–11–36. (20–12–36.) Droitwich. 26–9–36. (16–11–36.) Dudley. 15–10–36. Evesham. 11–5–36. (1–6–36.) Kidderminster. 15–10–36. (2–12–36.) King's Norton. 13–12–36. Martley. 26–10–36. (14–10–36.) Pershore. 22–10–35. (14–11–35.) Shipston on Stour. 20–12–34. Stourbridge. 29–11–34. Tenbury Wells. 29–8–36. Upton on Severn. 8–8–34. (12–12–35.) Worcester. 30–8–34. (26–1–37).

82. Kid 28 February 1837. PRO MH12\14016. WCRO Loc b251\Acc 403\Par 1.

83. Kid 5 June 1838. PRO MH12\14016. WCRO Loc b251\Acc 403\Par 1.

84. Wor 23 February 1848 PRO MH12\14205.

85. Repeated in PLB 3rd Annual Report, 1851. PRO ZHC1/1925.

86. W.E. Hickson. 1803–70. Son of a boot and shoe manufacturer from London. He retired from business in 1840 to concentrate on philanthropic works. A pioneer of popular education in general, and music education in particular. A strong supporter of National Education.

87. Letter to PLC, 13 August 1836.

88. NRC, 1861 Part I, p. 384.

89. Workhouse Visiting Society Journal. The only extant copies in the Bodleian Library, Oxford.

90. NRC, 1861 P.P. (2794–V) XXI, Part V.

91. SC on the Education of Pauper Children, 1861–2. P.P. (510) XLIX, p. 41.

92. Ibid., p. 5.

93. SC on the Poor Law Amendment Act, 1837–8. P.P. (681–1) XVIII. Part 1, p. 33.

94. 7 & 8 Vict. c.101. (1844).

95. PLC 'Official Circular', 31 January 1844. WCRO Loc b251\Acc 403\Par 67.

96. Included in APLC A. Doyle's Report. 1848. PRO MH32/17.

97. Bro 28 February 1848. PRO MH12\13908. WCRO Loc b251\Acc 400\Par 4.

98. Bro 17 April 1848. PRO MH12\13908. WCRO Loc b251\Acc 400\Par 4.

99. Per 30 January 1851. PRO MH12\14106. WCRO Loc b251\Acc 409\Par 5.

100. Per 11 November 1851. PRO MH12\14106. WCRO Loc b251\Acc 409\Par 5.

101. Per 16 March 1852. PRO MH12\14106. WCRO Loc b251\Acc 409\Par 5.
102. APLC E. Gulson's Report. 8 September 1854. PRO MH32/32.
103. APLC E. Gulson's Report. 27 February 1855. PRO MH32/32.
104. PLB 9th Annual Report. 1857. PRO ZHC1/2385.
105. APLC E. Gulson's Report, 1855. PRO MH32/32.
106. Obermann, 'The Education of Children in Poor Law Institutions in England and Wales during the Period 1834 to 1870', p. 71.
107. Kid 12 May 1857. PRO MH12\14021. WCRO Loc b251\Acc 403\Par 11.
108. Kid 9 February 1858. PRO MH12\14022. WCRO Loc b251\Acc 403\Par 11.
109. Coode was Assistant Secretary to the PLC, 1834 to 1848.
110. NRC, 1861, P.P. (2794–1) XXI. Part I. Vol. I. p. 384.
111. Webb, *English Poor Law History*, Part II, Vol. I, p. 114.
112. SC on the Education of Pauper Children, 1861–2. P.P. (510) XLIX, p. 9.
113. Ibid., p. 7.
114. Ibid., p. 9.
115. Ibid., p. 8.
116. Ibid., p. 9.
117. APLC E. Gulson's Report. 9-7-63. PRO MH32/33.
118. 25 & 26 Vict. c.43 (1866).
119. Included in Kid 13 March 1866. PRO MH12\14023. WCRO Loc b251\Acc 403\Par 17.
120. Ibid.
121. Kid 13 March 1866, ibid, gave details of the girls who: 'Left the workhouse 1 June 1863 to 1 January 1866. 12 to 16 years. 17. 8 to 12 years. 25. 2 to 8 years. 19 TOTAL: 61. Returned: Emily Mercer 13 – Very delicate, Sarah Ann Howell 11 – Deserted, Agnes Potter 10 – Returned with mother'.
122. Kid 4 December 1849. PRO MH12\14023. WCRO Loc b251\Acc 403\Par 8.
123. Dro 2 December 1850. WCRO Loc b251\Acc 401\Par 4. PRO MH12\13934.
124. Sto 9-5-62. PRO MH12\14143.
125. There were thirty boys from Stourbridge there in 1863, (17-4-63) sixteen in 1864 (16-12-64) and eighteen in 1865. (26-6-65) By 1866 (2-3-66) there was no mention of boys from Stourbridge at Quatt.
126. SC on the Education of Pauper Children, 1861–2. P.P. (510) XLIX, p. 33.
127. Ibid., p. 22.
128. Ibid., p. 39.
129. Ibid.
130. Ibid., p. 52.
131. Ibid., p. 68.
132. Ibid., pp. 68–9.
133. Ibid., pp. 69–70.
134. Ibid., p. 71.
135. PCCE Report, 1862. P.P. (3171) XLVII, pp. 336–7.
136. Wor 23 February 1848. PRO MH12\14205.
137. PLB 3rd Annual Report, 1851. PRO ZHC1/1925.
138. PCCE Minutes, 1852, p. 6.
139. Cited in NRC, 1861, P.P. (2794–1) XXI. Vol. I, Part I, pp. 364–5.
140. NRC, 1861 Part III. P.P. (2794–III) XXI, pp. 38–41.
141. Eve 22 February 1858. PRO MH12\14001.
142. Ship 12 May 1862. PRO MH12\14122.
143. SC on the Education of Pauper Children, 1861–2. P.P. (510) XLIX, p. 5.
144. Ibid., p. 72. Citing PCCE Minutes, 1857–8, p. 156.
145. H.G. Bowyer, letter to PLB 31 January 1867, PRO MH32/108. A. Doyle was cited by Obermann, 'The Education of Children in Poor Law Institutions in England and Wales during the Period 1834 to 1870', p. 237.
146. NRC, 1861. Part III. P.P. (2794–III) XXI, p. 8.
147. J.T. Graves Report. 10-11-51. PRO MH32/33.
148. Dro 18 May 1853. PRO MH12\13935. WCRO Loc b251\Acc 401\Par 6.
149. Dro 9 November 1853. H.M.I.'s Report. PRO MH12\13935. WCRO Loc b251\Acc 401\Par 6.
150. Dro 18 October 1854. H.M.I.'s Report. PRO MH12\13935. WCRO Loc b251\Acc 401\Par 6.
151. Dro 7 January 1857. PRO MH12\13936. WCRO Loc b251\Acc 401\Par 7.
152. SC on the Education of Pauper Children, 1861–2. P.P. (510) XLIX, p. 34.
153. SC on the Poor Law Amendment Act, 1837–8. P.P. (681–1) XVIII. Part 1, 3rd Report. Question 985.
154. PLC Instructional Letter. 5-3-42. WCRO Loc b251\Acc 403\Par 4.
155. Kid (Includes PLC Return.) 4 July 1838. PRO MH12\14017. WCRO Loc b251\Acc 403\Par 2.
156. Kid 26 November 1839. PRO MH12\14017. WCRO Loc b251\Acc 403\Par 2.
157. Kid 14 January 1840. PRO MH12\14017. WCRO Loc b251\Acc 403\Par 2.
158. Kid 16 June 1840. PRO MH12\14017. WCRO Loc b251\Acc 403\Par 2.
159. Kid 7 July 1840. PRO MH12\14017. WCRO Loc b251\Acc 403\Par 2.
160. Kid 14 July 1840. PRO MH12\14017. WCRO Loc b251\Acc 403\Par 3.
161. SC on the Poor Law Amendment Act, 1837–8. P.P. (681–1) XVIII. Part 1. Question 983.
162. Pressure for a training institution specifically for workhouse schoolmasters led to the founding of Kneller Hall Training School in

1852. In spite of the massive support for the training school idea and the appointment of Temple as its prestigious first Principal, the venture failed. The teachers trained at Kneller Hall did not generally go into workhouse schools, which were unattractive to them. Kneller Hall Training School closed in 1857.

163. Kin 3 January 1850. Copy of advertisement sent to National Society. PRO MH12\14041. BPL F1.
164. Wor 1 September 1853. PRO MH12\14207.
165. Kid 7 September 1858. PRO MH12\14022. WCRO Loc b251\Acc 403\Par 12.
166. Kin 16 January 1850. PRO MH12\14042. BPL F1.
167. Kid 14 November 1848. PRO MH12\14019. WCRO Loc b251\Acc 403\Par 7.
168. Kid 12 December 1848. PRO MH12\14019. WCRO Loc b251\Acc 403\Par 7.
169. Wor 5 June 1850. PRO MH12\14206.
170. Wor 8 June 1850. PRO MH12\14206.
171. Wor 2 January 1851. PRO MH12\14206.
172. Up 25 November 1853. PRO MH12\14185. WCRO Loc 251\Acc 414\Par 6.
173. Up 2 December 1853. PRO MH12\14185. WCRO Loc 251\Acc 414\Par 6.
174. Upt 17 December 1853. PRO MH12\14185. WCRO Loc 251\Acc 414\Par 6.
175. Ibid. They answered 18 ft 8 in × 15 ft × 8 ft 8 in.
176. Shi 27 May 1861. PRO MH12 14121.
177. Eve 5 December 1864. PRO MH12\14002.
178. Eve 24 July 1865. PRO MH12\14002.
179. Bro 28 June 1868. PRO MH12\13913. WCRO Loc b251\Acc 400\Par 7.
180. Kin 10 May 1850. PRO MH12\14041. BPL F1.
181. Sto 31 July 1868. PRO MH12\14144.
182. Sto 17 July 1868. PRO MH12\14144.
183. Sto 15 October 1868. PRO MH12\14144.
184. Sto 22 March 1869. She resigned. PRO MH12\14144.
185. Sto 27 February 1871. PRO MH12\14145.
186. Bro 10 August 1869. PRO MH12\13913. WCRO Loc b251\Acc 400\Par 7.
187. Shi 5 November 1869. PRO MH12\14124.
188. Shi 11 April 1871. H.M.I.'s Report. PRO MH12\14124.
189. Shi 24 April 1871. PRO MH12\14124.
190. Shi 3 August 1871. PLB letter to Guardians. PRO MH12\14124.
191. Kid 21 August 1860 and 11 September 1860. PRO MH12\14022. WCRO Loc b251\Acc 403\Par 13.
192. Kid Boys 12 August 1862, Girls 2 September 1862. PRO MH12\14023. WCRO Loc b251\Acc 403\Par 15.
193. Kid 3 October 1865. PRO MH12\14023. WCRO Loc b251\Acc 403\Par 17.
194. Sto 2 June 1852. PRO MH12\14139.
195. Sto 11 September 1852. H.M.I.'s Report. PRO MH12\14143.

196. Dro 19 July 1848. PRO MH12\13933. WCRO Loc b251\Acc 401\Par 4.
197. Per 13 August 1839. PRO MH12\14105. WCRO Loc b251\Acc 409\Par 2.
198. Kin 14 October 1868. PRO MH12\14045. BPL F1.
199. Wor 23 February 1848. PRO MH12\14205.
200. Wor 28 February 1848. PRO MH12\14205.
201. Wor 11 October 1852. PRO MH12\14207.
202. Kid Sanctioned, 7 April 1863. PRO MH12\14023, WCRO Loc b251\Acc 403\Par 15.
203. Wor 14 July 1840. PRO MH12\14203.
204. NRC 1861. P.P. (2794–IV) XXI. Part IV. Question 3213.
205. Dro 19 July 1848. PRO MH12\13933. WCRO Loc b251\Acc 401\Par 4.
206. Sir J.S. Pakington, 1799–1880. Born at Powick, Worcestershire. Lived at Westwood Park, near Droitwich. Educated at Eton and Oriel College, Oxford, but he did not graduate. A founder member of Droitwich Guardians. Conservative MP for Droitwich, 1837–74. Privy Council, 1852. Introduced Education Bills 1855 and 1857. Instrumental in setting up the NRC.
207. PCCE Minutes 1852–3. NRC, 1861, P.P. (2794–1) XXI. Vol. I, Part I, p. 354.
208. Webb, *English Poor Law Policy*, p. 113.
209. Bro 24 July 1850. WCRO Loc b251\Acc 400\Par 5.
210. Jellinger C. Symons. 1809–60. Born at West Ilsley, Berkshire. Father moved to Monkland, Herefordshire as vicar. Educated at Corpus Christi College, Cambridge. (BA) Commissioner on hand-loom weavers and miners, 1846. Appointed HMI for workhouse schools in February 1848. Wrote, amongst other books, *A Plea for Schools*, (1847) *Tactics of the Times, as regards the Condition and the Treatment of the Dangerous Class*, (1849) and *School Economy*, (1852).
211. SC on Poor Relief, 1861–2, P.P. (474–1) X. 4 Report. Question 12502, p. 56.
212. SC on Poor Relief, 1861–2. P.P. (474–1) X. 4 Report. Question 12503.
213. NRC, 1861, P.P. (2794–III) XXI. Part III, p. 38.
214. Digby, *Pauper Palaces*, p. 188.
215. APLC E. Gulson's Report, 12 September 1855. PRO MH32/32.
216. As indicated in Kid Reported 8 September 1863. PRO MH12\14023. WCRO Loc b251\Acc 403\Par 16.
217. PCCE, Memorandum included in E. Gulson's Report, 9 February 1863. MH32/33.
218. Webb, *English Poor Law History*, Part II, Vol. I, p. 114.
219. Shi 20 March 1847. HMI's Report. PRO MH12\14118.
220. Ibid.
221. Ibid.

222. Ibid.
223. Ibid.
224. Ibid.
225. Sto 20 March 1847. H.M.I.'s Report, PRO MH12\14118.
226. Sto 18 May 1853. PRO MH12\14140.
227. Wor 2 March 1861. PRO MH12\14209.
228. Ibid.
229. Dro 21 May 1856. PRO MH12\13936. WCRO Loc b251\Acc 401\Par 7.
230. NRC, 1861, Coode's Evidence. Referred to by APLC R. Weale in his evidence to SC on the Education of Pauper Children, 1861–2. P.P. (510) XLIX. p. 8.
231. Shi 20 March 1847. PRO MH12\14118.
232. Dro 29 November 1861. PRO MH12\13938. WCRO Loc b251\Acc 401\Par 9.
233. Sto 17 April 1864. PRO MH12\14143.
234. Bro 16 July 1867. PRO MH12\13913. WCRO Loc b251\Acc 400\Par 7.
235. Upt 10 April 1847. PRO MH12\14183. WCRO Loc 251\Acc 414\Par 4.
236. Sto 18 May 1853. PRO MH12\14140.
237. Sto 7 September 1859. Marginal Comment on PLB copy of minutes. PRO MH12\14142.
238. Dro 30 January 1861. PRO MH12\13938. WCRO Loc b251\Acc 401\Par 9.
239. Shi 20 March 1847. PRO MH12\14118.
240. Dro 21 May 1856. PRO MH12\13936. WCRO Loc b251\Acc 401\Par 7.
241. Eve 26 September 1859. PRO MH12\14001.
242. Shi 24 September 1859. PRO MH12\14121.
243. Dro 20 May 1866. PRO MH12\13939. WCRO Loc b251\Acc 401\Par 11.
244. SC on Poor Relief, 1861–2. P.P. (323) IX. 2nd Report. Question 4511.
245. Per 13 August 1839. PRO MH12\14105. WCRO Loc b251\Acc 409\Par 2.
246. Bro 28 February 1848. PRO MH12\13908. WCRO Loc b251\Acc 400\Par 4.
247. Dro 4 October 1848. PRO MH12\13933. WCRO Loc b251\Acc 401\Par 3.
248. Kid 12 December 1848. WCRO Loc b251\Acc 403\Par 7. PRO MH12\14019.
249. Dro 10 September 1851. PRO MH12\13934. WCRO Loc b251\Acc 401\Par 5.
250. Wor 11 October 1852. PRO MH12\14207.
251. Bro 4 February 1857. PRO MH12\13910. WCRO Loc b251\Acc 400\Par 5.
252. Lord Lyttelton. 1817–76. Baron Lyttelton of Frankley. Educated at Eton and Trinity College, Cambridge (BA/MA). Lord Lieutenant of Worcestershire. 'At the centre of the intellectual life and progress of the county'. (DNB Vol. XII, p. 374.) Principal of Queen's College, Birmingham (1845). President of Birmingham and Midland Institute (1853). Founder of St Peter's Training College, Saltley. Clarendon Royal Commission, Chief Commissioner (1861). Chief of Endowed Schools' Commission (1869–74).
253. Kid 25 May 1852, Sanctioned 13 September 1852. PRO MH12\14020. WCRO Loc b251\Acc 403\Par 9.
254. Kid 11 November 1856. PRO MH12\14021. WCRO Loc b251\Acc 403\Par 11.
255. Dud 24 September 1857. PRO MH12\13964. DPL.
256. Wor 9 April 1863. PRO MH12\14210.
257. Wor 1 September 1864. PRO MH12\14210.
258. Mar 18 July 1863. PRO MH12\14088. WCRO Loc b251\Acc 406\Par 1.
259. Dro 14 August 1861. PRO MH12\13938. WCRO Loc b251\Acc 401\Par 9.
260. Sto 31 August 1858. PRO MH12\14142.
261. Sto 17 April 1864. PRO MH12\14143.
262. Shi 20 March 1847. PRO MH12\14118.
263. Wor 30 September 1847. HMI's Report. PRO MH12\14210.
264. Wor 24 January 1848. HMI's Report. PRO MH12\14210.
265. SC on the Education of Pauper Children, 1861–2. P.P. (510) XLIX, p. 58.
266. Wor 28 June 1864. HMI's Report. Reported 1–9–64. PRO MH12\14210.
267. Eve 12 September 1866. HMI's Report. Reported. 18–2–67. PRO MH12\14002.
268. Dro 18 September 1867. PRO MH12\13940. WCRO Loc b251\Acc 401\Par 12.
269. PCCE Minutes 1847–8–9. p.v. Cited in SC on the Education of Pauper Children, 1861–2. P.P. (510) XLIX, p. 58.
270. PLB Circular, 25 January 1849. WCRO Loc b251\Acc 403\Par 69.
271. PLB 2nd Annual Report, 1850, p. 25. PRO ZHC1/1866.
272. Schedule I. Scholars' Books. Reading Lesson Books, 37; Grammar and Etymology, 11; Arithmetic, 11; Geography, 8; English History, 2; Mensuration, 1; Vocal Music, 2. TOTAL: 72. Schedule II. Teachers' Books. Reading and Composition, 4; Writing, 5; Grammar and Etymology, 6; Arithmetic, 8; Husbandry, 1; Domestic Economy, 6; Geography, 11; English History, 3; History of Scotland, 2; Preservation of Heal, 2; Principles of Teaching, 6; Mensuration, 1. TOTAL: 55. Maps; 115.
273. Black, Blackie, B. and FSS Cadell, Chambers, Cornwell, Deighton, Groombridge, Irish Board, Leitch, M'Phail, Oliver and Boyd, Parker, Ridgeway, Rivington, Simpkins and Marshall, Simmons and McIntyre, SPCK, SSBA, Sullivan, Taylor and Walton, The Government and Varty, and six map publishers: Chambers W. and A.K. Johnson, Smith and Sons. (for the Irish Board) SPCK, White (for SSBA) and Varty.
274. At Upton on Severn, in 1853, (19–5–53) an Irish Society reading book specifically for girls was recommended. (19–5–53) Greig's Domestic Economy was recommended, as a class book at Evesham, in 1857, (1–1–57) but the advice was clearly not heeded, because it

was recommended again in 1859. (1–6–59) In 1863, the HMI recommended, the SPCK publication, History of England, at Worcester, (9–4–63) (and at Stourbridge, (17–4–63) and Shipston on Stour (4–10–63)). In 1867, the SPCK again offered concessionary rates on books, and two unions, Evesham (12–4–67) and Bromsgrove, (23–8–67) availed themselves of this offer. From 1860, books published by the Irish Society were popular with HMIs, they were recommended at Worcester in 1848, (23–2–48) and at Martley in 1861 (23–11–61) and one very important aspect was religious education at Stourbridge in 1862 (19–5–62). At Droitwich, in 1861, (29–1–61) the HMI recommended, *Spelling taught by Transcription and Dictation*, by Richard Botterill (also recommended at Shipston on Stour, in 1861 (27–5–61)). *Progressive Exercise in Arithmetic*, by the same author, was also recommended in an attempt to solve teaching problems with the basic subjects. At Bromsgrove, in 1865, (15–8–65) problems with spelling led to Sullivan's *Spelling Book* being recommended. Maps and geography books were ordered at Evesham in 1868 (22–7–68). (Maps of England and the Holy Land were most popular.)

275. Dro 24 September 1867. PRO MH12\13940. WCRO Loc b251\Acc 401\Par 11 and 12.
276. Wor 23 February 1848. PRO MH12\14205.
277. Kid 22 November 1848. PRO MH12\14019. WCRO Loc b251\Acc 403\Par 7.
278. Bro 26 December 1854. PRO MH12\13910. WCRO Loc b251\Acc 400\Par 5.
279. SC on the Poor Law Amendment Act. 1837. P.P. (138) XVII. Part 1. Question 3668.
280. Ibid. Question 3669.
281. SC on the Education of the Poorer Classes, 1838. P.P. (589) VII. Question. 121.
282. 4 & 5 Will. IV. c.76. Section 19 (1834).
283. Kid 23 November 1841. PRO MH12\14017. WCRO Loc b251\Acc 403\Par 3.
284. Dro 23 June 1841. PRO MH12\13931. WCRO Loc b251\Acc 401\Par 2.
285. PLC Circular. 23 August 1847. WCRO Loc b251\Acc 403\Par 68.
286. Kid 20 July 1847. PRO MH12\14019. WCRO Loc b251\Acc 403\Par 7.
287. Upt 21 December 1853. PRO MH12\14185. WCRO Loc 251\Acc 414\Par 9.
288. Hon Charles Langdale (1787–1868). A Roman Catholic who became one of the first Catholic MPs after the Emancipation Act. He was MP for Beverley (1833–4) and MP for Knaresborough (1837–41). He was Chairman of the Catholic Poor Schools' Society.
289. NRC, 1861. P.P. (2794–V) XXI. Part V, p. 291.
290. Oberman, 'The Education of Children in Poor Law Institutions in England and Wales during the Period 1834 to 1870', p. 64.
291. Dud 9 December 1858. PRO MH12\13964. DPL/G/DU/1.4.

292. Dud 13 July 1859. PRO MH12\13964. DPL/G/DU/1.4 and 1.5.
293. Eve 12 July 1859. PRO MH12\14001.
294. Eve 19 July 1859. PRO MH12\14001.
295. As suggested by Roberts, *Paternalism in Early Victorian England*.
296. 25 & 26 Vict. c.43 (1862).
297. Bro 10 June 1862. PRO MH12\13912. WCRO Loc b251\Acc 400\Par 6.
298. 14 & 15 Vict. c.43 (1851).
299. SC on the Education of Pauper Children, 1861–2. P.P. (510) XLIX, p. 8.
300. Ibid., p. 25.
301. Ibid., p. 24.
302. Chesney, *The Victorian Underworld*, p. 243.
303. Crowther, *The Workhouse System 1834 to 1929*, p. 205.
304. 33 & 34 Vict. c.75 (1870).
305. F. Duke, 'Pauper Education' in D. Fraser (ed.), *The New Poor Law in the Nineteenth Century*, (Macmillan, 1976), p. 65.
306. Digby, *Pauper Palaces*.
307. Ross, 'The Care and Education of Pauper Children in England and Wales 1834–1896'.
308. Digby, *Pauper Palaces*, p. 180.
309. Webb, *English Poor Law History*, Part II, Vol. I, p. 264.
310. 33 & 34 Vict. c.75 (1870).
311. Ross, 'The Care and Education of Pauper Children in England and Wales 1834 to 1896', or Obermann, 'The Education of Children in Poor Law Institutions in England and Wales during the Period 1834 to 1870'.
312. Digby, *Pauper Palaces*.
313. Himmelfarb, *The Nature of Poverty in England in the Early Industrial Revolution*.

CHAPTER 7

1. Checkland (eds.), *The Poor Law Report of 1834*.
2. Ibid., p. 466.
3. PLC 11th Annual Report 1845. PRO ZHC1/1551.
4. 5 & 6 Vict. c.57 (1842).
5. 7 & 8 Vict. c.101 (1844).
6. Per 21 January 1845. PRO MH12\14104. WCRO Loc b251\Acc 409\Par 3.
7. Ibid.
8. Wor 10 June 1837. PRO MH12\14202.
9. 56 Geo. III, c.170 (1814).
10. Wor 10 June 1837. PLC letter to Guardians, PRO MH12\14202.
11. Wor 9 November 1838. PRO MH12\14202.
12. Wor 15 November 1838. PLC letter to Guardians. PRO MH12\14202.
13. Wor 16 November 1838. PRO MH12\14202.
14. Wor 20 January 1838. PLC letter to Guardians, PRO MH12\14202.
15. Wor 19 October 1839. PRO MH12\14202.

16. Ibid.
17. Ibid.
18. Kid 28 September 1852. PRO MH12\14020. WCRO Loc b251\Acc 403\Par 9.
19. Kid 22 February 1853. PRO MH12\14020. WCRO Loc b251\Acc 403\Par 9.
20. Bro 22 November 1864. PRO MH12\13912. WCRO Loc b251\Acc 400\Par 6.
21. 7 & 8 Vict. c.101 (1844).
22. Bro 18 November 1844. PRO MH12\13906. WCRO Loc b251\Acc 400\Par 2(ii).
23. Dro 6 November 1844. PRO MH12\13932. WCRO Loc b251\Acc 401\Par 3.
24. PLC Order, 25 January 1845. in PLC 11th Annual Report, 1845, PRO ZHC1/1551.
25. Dro 5 February 1845. PRO MH12\13932. WCRO Loc b251\Acc 401\Par 3.
26. In Per 21 January 1845. PRO MH12\14104. WCRO Loc b251\Acc 409\Par 3.
27. Bro 22 January 1845. PRO MH12\13907. WCRO Loc b251\Acc 400\Par 3.
28. Bro 26 May 1845. PRO MH12\13907. WCRO Loc b251\Acc 400\Par 3.
29. Per 2 April 1839. PRO MH12\14105. WCRO Loc b251\Acc 409\Par 2.
30. Bro 26 November 1851 and 3 December 1851. PRO MH12\13909. WCRO Loc b251\Acc 400\Par 5.
31. Factory inspection started in 1833.
32. Dro 28 August 1838. PRO MH12\13930. WCRO Loc b251\Acc 401\Par 1(ii).
33. Per 10 June 1850. PRO MH12\14106. WCRO Loc b251\Acc 409\Par 5.
34. Kid 24 April 1866, PRO MH12\14023. WCRO Loc b251\Acc 403\Par 17.
35. PLC Order, 25 January 1845 in PLC 11th Annual Report, PRO ZHC1/1551.
36. Bro 31 August 1846, PRO MH12\13907. WCRO Loc b251\Acc 400\Par 3.
37. Kid 25 November 1845. PRO MH12\14018. WCRO Loc b251\Acc 403\Par 6.
38. Kin 10 November 1845. PRO MH12\14040. BPL. F1 and Bro 10 November 1845. PRO MH12\13907. WCRO Loc b251\Acc 400\Par 2(ii).
39. Sto 8 March 1849. PRO MH12\14138 and Kid 25 September 1849. PRO MH12\14019. WCRO Loc b251\Acc 403\Par 8.
40. Bro 28 March 1849. PRO MH12\13909. WCRO Loc b251\Acc 400\Par 4.
41. Bro 26 March 1851. PRO MH12\13909. WCRO Loc b251\Acc 400\Par 5.
42. Bro 30 April 1851. PRO MH12\13909. WCRO Loc b251\Acc 400\Par 5.
43. Bro 7 May 1851. PRO MH12\13909. WCRO Loc b251\Acc 400\Par 5.
44. Ibid.
45. Bro 7 July 1846. PRO MH12\13907. WCRO Loc b251\Acc 400\Par 3.
46. PLC Circular 1845 in PLC 12th Annual Report 1846, PRO ZHC1/1662.
47. Ibid.
48. Bro 13 January 1845. PRO MH12\13907. WCRO Loc b251\Acc 400\Par 3.
49. Mar 23 September 1846, PRO MH12\14018.
50. PLC 13th Annual Report, 1847. PRO ZHC1/1748.
51. PLB 11th Annual Report, 1849. PRO ZHC1/1806.
52. Webb, English Poor Law History, Part II, Vol. 1, p. 298.
53. J.H. Stallard, London Pauperism Amongst Jews and Christians, (London, 1967), p. 101.
54. PLC Circular, 12 April 1844. in PLC 11th Annual Report, 1845, PRO ZHC1/1551.
55. Shi 12 June 1845. PRO MH12\14117.
56. Shi 29 May 1845. PRO MH12\14117.
57. Shi 4 June 1845. PLC letter to Guardians, PRO MH12\14117.
58. 7 & 8 Vict. c.112 (1845).
59. 8 & 9 Vict. c.83 (1850).
60. Kid 14 October 1851. PRO MH12\14020. WCRO Loc b251\Acc 403\Par 9.
61. Eve 22 May 1854. PRO MH12\14000.
62. Eve 4 January 1865. PRO MH12\140002.
63. Dro 2 November 1864. PRO MH12\13939. WCRO Loc b251\Acc 401\Par 10.
64. Dro 30 November 1864. PRO MH12\13939. WCRO Loc b251\Acc 401\Par 10.
65. Bro 2 January 1866, PRO MH12\13912. WCRO Loc b251\Acc 400\Par 7.
66. Bro 8 March 1847. PRO MH12\13908. WCRO Loc b251\Acc 400\Par 3.
67. Kid 7 March 1839. PRO MH12\14017. WCRO Loc b251\Acc 403\Par 2.
68. Per 25 April 1837. PRO MH12\14104. WCRO Loc b251\Acc 409\Par 1.
69. Ten 1 May 1838. PRO MH12\14168. WCRO Loc b251\Acc 409\Par 1.
70. Ten 31 July 1838. PRO MH12\14168. WCRO Loc b251\Acc 409\Par 1 and Ten 4 December 1838. PRO MH12\14168. WCRO Loc b251\Acc 409\Par 1.
71. Kid 19 August 1845. PRO MH12\14018. WCRO Loc b251\Acc 403\Par 6.
72. Bro 31 August 1846, PRO MH12\13907. WCRO Loc b251\Acc 400\Par 3.
73. Bro 8 March 1847. PRO MH12\13908. WCRO Loc b251\Acc 400\Par 4.
74. Dro 29 September 1847. PRO MH12\13933. WCRO Loc b251\Acc 401\Par 3.
75. Kin 6 August 1856, PRO MH12\14043. BPL. F1.
76. Kin 15 January 1862. PRO MH12\14044. BPL. F1.
77. Kin 18 March 1868. PRO MH12\14045. BPL. F1.
78. Kin 9 November 1870. PRO MH12\14045. BPL. F1.
79. Dro 9 November 1870. 24 November 1870. PRO MH12\13941. WCRO Loc b251\Acc 401\Par 13.

80. Dro 12 January 1848. PRO MH12\13933. WCRO Loc b251\Acc 401\Par 44.
81. Dro 22 October 1854. PRO MH12\13935. WCRO Loc b251\Acc 401\Par 6.
82. Kid 21 March 1869. PRO MH12\14024. WCRO Loc b251\Acc 403\Par 19.
83. Ibid.
84. 14 & 15 Vict. c.11 (1851).
85. Kin 22 March 1854. PRO MH12\14042. BPL. F1.
86. Kin 6 July 1870. PRO MH12\14045. BPL. F1.
87. 14 & 15 Vict. c.11 (1851)
88. Shi 26 February 1859. PRO MH12\14121.
89. Shi 5 March 1859. PRO MH12\14121.
90. Shi 7 November 1859. PRO MH12\14121.
91. Bro 2 July 1867. PRO MH12\13913. WCRO Loc b251\Acc 400\Par 6.
92. Dro 8 April 1840. PRO MH12\13931. WCRO Loc b251\Acc 401\Par 2.
93. Dro 15 April 1840. PRO MH12\13931. WCRO Loc b251\Acc 401\Par 2.
94. Wor 12 March 1841, PRO MH12\14203.
95. Sto 9 April 1856, PRO MH12\14141.
96. Kin 25 February 1864. PRO MH12\14044. BPL. F1.
97. Kin 13 January 1864. PRO MH12\14044. BPL. F1.
98. Bro 26 June 1852. PRO MH12\13910. WCRO Loc b251\Acc 400\Par 5.
99. Kid 26 September 1854. PRO MH12\14021. WCRO Loc b251\Acc 403\Par 10.
100. Dro 4 November 1857. PRO MH12\13936. WCRO Loc b251\Acc 401\Par 8.
101. Dro 5 October 1864. PRO MH12\13939. WCRO Loc b251\Acc 401\Par 10.
102. Dro 17 June 1865. PRO MH12\13939. WCRO Loc b251\Acc 401\Par 10.
103. Kin 1 November 1858. PRO MH12\14043. BPL. F1.
104. Bro 23 April 1851. PRO MH12\13909. WCRO Loc b251\Acc 400\Par 5.
105. Kin 24 September 1851. PRO MH12\14042. BPL. F1.
106. Bro 29 June 1853. PRO MH12\13910. WCRO Loc b251\Acc 400\Par 5.
107. Dro 28 July 1852. PRO MH12\13935. WCRO Loc b251\Acc 401\Par 5.
108. Dro December 1853. PRO MH12\13935. WCRO Loc b251\Acc 401\Par 6.
109. Kid 8 January 1861. PRO MH12\14023. WCRO Loc b251\Acc 403\Par 13.
110. Kid 5 April 1859. PRO MH12\14022. WCRO Loc b251\Acc 403\Par 12.
111. Kid 2 November 1870. PRO MH12\14024. WCRO Loc b251\Acc 403\Par 20.
112. PLC Order, 25 January 1845. in PLC 11th Annual Report, PRO ZHC1/1551.
113. In Wor 19 October 1839. PRO MH12\14202.
114. 4 & 5 Will. IV c.76 (1834).
115. F. Duke, 'Pauper Education', in D. Fraser, (ed.), *The New Poor Law in the Nineteenth Century*, p. 68.
116. e.g. Ross, 'The Care and Education of Pauper Children in England and Wales 1834 to 1896'.

CONCLUSION

1. A. Digby, 'The Operation of the New Poor Law – Social and Economic Life in Nineteenth-Century Norfolk' (Unpub. Ph.D. Thesis, University of East Anglia, 1971). The basis of *Pauper Palaces* (RKP, 1978) and M. Gibson, 'The Treatment of the Poor in Surrey Under the New Poor Law Between 1834 and 1871' (Unpub. Ph.D. Thesis, University of Surrey, 1978–9).
2. e.g. D. Ashforth, 'The Poor in Bradford c. 1834–1871' (Unpub. Ph.D. Thesis, University of Bradford, 1979); L.M. Shaw, 'Aspects of Poor Relief in Norwich 1825–1875' (Unpub. Ph.D. Thesis, University of East Anglia, 1980).
3. e.g. P.W. McKay, 'Education Under the Poor Law in Gloucestershire 1834–1909' (Unpub. M.Ed. Dissertation, University of Bristol, 1983); T. O'Brien, 'The Education and Care of Workhouse Children in some Lancashire Poor Law Unions 1834 to 1930' (Unpub. M.Ed. Dissertation, University of Manchester, 1976).
4. e.g. M.E. McKinnon, 'Poverty and Policy: the English Poor Law 1860–1910' (Unpub. D.Phil., University of Oxford, 1984).
5. e.g. Ross 'The Care and Education of Pauper Children in England and Wales 1834 to 1896'; Obermann, 'The Education of Children in Poor Law Institutions in England and Wales during the Period 1834 to 1870'.
6. e.g. A.M. Dickens, 'Architects and the Union Workhouse of the New Poor Law' (Unpub. Ph.D. Thesis, CNAA, 1983).
7. e.g. R.C. Mishra, 'The History of the Relieving Officer in England and Wales 1834 to 1948', (Unpub. Ph.D. Thesis, University of London (LSE), 1968).
8. e.g. Ross, 'The Care and Education of Pauper Children in England and Wales 1834 to 1896', intro.
9. A concept developed by Donajgrodski, in '"Social Police" and the Bureaucratic Elite, in *Social Control in Nineteenth-Century Britain* (Croom-Helm, 1977), pp. 51–77.
10. Goffman, *Asylums*, p. 69.
11. Himmelfarb, *The Idea of Poverty in England in the Early Industrial Revolution*.
12. Ross, 'The Care and Education of Pauper Children in England and Wales 1834 to 1896'.
13. Obermann, 'The Education of Children in Poor Law Institutions in England and Wales during the Period 1834 to 1870'.
14. Digby, *Pauper Palaces*.

BIBLIOGRAPHY

PRIMARY SOURCES

Manuscript Sources held at the Public Record Office

Poor Law Board and Poor Law Commission Papers held in the Public Record Office, Kew, London – Reference: MH – 12 – Union No. 526 Bromsgrove – 1834–8 – 13903 / 1839–40 – 13904 / 1841–2 – 13905 / 1843–4 – 13906 / 1845–6 – 13907 / 1847–8 – 13908 / 1849–51–13909 / 1852–5 – 13910 / 1856–61 – 13911 / 1862–6 – 13912 / 1867–71 – 13913. Union No. 527 – Droitwich – 1837–9 – 13930 / 1840–2 – 13931 / 1843–6 – 13932 / 1847–8 – 13933 / 1849–51 – 13934 / 1852–4 – 13935 / 1855–7 – 13936 / 1858–9 – 13937 / 1860–3 – 13938 / 1864–6 – 13939 / 1867–8 – 13940 / 1869–71 – 13941. Union No. 528 – Dudley – 1834–42 –13958 / 1843–4 – 13959 / 1845–7 – 13960 / 1848–50 – 13961 / 1851–2 – 13962 / 1853–5 – 13963 / 1856–8 – 13964 / 1859–62 – 13965 / 1863–6 – 13966 / 1867–8 – 13967 / 1869–71 – 13968. Union No. 529 – Evesham – 1834–8 – 13997 / 1839–42 – 13998 / 1843–7 – 13999 / 1848–51 – Missing / 1852–5 – 14000 / 1856–61 – 14001 / 1862–6 – 14002 / 1867–71 – 14003 / 1871–3 – 14004. Union No. 530 – Kidderminster – 1834–8 – 14016 / 1839–42 – 14017 / 1843–6 – 14018 / 1847–9 – 14019 / 1850–3 – 14020 / 1854–7 – 14021 / 1858–60 – 14022 / 1861–6 – 14023 / 1867–71 – 14024. Union No. 531 – King's Norton – 1834–42 – 14039 / 1843–61 – 14040 / 1847–50 – 14041 / 1851–51 – 14042 / 1856–9 – 14043 / 1860–7 – 14044 / 1868–71 – 14045. Union No. 532 – Martley – 1834–8 – 14079 / 1839–42 – 14080 / 1843–6 – 14081 / 1847–50 – 14082 / 1851–2 – 14083 / 1853–4 – 14084 / 1855–7 – 14085 / 1858–9 – 14086 / 1860–61 – 14087 / 1862–4 – 14088 / 1865–7 – 14089 / 1868–91 – 14090 / 1870–71 – 14091. Union No. 533 – Pershore – 1834–6 – 14103 / 1837 – 14104 / 1838–9 – 14105 / 1840–7 – Missing / 1848–53 – 14106 / 1854–9 – 14107 / 1860–6 – 14108 / 1867–71 – 14109. Union No. 534 – Shipston on Stour – 1834–8 – 14115 / 1839–42 – 14116 / 1843–6 – 14117 / 1847–9 – 14118 / 1850–3 – 14119 / 1854–7 – 14120 / 1858–61 – 14121 / 1862–6 – 14122 / 1867–8 – 14123 / 1869–71 – 14124. Union No. 535 – Stourbridge – 1834–9 – 14134 / 1840–2 – 14135 / 1843–4 – 14136 / 1845–7 – 14137 / 1848–50 – 14138 / 1851–2 – 14139 / 1853–4 – 14140 / 1855–6 – 14141 / 1857–9 – 14142 / 1860–6 – 14143 / 1867–9 – 14144 / 1870–1 – 14145. Union No. 536 – Tenbury Wells – 1834–8 – 14168 / 1839–42 – 14169 / 1843–9 – 14170 / 1850–5 – 14171 / 1856–64 – 14172 / 1865–71 – 14173. Union No. 537 – Upton on Severn – 1834–7 – 14179 / 1838–40 – 14180 / 1841–2 – 14181 / 1843–6 – 14182 / 1847–9 – 14183 / 1850–2 – 14184 / 1853–5 – 14185 / 1856–9 – 14186 / 1860–3 – 14187 / 1864–6 – 14188 / 1867–8 – 14189 / 1869–71 – 14190. Union No. 538 – Worcester – 1834–9 – 14202 / 1840–2 – 14203 / 1843–6 – 14204 / 1847–8 – 14205 / 1849–51 – 14206 / 1852–4 – 14207 / 1855–9 – 14208 / 1860–2 – 14209 / 1863–6 – 14210 / 1867–9 – 14211 / 1870–1 – 14212.

Printed Sources held at the Public Record Office – Parliamentary Papers

NRC – Report – [2974–1] XXI, Part I, 1861 / NRC – Assistant Commissioners' Reports – [2974–II], XXI, Part II, 1861 / NRC – Assistant Commissioners' Reports – [2974–III], XXI, Part III, 1861 / NRC – Assistant Commissioners' Reports [2974–IV], XXI, Part IV, 1861 / NRC – Answers To Questionnaires – [2974–V], XXI, Part V, I, 1861 / NRC – Minutes of Evidence – [2974–VI], XXI, Part VI, 1861 / Education, Poorer Classes (England and Wales), SC Report (Slaney), (589)VII, 1837–8 / Education of Destitute and Neglected Children, SC Report (Stafford-Northcote), (460)VII, Index (460–I), 1861/ Education in Pauper Schools – Poor Law Inspectors' Reports, (510)XLIX, 1834–64 / 1851 Census – Worcestershire – [1631]LXXXV, 1852–3 / 1851 Census – Religious Worship, [1690]LXXXIX, 1852–3 / 1851 Census – Education [1692] XC, IUP Population Vol. 11.

APLC's Correspondence held at the Public Reference Office, Kew – Reference MH – 32.
APLC Charles Ashe A'Court 1–4 / APLC Edward Gulson 28–32 / APLC John T. Graves 33 / APLC Richard Hall 34–5 / APLC W.H.T.Hawley 39 / APLC James Kay 48–50 / APLC Charles Mott 56 / APLC Alfred Power 63 / APLC E.C. Tufnell 69 / APLC Alfred Austin 74 / APLC Sir John Walsham, Bart 76 / APLC Robert Weale 85.

PLC Annual Reports held at the House of Lords Library
1835 – 1st / 1836 – 2nd.

PLC Annual Reports held at the Public Records' Office, Kew, London – Reference: ZHC1
1837 – 3rd – 1150 / 1838 – 4th – 1295 / 1839 – 5th – 1249/1295 / 1840 – 6th – 1295 / 1841 – 7th – 1339 / 1842 – 8th – 1386 / 1843 – 9th – 1434 / 1844 – 10th – 1493 / 1845 – 11th – 1551 / 1846 – 12th – 1662 / 1847 – 13th – 1748.

PLC Annual Reports held at the Public Records' Office, Kew, London
1849 – 1st – 1806 / 1850 – 2nd – 1866 / 1851 – 3rd – 1925 / 1852 – 4th – 1984 / 1853 – 5th – 2069 / 1854 – 6th – 2155 / 1855 – 7th – 2233 / 1856 – 8th – 2300 / 1857 – 9th – 2385 / 1858 – 10th – 2442 / 1859 – 11th – 2489 / 1860 – 12th – 2591 / 1861 – 13th – 2666 / 1862 – 14th – 2736 / 1863 – 15th – 2806 / 1864 – 16th – 2893 / 1865 – 17th – 1962 / 1866 – 18th – 3039 / 1867 – 19th – 3120 / 1868 – 20th – 3222 / 1869 – 21st – 3303 / 1870 – 22nd – 3385 / 1871 – 23rd – 3454.

Other Poor Law Papers held at the Public Record Office, Kew, London : ZHC1.
Pauperism in Industrial Districts – 1840 – 1318 / Children in Workhouses – 1841 – 1349 / Orphaned and Destitute Children – 1844 – 1514 / The Law Concerning Bastards – 1844 – 1493 / Emigration – 1847 – 1639 / Workhouse Schools – 1847 – 1683 / Emigration – 1847–8 – 1762 / Expenditure – 1847–8 – 1765 / Children in Workhouses – 1847–8 – 1768 / Parochial Schools – 1849 – 1823 / Expenditure – 1850 – 1889 / Education and Training – 1851 – 1948 / Numbers of Pauper Children – 1852 – 1984 / Children's Returns – 1852–3 – 2103 / Emigration to Canada – 1854–5 – 2255 / Children's Returns – 1856 – 2322 / Children's Returns – 1862 – 2761 / Inspection – 1867–8 – 3233 / Boarding-Out in Evesham – 1868–9 – 3328 / Boarding-Out – 1870 – 3393.

MANUSCRIPT SOURCES HELD AT WORCESTER COUNTY RECORD OFFICE

Worcestershire Poor Law Union Papers held at Worcester County Records' Office, St Helen's Church, Fish Street, Worcester
Union No 526 – Bromsgrove Location b251 Accession No 400 – 1836–8 – Parcel 1(i) / 1838–40 – Parcel 1(ii) / 1840–2 – Parcel 2(i) / 1842–4 – Parcel 2(ii) / 1844–7 – Parcel 3 / 1847–50 – Parcel 4 / 1850–6 – Parcel 5 / 1856–65 – Parcel 6 / 1865–71 – Parcel 7 / 1871–6 – Parcel 8 / Union No 527 – Droitwich Location b251 Accession No 401 – 1836–8 – Parcel 1(i) / 1838–40 – Parcel 1(ii) / 1840–4 – Parcel 2 / 1844–8 – Parcel 3 / 1848–50 – Parcel 4 / 1850–3 – Parcel 5 / 1853–5 – Parcel 6 / 1855–7 – Parcel 7 / 1857–9 – Parcel 8 / 1859–62 –Parcel 9 / 1862–4 – Parcel 10 / 1865–7 – Parcel 11 / 1867–9 – Parcel 12 / 1869–72 – Parcel 13 / Union No 530 – Kidderminster Location b251 Accession No 403 – 1836–8 – Parcel 1 / 1838–40 – Parcel 2 / 1840–1 – Parcel 3 / 1842–4 – Parcel 4 / 1844–5 – Parcel 5 / 1845–7 – Parcel 6 / 1847–9 – Parcel 7 / 1849–51 – Parcel 8 / 1851–4 – Parcel 9 / 1854–6 – Parcel 10 / 1856–8 – Parcel 11 / 1858–9 – Parcel 12 / 1859–61 – Parcel 13 / 1861–2 – Parcel 14 / 1862–3 – Parcel 15 / 1863–4 – Parcel 16 / 1864–6 – Parcel 17 / 1866–7 – Parcel 18 / 1867 9 – Parcel 19 / 1869–72 – Parcel 20 / Union No 532 – Martley Location b251 Accession No 406 – 1863–5 – Parcel 1 / 1865–8 – Parcel 2 / 1868–72 – Parcel 3 / Union No 533 – Pershore Location b251 Accession No 409 – 1835–7 – Parcel 1 / 1837–41 – Parcel 2 / 1841–4 – Parcel 3 / 1844–6 – Parcel 4 / 1846–9 – Parcel 5 / 1849–52 – Parcel 6 / 1852–6 – Parcel 7 / 1856–60 – Parcel Missing / 1860–66 – Parcel 8 / 1866–70 – Parcel 9 / 1870–3 – Parcel 10 / Union No 536 – Tenbury Wells Location b251 Accession No 413 – 1836–9 – Parcel 1 / 1839–41 – Parcel 2 / 1841–6 – Parcel 3 / 1847–51 – Parcel 4 / 1851–5 – Parcel 5 / 1855–61 – Parcel 6 / 1861–7 – Parcel Mising / 1867–72 – Parcel 7 / Union No 537 – Upton on Severn Location 251 Accession No 414 – 1835–7 – Parcel 1 / 1838–40 – Parcel 2 / 1840–3 – Parcel 3 / 1843–8 – Parcel 4 / 1848–53 – Parcel 5 / 1853–9 – Parcel 6 / 1859–63 – Parcel 7 / 1864–8 – Parcel Missing / 1869–71 – Parcel 8.

MANUSCRIPT SOURCES KEPT AT OTHER RECORD OFFICES

Dudley Poor Law Union Papers held at Dudley Public Library, Local Studies Department – Union No. 528 – Dudley Board Of Guardians' Minutes – Ref. 251.

King's Norton Poor Law Union Papers held at Birmingham Public Library, Local Studies Department – Union No. 531 – King's Norton Board Of Guardians' Minutes – Ref. File F1.
Herefordshire Poor Law Papers held at Hereford County Record Office, Harold Street, Hereford – Bromyard Admissions and Discharge Registers – Ref. K42.

OTHER PRINTED PRIMARY SOURCES

Hansard – Speech of Edward Baines to the House of Commons – 12th July 1853, Vol. 129. c.138 / 1867, Vol. 85, c.163.

SECONDARY SOURCES – PRE-1909 PUBLISHED SOURCES

Aschrott, P.F., *The English Poor Law Past and Present*, 1902.
Adshead, J., *Distress in Manchester: Evidence of the State of the Labouring Classes in 1840–2*. (Reprinted in *Focal Aspects of the Industrial Revolution 1825–42*, by Irish Universities Press, Shannon, 1971.)
Arnold, M., *Reports on Elementary Schools 1852–82*, HMSO, 1908.
Ashberry, P., 'The Wycliffe-Wilson System of Isolated Homes for the Training of Workhouse Children', in *Poor Law Conferences 1895–6*, 1896.
Barnett, H.O., 'Verdict on the Barrack Schools', *Nineteenth Century*, January 1897.
Barnett, S.A., *New Poor Law or No-Poor Law*, 1909.
Bartley, G.C.T., *Schools For the Nation*, 1871.
Baxter, G.R.W., *The Book of Bastilles*, 1841.
Bentham, J., *Pauper Management Improved*, 1785.
——, *The Works of Jeremy Bentham*, (ed. Bowring, J.) 1859.
——, 'Panopticon or Inspection House' (1840) in *The Works of Jeremy Bentham*, (ed. Bowring, J.) 1859, Vol. IV, pp. 39.
Brougham, H.P., *Practical Observations Upon the Education of the People*, 1825. (Reprinted in *Focal Aspects of the Industrial Revolution 1825–42*, by Irish Universities Press, Shannon, 1971.)
Burritt, E., *Walks in the Black Country*, 1868. (Republished by Roundwood Press, Kineton, 1976.)
Butler, H., *What is the Harm?*, 1864, Cited by Smith, F.B., *The People's Health – 1830–1910*, Croom-Helm, 1979, p. 70.
Chance, Sir W., *Children Under the Poor Law*, 1897.
——, *Our Treatment of the Poor*, 1898.
Engels, F., *The Condition of the Working-Class in England in 1844*, 1845. (Translated by Henderson, W.O. And Chaloner, W.H., Panther, 1969.)
Fawcett, H., *Pauperism*, 1871.
Fletcher, J., *The Farm Schools System on the Continent and its Applicability to the Prevention and Reformatory Education of Criminal and Pauper Children in England and Wales*, no date.
Godwin, G., *Town Swamps and Social Bridges*, 1859. (Reprinted by Leicester University Press, 1972.)
Greenwood, J., *The Seven Curses of London*, 1869. (Reprinted by Blackwell, 1981.)
——, 'A Night in the Workhouse', *Pall Mall Gazette*, (1866). (Reprinted in Keating, P. (ed.), *Into Unknown England*, Fontana, 1976.)
Helps, A., *The Claims of Labour*, 1845. (Reprinted by Irish Universities Press, Shannon, 1971.)
Hill, A., *Some Thoughts on Pauperism*, 1856.
——, *Training Up the Children*, 1856.
Hill, F.D., *Children of the State*, 1889.
Hill, F., *National Education*, no date.
Hopkirk, M., *Nobody Wants Sam*, 1849.
Johnson, W., *England As It Is*, 1851. (Reprinted by Irish Universities Press, Shannon, 1971.)
Kay, J. (Shuttleworth), 'On the Establishing of Pauper Schools', *Journal of the Royal Statistical Society*, cited by Digby, A., *Pauper Palaces*, RKP, 1978, p. 180.
Kay-Shuttleworth, J., *The Punishment of Children in Workhouses*, no date.
——, *Four Periods of Public Education*, 1862.
Laffan, T., *The Medical Profession*, Dublin, 1887.
Liveing, S., *A Nineteenth-Century Teacher*, 1876.
London, J., *People of the Abyss*, 1903. (Republished by Journeyman Press, 1980.)
Lonsdale, Miss S., *The English Poor Law*, no date.
Mackay, S., *History of the Poor Law*, 1899.
Malthus, T., *First Essay on Population, 1798*. (Reprinted by Penguin, 1970.)

Mayhew, H., *London Labour and London Poor*, 1862. (Reprinted by Harvester Press, 1968.)

Nicholls, Sir G., *A History of the English Poor Laws*, 1854.

Parkinson, R., *On the Present Condition of the Labouring Poor in Manchester*, 1841. (Reprinted in *Focal Aspects of the Industrial Revolution 1825–42*, by Irish Universities Press, Shannon, 1971.)

Pashley, R., *Pauperism and the Poor Laws*, 1852.

Peek, F., *Social Wreckage*, 1883.

Pratt, J.T., *The Act for the Amendment and Better Administration of the Law relating to the Poor in England and Wales*, 1834.

Protheroe, G.W., *Select Statutes and Other Constitutional Documents*, 1906.

Redlich, J. and Hirst, F.W., *The History of Local Government in England*, 1903. (Reprinted by Macmillan, 1970, ed. Keith-Lucas, B.)

Rowntree, S.B., *Poverty*, 1901.

Senior, Nassau W., *Suggestions on Popular Education*, 1861.

Smith, A., *An Inquiry into the Nature and the Cause of the Wealth of Nations*, 1776. (Reprinted by Penguin, 1970.)

Stallard, J.H., *London Pauperism*, 1867.

Stewart, A.P. and Jenkins, E., *Sanitary Reform*, 1867. (Reprinted by Leicester University Press, 1969.)

Symons, J.C., *School Economy*, no date.

Tufnell, E.C., *Reports on the Education of Pauper Children*, 1841.

Twining, L., *Recollections of Workhouse Visiting*, 1880.

Urquhart, D., *Wealth and Want*, 1845. (Reprinted by Irish Universities Press, Shannon, 1971.)

Walker, T., *Observations on the Nature, Extent and Effect of Pauperism and the Means of Reducing it*, 1826, cited by Webb, S. and B., *English Poor Law History*, Part II, Longman-Green, 1929, p. 13.

Whitmore, W., *Memoir Relating to the Industrial School at Quatt*, 1849.

Lancet

Anonymous. Comment: 31 December 1836, p. 507, 18 March 1837, p. 896. Letter:4 February 1871, p. 181. 'Observations on Epidemic Ophthalmia', 3 May 1851,p. 489.

Clifton, Comment: 28 November 1835, pp. 337–8.

Edmonds, T.R., 'Mortality of Infants in England', 30 July 1836, p. 691.

Headland, Comment: 28 November 1835, pp. 337–8.

Kirby, Dr, 31 October 1835, p. 178.

Leading Article – 3 October 1835, p. 49, 12 September 1835, p. 786, 26 December 1835, pp. 508–10, 2 March – 1842, p. 16, 1 April 1871, p. 457.

Magendie, F., 'Physical Conditions of the Tissues of the Human Body', 8 November 1834, p. 810.

Moss, W., 4 April 1835, Vol. II, p. 35.

Stewart, L., Comment: 28 November 1835, pp. 337–8

Thompson, A., 'Lecture', 9 May 1835.

Wardrop, 'Clinical Observations on Various Diseases', 3 January 1835, p. 515.

Contemporary Local Newspapers. Held by Berrow's Newspapers Limited, Worcester.

Worcester Herald – 13 May 1865, 31 May 1865, 31 August 1865. Copies of the *Worcester Herald, Journal and News* for the period 1780–1834 were used in compiling a price index for wheat.

Journal of the Workhouse Visiting Society. Held only at the Bodleian Library, Oxford. Anonymous – 'Christmas Day and Kirkdale Industrial School', January (1859), Vol. i, pp. 25–7. 'Industrial Training and the Pauper Schools', May (1859), Vol. ii, pp. 31–50. 'Sunday Schools in Workhouses', May (1859), Vol. ii, p. 60. 'Workhouse Schools', February 1860, Vol. v, pp. 145–50, November (1860), Vol. x, p. 324, July (1863), Vol. xxvi, pp. 95–7. 'A Christmas Tree in a Workhouse School', February (1860), Vol. v, pp. 155–60. 'Training of Pauper Children', May (1860), vol. vii, pp. 219–23. 'The Separation of Orphan Children in Pauper Schools', May (1860), Vol. vii, p. 223. 'The Norwich Pauper Homes', July (1860), Vol. viii, pp. 234–44, 'Industrial Homes for Young Women', September (1860), Vol. ix, pp. 261–2, May (1861), Vol. xiii, pp. 393–400, May (1863), Vol. xxv, pp. 33–59, April (1864), Vol. xxix, pp. 165–83. 'Proposed Plans for Visitors to District and other Pauper Schools', September (1860), Vol. ix, pp. 281–3. 'Pauper Schools', September (1860), Vol. ix, pp. 281–3. 'Reports on Girls from the Union of Bristol', January (1861), Vol. xi, pp. 347–8. May (1861), Vol. xiii, pp. 408–10, November (1861), Vol. xvi, p. 511, June (1862), Vol. xix, pp. 639–40, November (1862), Vol. xxii, pp. 727–8, March (1863), Vol. xxiv, p. 23, April (1864), Vol. xxix, pp. 183–5, July (1864), Vol. xxx, pp. 218–9, October (1864), Vol. xxxi, p. 256. 'Visits to Pauper Girls and Girls in Service', March (1861), Vol. xii, pp. 380–1. 'The Workhouse Child', March (1861), Vol. xii, pp. 389–90, March (1863), Vol. xxiv, pp. 931–2. 'The Girl From the Workhouse', November (1862), Vol. xxii, pp. 729–36. 'The Bradden House for Workhouse Girls', November (1863), Vol. xxii, pp. 23–9. 'A Railway Trip for Workhouse Children', October (1863), Vol. xxvii,pp. 128–9. 'The Cowley School', July (1864), Vol. xxiv, pp. 90–2. 'The Children's Establishment at Limehouse', April (1864), Vol. xxiv, pp. 193. 'Industrial Homes for Workhouse Girls at Sheffield and Bradford', January (1865), Vol. xxxii, p. 262.

Archer, H., 'Country Workhouse Schools', January (1861), Vol. xi, pp. 352–3.

Archer, H., 'A Scheme for Befriending Orphan Pauper Girls', January (1862),pp. 525–33.
Edwards, S.V., 'Suggestions Respecting the Orphan Children in Workhouse Schools', March (1863), Vol. xxiv, pp. 13–17.
Lloyd, W.R., 'Workhouse Schools', November (1859), Vol. iv, pp. 111–9.
O'Shaughnessy, M.S., 'On the Rearing of Pauper Children Out of the Workhouse', January (1863), Vol. xxiii, pp. 760–9.
Roberts, M.J., 'A Plea for Workhouse Children', November (1861), Vol. xvi,pp. 518–20.
Sheppard, G.W., 'Homes For Workhouse Boys', February (1860), Vol. v, pp. 157–8.
Tufnell, E.C., 'Papers and Discussions on Education', July (1862), Vol. xx, pp. 667–76.
Twining, L., 'Workhouse Education', September (1861), Vol. xv, pp. 461–70.
The Builder – various editions of this journal were used to provide examples of workhouse architecture.

SECONDARY SOURCES – POST-1909 PUBLISHED SOURCES

Abel-Smith, B., A History of the Nursing Profession, Heinemann, 1966.
Anderson, M., 'Urban Migration in Nineteenth Century Lancashire, Annales de Demographie Historique, 1974, pp. 13–26.
Anstruther, I, The Scandal of the Andover Workhouse, Alan Sutton, Gloucester, 1984.
Armstrong, M., Stability and Change in an English County Town: York 1841–51, CUP, 1974.
Ashforth, D., 'The Urban Poor Law', in Fraser, D., Urban Politics in Victorian England, Leicester University Press, 1976, pp. 128–48.
Ayers, G.M., England's First State Hospitals 1867–1930, Wellcome, 1971.
Bettey, J.H., Rural Life in Wessex 1500–1900, Moonraker, Bradford, 1977.
Blaug, M., 'The Myth of the Old Poor Law and the Making of the New', Journal of Economic History, 23, (1963), pp. 151–84.
Blaug, M., 'The Poor Law Report Re-examined', Journal of Economic History, 24, (1964), pp. 229–45.
Boothroyd, H.E., The History of the Inspectorate, 1923.
Bowley, M., Nassau Senior, 1937.
Browning, A. (ed.), English Historical Documents 1660–1714, Vol. viii, Eyre and Spottiswoode, 1953.
Brundage, A., 'Reform of the Poor Law Electoral System 1834–94', Albion, 7, Autumn (1975), pp. 201–15.
——, The Making of the New Poor Law 1832–9, Hutchinson, 1978.
Burton, J.H., Benthamania, 1937.
Checkland, S.G. and E.O.A. (eds.), The Poor Law Report of 1834, Penguin, 1974.
Chesney, K., The Victorian Underworld, Penguin, 1970.
Cole, G.D.H. and Postgate, R., The British Common People 1746–1946, Methuen, 1961.
Collins, P., Dickens and Crime, Macmillan, 1965.
Costin, W.C. and Watson, J.S., The Law and Working of Constitutional Documents 1660–1914, Black, 1952.
Crossick, G., An Artisan Elite in Victorian Society, Croom-Helm, 1978.
Crowther, M.A., 'The Later Years of the Workhouse', in Thane, P., The Origins of British Social Policy, Croom-Helm, 1978, pp. 36–56.
Crowther, M.A., The Workhouse System 1834–1929, Methuen, 1981.
D'Entreve, A., 'Negative Liberty' reprinted in Open University Reader Understanding Society, Open University Press, 1970, pp. 30–5.
Digby, A., 'The Rural Poor Law' in Fraser, D., Urban Politics in Victorian England, Leicester University Press, 1976, pp. 149–60.
——, Pauper Palaces, RKP, 1978.
——, The Poor Law in Nineteenth-Century England and Wales, Historical Association, 1982.
Donajgrodski, A.P., Social Control in Nineteenth-Century Britain, Croom-Helm, 1977.
——, '"Social Police" and the Bureaucratic Elite' in Social Control in Nineteenth-Century Britain, Croom-Helm, 1977, pp. 51–76.
Drake, M. (ed.), Population in Industrialisation, Harper and Rowe, 1969.
Duke, F., 'The Poor Law Commissioners and Education', Journal of Educational Administration and History, Vol. III(i), (1970), pp. 7–14.
——, 'Pauper Education', in Fraser, D., The New Poor Law in the Nineteenth Century, Macmillan, 1976. pp. 45–86.
Durey, M., 'Biographical Details of Her Majesty's Inspectors of Schools Appointed Before 1870', History of Education Society Bulletin, 28, Autumn, (1981).
——, The Return of the Plague, Gill and Macmillan, 1979.
Edsall, N.C., The Anti-Poor Law Movement, Manchester University Press, 1971.
Edwards, D.L., Leaders of the Church of England 1828–1978, Hodder and Stoughton, 1978.

Ensor, Sir R.C.K., *England 1870–1914*, OUP, 1980.

Erickson, C., *Emigration From Europe 1815–1914*, Black, 1976.

Evans, A.J. (ed.), *Social Policy 1830–1914*, RKP, Oxford, 1980.

Finer, S.E., *The Life and Times of Sir Edwin Chadwick*, Methuen, 1952.

Flinn, M.W., 'Medical Services Under the New Poor Law', in Fraser, D., *The New Poor Law in the Nineteenth Century*, Macmillan, 1976, pp. 45–66.

Fraser, D., *The Evolution of the British Welfare State*, Macmillan, 1973.

—— (ed.), *The New Poor Law in the Nineteenth Century*, Macmillan, 1976 (i).

——, 'The Poor Law as a Political Institution', in Fraser, D., *The New Poor Law in the Nineteenth Century*, Macmillan, 1976, pp. 45–66, pp. 111–27.

——, *Urban Politics in Victorian England*, Leicester University Press, 1976.

——, *Power and Authority in the Victorian City*, Blackwell, 1979.

Gash, N., *Aristocracy and People*, Arnold, 1979.

Goffman, E., *Asylums*, Penguin, 1968.

Golding, P. and Middleton, S., *Images of Welfare*, Blackwell, 1982.

Griggs, C., *The Trades Union Congress and the Struggle For Education*, Falmer, Lewes, 1983.

Halevy, E., *The Liberal Awakening 1815–30*, Benn, 1961.

——, *The Age of Peel and Cobden*, Benn, 1970.

——, *Victorian Years 1841–95*, Benn, 1962.

Hammond, J.L. and B., *The Village Labourer*, (1911), reprinted by Longman (Rule, J. (ed.)), 1979.

——, *The Town Labourer*, (1917), reprinted by Longman (Rule, J. (ed.)), 1979.

——, *The Skilled Labourer*, (1919), reprinted by Longman (Rule, J. (ed.)), 1979.

Heafford, M., 'Woman Entrants to a Teacher Training College 1852–60', *History of Education Society Bulletin*, 23, Spring (1979), pp. 14–21.

Henriques, U., 'Bastardy and the New Poor Law', *Past and Present*, 37, July (1967), pp. 103–29.

Henriques, U., 'How Cruel Were the Victorian Poor Laws?', *Historical Journal*, 11, (1968), pp. 365–71.

Himmelfarb, G., *The Idea of Poverty in the Early Industrial Revolution*, Faber, 1984.

Hobsbawm, E., 'The British Standard of Living 1790–1850', reprinted in Taylor, A.J. (ed.), *The Standard of Living in the Industrial Revolution*, Methuen, 1975.

——, *Labouring Men*, Weidenfeld and Nicolson, 1964.

——, 'The Labour Aristocracy in the Nineteenth Century', reprinted in *Labouring Men*, 1964, pp. 272–315.

Hodgkinson, R.G., *The Origins of the National Health Service*, Wellcome, 1967.

Holderness, B.A., '"Open" and "Closed" Parishes in England in the Eighteenth and Nineteenth Centuries', *Agricultural History Review*, XX, (1972), pp. 126–39.

Holman, R., 'Prevention: the Victorian Legacy', *British Journal of Social Work*, 16, Feb (1986), pp. 1–23.

Hopkins, E., 'Were the Webbs Wrong about Apprenticing in the Black Country?', *West Midland Studies*, 6, (1973), pp. 29–31.

Horn, P., *Education in Rural England 1800–1914*, Gill and Macmillan, 1978.

——, *The Rise and Fall of the Victorian Servant*, Alan Sutton, Gloucester, 1986.

Horne, D.B. and Ransome, N. (eds.), *English Historical Documents 1714–83*, Eyre and Spottiswoode, Vol. X, 1957.

Howe, G.M., *Man, Environment and Disease in Britain*, David and Charles, Newton Abbot, 1972.

Hurt, J.S., *Education in Evolution*, Palladin, 1971.

——, *Education and the Working Classes*, RKP, 1979.

——, (ed.), *Childhood, Youth and Education in the Nineteenth Century*, History of Education Society, 1981.

James, P., *Population Malthus*, RKP, 1979.

Johnson, H.J.M., *British Emigration Policy 1815–30*, OUP, 1972.

Johnson, R., 'Educational Policy and Social Control in Early Victorian England', *Past and Present*, 49, November (1970).

——, 'Education and the Educators: "Experts" and the State 1833–9', in Donajgrodski, A.P., *Social Control in Nineteenth-Century Britain*, Croom-Helm, 1977.

Keating, P. (ed.), *Into Unknown England*, Fontana, 1976.

Keith-Lucas, B. (ed.), *The History of Local Government in England* by Redlich, J. and Hirst, F.W. (1903), Macmillan 1970.

Keith-Lucas, B., *The Unreformed Local Government System*, Croom-Helm, 1980.

Kitson-Clarke, G., *The Making of Victorian England*, Methuen, 1971.

Krause, J.T., 'English Population Movements Between 1700 and 1850', in Drake, M. (ed.), *Population in Industrialisation*, Harper and Rowe, 1969.

Lawson, J. and Silver, H., *A Social History of Education in England*, Methuen, 1973.

Levy, S.L., *Nassau Senior*, David and Charles, Newton Abbot, 1970.

Liveing, S., *A Nineteenth-Century Teacher*, 1928, cited by Webb, S. and B., *English Poor Law History*, Part II, Longman-Green, 1929, pp. 283–4.

Longmate, N., *The Workhouse*, Temple-Smith, 1974.

McCord, N. 'Poor Law and Philanthropy', in Fraser, D., *Urban Politics in Victorian England*, Leicester University Press, 1976, pp. 87–110.

McCrory, P., 'Poor Law Education and the Urban Pauper Child: the Theory and Practice of the Urban District School 1840–1896', in Hurt, J.S. (ed.), *Childhood, Youth and Education in the Nineteenth Century*, History of Education Society, 1981,pp. 83 100.

McKisack, M.,*The Fourteenth Century 1307–1399*, OUP, 1959.

Manton, J., *Mary Carpenter and the Children of the Streets*, Heinemann, 1976.

Masters, A., *Bedlam*, Joseph, 1977.

Mathias, P., *The First Industrial Nation*, Harper and Rowe, 1969.

Mellett, D.J., 'Bureaucracy and Mental Illness: The Commissioners on Lunacy 1845–90', *Journal of Medical History*, 25, (1981), pp. 236–46.

Middleton, A. and Weitzman, S., *A Place For Everyone*, Gollancz, 1976.

Mills, D., *Lord and Peasant in Nineteenth-Century Britain*, Croom-Helm, 1980.

Myers, A.R. (ed.), *English Historical Documents 1327–1485*, Vol. IV, Eyre and Spottiswoode, 1969.

Parry-Jones, W.L., *The Trade in Lunacy*, RKP, 1972.

Paz, D,G., *The Politics of Working-Class Education in Britain 1830–50*, Manchester University Press, 1980.

Phillips, R.J., 'E.C. Tufnell: Inspector of Poor Law Schools 1847 to 1874', *History of Education*, Vol. 5(3), (1976), pp. 227–40.

Poynton, J.R., *Society and Pauperism: English Ideas on Poor Relief 1795–1834*, RKP, 1969.

Redford, A., *Labour Migration in England*, 1926, (reprinted by Manchester University Press, 1976 ed. Challoner, W.H.).

Roach, J., *Social Reform in England*, Batsford, 1978.

Robson, A.H., *The Education of Children Involved in Industry 1833–76*, Kegan Paul, 1931.

Roberts, D., 'How Cruel Were the Victorian Poor Laws?', *Historical Journal*, 6, (1963), pp. 97–107.

——, *Victorian Origins of the British Welfare* State, Archon, 1969.

——, *Paternalism in Early Victorian England*, Croom-Helm, 1979.

Rose, M.E., *The English Poor Law 1780–1830*, David and Charles, Newton Abbot, 1971.

——, *The Relief of Poverty 1834–1914*, Macmillan, 1972.

——, (ed.), *The Poor and the City: The English Poor Law: its Urban Context 1834–1914*, Leicester University Press, 1985.

Ross, A.M., 'Kay-Shuttleworth and the Training of Teachers for Pauper Schools', *British Journal of Educational Studies*, Vol. XV, (1967), pp. 275–83.

Rude, G., *The Crowd in History*, Lawrence and Wishart, (1964) 1985.

Ryder, J. and Silver, H., *Modern English Society*, Methuen, 1970.

Seaborne, M., *The English School*, RKP, 1971.

Selleck, R.J.W., 'Mary Carpenter: A Confident and Contradictory Reformer', *History of Education*, 14, 1985, pp. 101–15.

Simon, B., *Two Nations and the Educational Structure 1780–1870*, Lawrence and Wishart, 1974.

Skultans, V., *Madness and Morals*, RKP, 1975.

——, *English Madness 1580–1890*, RKP, 1979.

Smith, F., *The Life and Times of Sir James Kay-Shuttleworth*, Murray, 1923.

Smith, F.B., *The People's Health 1830–1910*, Croom-Helm, 1979.

Snell, K.D.M., *Annals of the Labouring Poor 1660–1900*, CUP, 1985.

Steintrager, J., *Bentham*, Allen and Unwin, 1977.

Sutherland, G., *Elementary Education in the Nineteenth Century*, Irish Universities Press, 1971.

Taylor, A.J. (ed.), *The Standard of Living in Britain in the Industrial Revolution*, Methuen, 1975.

Thane, P., *The Origins of British Social Policy*, Croom-Helm, 1978.

Thomas, E.G., 'Pauper Apprentices', *Local Historian*, 14 August (1981), pp. 400–6.

Thompson, E.P., *The Making of the English Working Class*, Penguin, 1963.

—— and Yeo, E. (eds.), *The Unknown Mayhew*, Penguin, 1971.

Tobias, J.J., *Crime and Industrial Society in the Nineteenth Century*, Batsford, 1977.

Tranter, N.L. (ed.), *Population and Industrialisation*, Black, 1973.

Treble, J,H., *Urban Poverty in England*, Batsford, 1979.

Tropp, A., *The Schoolteachers: The Growth of the Teaching Profession in England and Wales from 1800 to the Present Day*, Heinemann, 1957.

Tucker, R., 'Real Wages of Artisans in London 1729–1935', (1936), reprinted in Taylor, A.J. (ed.), *The Standard of Living in the Industrial Revolution*, Methuen, 1975, pp. 21–35.

Webb, S. and B., *English Poor Law Policy*, Cass, 1910.

——, *English Poor Law History*, Longman-Green, 1929.

Wohl, A.S., *Endangered Lives*, Methuen, 1983.

Wood, P., *Poverty and the Workhouse in Victorian England*, Alan Sutton, Gloucester, 1993.

Woodward, J., *To Do the Sick No Harm*, RKP, 1974.
Woodward, Sir L., *The Age of Reform*, OUP, 1979.

UNPUBLISHED WORKS

Ashforth, D., 'The Poor in Bradford *c*. 1834–1871', unpublished Ph.D. Thesis, University of Bradford, 1979.

Baker, G.F., 'The Care and Education of Children in Union Workhouses in Somerset 1834 to 1870', unpublished M.A. Dissertation, University of London, 1960.

Boyson, R., 'The History of Poor Law Administration in North-East Lancashire 1834–71', unpublished M.A. Dissertation, University of Manchester, 1960.

Caplan, M., 'The Administration of the Poor Laws in the Unions of Southwell and Basford 1836 to 1871', unpublished Ph.D. Thesis, University of Nottingham, 1967.

Cooke, F., 'The Organisation and Work of the Inspectorate of Workhouse Schools 1846–1904, unpublished M.Ed. Dissertation, University of Manchester, 1980.

Crooke, M.E., 'The Care and Education of Children in the Hull Poor Law Unions Schools 1834 to 1861', unpublished M.Ed. Dissertation, University of Hull, 1980.

Dickens, A.M., 'Architects and the Union Workhouse of the New Poor Law', unpublished Ph.D. Thesis, CNAA, 1983.

Digby, A., 'The Operation of the New Poor Law – Social and Economic Life in Nineteenth-Century Norfolk', unpublished Ph.D. Thesis, University of East Anglia, 1971.

Duke, F., 'The Education of Pauper Children: Policy and Administration 1834–58', unpublished M.A. Dissertation, University of Manchester, 1968.

Gibson, M., 'The Treatment of the Poor in Surrey Under the New Poor Law Between 1834 and 1871', unpublished Ph.D. Thesis, University of Surrey, 1978–9.

Hughes, D.B., 'The Education of Pauper Children in Monmouthshire 1834 to 1929', unpublished M.A. Dissertation, University of Cardiff, 1967.

McCrory, P., 'Poor Law Education and the Urban Pauper Child: A Study of the Poor Law District School', unpublished M.Ed. Dissertation, University of Leicester 1983.

McKay, P.W., 'Education Under the Poor Law in Gloucestershire 1834–1909', unpublished M.Ed Dissertation, University of Bristol, 1983.

McKinnon, M.E., 'Poverty and Policy: the English Poor Law 1860–1910', unpublished D.Phil., University of Oxford, 1984.

Mosley, J.V., 'Poor Law Administration in England and Wales 1834 to 1850', unpublished Ph.D. Thesis, University of London (External), 1975.

Obermann, S.P., 'The Education in Poor Law Institutions in England and Wales during the Period 1834 to 1870', unpublished Ph.D. Thesis, Queen's University, Belfast, 1982.

O'Brien, T., 'The Education and Care of Workhouse Children in some Lancashire Poor Law Unions 1834 to 1930', unpublished M.Ed. Dissertation, University of Manchester, 1976.

Pigott, D.A., 'The Education of Agricultural Workers and their Children during the Late 19th and Early 20th Centuries, with particular Reference to Southern Lincolnshire and Norfolk', unpublished Ph.D. Thesis, University of Birmingham, 1980.

Richards, P.R., 'The State and the Working Class', unpublished Ph.D. Thesis, University of Birmingham, 1976.

Ross, A.M., 'The Care and Education of Pauper Children in England and Wales 1834 to 1896', unpublished Ph.D. Thesis, University of London, 1955.

Russell, V.J, 'Poor Law Administration 1840 to 1843 With Special Regard to the Cardiff Union', unpublished M.A. Dissertation, University of Cardiff, 1967.

Shaw, L.M., 'Aspects of Poor Relief in Norwich 1825–1875', unpublished Ph.D. Thesis, University of East Anglia, 1980.

Thomas, J.E., 'Poor Law Administration in West Glamorgan 1834 to 1930', unpublished M.A. Dissertation, University of Wales, 1952.

Thompson, R.T., 'The New Poor Law in Cumberland and Westmorland 1834–71', unpublished Ph.D. Thesis, University of Newcastle Upon Tyne, 1976.

Woods, J.E., 'The Development of the Education of Pauper Children in Workhouse Schools 1834 to 1870', unpublished M.Ed. Dissertation, University of Leicester, 1975.

Computer Programmes

'Super-Diet' written by Surrey University Computer Service and belonging to Worcester College of Higher Education was used for dietary analysis of workhouse dietaries.

INDEX

UNIVERSITY OF WOLVERHAMPTON LEARNING RESOURCES